Enhancing Safety, Security, and Service in Organizations:

Communication, Leadership, and Performance

Darcia Roache
Capilano University, Canada

IGI Global
Scientific Publishing
Publishing Tomorrow's Research Today

Published in the United States of America by
IGI Global Scientific Publishing
701 East Chocolate Avenue
Hershey, PA, 17033, USA
Tel: 717-533-8845
Fax: 717-533-7115
Website: https://www.igi-global.com E-mail: cust@igi-global.com

Library of Congress Cataloging-in-Publication Data

Names: Roache, Darcia Ann-Marie, 1970- editor.
Title: Enhancing safety, security, and service in organizations : communication, leadership, and performance / [edited by] Darcia Roache.
Description: Hershey, PA : IGI Global Scientific Publishing, [2026] | Includes bibliographical references and index. | Summary: "The objective of this book is to provide a comprehensive framework for understanding and implementing effective strategies that improve safety and security while enhancing service quality within organizations"-- Provided by publisher.
Identifiers: LCCN 2024055635 (print) | LCCN 2024055636 (ebook) | ISBN 9798337304823 (hardcover) | ISBN 9798337304830 (paperback) | ISBN 9798337304847 (ebook)
Subjects: LCSH: Total quality management. | Customer services. | Customer relations. | Consumer protection. | Business enterprises--Security measures.
Classification: LCC HD62.15 .E54 2025 (print) | LCC HD62.15 (ebook) | DDC 658.5/62--dc23/eng/20250124
LC record available at https://lccn.loc.gov/2024055635
LC ebook record available at https://lccn.loc.gov/2024055636

British Cataloguing in Publication Data
A Cataloguing in Publication record for this book is available from the British Library.

To the leaders, professionals, and everyday heroes who tirelessly champion safety, uphold security, and strive for excellence in service across organizations worldwide.

This work is dedicated to those who understand that true leadership is measured not just by performance, but by the care, courage, and clarity with which we protect and serve others.

May this book inspire continued commitment to creating environments where people can thrive—secure, supported, and empowered.

Table of Contents

Detailed Table of Contents

Globally, the beauty industry stands out as one of the most competitive and dynamic sectors, consistently demonstrating resilience compared to other non-essential consumer goods markets. The COVID-19 pandemic and changing customer purchasing approaches have left many companies struggling to survive. In response, VITALUXE ESSENTIALS Health has formulated new strategies, aiming to maintain its competitive edge through the expertise and support of a management and strategy consulting firm. Real-world case study interventions, like this one, allow for the examination of complex, dynamic business environments in their natural contexts, providing rich insights that theoretical models or controlled experiments may not capture. Unlike purely academic research, which can sometimes lack immediate applicability, case study interventions focus on solving current problems faced by businesses. This relevance ensures that the findings are not only theoretically sound but also pragmatically valuable to stakeholders, including managers, employees, and consultants.

This study found that applying specific theories to local industry problems can improve health, wellness, and safety standards. We can enhance industry effectiveness and durability by aligning industry practices with employee, supervisor, and stakeholder needs. This alignment benefits and is necessary for everyone. This is a call for collaboration to change industry protocols. Multiple theories show that organizational practices affect performance. This article discusses a crucial opportunity to protect minority construction workers and improve safety, health, and well-being. This study enhances industry knowledge of health, wellness, and safety by examining Schein's

communities in cyber-focused partnerships can positively impact organizations and the cybersecurity workforce as a whole.

Saksham Sharma, School of Computer Engineering, Kalinga Institute of Industrial Technology (KIIT), Bhubaneswar-751024, Odisha, India
Ravi Raj Shrivastava, School of Computer Engineering, Kalinga Institute of Industrial Technology (KIIT), Bhubaneswar-751024, Odisha, India
Aashish Sahu, School of Computer Engineering, Kalinga Institute of Industrial Technology (KIIT), Bhubaneswar-751024, Odisha, India
Sidhant Mishra, School of Computer Engineering, Kalinga Institute of Industrial Technology (KIIT), Bhubaneswar-751024, Odisha, India
Kaustubh Srivastava, School of Computer Engineering, Kalinga Institute of Industrial Technology (KIIT), Bhubaneswar-751024, Odisha, India
Hitesh Mohapatra, School of Computer Engineering, Kalinga Institute of Industrial Technology (KIIT), Bhubaneswar-751024, Odisha, India

Cloud computing in smart cities has gradually transformed public security and emergency management. This report reviews the importance of cloud enabled safety systems with bonus details on IoT, big data, AI, and mobile technology. These benefits include; able to predict, and prevent crimes, quick and effective response to incidences, sharing of information, and citizens' participation in safety apps. However, issues such as data privacy, artificial intelligence preconceptions, the digital divide, and cybersecurity issues are also explored. Both, Dubai and Singapore's cases are viable examples can be used here. The dependence on technology for smart cities; ethical innovation, and public involvement for safe, equal and resilient smart cities is emphasized.

Nigeria's telecommunication sector is strongly impacted by customer satisfaction and more so the sector is a competitive landscape where companies are vying to maintain their market share, ensure consumer satisfaction, and cultivate enduring service quality. Service quality is a major factor in determining customer satisfaction, especially regarding mobile service offerings, network reliability, data speed, and coverage. Therefore, this study examined the service quality and customer satisfaction of selected telecommunication firms in Nigeria. The study employed quantitative methods and survey research while the population for the study consisted of ninety-four service team members selected from three (3) telecommunication firms with the largest number of subscribers in Nigeria. The study concluded that service quality affects customer satisfaction of selected telecommunication firms in Nigeria. It was recommended that firms should place more effort into improving the quality of products and services to improve customer satisfaction and help reduce customer attrition.

In an era, full of digital interactions and online connectivity, the importance of web security has become increasingly paramount. As our lives become more intertwined with the virtual realm, protecting sensitive data and countering cyber threats have gained unprecedented importance. Web security, comprising an extensive array of

Foreword

I commend Dr. Darcia Roache and her collaborators in their authorship of this well-named book which is generous in its insights for enhancing safety, security and service in organizations. I am guessing that most educated adolescents would provide at least vague recitation of Abraham Maslow's Hierarchy of Human Needs. Because of the pervasive appreciations of those needs, people in our organizations also will understand and experience various articulations of human needs. It must also be recognized that in our efforts to rush forward in pursuit of production, we sometimes forget these basic needs. We forget to provide self-care, to think of the "least among us," and appreciate the benefits of creating environments of grace, integrity and consideration. We know that the needs for safety and security of person, community, and workplaces are foundational to our exercise of liberty, operational efficiencies, wholesome development of social relationships, and honouring of diversity. There is an Asian saying that "as the load of the ox increased, the ox bowed its head to the ground." I wonder if this means that the oxen failed to gain the benefits and economies of seeing the larger picture and fundamental facets of the constitution of the pathways to successful performance. Is it possible that organizations, as their best, are ones that habituate the awareness and practices associated with fulfilling fundamental human needs?

As organizations create safe places for work and relationships, they move forward in their efforts to achieve their mandates. Recall that "driving fear out of the workplace" was one of the cornerstone facets of Deming's early total quality management thinking. It is difficult to sustain performance, retain talented persons and attract resources in fear-laced, risky and toxic environments. Likewise, service that is grounded in principled mission and purpose will be more likely to be experienced as authentic and regenerative for organizations. Of course, the problem with communications in our organizations is that "it" (communications) is too often assumed to have take place. In challenging times, the importance of truth and trust is often forsaken. Communication and conspiring (breathing together) are essential to thriving and productive human workplaces. So, as the authors of this collection reinforce, we need to be explicit in our attention to safety, security, service, and communications to perform well. Leaders help organizations to define their realities, to safeguard the organizational community, and make space for caring and good work.

Leading well is a daunting and even tricky role. We want to show production and yet we need to pay constant attention to organizational production capacity. This is an ever-present tension of our attentions. There is a need to maximize efficiency in performance but to do so without diminishing relational capital, dignity and inclusion, community (belongingness) or freedoms. You will see these themes in the chapters of this book. Efforts to enhance communications, to provide timely and systemic support for employees, to acknowledge diversity and unconscious bias are critical leader activities.

How do we adapt the way we do things in our organizations in a fashion that makes visible our buying into the positive organizational researchers' findings that wellbeing, health, sense of safety are correlated with preferred performance outcomes? The authors commend strategic and adaptive frames of mind and heart that orient leaders' work with their constituents and industries such that they humanize, innovate, initiate and institutionalize to achieve well-doing and wellbeing. The character and integrity of an organization is marked by how key leaders "treat" followers and how the organization's leaders deal with chronic or episodic disruptions. Insights and reflexive practice with respect to compassion in the workplace-under-stress are invaluable and readers will benefit from chapters which address these circumstances.

How do organizations contend with the myriad technological challenges of the 21st Century, with its threats and uncertainties? I commend the authors in this book for providing concrete descriptions and their expert exegesis of cases that pertain to these difficult and even wicked issues. How do we serve, communicate, and operationalize the transformations we seek in the organizations we lead or that we send our students into? These are questions that require practical wisdom and well-considered understandings. You will find that the international scholars and practitioners assembled to contribute to this book have much to offer as we seek to enhance safety, security and service in ways that matter to us and our organizations.

Thank you Dr. Roache and contributing authors for this wide-ranging but intentional set of chapters.

Keith Walker

Department of Educational Administration, University of Saskatchewan, Saskatoon, Canada

Preface

As the editor of Enhancing Safety, Security, and Service in Organizations: Communication, Leadership, and Performance I am elated to present this edited reference book that presents a multidisciplinary exploration of how organizations across diverse sectors can navigate complex challenges while cultivating environments of safety, equity, and operational excellence. This edited volume draws together research and applied insights from scholars and practitioners across the globe to address pressing organizational concerns from employees' safety and security in organizations, building inclusive workplace, organizational citizenship behavior, strategic innovations in service and adaptive leadership, health, well-being and cybersecurity, cloud security, and artificial intelligence in organizations.

Amidst global shifts triggered by health crises, digital transformation, and evolving social expectations, the need for resilient, inclusive, and strategically agile organizations has never been more urgent. This book synthesizes emerging theories, real-world case studies, and innovative frameworks to support leaders, managers, and policy-makers in creating high-performing, people-centered institutions.

CHAPTER OVERVIEW

Chapter 1: Employees Safety and Security in Organizations: Is it Leadership or Communication?

Dr. Darcia Roaache, Capilano University, Canada. Yorkville University, Canada, & University of the Fraser Valley, Canada.

Ensuring employee safety and security is no longer just a compliance issue, it's a leadership and communication imperative. This study investigates how these two forces intersect to protect the physical, psychological, and emotional well-being of employees. Through structured interviews with leaders from the U.S., Canada, Dubai, and Jamaica, the research uncovers that safety protocols are only truly effective when strong leadership is paired with clear, responsive communication. It explores how leadership styles, especially transformational and transactional, work in tandem with communication strategies to build a secure work culture. The key takeaway: leadership and communication must be integrated, not isolated. The study culminates in a practical *Leadership and Communication Framework for Employees' Safety and Security*, offering organizations a roadmap to create environments where employees feel safe, valued, and empowered to thrive.

Chapter 2: Building Inclusive Workplace: Enhancing Safety, Security, and Service Quality to Address Workplace Discrimination

Dr. Jimmy Thankachan, Christ University; Mr. Akummeren Sanglir, Christ University; Dr. Sunita Kumar, Christ University.

This chapter explores how workplace inclusivity and anti-discrimination efforts are not just ethical imperatives but strategic levers for organizational performance. Centered on a compelling case study of IT professionals from Northeast India, it uncovers the harsh realities of racial stereotyping, exclusion, and their toll on employee well-being, morale, and career advancement. The chapter argues that tackling such discrimination requires more than token measures it demands zero-tolerance policies, transparent grievance systems, and a deep commitment to meritocracy. Through actionable insights, including the implementation of cross-cultural training and inclusive leadership practices, the chapter demonstrates how fostering respect, and dismantling stereotypes can lead to stronger team cohesion, enhanced innovation, and sustained productivity. By showing that employees who feel seen and valued contribute more meaningfully, this chapter positions inclusivity not just as a moral choice but as a business-critical strategy for sustainable growth in today's globalized workplaces.

Chapter 3: Organizational Citizenship Behavior, Enhancing Workplace Dynamics

Dr. José G Vargas-Hernandez, Universidad Cristóbal Colón; Dr. Mario A. García-Camacho, División de Ingeniería en Gestión Empresarial, Tecnológico Nacional de México, ITS Fresnillo; Prof. Omar C. Vargas-González, Computer Systems, Tecnológico Nacional de México /Campus Ciudad Guzmán

In *Organizational Citizenship Behavior: Enhancing Workplace Dynamics*, the authors explore the definitions, dimensions, causes, and effects of Organizational Citizenship Behavior (OCB). Through a comprehensive literature review and empirical analysis, the study demonstrates how OCB contributes to organizational effectiveness and employee satisfaction. The research outlines its methodology, analyzes the relationship between OCB and performance, and interprets findings within existing theoretical frameworks. The essay concludes by emphasizing the importance of promoting OCB as a strategy for achieving long-term organizational success.

Chapter 4: Strategic Innovations in Service and Adaptive Leadership Response in Retail Health and Beauty

Dr. Darrell Norman Burrell, Marymount University; Lauren C. Conley, Marymount University; Dr. Delores Springs, Capitol Technology University; Dr. Amalisha Sabie-Aridi, Capitol Technology University; Prof. Quatavia McLester, Capitol Technology University; Dr. Kim L Brown-Jackson, Claremont Lincoln University; Dr. Marlena Daryousef, Colorado Technical University; Dr. Terrence Duncan, Liberty University; Dr. William Quisenberry, Purdue University Global; Dr. Maria R. Mondala-Duncan, Marymount University; Dr. Brian Douglas, Clinton College

Strategic Innovations in Service and Adaptive Leadership Response in Retail Health and Beauty examines how the highly competitive beauty industry, particularly amid challenges like the COVID-19 pandemic and shifting consumer behaviors, demands innovative strategies for survival and growth. The chapter focuses on VITALUXE ESSENTIALS Health's collaboration with a management consulting firm to develop adaptive strategies that sustain competitiveness. Using a real-world case study approach, the research provides practical insights into navigating complex business environments, offering valuable lessons for managers, employees, and consultants by bridging theory and actionable solutions in dynamic market conditions.

Chapter 5: Safeguarding the Health, Well-Being, and Safety of Minority Construction Professionals from the Impact of COVID-19

Dr. Thomas C. Gibbs III, Capitol Technology University.

This study highlights the importance of applying organizational and cultural theories to improve the health, safety, and well-being of minority construction professionals, particularly in the context of COVID-19. By aligning industry practices with the needs of employees, supervisors, and stakeholders, the construction sector can become more effective and resilient. The study calls for collaborative efforts to reform industry protocols and emphasizes that organizational culture significantly impacts performance. Drawing on multiple theoretical frameworks, including Schein's organizational culture theory, Denison's model, and Equity Theory, the research provides valuable insights into protecting vulnerable workers and fostering a safer, more inclusive construction industry.

Chapter 6: Adapting Mental Health Services in Crisis A Case Study of Mental Health Organizations' Response to COVID-19

Mr. Roger Tshiondo Muntu, Marymount University.

This chapter explores how mental health organizations responded to the COVID-19 crisis, highlighting the financial and operational challenges they faced and the strategies they used to adapt. It focuses on the rapid shift to remote care through telehealth, which led to reduced service volume and revenue. The chapter underscores the role of transformational leadership and change management—especially Kotter's Eight-Step Model—in navigating these disruptions. It also emphasizes the value of data-driven decision-making and leadership development for sustaining services and building resilience. Practical recommendations are offered to strengthen crisis preparedness, integrate technology, and ensure equitable access to care, advocating for ongoing innovation in mental health service delivery.

Chapter 7: A Qualitative Analysis of Cybersecurity Partnerships in Underserved Communities

Allison Fullwood, Capitol Technology University; Dr. Eugene J Lewis, Capitol Technology University.

A Qualitative Analysis of Cybersecurity Partnerships in Underserved Communities explores the historical and ongoing lack of cybersecurity partnerships in underserved areas and its impact on workforce diversity. Through exploratory research, the study identifies critical gaps that hinder inclusion and examines how building partnerships in these communities can enhance organizational problem-solving and innovation. Emphasizing the importance of diverse perspectives in addressing complex cyber threats, the paper offers insights into how inclusive collaboration can strengthen both organizations and the broader cybersecurity workforce.

Chapter 8: Cloud-Driven Public Safety in Smart Cities Transforming Security and Overcoming Challenges

Mr. Saksham Sharma, School of Computer Engineering, KIIT Deemed to Be University; Mr. Ravi Raj Shrivastava, School of Computer Engineering, KIIT Deemed to Be University; Mr. Aashish Sahu, School of Computer Engineering, KIIT Deemed to Be University; Mr. Sidhant Mishra, School of Computer Engineering, KIIT Deemed to Be University; Mr. Kaustubh Srivastava, School of Computer Engineering, KIIT

Deemed to Be University; Dr. Hitesh Mohapatra, School of Computer Engineering, KIIT Deemed to be University

In *Cloud-Driven Public Safety in Smart Cities: Transforming Security and Overcoming Challenges*, Sharma and his co-authors examine how cloud computing is reshaping public safety and emergency management in smart cities. The report highlights the integration of cloud-enabled systems with IoT, big data, AI, and mobile technologies, demonstrating their capacity to predict and prevent crimes, facilitate rapid emergency responses, enhance information sharing, and engage citizens through safety apps. While showcasing successful implementations in cities like Dubai and Singapore, the report also addresses critical challenges, including data privacy concerns, AI biases, cybersecurity vulnerabilities, and the digital divide. Emphasizing the need for ethical innovation and inclusive public participation, the authors argue that the future of smart city security lies in balancing technological advancement with equity, resilience, and responsible governance.

Chapter 9: Customer Satisfaction in Indigenous Telecommunication Companies in Nigeria: Role of Service Quality

Dr. Timilehin Olasoji Olubiyi, Babcock University, Ilishan-Remo, Nigeria; Dr. Adedayo Olufemi Ogunberu, Babcock University Ilishan Remo Ogun State Nigeria; Dr. Omolade Sunday Adeyemi, Oduduwa University Ipetumodu, Ile-Ife, Osun State, Nigeria; Prof. Adekunle Oluwole Binuyo, Babcock University Ilishan Remo Ogun State Nigeria; Dr. Balraj Verma, Chitkara University, Punjab, India; Dr. Bibin Xavier, Marian College Kuttikkanam Autonomous.

This study investigates customer satisfaction in Nigeria's competitive telecommunications sector, focusing on service quality factors such as mobile services, network reliability, data speed, and coverage. Using a quantitative survey of 94 service team members from three major telecom firms, the research found that service quality significantly influences customer satisfaction. The study recommends that companies enhance their product and service quality to boost customer satisfaction and reduce customer churn.

Chapter 10: Web Security Framework for Vulnerability Detection and Policy Enforcement

Ms. Akshita Sharma, Department of Computer Science & Engineering, Sharda School of Engineering & Technology; Mr. Astitva Bhardwaj, Department of Computer Science & Engineering, Sharda School of Engineering & Technology; Mr. Dharm Raj, Department of Computer Science & Engineering, Sharda School of Computing

Science & Engineering; Dr. Amrit Kumar Agrawal, Department of Computer Science & Engineering, Sharda School of Computing Science & Engineering; Mr. Murari Kumar Singh, Department of Computer Science & Engineering, Sharda School of Computing Science & Engineering; Dr. Anil Kumar Sagar, Department of Computer Science & Engineering, Sharda School of Computing Science & Engineering

This paper highlights the critical importance of web security in today's digitally connected world, focusing on protecting sensitive data from various cyber threats. It provides an overview of common web attacks such as cross-site scripting and SQL injections, emphasizing the need for tailored defense strategies. The study reviews current tools and techniques used for vulnerability detection and policy enforcement and concludes with insights into recent advancements and future directions in web security measures.

These chapters illuminate how communication, leadership, and strategic planning can converge to foster safe, inclusive, and high-performing organizations. This book is a timely contribution for academics, professionals, and policy-makers invested in the future of organizational development across sectors.

As the editor, together with the contributing authors and co-authors, we are confident that *Enhancing Safety, Security, and Service in Organizations: Communication, Leadership, and Performance* will make a significant impact on the academic community, business organizations, and industry professionals. Emphasizing the vital role of communication alongside leadership and performance, the book provides practical insights and research-driven strategies to foster safer, more secure, and service-oriented workplaces. We believe it will serve as a valuable resource for those striving to create resilient, high-performing organizations through effective communication and informed leadership.

Darcia Roache
Capilano University, Canada

Acknowledgement

It is with great gratitude and humility that I acknowledge the many individuals and institutions whose contributions made this volume, *Employees' Safety and Security in Organizations: Is it Leadership or Communication?*, possible.

First, I extend my heartfelt appreciation to my esteemed authors. Your commitment to academic rigor, critical analysis, and thoughtful reflection is evident in each chapter. The depth and diversity of your contributions have significantly enriched this volume, offering multifaceted perspectives on one of the most pressing concerns in contemporary organizational life. Your work has not only enhanced the intellectual quality of this book but also helped advance the ongoing conversation around leadership, communication, and workplace safety.

I am deeply honored by the contribution of Professor Keith Walker, who graciously accepted the invitation to write the foreword. His ability to frame the themes of this book with such clarity, wisdom, and academic insight has set the stage for the discussions that follow. Thank you for lending your voice to this work and for your long-standing dedication to advancing scholarship in the field. As my former PhD Supervisor, you have molded my research and writing interest.

A very special and personal note of thanks is owed to Mr. Richard Muschette, Captain and Aerospace Engineer. Our frequent and engaging discussions, particularly those centered on safety and security in the aviation sector served as the conceptual foundation for this book. Your depth of knowledge, practical insight, and passion for the subject have been both inspirational and instrumental. It is through these conversations that the initial vision for this book took shape, and for that, I am sincerely grateful.

To the team at IGI Global, thank you for your continued support, professionalism, and guidance throughout the editorial and production process. Your commitment to publishing scholarship that bridges research and practice is commendable. From manuscript preparation to final proof, your attention to detail and collaborative approach ensured that this work reached its full potential.

I would also like to acknowledge the many research participants who contributed their time, experiences, and insights to the study at the core of this project. Their candid reflections and perspectives provided essential grounding to the theoretical frameworks and arguments explored in the book. Without their voices, the research would have lacked the depth and authenticity that make it truly meaningful.

To my family, thank you for your unwavering support, patience, and encouragement throughout this demanding yet fulfilling journey. Your understanding during late nights, tight deadlines, and moments of uncertainty sustained me and made this endeavor possible.

Lastly, I give all glory and thanks to my Lord and Savior, Jesus Christ. It is through His grace, strength, and divine guidance that this work was not only envisioned but brought to completion. In every step of the process, I have been reminded of the power of faith, perseverance, and purpose. May this book be used in service of greater understanding and meaningful impact.

To all who contributed in ways both large and small, thank you. This book is as much yours as it is mine.

Dr. Darcia Roache, PhD. DBA. MBA. BSc.

Editor

Section 1
Employees and Workplace Safety and Security

Chapter 1
Employees' Safety and Security in Organizations, Is It Leadership or Communication?

Darcia Ann Marie Roache
https://orcid.org/0009-0007-7172-7695
University of Saskatchewan, Canada & Capilano University, Canada & University Canada West, Canada

ABSTRACT

Employees' safety and security in organizations are critical components of a healthy and productive work environment. The study explores the roles that leadership and communication play in ensuring the physical, psychological, and emotional well-being of employees. While leadership is often seen as the guiding force in setting safety policies and fostering a secure work culture, effective communication acts as the conduit through which these policies are implemented and reinforced. The study explores the interplay between leadership styles such as, transformational and transactional and communication strategies, highlighting how they contribute to creating an environment where employees feel safe and secure. The literature identifies factors, such as leadership styles, employee engagement, communication responsiveness, and crisis leadership, that influence both leadership and communication efforts.

DOI: 10.4018/979-8-3373-0482-3.ch001

INTRODUCTION

The safety and security of employees have become central to organizational success in an evolving and often unpredictable work environment. According to Kelloway and Barling (2010) a secure workplace, physically, emotionally, and digitally is no longer a merely regulatory obligation, Tamers (2020) said is a critical component of operational efficiency, reputation management, and employee satisfaction. Consensus on the importance of safety is an ongoing debate over what drives it more effectively, strong leadership or clear communication (Payne et al., 2024). Research shows that both are vital however, understanding which one holds greater weight or whether their combination is the key to assist organizations better design and implement their safety strategies. Men and Yue (2019) said that communication is a strategic tool for building strong leader-employee relationships and cultivating a positive workplace culture, however, Poor communication can undermine organizational performance even when leadership is strong (Clampitt et al., 2000).

The role of leadership in safety and security in organizations add value to the effective operations and management of organizations. Leaders not only set the tone for safety culture but also influence employee behavior, compliance with safety regulations, and the proactive identification of risks (Quansah et al., 2023). Leadership in an organization is the driving force behind vision, culture, and policy (Tasi, 2011). When leaders prioritize safety, it is more likely to become a core part of organizational culture (Naji et al., 2021).

According to Cooper (2000) leadership as safety in organization contributes to the development and reinforcement of a safety culture, where there are shared beliefs, practices, and attitudes that exist at an organization regarding safety. Reason (1997) said leaders establish this culture through communication, policy enforcement, and by serving as role models. According to Reason (1997), a strong safety culture reduces human error and enhances organizational resilience. Transformational leadership, which emphasizes motivation and engagement, has been shown to positively correlate with safety compliance and participation (Barling et al., 2002). Leaders who prioritize safety are proactive in identifying hazards and fostering an environment where employees feel safe to report near-misses and unsafe conditions (Haas et al., 2020). Such transparency prevents accidents and promotes continuous improvement in organization (Cooper, (2000). Leaders should be strategic in their security management in organizations. Security encompasses not just physical protection, but also cybersecurity, data protection, and emergency preparedness (Adamaas et al., 2024). Strategic leaders are responsible for assessing threats, allocating resources, and developing policies that mitigate risk. According to Garcia (2001), effective security leadership involves risk assessment, strategic planning, and staff training.

Leaders must align security goals with organizational objectives while ensuring compliance with laws and standards such as ISO 27001 or OSHA regulations.

In sectors such as critical infrastructure and national defense, leadership decisions can have far-reaching implications and such employees' safety and security in organizations involve effective communication and leadership. Fischer and co-authors (2018) postulated that clear command structures, defined responsibilities, and rehearsed contingency plans are vital to maintaining operational continuity and public safety. The study explores employees' safety and security in organizations and the effects of leadership communication in the process.

Purpose Statement

The purpose of this study is to explore the role of leadership and communication in ensuring employee safety and security within organizations, with the aim of determining whether effective leadership or clear communication has a more significant impact on creating and maintaining a safe and secure workplace environment. Ciekanowski et al. (2025) stated that "an effective leader not only ensures compliance with norms and procedures but primarily builds a work environment where safety becomes an integral part of the organization's daily operations" (p.1).

Problem Statement

Despite the increasing emphasis on workplace safety and security, many organizations continue to experience incidents that compromise employee well-being. While both leadership and communication are recognized as critical factors in promoting a safe work environment, it remains unclear which plays a more pivotal role (Molnar et al. 2019; Vidman & Strömberg, 2020). The lack of clarity regarding whether strong leadership or effective communication (Locker & Findlay, 2009) is more influential in ensuring employee safety and security creates a gap in both theory and practice. This ambiguity hinders organizations from prioritizing the most impactful strategies, potentially putting employees at continued risk.

Significance of the Chapter

This chapter is significant as it explores the critical factors that contribute to employee safety and security in organizations, focusing on the roles of leadership and communication. An understanding of these elements has a greater impact essentially for organizations aiming to create safer work environments. This study provides valuable insights for policymakers, leaders, managers, and human resource professionals on the importance of leadership and effective communication in ensuring safety and security for employees in organizations. The findings might assist organizations allocate resources more effectively, enhance training programs, and develop targeted strategies that foster a culture of safety and security. Ultimately, the chapter contributes to the broader discourse on workplace well-being and offers practical guidance for reducing risks and promoting a secure organizational climate.

RESEARCH METHOD

This qualitative study employed a case study approach, utilizing a standardized set of interview questions to explore the topic: *Employees' Safety and Security in Organizations, Is It Leadership or Communication*?. The study sample consisted of 10 participants drawn from business organizations and institutions across the United States, Canada, Dubai, and Jamaica. NVivo 10 qualitative analysis software was used to facilitate the coding, categorization, and identification of emerging themes. Data analysis was conducted using the constant comparison method to ensure a rigorous and systematic interpretation of the interview responses.

RESEARCH QUESTIONS

The study was guided by one main question and three sub-questions. Participants were asked structured questions.

Primary Research Question

To what extent do leadership and communication individually and collectively influence employees' safety and security in organizations?

Sub-Questions

RQ1: How does leadership style impact on employees' perception of safety and security in the workplace?
RQ2: To what extent does organizational communication influence employees' compliance with safety and security protocols?
RQ3: Can effective communication compensate for weak leadership in ensuring workplace safety and security, or are both equally indispensable?

REVIEW OF LITERATURE

This section presents a concise review of the existing literature pertinent to the research topic: *Employees' Safety and Security in Organizations, Is It Leadership or Communication*?. It aims to explore empirical findings and scholarly articles that inform organizational leadership, communication practices, and employees' safety and security in organizations.

Empowerment and Engagement

Engaged employees are more likely to follow safety procedures and contribute to a secure workplace. Leaders who empower employees through training, feedback, and involvement in decision-making foster a sense of ownership over safety outcomes (Baczyńska et al., 2024; Kapp, 2012; Quansah et al., 2023). Empowerment reduces the likelihood of negligence and improves morale. According to Quansah et al. (2023) leadership that emphasizes psychological safety, a belief that one can speak up without fear of punishment enhances risk communication. Edmondson (1999) found that psychological safety improves team learning and responsiveness, key elements in high-reliability organizations (Weick & Sutcliffe, 2001).

Crisis Leadership

During emergencies, effective leadership is critical to managing the response and minimizing harm. Crisis leadership demands clear communication, rapid decision-making, and emotional intelligence (Marshall et al., 2019). Leaders must manage panic, provide direction, and coordinate recovery efforts. Studies from the COVID-19 pandemic have shown that transparent, empathetic leadership helped organizations and governments maintain trust and order during uncertainty (Gigliotti, 2020; Marshall et al., 2020; Roache et al., 2020; Roache, 2023). Despite its importance, leadership in safety and security faces challenges such as resource constraints, resistance to change, and evolving threats (Sott & Bender, 2025). Leaders' continuous adaptation and upgrading of their skills and knowledge should be given priority in organizations. Investment in leadership development programs, scenario-based training, and cross-functional collaboration is essential (Sott & Bender, 2025). According to Roache (2023), when leaders communicate effectively it aids their planning, organizing, and controlling skills in the organizations. Roache further stated that leadership styles impact the organizations' performance negatively or positively. Leadership is indispensable to establishing and maintaining safety and security in any organization (Naji et al., 2021). Through vision, communication, and active engagement, leaders create environments where safety is a shared responsibility. As threats evolve, leadership strategies must remain adaptive, informed, and committed to the well-being of individuals and society at large.

Leaders' tone and communication styles influence how serious safety is taken across departments and job functions (Cakis, 2023). An active demonstration for safety, participating in inspections, speaking about security in meetings, or responding to incidents, leaders show employees that their well-being is a priority (Clarke, 2013; Zohar, 2002). Moreover, leaders make strategic decisions about where to allocate resources. Organizations might face budgetary constraints, but if safety is prioritized by leaders, they will ensure investments in personal protective equipment, cybersecurity systems, mental health support, or ergonomic workstations for their employees to benefit. Without such leadership commitment, even the most well-drafted safety policies may never be fully implemented. Leadership plays a pivotal role in shaping safety and security within organizations. Whether in corporate settings, public institutions, or high-risk industries such as construction, healthcare, and aviation, effective leadership is central to creating and maintaining a safe and secure environment (Ayiei eta al., 2020; Syed-Yahya et al., 2022). Leadership also influences employee behavior indirectly. Employees tend to mirror the attitudes of their supervisors or executive team. When safety is embedded in performance evaluations, leadership development, and organizational goals, it becomes a shared responsibility rather than an administrative burden.

Formal and Informal Communications

Formal communication follows official channels and structures established by an organization. It is typically documented, regulated, and used for operational, strategic, and compliance purposes. (Langton et al., 2023; McShane et al., 2024) Example, such as Memos, reports, and official emails, policies and procedures, organizational charts and meeting minutes, and company newsletters and performance reviews. There are advantages, clear, consistent messaging, accountability and traceability, and supports compliance and standardization (Guo & Sanchez, 2009; Langton et al., 2023; Locker & Findlay, 2009). However, limitations where communication can be rigid or slow to adapt and may create communication silos.

Informal communication is often referred to as the "grapevine," occurs outside official channels and is more spontaneous, flexible, and personal (Langton et al., 2023; Locker & Findlay, 2009). It plays a key role in shaping organizational culture and fostering trust among employees, an example includes casual conversations between colleagues. Advantages could be seen as: encourage relationship-building, speed up information sharing, and assist with identifying issues not captured in formal channels (Langton et al., 2023; Locker & Findlay, 2009; McShane et al., 2024).

Also, limitations that can lead to misinformation or rumors, and lacks documentation or control (Langton et al., 2023; Locker & Findlay, 2009; McShane et al., 2024).

Direction of Communications

Langton et al. (2023) postulated that communication can flow vertically, upwardly (bottom-up), and laterally in organizations and is used by leaders to provide instructions, inform employees of 'policies and procedures' (p. 234), identify problems, and provide feedback.

Top-Down/Downward Communication

Flows from senior management to lower-level employees. It is typically directive in nature and used to provide guidance, assign tasks, communicate goals, and share decisions such as strategic updates and organizational changes (Langton et al., 2023; McShane et al., 2024). The benefits of downward communication, ensure alignment with leadership vision, establish authority and clarity, and facilitate consistent messaging (Langton et al., 2023; McShane et al., 2024). The top-down approach to communication is that it provides limitations, the authors stated, as an employee can feel one-sided or authoritarian and that might limit his or her input or feedback in the organizational decisions. Leaders have a responsibility to explain reasons for organizational decisions but might be too busy to explain (Hakanen et al., 2011; Meier & Semmer, 2008). According to Langton et al., (2023) "managers might think that sending a message one time is enough to get through to lower-level employees" (p. 234). However, that might not be the case, as "managerial communication must be repeated several times and through a variety of different media to be truly effective" (Langton et al., 2023, p. 234; Meier et al., 2008). Needless to say, when leaders explain information to employees it increases their commitment and support of decisions (Hakanen et al., 2011).

Bottom-Up Communication

Bottom-up or upward communication originates from employees and moves upward to supervisors, managers, and executives. The value of this hierarchical method is, it "flows to a higher level in group or organizations and is used to provide feedback to higher-ups, informing them of progress towards goals (Langton et al., 2023, p. 235). The bottom-up approach provides feedback, suggestions, concerns, and ideas from those on the front lines. The upward communication has boasted examples such as, employee surveys or feedback forms, team meetings and brainstorming sessions, and direct conversations with supervisors (Langton et al., 2023; McShane et al., 2024).

Research suggests that advantages include, encourages employee engagement and innovation, assists leaders stay connected with operational realities, and builds trust and transparency among leaders and employees within the organization (Guo & Sanchez, 2009; Langton et al., 2023; Locker & Findlay, 2009; McShane et al., 2024). Upward communication is not without limitations, as it may be filtered or diluted through layers of hierarchy and requires a supportive culture to be effective (Guo & Sanchez, 2009; Langton et al., 2023; Locker & Findlay, 2009; McShane et al., 2024). Organizational leaders have a responsibility to strive to balance these communication channels as each type plays a distinct role in maintaining a healthy organizational climate that ensures strategic clarity and consistency and captures employee sentiment and fosters engagement (Guo & Sanchez, 2009; Langton et al., 2023; Locker & Findlay, 2009; McShane et al., 2024). According to Langton et al. (2023) and McShane (2021) when managed effectively, these communication types contribute to a work environment that is not only well-informed but also inclusive and responsive.

Lateral Communication

Lateral communication, also known as horizontal communication, refers to the flow of information between employees or departments at the same organizational level (Langton et al., 2023). Unlike top-down or bottom-up communication, which moves vertically through the hierarchy, lateral communication moves side-to-side, facilitating collaboration, coordination, and problem-solving among peers Guo & Sanchez, 2009; Langton et al., 2023; Locker & Findlay, 2009; McShane et al., 2024). Lateral communication plays a vital role in promoting operational efficiency, reducing misunderstandings, and fostering a culture of teamwork and organizations rely on cross-functional collaboration or project-based teams within organizations (Guo & Sanchez, 2009; Langton et al., 2023; Locker & Findlay, 2009; McShane et al., 2024). Communication regardless of the type is essential to the workplace and employees' safety and security.

Digital Communication and Workplace Safety

Remote and hybrid work environments give increasingly more importance to digital communication which has become central to maintaining organizational efficiency, culture, and workplace safety. As physical presence decreases, the reliance on digital platforms for sharing safety information, emergency protocols, mental health resources, and leadership messaging becomes essential (Fitzpatrick,

2023; Simon et al., 2015). The digitized work environment has accelerated by the COVID-19 pandemic and has become central to organizational functioning. Digital communication not only improves efficiency and connectivity in organization but is vital for ensuring workplace safety, especially in remote and hybrid settings (Battisti et al., 2022; Kraemer & Swanson, 2021). As traditional safety protocols evolve to include mental well-being, cybersecurity, and remote ergonomics, digital tools offer innovative ways to inform, engage, and protect employees.

Digital Communication in Organizations

Organizations have transitioned from primarily face-to-face communication to digital platforms such as email, video conferencing, chat applications, and collaborative tools. These changes are particularly pronounced in remote and hybrid environments where physical presence is limited. According to Wang et al. (2021), remote work has prompted organizations to rely heavily on digital tools to maintain organizational culture, disseminate critical updates, and ensure the continuity of operations, including safety procedures.

Kraemer and Swanson (2021) highlight how digital communication tools enable both real-time updates and asynchronous communication, which are essential in disseminating emergency protocols and health-related information in distributed or hybrid workplaces. Their findings underscore the importance of using digital platforms to ensure that all employees, regardless of time zone or location, receive consistent and timely safety communication. Leonardi's research also discusses how digital communication technologies collaboration platforms, messaging apps, and intranet systems are central to real-time and time-independent communication, especially in the context of remote and hybrid work (Leonardi, 2021). The article emphasizes that these tools are essential for delivering critical updates, including safety and health protocols, ensuring equitable access to information across different geographies and time zones.

Enhancing Physical and Psychological Safety

Workplace safety has broadened to include psychological and emotional well-being, particularly as remote work blurs the boundaries between personal and professional life. Digital platforms now serve as conduits for promoting mental health through virtual check-ins, teletherapy, mindfulness sessions, and wellness webinars (Ford et al., 2021). Managers can use video conferencing tools to provide support and build trust, which is crucial in reducing employee stress and anxiety during times of uncertainty. Moreover, digital communication supports ergonomic safety in remote settings. Employees working from home may face risks due to improper seating, poor lighting, or inadequate workstations (Milaković et al., 2023; Snodgrass et al., 2022). Organizations can mitigate these risks by distributing ergonomic guidelines via email, offering virtual workstation assessments, or reimbursing home-office setups all facilitated through digital communication channels.

Cybersecurity and Information Safety

Another critical dimension of workplace safety in digital environments is cybersecurity. With the rise of remote work, employees often access sensitive data through personal or unsecured networks, increasing the risk of breaches. Digital communication plays a central role in educating employees about cybersecurity best practices, phishing risks, and data protection protocols. According to Choudhury et al. (2020), organizations that frequently communicate about cybersecurity tend to have fewer incidents of human-error-related breaches. Companies can use digital tools to implement two-factor authentication, distribute secure access credentials, and issue automatic security updates. Regular webinars and e-learning modules on cybersecurity awareness can also foster a culture of vigilance and responsibility among employees.

Challenges in Digital Communication for Safety

Digital communication has redefined the way organizations approach workplace safety. In remote and hybrid work environments, it ensures that all employees, regardless of physical location, are informed, supported, and protected. When used effectively, digital communication not only enhances physical and psychological safety but also fosters a culture of transparency and engagement. However, to maximize its benefits, organizations must address challenges such as digital fatigue, inequality, and overload through inclusive and strategic communication practices. Despite its advantages, digital communication is not without challenges. Information overload can lead to important safety messages being overlooked. In a sea of emails and notifications, safety communication must be clear, concise, and prioritized. Additionally, digital fatigue, caused by continuous screen time and online interactions can diminish engagement and responsiveness to critical safety content (Wang et al., 2021). Digital inequality poses another concern. Not all employees have equal access to high-speed internet, digital devices, or the technical literacy required to engage with online safety programs. Organizations must ensure inclusivity by providing technical support, mobile-friendly content, and alternative formats where necessary.

Importance of Communication in Safety and Security

Communication is the mechanism through which safety policies are operationalized. According to (McShane et al. 2021) leadership might create a strong safety vision, however, communication ensures that vision to be understood, embraced, and acted upon throughout the organization. Without clear and consistent communication, employees may not know what is expected of them, how to follow safety procedures, or whom to contact in case of emergencies (Findlay & Locker, 2009; Guo, 2009). Effective communication involves both one-way messaging, such as distributing policy documents or sending alerts, and two-way engagement, including feedback mechanisms and whistleblowing systems (Daft, 2010; Locker & Findlay, 2009). Employees must feel comfortable and empowered to report hazards or raise concerns without fear of retaliation. Creating these feedback loops and ensuring they are accessible and confidential is essential for early risk detection and proactive action.

When communication is effective it informs policies and regulations of any successful organization. It enables coordination, promotes a positive culture, and ensures that employees are informed, engaged, and aligned with organizational goals (McShane et al., 2021; Men, 2014; Mumby & Kuhn, 2019). Communication is a process, model, and a network that flows through channels, and between sender and receiver (McShane et al., 2021; McShane & Warner, 2024). Organizational communication can be categorized into several types, for example, formal and informal communication, as well as top-down and bottom-up communication. Training is another major area where communication plays a critical role (Mehner et al., 2025). Safety training must be more than a checkbox item during onboarding. It should be an ongoing, interactive, and engaging process, using multiple communication channels, face-to-face meetings, emails, mobile apps, and even virtual reality simulations where applicable. Reinforcement through visual cues (like signage), reminders, and regular briefings can further strengthen the safety culture (Daft, 2010; Guo, 2009; Kotler & Armstrong, 2006). Employee safety and security are among the most crucial responsibilities of any organization. Leadership and communication play indispensable roles in fostering a safe working environment (Roache, 2023). It is through the combination of these two elements that organizations can truly protect their employees and build resilient, high-trust workplaces.

Leadership and Safety and Security in Organizations

Leadership plays a foundational role in shaping the safety and security culture within organizations. While policies and procedures provide a framework for action, it is leadership that determines whether safety and security are taken seriously or treated as mere formalities. Effective leadership not only initiates and enforces safety protocols but also inspires a shared sense of responsibility and vigilance among employees. The complex of the workplace environments, ranging from corporate offices to industrial plants, leaders must proactively manage risks, promote a safety-first culture, and respond decisively to threats. Leadership role in ensuring organizational safety and security is paramount.

Leadership as the Driver of Safety Culture

The safety culture of an organization refers to the shared attitudes, perceptions, and values that employees hold regarding safety. This culture is heavily influenced by leadership. Research has shown that leaders consistently emphasize the importance of safety, recognize safe behaviors, and model compliance with safety standards (Molnar, 2019; Molnar et al., 2022; Omidi et al., 2023). They embed those values into the organizational mindset

Leaders who downplay safety protocols or ignore violations contribute to a culture of complacency or risk tolerance. Leadership is responsible for crafting the strategic vision around safety and security (Thompson et al., 2024). This includes setting safety objectives, defining acceptable risk levels, and developing comprehensive safety policies. These policies should align with national laws, industry standards, and organizational values. Effective leaders ensure that these policies are not just theoretical documents but translated into practical procedures, delegate authority to safety officers, and create systems to monitor compliance (Molnar et al., 2022; Omidi et al., 2023). Moreover, strategic leaders engage stakeholders, from HR to operations, in building cross-functional safety plans, ensuring alignment and shared accountability (Thompson et al., 2024; Uhl-bien et al., 2023).

Empowering and Training Employees

Another important dimension of leadership is employee empowerment. Safety cannot be managed top-down alone; it requires participation at every level. Strong leaders create environments where employees feel confident to report hazards, suggest improvements, and intervene in unsafe situations. This is closely tied to training. Leaders must ensure that employees receive regular and meaningful training in both safety and emergency procedures. Training should be role-specific and evolve in response to new threats, such as cybersecurity issues, remote work risks, or public health emergencies like pandemics. When leadership is involved in training, whether by attending sessions, giving opening remarks, or participating in drills, it reinforces the value of safety and security for everyone in the organization.

Leadership Styles in Organizations

Leadership is a cornerstone of organizational success. It determines how goals are set, how teams are managed, and how organizations respond to challenges and change. However, leadership is not a one-size-fits-all concept. Different situations call for different approaches, and leaders often adopt distinct styles to influence, guide, and motivate their teams. The choice of leadership style significantly enhances organizational effectiveness. Transformational leaders inspire impacts employee morale, productivity, innovation, and overall and motivate employees to exceed expectations by focusing on vision, change, and personal development (Roache, 2023; Roache 2024). They lead by example, emphasize innovation, and build commitment to organizational goals (Roache, 2024), Transactional leaders focus on structure, rules, and performance-based rewards and punishments. Their primary concern is maintaining efficiency and achieving short-term goals (Roache, 2023; Roache 2024). Laissez-faire leaders offer minimal guidance, allowing employees to make decisions and manage their own work (Ahmed et al., 2021). This style trusts team members to be self-motivated and responsible.

The most effective leaders often adopt a situational leadership approach, adjusting their style based on the team's needs, the nature of the task, and the organizational environment. A transformational leader may shift to a transactional approach during a performance review cycle. Similarly, an autocratic style may be necessary during a crisis but should transition to a democratic style during planning and development phases. Leaders who understand and can flexibly apply various leadership styles are more likely to build high-performing teams, foster innovation, and respond effectively to both opportunities and challenges.

Middle Managers and Team Supervisors in Workplace Safety and Security

Workplace safety and security are critical components of organizational success, directly influencing employee well-being, productivity, and regulatory compliance. While senior leadership typically sets the strategic direction for safety policies, the practical implementation and daily enforcement often relies heavily on middle managers and team supervisors. These roles serve as the vital link between upper management's safety goals and frontline employee behavior, shaping the safety culture within organizations.

Middle Managers Contribution in Organization Safety and Security

Middle managers hold a pivotal role in translating organizational safety policies into operational practices. According to Mullen and Kelloway (2009), middle managers act as "safety intermediaries," facilitating communication between senior leadership and employees. They are responsible for ensuring that safety protocols are understood and implemented consistently within their departments. Research indicates that the allocation of resources such as training programs, personal protective equipment (PPE), and safety audits aid maintaining a safe work environment and that the commitment of middle managers to safety has a strong impact on safety outcomes (Huang et al., 2006). A study by Barling et al. (2002) found that middle managers' safety-specific transformational leadership positively influenced employee safety behaviors, and reduced injury rates. By modeling safety values and holding employees accountable, middle managers reinforce the importance of compliance with safety standards. Additionally, Clarke (2013) posited that middle managers often lead investigations of workplace incidents to identify root causes and develop corrective actions. Their role in reporting safety metrics and incidents upward allows for informed decision-making at the strategic level, thus enabling continuous improvement in workplace safety systems.

Contributions of Supervisors Organization Safety and Security

Team supervisors operate on the frontline of workplace safety, directly overseeing the daily activities of employees, monitor compliance with safety procedures, and promptly address hazards (Griffin & Neal, 2000). Studies demonstrate that supervisors' safety-specific feedback and interventions are crucial in preventing unsafe behaviors and accidents (Christian et al., 2009). Effective supervisors not only enforce rules but also cultivate an environment where employees feel empowered to report safety concerns without fear of retaliation (Zohar & Luria, 2003). This open communication is essential for identifying latent hazards that may not be visible at higher organizational levels. Nahrgang et al. (2011) stated that among the work of supervisors, one can find their ability to recognize and mitigate risks before incidents occur reflects their critical role in proactive safety management.

Supervisors are contributory to building a positive safety culture by consistently reinforcing safety norms and demonstrating commitment through their actions. Effective leaders as supervisors influence and enhance employees' safety motivation and participation in safety initiatives (Neal & Griffin, 2006). Supervisors often conduct on-the-job safety training and refreshers, ensuring that safety knowledge is maintained and updated regularly (Wu et al., 2008). The synergistic impact of middle managers and supervisors is discussed in literature. The literature suggests that the safety performance of an organization is significantly improved when middle managers and supervisors work in alignment to promote safety culture and practices. Hofmann and Mark (2006) argue that middle managers create the framework and allocate resources for safety, while supervisors ensure effective implementation and day-to-day adherence. This synergy fosters a comprehensive safety climate that extends from policy to practice.

Leadership style is one of the most significant factors influencing organizational success, employee engagement, and culture. While no single style is universally superior, each has its strengths and limitations depending on the situation (Roache, 2023). Effective leaders are those who are self-aware, adaptable, and capable of choosing the right style for the right moment. In a world of constant change and complexity, leadership agility, rather than adherence to a single style, may ultimately be the most valuable trait of all. Communication is the lifeblood of any organization. According to Roache, (2023) "communication effectiveness has been a guide for leaders as they have planned, organized, controlled and led the organizations" (p. 17). It is the process through which information, ideas, instructions, and feedback are shared among individuals and groups to achieve common goals. In organizational settings, effective communication is crucial for coordination, decision-making, conflict resolution, employee engagement, and overall efficiency. As workplaces become more complex and diverse, the ability to communicate clearly, respectfully, and strategically becomes even more important. This essay explores the role of communication in organizations, its various forms, common barriers, and strategies to enhance its effectiveness.

RESEARCH FINDINGS

The ten participants unanimously agreed that leadership styles critically shape how employees perceive their safety and security in organizations. Participants shared that leadership styles impact their perceptions of safety and security positively or negatively in organization. Different styles in leadership require an understanding that employees' roles are essential in the working environment therefore leaders should ensure the inclusion of safety and security as a priority in organizations' productivity, collaboration, and staff morale. The emergent themes from the study are explained below:

Theme 1: Leadership Styles That Include Inspiration and Support, and Workplace Policy

When asked "*How does leadership style impact employees' perception of safety and security in the workplace,* Participant 9 postulated that "transformational leaders, who inspire, support, and engage their employees often create an environment where safety is a shared value. This builds trust and psychological safety. In contrast, laissez-faire leaders, who are less involved, may cause uncertainty and lower safety perceptions due to lack of direction and enforcement. "Transactional leaders, who focus on clear rules and reward punishment systems, may improve compliance but not necessarily enhance intrinsic safety perceptions" (Participant 10).

Other perspectives were that the situation varies based on the type of leadership style and an adaptation to various leadership styles dependent on the immediate circumstances or situations (Participants 1-3). Leaders should use each leadership style to the advantage of the organization and set the tone from their hierarchical position. According to Participant 6, leadership style impacts workplace safety and impactful leaders prioritize workplace safety and allocate resources to ensure that workers are kept safe. This argument was supported by Participant 5 that They make sure staff are trained in safety procedures and have procedures in place that monitor compliance. If leaders take safety seriously, workers will follow suit. Training changes leaders and employees' behavior in organizations. Empirical research on leadership and organizational safety found that transformational leadership has been found to have positive associations with occupational safety outcomes, such as lower injury rates (Molnar et al., 2019). The strong link between transformational leadership and safety participation is that the empowering, inspiring, and trust-based behaviors of these leaders increases employees' willingness to exceed their formal role responsibilities (Clarke (2013)

Participant 2 stated that "transformational and transactional leadership among others help promote a safe cultural environment among employees because they ensure that workers are encouraged to raise their concern on safety and security". Transactional leaders are strict and able to establish clear safety and security guidelines for employers to follow. Participant 6 shared that "leadership plays a crucial role in shaping workplace safety culture. Leaders who recognize their employees and the future or mission and vision of the organization inspire employees to prioritize all forms of safety and compliance measures. "Safety comes in different forms, such as, "personal safety, organizational safety to the point where, CCTVs, Security Guards, safety signage among things are implemented" (Participant 5). Supporting employees by encouraging them to behave safely, making suggestions for improving safety, and communicating when nonsafe situations are identified shows concerns for employees (Clarke, 2013; Molnar, 2019, Tsai, 2011)

Participant 10 perspectives were, "a leader is responsible for cultivating safety and security in the workplace according to some establishments code of ethics and workplace policy. However, how this conducted depends on the leadership style of the individual leader". A participant shared, "from my experience, the leaders I have worked with were more desirous to get the job done. Although my colleagues complained about safety issues in the workspace they were never taken seriously, instead, supervisors would simply report that they would analyze the problem, but there was no resolution". Research has shown that leadership styles significantly impact employees' views of safety and security in the workplace. Transformational leadership has a robust impact, while transactional leadership influences safety culture (Clarke, 2013; Hadley, 2025; Molnar, 2019). Passive-avoidant leadership is negatively associated with safety perception (Hadley, 2025). Leadership styles mold employees' safety behavior by influencing motivation, responsibility, and collaboration on safety matters (Hadley, 2025). A positive safety climate can improve safety practices and promote active discussion of safety and security in the workplace.

In conclusion, the research findings revealed that employees feel safer when leaders are proactive, communicative, and visibly committed to safety in organizations, regardless of their leadership styles.

Theme 2: Effective Communication, Decision-making process, Safety Compliance, Training and Development

When asked, *to what extent does organizational communication influence employees' compliance with safety and security protocols.* It was revealed that organizational communication strongly influences safety compliance. Clear, consistent, and transparent communication ensures that employees understand safety expectations, procedures, and consequences, the finding gleaned. Regular updates and feedback mechanisms help maintain high levels of awareness and adherence (Participant 5). The finding revealed that creating and establishing an environment where employees clearly understand their roles and responsibilities involving policies, practices, and policies on safety and security influences employees' compliance. Effective communication builds trust and collaboration and when leaders outline clear expectations, there is a greater chance of compliance on safety issues, (Participant 6).

The findings revealed that clear and consistent communication ensures employees understand and follow the organizations' safety protocols. Participant 5 shared that "diagonal, horizontal and vertical (downward) and upward communication methods are important in two-way communication (feedback loops) which increases compliance by making employees feel heard and having a voice in activities of the organization and the decision-making process". Two-way communication increases clear understanding of organization goals and needs. Organizations are better able to engender clear understanding of issues and engender corporation and goodwill. Participants 2 said "miscommunication or lack of information can lead to misunderstandings, increased risk-taking, and non-compliance. Hence, effective communication boosts awareness and accountability, directly improving safety protocol compliance". This Participant 8 said, "effective communication builds trust and collaboration. When leaders outline clear expectations, there is a greater chance of compliance". Organizations require standard operations procedures in the environment for workers and ensuring that the necessary protective gear is available and thus enforcement safety and security at all levels with educational awareness (Participant 6). The participant further stated, "to a great extent, if employees are aware, they will be more knowledgeable and compliant. Avenues that can be used to assist with remaining/becoming informed include training and development, newsletters, signage, and regular updates/meetings." The finding revealed that communication allows individuals with the necessary information they need to respond to the established organizations' protocols. The protocols should be communicated regularly alongside the practice of what is expected of everyone (Participant 10).

Literature revealed that organizational communication positively influences employees' safety, compliance, and participation (Lee et al., 2019). Effective and transparent communication creates a safe and productive workplace (Lee et al., 2019). The organizational climate should include leadership commitment to safety and security protocols which might influence employees' compliance.

Theme 3: Leadership, Communication, Employee trust in Fostering Safety Culture

The participants were asked which *component has a greater effect on fostering a culture of safety and security, leadership practices or internal communication strategies*? In responding, they postulated that leadership and communication are essential in organization, while leadership sets the tone for safety culture, strong leadership without effective communication can lead to confusion, while good communication without leadership may lack enforcement. The ten participants collectively agreed that leadership has a foundational impact, while communication amplifies and reinforces that foundation. Internal communication strategies driven by solid leadership practices can greatly affect and foster a culture of safety. Participant 9 said "an ineffective or "lame" leadership will be unable to effectively promote a safe and secure workplace environment among employees even with the best internal communication strategies". Transactional leadership practices, for example, can create and establish clear workplace guidelines for employees to follow.

When asked, "*which has a greater effect on fostering a culture of safety and security—leadership practices or internal communication strategies*, Participant 1 alluded that leadership typically has a slightly greater impact. "Leadership sets the tone and priorities of an organization; if leaders prioritize safety and model safe behavior, it becomes embedded in the culture. However, "without effective communication, even good leadership practices can fail to resonate and conversely, strong communication cannot fully make up for poor leadership (Participant 6). According to Roache (2023) in her study on *transformational leadership style: Management and communication taxonomies for organizational effectiveness* found that "… when goals differ, clear communication is more essential for individuals to work organizational solutions that are acceptable and possible for all persons involved" (P.17).

Effective communication has a greater influence on safety practices, as people are more interested in keeping themselves and others safe, despite leadership style. "Self-preservation takes precedence over leadership style. However, leadership can still influence the rate of compliance' (Participant 2). This study reinforced the importance of how employees often view leadership as the driving force behind safety values, while communication is the mechanism through which those values are enacted. Employees trust and follow leaders who visibly support safety initiatives. They also appreciate timely and clear communication about risks, policies, and expectations. Employees cited leadership commitment as the most important indicator of a safe workplace. It became apparent through the study of Al-Mekhlafi, (2024) that employees perceive effective communication as essential for building healthy relationships and promoting a safe and secure work environment. Leaders who communicate well might inspire team members and create environments that promote loyalty, innovation, and sustained success (Toseef, 2022). Effective leadership is significant and the "key in opening the many doors" for a safe and secure working environment (Participant 9). Employees perceive leadership which operates on the ideals of transparency and engagement with employees on issues of safety and security to be of more important vis-a vis communication.

The findings revealed that once employees are guided and knowledgeable, they will know how to proceed during certain catastrophic experiences in the organizations. Participant 4 in support of the findings' perspectives were "protocols shared for the standard operating procedures are more important for promoting a safe and secure environment as opposed to whether a leader is autocratic or transformational".

Theme 4: Safety-First Culture, OSHA Workplace Safety Policies, Organizational Success

The findings revealed that internal communication to a limited extent might compensate temporarily for weak leadership. Some participants stated that both are equally indispensable as leadership influences compliance through effective communication, workplace policies, monitoring, and compliance. While communication can support safety in the short term, sustained safety requires strong leadership. The participants collaboratively shared that effective communication to include detailed procedures, safety alerts, and training can help maintain basic compliance even when leadership is weak. However, without strong leadership to model behavior, enforce standards, and create a safety-first culture, communication alone may not inspire the deeper commitment needed for long-term safety performance.

When asked can effective internal communication compensate for weak leadership in ensuring workplace safety, participant 1 said "weak leadership cannot be overlooked nor deliberately accepted but believe that effective communication can partially compensate for weak leadership but cannot fully replace it. Weak leadership undermines workplace safety, even with strong communication (Participant 1). The Participant further explained that the "leader would be interested in developing policies such OSHA workplace safety policies. In a practical sense, the participants perspectives were, organizations need strong and effective leadership and effective communication to achieve growth and development for organizational success (Participants 5-8). Effective communication is essential for workplace safety and security and can compensate for weak leadership. Unblemished and honest communication is critical during times of uncertainty and can strengthen workplace safety (Mohamed, 2024). While both are indispensable, "weak leaders do not necessarily communicate. However, "if a strong HR team deals with effective communication of policies surrounding safety and security, the leadership style(s) should ideally influence workplace safety and security" (Participant 6).

In conclusion, Figure 1: illustrates the framework developed from the participants' responses. The framework depicted that leadership and communication are exclusive for employees' safety and security in organizations.

Figure 1. Darcia Roache' framework for leadership and communication for organizational and employees' safety and security

Developed by (Roache, 2025)

Summary of the Framework

Leadership Styles - The framework demonstrates that leadership styles provide a balanced and dynamic approach to fostering a safe and secure workplace. Transactional leadership offers the structure and accountability needed to enforce safety protocols, while transformational leadership serves to inspire, support, and encourage employees to actively engage in maintaining a positive safety culture. Together, these styles create an environment where safety is not only managed but deeply valued, empowering organizations to protect their people and promote long-term well-being.

Communication – Roache's Leadership and Communication Framework underscores the importance of aligning leadership practices with clear communication to ensure organizational and employee safety and security. Central to this alignment are structured training programs, consistent monitoring, and a strong emphasis on compliance. These elements work together to reinforce safety expectations, build awareness, and cultivate a proactive safety culture. By integrating leadership with effective communication strategies, organizations can create a secure environment where employees are well-informed, engaged, and committed to upholding safety standards.

Organizational Safety and Security as illustrates in the framework *reinforces* the vital connection between strong leadership, effective communication, and a resilient safety culture. By promoting awareness, consistently enforcing safety protocols, and engaging employees at all levels, organizations can build a secure workplace where safety is deeply embedded in daily operations. This integrated approach not only strengthens compliance and reduces risk but also drives organizational success by fostering trust, well-being, and a shared commitment to safety.

FINDINGS AND IMPLICATONS

Findings

The qualitative data analysis revealed that while both leadership and communication are integral to organizational safety and security, leadership emerged as the more decisive factor in shaping a strong safety culture. Participants reported that leaders who actively engage in safety-related practices, such as setting clear expectations, visibly supporting safety protocols, and responding promptly to risks, enhance employees' sense of security. Effective communication was acknowledged as a key enabler; however, its impact was significantly amplified when delivered through credible and committed leadership. A recurring theme among responses was that leadership sets the tone, and employees' trust in leadership directly influenced their engagement with safety initiatives. From the data, the *Roache's Leadership and Communication Framework for Organizational and Employees' Safety and Security* was developed. This framework illustrates how leadership behaviors, such as visible commitment to safety, and strategic decision-making, interact with clear, consistent, and inclusive communication practices could create a psychologically safe and secure work environment.

Implications

These findings have important implications for organizational policy and practice. First, it highlights the need for leadership development initiatives that equip managers with the skills to lead safety efforts, communicate effectively, and foster a culture of accountability. Second, the results suggest that organizations must go beyond information dissemination by embedding safety communication within effective leadership behavior and the appropriate styles. Finally, given the dynamic nature of organizational threats, from public health emergencies to cybersecurity risks, leaders must adopt a proactive and adaptive approach, ensuring that safety and security remain strategic priorities aligned with employee well-being and organizational sustainability.

CONCLUSION

Communication is a critical enabler of success in modern organizations. It connects people, drives collaboration, and ensures that objectives are met efficiently and ethically. The findings of this study underscore the critical interdependence between leadership and communication in fostering a safe and secure organizational environment for employees. Strong leadership provides the vision, structure, and authority necessary to prioritize employee safety and effective communication ensures that policies are clearly articulated, understood, and consistently reinforced across all levels of the organization. The insights gathered from leaders across diverse cultural and organizational contexts as participated in the study revealed that a one-dimensional approach, that relying solely on leadership or communication is insufficient.

Instead, a cohesive and collaborative strategy that integrates both elements is vital for building trust, encouraging compliance, and promoting a culture of safety. The development of the *Roache's Leadership and Communication Framework* offers a practical guide for organizations seeking to enhance employee well-being by aligning leadership practices with transparent, responsive, and inclusive communication strategies. Ultimately, the study affirms that when leadership and communication work in tandem, organizations are better equipped to protect, engage, and empower their workforce.

REFERENCES

Admass, W. S., Munaye, Y. Y., & Diro, A. A. (2024). Cyber security: State of the art, challenges and future directions. *Cyber Security and Application Journal, 2*, 1–10. DOI: 10.1016/j.csa.2023.100031

Ahmed, I. Z., Abid, G., Arshad, M., Ashfaq, F., Athar, M. A., & Hassan, Q. (2021). Impact of authoritative and laissez-Faire leadership on thriving at work: The moderating role of conscientiousness. *European Journal Investigation in Health. European Journal of Investigation in Health, Psychology and Education, 11*(3), 667–685. DOI: 10.3390/ejihpe11030048

Al-Mekhlafi, A. B. A. (2024). The importance of effective human resources management in creating a more secure work environment by improving safety culture. *International Journal of Intellectual Human Resource Management, 5*(01), 14–23.

Baczyńska, A., He, H., He, T., Li, X., & Xinyi He, X. (2024). Servant leadership and employees' work safety behavior: The moderating role of corporate social responsibility to employees. *International Journal of Organizational Leadership, 13*(4), 778–801.

Barling, J., Loughlin, C., & Kelloway, E. K. (2002). Development and test of a model linking safety-specific transformational leadership and occupational safety. *The Journal of Applied Psychology, 87*(3), 488–496. DOI: 10.1037/0021-9010.87.3.488 PMID: 12090606

Battisti, E., Alfiero, S., & Leonidou, E. (2022). Remote working and digital transformation during the COVID-19 pandemic: Economic-financial impacts and psychological drivers for employees. *Journal of Business Research, 150*, 38–50. DOI: 10.1016/j.jbusres.2022.06.010 PMID: 35706830

Cakir, M. S., Wardman, J. K., & Trautrims, A. (2023). Ethical leadership supports safety voice by increasing risk perception and reducing ethical ambiguity: Evidence from the COVID-19 pandemic. *Risk Analysis, 43*(9), 1902–1916. DOI: 10.1111/risa.14053 PMID: 36261397

Choudhury, P., Foroughi, C., & Larson, B. Z. (2020). Work-from-anywhere: The productivity effects of geographic flexibility. *Strategic Management Journal, 42*(4), 655–683. DOI: 10.1002/smj.3251

Christian, M. S., Bradley, J. C., Wallace, J. C., & Burke, M. J. (2009). Workplace safety: A meta-analysis of the roles of person and situation factors. *The Journal of Applied Psychology, 94*(5), 1103–1127. DOI: 10.1037/a0016172 PMID: 19702360

Ciekanowski, Z. S., Żurawski, S., Wysokińska, A., & Kacprzak, A. (2025). The Role of a leader in shaping the safety culture of an organization. *European Research Studies*, *28*(1), 589–598. DOI: 10.35808/ersj/3923

Clampitt, P. G., DeKoch, R. J., & Cashman, T. (2000). A strategy for communicating about uncertainty. *The Academy of Management Perspectives*, *14*(4), 41–57. DOI: 10.5465/ame.2000.3979815

Clarke, S. (2013). Safety leadership: A meta-analytic review of transformational and transactional leadership styles as antecedents of safety behaviours. *Journal of Occupational and Organizational Psychology*, *86*(1), 22–49. DOI: 10.1111/j.2044-8325.2012.02064.x

Cooper, M. D. (2000). Towards a model of safety culture. *Safety Science Journal*, *36*, 111–136. DOI: 10.1016/S0925-7535(00)00035-7

Daft, R. L. (2010). *Management* (9th ed.). South-Western. Cengage Learning

Fischer, R. J., Halibozek, E. P., & Walters, D. C. (2018). Contingency Planning Emergency Response and Safety. *International Security*, *2019*, 249–268. DOI: 10.1016/B978-0-12-805310-2.00011-1

Fitzpatrick, P. J. (2023). Improving health literacy using the power of digital communications to achieve better health outcomes for patients and practitioners. *Frontiers in Digital Health*, *17*(5), 1–13. DOI: 10.3389/fdgth.2023.1264780 PMID: 38046643

Ford, M. T., Matthews, R. A., Wooldridge, J. D., Mishra, V., Kakar, U., & Strahan, S. R. (2021). How do occupational stressor-strain effects vary with time? A review and meta-analysis of the relevance of time lags in longitudinal studies. *Work and Stress*, *35*(2), 104–130. DOI: 10.1080/02678373.2020.1837731

Griffin, M. A., & Neal, A. (2000). Perceptions of safety at work: A framework for linking safety climate to safety performance, knowledge, and motivation. *Journal of Occupational Health Psychology*, *5*(3), 347–358. DOI: 10.1037/1076-8998.5.3.347 PMID: 10912498

Guo, K. L. (2009). Effective communication in health care: Strategies to improve outcomes. *The Health Care Manager*, *28*(3), 222–229. DOI: 10.1097/HCM.0b013e3181b3e2b2

Guo, K. L., & Sanchez, Y. (2009). Workplace communication. *Organization Development Journal*, *27*(4), 9–22.

Haas, E. J., Demich, B., & McGuire, J. (2020). Learning from Workers' Near-miss Reports to Improve Organizational Management. *Mining, Metallurgy & Exploration, 37*(3), 873–885. DOI: 10.1007/s42461-020-00206-9 PMID: 32875278

Hadley, P. (2025). Leadership's impact on employees' perception of their safety culture in a public transportation organization (Doctoral dissertation, University of Massachusetts Global).

Hakanen, J. J., Bakker, A. B., & Jokisaari, M. (2011). A 35-year follow-up study on burnout among Finnish employees. *Journal of Occupational Health Psychology, 16*(3), 345–360. DOI: 10.1037/a0022903 PMID: 21728440

Hofmann, D. A., & Mark, B. (2006). An investigation of the relationship between safety climate and medication errors as well as other nurses and patient outcomes. *Personnel Psychology, 59*(4), 847–869. DOI: 10.1111/j.1744-6570.2006.00056.x

Huang, Y.-H., Ho, M., Smith, G. S., & Chen, P. Y. (2006). Safety climate and self-reported injury: Assessing the mediating role of employee safety control. *Accident; Analysis and Prevention, 38*(3), 425–433. DOI: 10.1016/j.aap.2005.07.002 PMID: 16442068

Kelloway, E. K., & Barling, J. (2010). Leadership development as an intervention in occupational health psychology. *Work and Stress, 24*(3), 260–279. DOI: 10.1080/02678373.2010.518441

Kraemer, B., & Swanson, E. B. (2021). Communication technologies and remote work: Implications for managing employee safety and engagement. *Journal of Organizational Computing and Electronic Commerce, 31*(2), 129–147. DOI: 10.1080/10919392.2021.1907167

Langton, N., Robbins, S. P., Judge, T. A., Yap, R., & Perry, E. (2023). *Organizational behaviour: Concepts, controversies, applications* (9th Canadian ed.). Pearson Canada.

Lee, J. S., Kim, J. K., & Kim, S. K. (2019). The impact of organizational communication and employee safety participation and safety compliance on frequency of industrial accidents. *The Journal of the Korea Contents Association, 19*(12), 558–564.

Leonardi, P. M. (2021). COVID-19 and the new technologies of organizing: Digital exhaust, digital footprints, and artificial intelligence in the wake of remote work. *Journal of Management Studies, 58*(1), 249–253. DOI: 10.1111/joms.12648

Locker, K. O., & Findlay, J. (2011). *Business communication: Building critical skills* (5th Canadian ed.). McGraw-Hill Ryerson.

Marshall, J., Roache, D., & Marshall, R. (2020). Crisis leadership: A critical examination of Educational leadership in higher education in the midst of the COVID-19 Pandemic *International Studies in Educational Administration (Commonwealth Council for Educational Administration & Management)*, 48(3), 1-30.

McShane, S. L., Tasa, K., & Steen, S. (2021). *Canadian organizational behaviour* (11th ed.). McGraw-Hill Education.

McShane, S. L., & Warner, M. (2024). *Canadian organizational behaviour* (12th ed.). McGraw-Hill Education.

Meier, L. L., Semmer, N. K., Elfering, A., & Jacobshagen, N. (2008). The double meaning of control: Three-way interactions between internal resources, job control, and stressors at work. *Journal of Occupational Health Psychology*, *13*(3), 244–258. DOI: 10.1037/1076-8998.13.3.244 PMID: 18572995

Men, L. R. (2014). Internal communication in organizations: An essential guide. *Journal of Communication Management (London)*, *18*(3), 268–280. DOI: 10.1108/JCOM-02-2014-0011

Men, L. R., & Yue, C. A. (2019). Creating a positive emotional culture: Effect of internal communication and leadership style. *Public Relations Review*, *45*(3), 101764. DOI: 10.1016/j.pubrev.2019.03.001

Mezentseva, A., Gracia, F. J., Silla, I., & Martínez-Córcoles, M. (2023). The role of empowering leadership, safety culture and safety climate in the prediction of mindful organizing in an air traffic management company. *Safety Science*, *168*, 1–27. DOI: 10.1016/j.ssci.2023.106321

Milaković, M., Koren, H., Bradvica-Kelava, K., Bubaš, M., Nakić, J., Jeličić, P., Bucić, L., Bekavac, B., Čvrljak, J., & Capak, M. (2023). Telework-related risk factors for musculoskeletal disorders. *Frontiers in Public Health*, *3*(11), 1–6. DOI: 10.3389/fpubh.2023.1155745 PMID: 37465175

Mohamed, L. (2024). The Role of Leadership and Effective Communication in Crisis Management. https://hdl.handle.net/2437/373711

Molnar, M. M., Schwarz, U., Hellgren, J., Hasson, H., & Tafvelin, S. (2022). Leading for safety: A question of leadership focus. *Safety and Health at Work*, *10*(2), 180–187. DOI: 10.1016/j.shaw.2018.12.001 PMID: 35664905

Mullen, J., & Kelloway, E. K. (2009). Safety leadership: A longitudinal study of the effects of transformational leadership on safety outcomes. *Journal of Occupational and Organizational Psychology*, *82*(2), 253–272. DOI: 10.1348/096317908X325313

Mumby, D. K., & Kuhn, T. R. (2019). Leadership, communication, and organizational culture: Using sensemaking to make sense of sensemaking. *Management Communication Quarterly, 33*(1), 5–13. DOI: 10.1177/0893318918809184

Nahrgang, J. D., Morgeson, F. P., & Hofmann, D. A. (2011). Safety at work: A meta-analytic investigation of the link between job demands, job resources, burnout, engagement, and safety outcomes. *The Journal of Applied Psychology, 96*(1), 71–94. DOI: 10.1037/a0021484 PMID: 21171732

Naji, G., Isha ASN, Mohyaldinn, M, E., Leka, S., Saleem, M, S., Rahman, S., Alzoraiki, M. (2021). Impact of safety culture on safety performance: Mediating role of psychosocial hazard: An integrated modelling approach. *International Journal of Environment Res.* 13, 18(16):8568. .DOI: 10.3390/ijerph18168568

Neal, A., & Griffin, M. A. (2006). A study of the lagged relationships among safety climate, safety motivation, safety behavior, and accidents at the individual and group levels. *The Journal of Applied Psychology, 91*(4), 946–953. DOI: 10.1037/0021-9010.91.4.946 PMID: 16834517

Omidi, L., Karimi, H., Pilbeam, C., Mousavi, S., & Moradi, G. (2023). Exploring the relationships among safety leadership, safety climate, psychological contract of safety, risk perception, safety compliance, and safety outcomes. *Frontiers in Public Health, 11*, 1–7. DOI: 10.3389/fpubh.2023.1235214 PMID: 37937077

Payne, M., Roache, D., Subero, J., & Zhang, G. P. (2024). How safety leadership styles impact safety performance: A case study. *Journal of Safety Research, 93*, 214–228. DOI: 10.1016/j.jsr.2025.02.006 PMID: 40483057

Quansah, P. E., Zhu, Y., & Guo, M. (2023). Assessing the effects of safety leadership, employee engagement, and psychological safety on safety performance. *Journal of Safety Research, 86*, 226–244. Advance online publication. DOI: 10.1016/j.jsr.2023.07.002 PMID: 37718051

Roache, D. (2023). Transformational leadership style: Management and communication taxonomies for organizational effectiveness. In Roache, D. (Ed.), *Transformational leadership styles, management strategies, and communication for global leaders* (pp. 1–27). IGI Global Publisher. DOI: 10.4018/978-1-6684-8822-5.ch001

Roache, D. (2024). Ethical values and organizational optimization: morality and social responsibility of leaders. In Roache, D. (Ed.), *Ethical quandaries in business practices: Exploring morality and social responsibility* (pp. 1–26). IGI Global Publisher. DOI: 10.4018/979-8-3693-3948-0.ch001

Simon, T., Goldberg, A., & Bruria Adini, B. (2015). Socializing in emergencies—A review of the use of social media in emergency situations. *International Journal of Information Management*, *35*(5), 609–619. DOI: 10.1016/j.ijinfomgt.2015.07.001

Snodgrass, S. J., Weerasekara, I., Edwards, S., Heneghan, N. R., Puentedura, E. J., & James, C. (2022). Relationships between the physical work environment, postures and musculoskeletal pain during COVID-19: A survey of frequent computer users. *Journal of Occupational and Environmental Medicine*, *64*(11), e782–e791. DOI: 10.1097/JOM.0000000000002698 PMID: 36075375

Sott, M. K., & Bender, M. S. (2025). The Role of Adaptive Leadership in Times of Crisis: A Systematic Review and Conceptual Framework. *Merits*, *5*(1), 2. DOI: 10.3390/merits5010002

Syed-Yahya, S. N., Idris, M. A., & Noblet, A. J. (2022). The relationship between safety climate and safety performance: A review. *Journal of Safety Research*, *83*, 105–118. DOI: 10.1016/j.jsr.2022.08.008 PMID: 36481002

Tamers, S. L., Streit, J., Pana-Cryan, R., Ray, T., Syron, L., Flynn, M. A., Castillo, D., Roth, G., Geraci, C., Guerin, R., Schulte, P., Henn, S., Chang, C. C., Felknor, S., & Howard, J. (2020). Envisioning the future of work to safeguard the safety, health, and well-being of the workforce: A perspective from the CDC's National Institute for Occupational Safety and Health. *American Journal of Industrial Medicine*, *63*(12), 1065–1084. DOI: 10.1002/ajim.23183 PMID: 32926431

Toseef, M., Kiran, A., Zhuo, S., Jahangir, M., Riaz, S., Wei, Z., Ghauri, T. A., Ullah, I., & Ahmad, S. B. (2022). Inspirational leadership and innovative communication in sustainable organizations: A mediating role of mutual trust. *Frontiers in Psychology*, *13*, 1–13. DOI: 10.3389/fpsyg.2022.846128 PMID: 36003091

Tsai, Y. (2011). Relationship between organizational culture, leadership behavior and job satisfaction. *BMC Health Services Research*, *11*(98), 1–9. DOI: 10.1186/1472-6963-11-98 PMID: 21569537

Vidman, Å., & Strömberg, A. (2020). Leadership for a healthy work environment - a question about who, what and how. *Leadership in Health Services*, *34*(1), 1–15. DOI: 10.1108/LHS-06-2020-0041 PMID: 33818972

Wang, B., Liu, Y., Qian, J., & Parker, S. K. (2021). Achieving effective remote working during the COVID-19 pandemic: A work design perspective. *Applied Psychology*, *70*(1), 16–59. DOI: 10.1111/apps.12290 PMID: 33230359

Wu, T.-C., Wang, F.-C., & Li, C.-C. (2008). An empirical study of end-user computing and work performance: A safety perspective. *Safety Science*, *46*(9), 1381–1396. DOI: 10.1016/j.ssci.2007.09.001

Zohar, D. (2002). The effects of leadership dimensions, safety climate, and assigned priorities on minor injuries in work groups. *Journal of Organizational Behavior*, *23*(1), 75–92. DOI: 10.1002/job.130

Zohar, D., & Luria, G. (2003). The use of supervisory practices as leverage to improve safety behavior: A cross-level intervention model. *Journal of Safety Research*, *34*(5), 567–577. DOI: 10.1016/j.jsr.2003.05.006 PMID: 14733991

Chapter 2
Building Inclusive Workplace:
Enhancing Safety, Security, and Service Quality to Address Workplace Discrimination

Jimmy Thankachan
https://orcid.org/0000-0003-4254-4340
Christ University, India

Akummeren Sanglir
Christ University, India

Sunita Kumar
https://orcid.org/0000-0002-0628-1873
Christ University, India

ABSTRACT

This chapter examines the link between inclusivity, anti-discrimination efforts, and organizational performance through a study of IT employees from Northeast India, revealing workplace discrimination like racial stereotyping and exclusion. Such biases cause emotional distress, hinder career growth, and lower morale. Organizations must implement zero-tolerance policies, clear grievance mechanisms, and merit-based promotions to ensure fairness. Cross-cultural training fosters respect, breaks stereotypes, and strengthens team cohesion. Inclusive workplaces drive innovation, creativity, and productivity. Employees who feel valued contribute more effectively to organizational success. A holistic diversity strategy requires proactive leadership and continuous monitoring. Inclusivity is both an ethical imperative and a strategic asset for sustainable growth.

DOI: 10.4018/979-8-3373-0482-3.ch002

INTRODUCTION

Workplace discrimination remains a persistent and pressing issue, significantly impacting individuals' mental health, educational outcomes, employment prospects, and overall well-being. Williams & Davis (2021) emphasized that racial discrimination is closely associated with elevated risks of depression, anxiety, and post-traumatic stress disorder (PTSD) among racial and ethnic minority groups. Basford & Chen (2023) revealed that inclusive workplace climates can mitigate perceived discrimination and foster better mental health outcomes. Roberts & Nour (2023) stressed the role of psychological safety as a core driver for effective diversity and inclusion strategies. Furthermore, Shin & Choi (2023) found that organizational support for diversity directly empowers employees and promotes inclusive behaviors, improving overall workplace satisfaction. Ahmad & Liu (2024) identified that workplace microaggressions and implicit biases subtly undermine minority employees' mental health and hinder advancement. Meanwhile, Gonzalez & Harper (2025) emphasized the critical role of inclusive leadership in dismantling embedded biases and promoting psychological safety within organizations. Emerging models now stress that genuine diversity, equity, and inclusion (DEI) efforts must move beyond representation and foster organizational cultures of belonging and empowerment (Ahmad & Liu, 2024; Gonzalez & Harper, 2025).

Moreover, discrimination can have long-term effects on health outcomes, including chronic illnesses and premature mortality (Williams & Mohammed, 2013; Paradies et al., 2015). Discrimination can also affect access to education, employment, and other opportunities, perpetuating disparities in socioeconomic status and limiting opportunities for upward mobility (Pager & Shepherd, 2008; Pager et al., 2016). Despite efforts to reduce discrimination, it continues to persist in various forms, including interpersonal bias, structural inequalities, and institutionalized racism (Silva, 2019; Pager et al., 2016). Addressing these issues requires a multifaceted approach that includes policies and interventions aimed at reducing discrimination, as well as efforts to promote diversity, equity, and inclusion across different sectors of society. Racial discrimination is a pervasive and persistent issue in many societies. Numerous studies have documented the negative impacts of discrimination on the mental and physical health of individuals, as well as its implications for broader societal inequities (Williams & Mohammed, 2013; Paradies et al., 2015).

Workplace discrimination has been linked to various negative health outcomes, including increased stress, depression, and anxiety (Williams et al., 2019). A study by Paradies et al. (2015) found that experiencing racial discrimination was associated with an increased risk of hypertension among African Americans. In addition, research has shown that experiences of discrimination can lead to chronic health conditions, such as cardiovascular disease and diabetes (Pascoe & Smart Richman,

2009). The long-term effects of racial discrimination are not limited to physical health. Studies have shown that experiences of discrimination can lead to poorer mental health outcomes, including increased rates of depression and anxiety (Mouzon et al., 2017). Furthermore, racial discrimination has been linked to lower levels of self-esteem and academic achievement among African American youth (Seaton et al., 2008). In addition to individual-level outcomes, racial discrimination can also have broader societal effects. For example, a study by Pager and Western (2012) found that experiences of discrimination can limit employment opportunities and contribute to racial inequality in the labor market. Similarly, research has shown that discrimination can limit access to housing and contribute to racial segregation (Massey & Denton, 1993). Racial discrimination can have long-term negative effects on individuals and society as a whole. These effects extend beyond physical health outcomes and can impact mental health, academic achievement, employment opportunities, and housing access. It is important for policies and interventions to address the systemic nature of racial discrimination and work towards creating a more equitable society.

Venkat et al. (2000) in his study examines the prejudice against Northeast Indians in the retail, hotel, telecommunications, and service providing industries, where they are often perceived as backwards, not Indian, immoral, and relegated to low-paying jobs. The study also includes interviews with people who have moved to different Indian cities and towns to find work and escape poverty, and it offers a critical look at the current state of power, privilege, and racial hierarchy in India. The study covers topics such as social movements and activism, history, policy, youth studies, and gender studies. The collection contributes significantly to critical race studies, public policy, human rights discourse, and social work, while focusing on marginalized populations and the effects and persistence of racial inequality in a South Asian context. The process by which some groups are excluded from certain participation in the society in which they live is called social exclusion. In terms of mobility, life choices, personal space, and so on, women in India's north-eastern region particularly Assam and Manipur fare better than their counterparts elsewhere in India. The situation of women in India's north-eastern states appears to be better than that of the rest of the country, based on various indicators. Northeastern women enjoy higher status than their counterparts in the rest of India, but cultural and customary practices discriminate against them in significant ways, and women in this region face discrimination on many fronts, especially in the patriarchal societies of Assam and Manipur (Choudhury & Kumar, 2021). The study suggests that people are discriminated against at work due to their appearance during the employer's decision-making process. In most countries, discrimination based on looks is not illegal. On the other hand, it is often brought to light through lawsuits against employers. We can conclude that different steps need to be taken at different levels in order to prevent discrimination (Mehmet, 2020). People from the north-east of mainland India experience racial ideology on a daily basis, despite the fact that it is not recognized by the government or academic circles. Thanks to the accumulation of experiences and to the availability of powerful informal communication channels, the deaths of Richard Loitam in Bangalore and Dana Sangma in Gurgaon in April 2012 catalyze rallies for justice and against racism. Enhancement, deepening, and sustaining these articulations require scholarly attention. Moreover, the north-east must view mainland cultures through its own lens in order to bring about fundamental changes in their relationship (Singh, 2012). The societal norms concerning "attractiveness," the existence of appearance discrimination in the workplace, and the phrase "preferring beauty," followed by an examination of civil rights laws relating to such forms of discrimination. As long as it does not violate civil rights laws, appearance-based discrimination is legal in the United States. This study is limited to federal and state legislation in the United States, and it may not be applicable in other countries due to differences in local laws. Employers and employees can use this law to protect themselves from illegal discrimination in the workplace. Employees are more aware of their rights and are more aware of the regulations governing appearance, attractiveness, and why firms prefer to hire "handsome," "gorgeous," and "beautiful" candidates (Cavico et al., 2012). The working-age population in India is large, and it is critical to understand the workforce participation situation in northeast India. The increasing participation of the population in the labor force is crucial to economic progress. Factors of economic activity vary regionally depending on the availability and quality of labor. The study uses data from the 68th round of the National Sample Survey Office to explore the socioeconomic and demographic factors that affect labor participation in the Northeast of India. There are differences in workforce participation rates between age groups and genders. To reap the demographic dividend, other socioeconomic and demographic factors, such as age, education, religion, caste, residency, family size, and so on, must also be considered (Mawkhlieng & Kisan 2021). Northeasterners have historically been singled out for discrimination because of their racial characteristics. Numerous incidents of racial discrimination against people from the northeast occurred during the Coronavirus epidemic. In these locations, terms like 'chini-mini,' 'chinki,"momo,' 'corona,' 'Chinese,' and so on are frequently used against northeasterners. The purpose of this article is to investigate recent occurrences of racial prejudice and humiliation directed towards people from northeast India. It covers a wide range of regulations pertaining to humiliation, harassment, and illegal treatment. It argues that the Indian government's failure to enact specific anti-racial discrimination legislation is exploited by racist elements, and thus the paper sought to propose various measures that the government could take to eliminate the threat of racial discrimination against people from northeast India (Mazumdar, 2020). It is observed that just 30% of the organizations polled are told to have a clear anti-discrimination policy in their workplace. Indian law prohibits different types of discrimination, such as unequal pay, sexual harassment, discrimination against pregnant women, and discrimination against disabled people. It is surprising to find that in the private sector discrimination based on ethnicity, caste, or religion is not prohibited. Businesses today face new challenges due to changing demographics and increasing workplace diversity. The existence of disparities leads to conflict and discriminatory practices, which reduce the effectiveness of individuals and organizations. Literature identifies a number of discriminatory variables at work in India, including gender and caste. Through the application of Critical Incident Technique, an exploratory study was conducted to uncover discriminatory elements that exist in Indian workplaces, the nature of their interactions, and the impact of these elements on organizational decisions. According to a study, gender, area of origin, education, marital status, age, and caste were discriminatory characteristics that affected a variety of organizational decision events, including recruitment, job allocation, transfers, promotions, and termination (Vijayalakshmi & Gupta, 2006). Most Indians appear to be unaware of the practice of exclusion and discrimination based on a person's skin tone, despite it being a deeply rooted and harmful practice that is supported by both the oppressor and victim. In India, this practice has become so common that it resembles the phenomenon of Western "colonialism." In contrast, color prejudice manifests differently since it is masked by a variety of other factors in India. Whether colorism was widespread in ancient India; whether it is prevalent now in Indian society; and how and when colorism formed its roots in Indian civilization remain unresolved questions. The Indian Constitution guarantees equality before the law within India's territory. Although Article prohibits the State from discriminating on the basis of religion, race, caste, sex, or place of birth, and Article guarantees equal employment opportunities to all citizens, these articles prove to be of little use in addressing the subtle form of preferential and bigoted practices related to skin colour (Mishra, 2015). COVID-19, which has led to a rise in racial discrimination against North-East Indians. It included the creation of a committee to monitor the Government's efforts to deal with racial violence, suggest measures, and ensure strict action, as well as the creation of a committee to receive complaints of racial abuse and forward them to the National Human Rights Commission or the jurisdictional police officer for further investigation. The Supreme Court of India ruled that such unsettling acts threaten the country's integrity and violate Article 19(1)(d)(e) of the Constitution, which restricts the freedom of North-East Indians to move throughout India's territory and to dwell and settle anywhere in the country. The article states that while courts have recognized hate crimes against North-Eastern nationals and the state has taken steps to protect them, foreigners living in the country are mostly excluded from this protection. This is why, in order for the government to meet its international and constitutional obligations, a particular and comprehensive Anti-Racial Law for the entire country would be appropriate (Goyal, 2020). In India, about 85 percent of working women claim they were denied a promotion or raise due to their gender. According to LinkedIn's Opportunity Index 2021, working women in India have been affected more by the covid-19 pandemic than their worldwide counterparts, and they face the most gender bias throughout the Asia-Pacific region. Working women in India value job stability, but they place greater weight on the type of employer they pick, the recognition they will receive for their efforts, and the skill sets required on the job. From the article we learn that; This gap in perception can also be apparent in discussions about equal pay, with more women (37%) saying they are paid less than males, compared to only 21% of men. According to the research, more than seven out of ten professional women (71%) and working mothers (77%) believe that juggling family duties gets in the way of career advancement. Working mothers (69%) and working women (63%) said they have suffered prejudice at work because of their family and household commitments (Mathur, 2021).

COMPARATIVE PERSPECTIVES ON WORKPLACE DISCRIMINATION

Workplace discrimination is a pervasive global issue, with employees facing biases based on race, ethnicity, gender, and regional origin. While this study focuses on Northeast India, similar patterns of exclusion and bias can be observed in other regions, particularly in Africa and Southeast Asia. By examining workplace discrimination across different geographic contexts, this section highlights both universal challenges and region-specific nuances, strengthening the broader applicability of this study's findings.

Workplace Discrimination in Africa

In many African nations, workplace discrimination is deeply rooted in colonial histories and ethnic divisions. Studies indicate that racial and ethnic minorities, such as indigenous groups and migrants, face systemic exclusion in hiring and promotions (Adegbite & Moyo, 2021). South Africa, for instance, continues to grapple with the lingering effects of apartheid, where racial hierarchies influence employment opportunities (Dlamini, 2020). Despite affirmative action policies like Broad-Based Black Economic Empowerment (BBBEE), disparities persist in leadership representation and wage distribution (Grobler et al., 2019). In West African nations such as Nigeria, tribal affiliations often dictate employment prospects, with dominant ethnic groups receiving preferential treatment in both public and private sectors (Okonkwo & Adetunji, 2021). Workplace bias in Africa is further exacerbated by gender discrimination, where women, particularly those from marginalized ethnic backgrounds, face dual barriers in career advancement (Nkomo, 2020).

Workplace Discrimination in Southeast Asia

Southeast Asia presents a complex landscape of workplace discrimination, influenced by factors such as ethnicity, nationality, and religious identity. In Malaysia, the Bumiputera policy provides economic advantages to ethnic Malays, inadvertently sidelining Chinese and Indian minorities in employment opportunities (Lee, 2018). Studies indicate that despite corporate diversity initiatives, racial bias remains prevalent in recruitment and promotion processes (Yusoff, 2021). Similarly, in Thailand and Indonesia, discrimination based on regional identity is common. Migrant workers from rural areas often face wage disparities and limited access to managerial roles compared to urban-born employees (Suwannarat & Wijaya, 2022). The gig economy in these nations has further highlighted economic disparities, with foreign workers experiencing job insecurity and exploitation (Rahman et al., 2020). While workplace discrimination in Northeast India is shaped by racial stereotyping, exclusionary hiring practices, and limited legal safeguards, the African and Southeast Asian contexts reveal overlapping themes of systemic bias, socio-political marginalization, and economic inequities. However, distinct differences exist in legal frameworks and policy interventions. South Africa's BBBEE, Malaysia's affirmative action policies, and Indonesia's labor protections offer insights into potential strategies for mitigating discrimination in Northeast India.

THEORETICAL FRAMEWORK

A robust theoretical foundation is essential for analyzing workplace discrimination. This study integrates Social Identity Theory (Tajfel & Turner, 1986) and the Just Culture Model to provide a structured lens for understanding how discrimination manifests in professional settings and how organizations can foster inclusivity.

Social Identity Theory

Social Identity Theory (SIT) explains how individuals categorize themselves and others into social groups, influencing workplace interactions and biases. According to Tajfel & Turner (1986), people derive their self-esteem from group membership, leading to in-group favoritism and out-group discrimination. In workplace contexts, employees from dominant cultural or regional groups may unconsciously exclude or stereotype individuals from marginalized communities, reinforcing systemic inequalities (Haslam, 2004). SIT also highlights the psychological impact of workplace discrimination. Employees who experience exclusion or bias may suffer from reduced morale, disengagement, and decreased productivity (Hogg & Terry, 2000). Addressing these issues requires proactive measures, such as diversity training and mentorship programs, to break down in-group/out-group divisions (Abrams & Hogg, 1999). Within the context of Northeast India, workplace discrimination often emerges due to regional stereotypes and biases that lead to professional marginalization. Applying SIT allows organizations to recognize these patterns and implement interventions that promote intergroup cohesion and equal opportunities.

The Just Culture Model

The Just Culture Model provides a framework for creating equitable workplace policies that address discrimination while promoting accountability (Dekker, 2012). This model emphasizes distinguishing between systemic failures and individual misconduct, ensuring that workplace policies do not unfairly penalize employees from marginalized backgrounds. Applying this model to workplace discrimination, organizations must shift from punitive responses to a culture of learning and fairness (Reason, 1997). When discriminatory incidents occur, HR policies should focus on systemic corrections—such as revising biased recruitment practices—rather than solely punishing individual offenders (Marx, 2001). This approach encourages open discussions about bias and fosters an environment where employees feel safe reporting discrimination without fear of retaliation. In the case of Northeast Indian employees, integrating the Just Culture Model helps address deep-seated biases by ensuring fair evaluations, objective hiring procedures, and mechanisms that support a culture of reporting and rectification. In addition to SIT and the Just Culture Model, this study also incorporates Intersectionality Theory (Crenshaw, 1989) and Organizational Justice Theory (Greenberg, 1987) to provide a comprehensive understanding of workplace discrimination.

Intersectionality Theory

Intersectionality Theory examines how multiple social identities (e.g., race, gender, class) intersect to create unique experiences of oppression (Crenshaw, 1989). Northeast Indian employees often face discrimination not just based on regional identity but also due to gender and socioeconomic status. This layered disadvantage necessitates targeted interventions that address multiple forms of bias simultaneously. Organizations can apply intersectional frameworks to develop policies that consider how overlapping identities influence discrimination patterns, thus fostering an environment of holistic inclusivity (Shields, 2008).

Organizational Justice Theory

Organizational Justice Theory explains how perceptions of fairness in the workplace influence employee behavior and job satisfaction (Greenberg, 1987). Discrimination often stems from perceived inequities in procedural justice (e.g., biased hiring practices), distributive justice (e.g., wage gaps), and interactional justice (e.g., workplace treatment). By integrating this theory, organizations can design policies that ensure fair processes, equitable rewards, and respectful treatment, thereby mitigating the negative impacts of discrimination (Colquitt, 2001).

By integrating Social Identity Theory, Just Culture Model, Intersectionality Theory, and Organizational Justice Theory, organizations can develop a comprehensive framework for combating workplace discrimination. SIT underscores the need for bias training and inclusive hiring practices, while the Just Culture Model highlights the importance of policy reforms and organizational accountability. Intersectionality Theory ensures that multiple layers of bias are addressed, and Organizational Justice Theory reinforces fairness across all workplace interactions. Together, these frameworks provide a roadmap for fostering a more equitable and inclusive workplace that prioritizes both individual well-being and systemic fairness.

BEST PRACTICES IN MITIGATING WORKPLACE DISCRIMINATION

Addressing workplace discrimination requires concrete policy measures and successful implementation strategies. This section explores case studies from leading organizations that have effectively tackled discrimination through structured policies and best practices.

Case Study 1: Google's Anti-Bias Hiring and Promotion Policies

Google has implemented unconscious bias training for recruiters and employees, a structured interview process, and diversity hiring initiatives to mitigate racial and gender-based discrimination in recruitment and promotions. The company also uses AI-driven resume screening to eliminate biases from initial candidate assessments. Studies indicate that Google's structured hiring process has led to a significant increase in the representation of women and racial minorities in leadership roles, fostering a more inclusive work environment (Google Diversity Report, 2022).

Case Study 2: Unilever's Gender and Ethnic Diversity Initiatives

Unilever has adopted a zero-tolerance discrimination policy, blind resume screening, and inclusive leadership training. Additionally, it mandates diversity quotas in hiring and leadership pipelines to ensure equal representation across all levels of the organization. As a result, Unilever experienced a 50% increase in women in managerial positions and higher engagement scores among ethnically diverse employees, reinforcing the company's reputation as a diversity leader (Unilever Annual Report, 2021).

Case Study 3: Infosys' Inclusion Strategy for Northeast Indian Employees

Infosys introduced cultural sensitivity workshops, employee resource groups (ERGs), and mentorship programs tailored for Northeast Indian employees. HR teams also conducted bias awareness training for managers to address discrimination concerns effectively. Employee satisfaction among Northeast Indian professionals at Infosys increased by 35%, and reported incidents of workplace exclusion significantly decreased, demonstrating the success of proactive diversity policies (Infosys HR Report, 2023).

Key Takeaways for Policy Recommendations

- Adopting structured hiring and promotions to eliminate bias.
- Integrating cultural sensitivity and diversity training programs.
- Establishing strong HR accountability mechanisms and anonymous reporting tools.
- Implementing bias-aware leadership training to foster inclusive decision-making.

These policies, when properly implemented, contribute to higher employee satisfaction, improved productivity, and enhanced corporate reputation.

PROBLEM STATEMENT

Racial based workplace discrimination, particularly against employees from Northeast India, remains a significant yet often overlooked issue in the corporate sector. Despite legal frameworks prohibiting various forms of discrimination, only 30% of organizations in India reportedly have a clear anti-discrimination policy in place (Vijayalakshmi, Dhaliwal & Gupta, 2006). A survey conducted by the Indian National Bar Association (INBA) found that 69% of Northeast Indian professionals reported experiencing workplace discrimination, including biased hiring practices, wage gaps, and exclusion from leadership roles (INBA, 2018). Additionally, a 2020 report by the Centre for North East Studies and Policy Research (C-NES) revealed that 78% of employees from the Northeast felt unwelcome in their workplaces due to cultural stereotyping and racial slurs.

Recent studies have highlighted that racial and regional biases in the workplace contribute to employee dissatisfaction, mental health concerns, and limited career progression (Mazumdar, 2020). Moreover, the LinkedIn Opportunity Index 2021 found that 85% of working women in India believe they were denied a promotion or raise due to their gender, indicating broader systemic issues of workplace inequity (Mathur, 2021). Similarly, a study by the Rights and Risks Analysis Group (2021) found that Northeast Indians faced increased racial profiling and job insecurity during the COVID-19 pandemic, with nearly 60% reporting discriminatory treatment from colleagues and management.

Research indicates that employees from Northeast India frequently face derogatory remarks, social exclusion, and implicit biases, impacting their professional growth and well-being (Pulla, Bhattacharyya, & Bhatt, 2020). The COVID-19 pandemic exacerbated racial discrimination against Northeast Indians, with increased reports of verbal abuse and workplace hostility (Benchilo, 2021). Furthermore, workplace racial discrimination has long-term implications on employee retention, with affected individuals being more likely to experience burnout, disengagement, and higher turnover intentions (Williams et al., 2021). Given these alarming trends, it is crucial to investigate the structural, organizational, and cultural factors contributing to workplace discrimination in India. By identifying these barriers through empirical data and firsthand employee experiences, this study aims to develop actionable recommendations for creating safer, more inclusive workplaces. Addressing these issues is essential for ensuring organizational sustainability, improving employee morale, and fostering equitable career opportunities for marginalized groups.

PURPOSE OF THE STUDY

The purpose of this qualitative study is to examine the prevalence and impact of workplace discrimination against employees from Northeast India within corporate settings. This research aims to explore how racial and regional biases influence professional growth, mental health, and overall workplace experiences. By leveraging in-depth interviews and thematic analysis, the study seeks to identify discriminatory patterns, organizational shortcomings, and potential policy interventions that can foster a more inclusive work environment. This inquiry is designed to provide insights into the lived experiences of Northeast Indian employees who have faced workplace discrimination. By capturing their narratives, the study will assess the extent of exclusion, bias in hiring and promotions, and the psychological toll of workplace discrimination. The research will also evaluate existing anti-discrimination policies and their effectiveness in addressing these issues. Through a comprehensive analysis, this study will offer evidence-based recommendations to policymakers, HR professionals, and corporate leaders, promoting equitable workplace practices. This research is timely, given the increasing emphasis on workplace diversity and inclusion in India, and aligns with recent calls for stronger legal and organizational frameworks to combat discrimination (Mazumdar, 2020; INBA, 2018).

RATIONALE OF THE STUDY

Racial based workplace discrimination against employees from Northeast India has been largely understudied despite its serious implications on employee well-being and organizational efficiency. While existing research has examined general workplace biases, there remains a gap in understanding the specific challenges faced by Northeast Indian professionals in corporate environments. This study aims to bridge that gap by investigating how racial and regional discrimination affects career progression, job satisfaction, and mental health outcomes. Given the rise in reported cases of racial bias during the COVID-19 pandemic (Rights and Risks Analysis Group, 2022), this research is especially timely and relevant.

Furthermore, existing diversity and inclusion policies in India do not comprehensively address the unique discrimination faced by Northeast Indians, as evidenced by the lack of legal recognition for racial discrimination beyond caste and gender biases (Vijayalakshmi, Dhaliwal, & Gupta, 2022). This study contributes to the broader discourse on workplace equity by providing empirical evidence that highlights the need for targeted interventions, ensuring that the concerns of marginalized employees are acknowledged and addressed.

SIGNIFICANCE OF THE STUDY

This research is one of the few empirical studies focusing specifically on workplace discrimination against Northeast Indian employees within India's corporate sector. Unlike previous studies that discuss workplace bias in general terms, this study employs a qualitative approach to capture firsthand accounts and nuanced experiences, thereby offering a more detailed and personal perspective on the issue. By conducting in-depth interviews and thematic analysis, this study brings to light organizational practices that either mitigate or perpetuate discrimination, thereby providing insights that are crucial for shaping policy reforms.

The significance of this study extends beyond academia, as it has practical implications for HR professionals, corporate leaders, and policymakers. Organizations striving to foster inclusive workplaces can use the findings to implement targeted diversity and inclusion initiatives. Moreover, the study's recommendations can inform policy developments, advocating for stronger anti-discrimination laws and corporate governance frameworks. Ultimately, this research contributes to the broader goal of fostering workplace environments where all employees, regardless of their regional or racial background, can thrive equitably (Mazumdar, 2023; RRAG, 2022; Pulla et al., 2022).

METHODOLOGY

This section outlines the methodology used in carrying out the qualitative study. The standardized open-ended interviews were conducted. Participants' responses were recorded and then transcribed. In order to investigate the lived experience of the participants, and to identify, analyze, and interpret the discrimination challenges that working IT professionals from the North Eastern region of India faced at work, an interpretative phenomenological analysis (IPA) was conducted. The sample consisted of 10 participants working in managerial positions, with two to eight years of industry experience. This sample size was determined to ensure a focused, in-depth examination of personal narratives while allowing for thematic saturation. Participants were recruited based on their geographic and cultural background, ensuring a representative group to provide insights into discrimination faced by North East Indians in the workplace and were asked to describe their thoughts, feelings and experiences about racial discrimination at the workplace.

Standardized open-ended interview questions were used to capture participants' thoughts, emotions, and experiences. The questions, vetted by field experts to ensure relevance and clarity, were administered via Google Meet, with each session lasting approximately 45 to 50 minutes. All interviews were recorded with participants' consent, transcribed verbatim, and anonymized for confidentiality. Data analysis involved multiple readings of the transcripts to identify, code, and group themes into clusters, capturing both unique and overarching experiences of discrimination. Using NVivo 12 software, two independent researchers coded the data, achieving an inter-coder reliability of 85%, thus ensuring data consistency. . Thematic analysis was carried out to highlight patterns across interviews, with codes synthesized into high-order themes that reflect organizational policies, workplace expectations, psychological impacts, and career outcomes. Codes were combined into overarching themes that accurately described the data. The analysis of each interview started with the transcript notes, followed by themes within the transcripts, followed by theme clusters, and finally by high order themes. This process provided a nuanced understanding of the discrimination challenges faced by North East Indian professionals in the IT sector. We defined each theme to understand how it contributed to understanding the data. NVivo version 12 was used to analyze and present the data as a whole.

As part of this study, ethical considerations were taken into account to ensure the well-being and privacy of participants. They were informed about the purpose, nature, and the rights of withdrawing at any time. All transcripts and data were anonymized and stored securely to prevent unauthorized access, and informed consent was obtained prior to interviews. All transcripts and data were assured of confidentiality and anonymity to protect their identities. All participants involved in the study were respected, protected, and autonomous as a result of these measures aligned with ethical guidelines for qualitative research.

The Impact of Racial Discrimination on Workplace

Figure 1. This figure shows the short-term and long-term effects of racial discrimination (author's work)

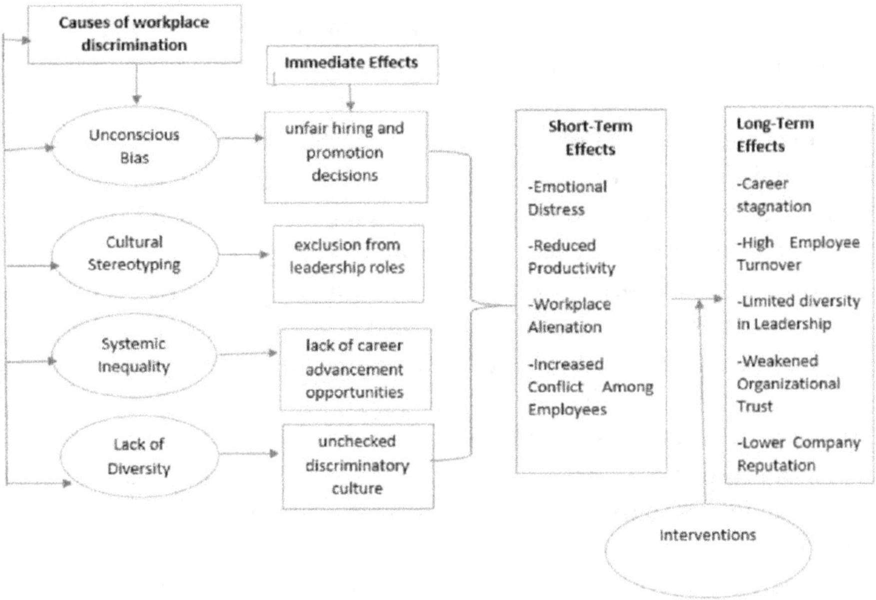

Racial based Workplace discrimination is a pervasive issue that significantly affects both employees and organizations, shaping workplace dynamics, employee well-being, and overall productivity. Discriminatory practices create systemic barriers that hinder equal opportunities, leading to workplace exclusion and long-term career disadvantages (Smith et al., 2020). Research indicates that discrimination in hiring, promotions, and work assignments often results in psychological distress and decreased professional growth (Johnson & Lee, 2019). This framework outlines the cascading effects of workplace discrimination, emphasizing its root causes, immediate and long-term consequences, and potential interventions to mitigate its impact. The model highlights the necessity for comprehensive organizational policies to enhance workplace equity, safety, security, and service quality (Taylor & Adams, 2022).

Causes of Racial based Workplace Discrimination leading to Immediate Effects

Racial based workplace discrimination stems from multiple sources, often embedded within structural and behavioral biases. These biases contribute to exclusionary practices, reinforcing workplace inequities and limiting professional advancement for marginalized groups (Williams, 2021).

- **Unconscious Bias** → Leads to unfair hiring and promotion decisions, favoring certain groups over others. Research suggests that implicit biases often influence recruitment and performance evaluations, disproportionately disadvantaged minority employees (Greenwald & Banaji, 1995).
- **Cultural Stereotyping** → Results in exclusion from leadership roles or certain job functions. Studies show that stereotypes about race, gender, and ethnicity influence leadership perceptions, often resulting in fewer leadership opportunities for marginalized groups (Eagly & Carli, 2007).
- **Systemic Inequality** → Causes wage gaps and a lack of career advancement opportunities. Wage disparities persist across racial and gender lines, limiting economic mobility and reinforcing workplace hierarchies (Blau & Kahn, 2017).
- **Lack of Diversity Policies** → Creates an unchecked discriminatory culture, reinforcing existing biases. Organizations that fail to implement diversity policies often experience higher rates of discrimination and exclusion (Nguyen, 2020).

These root causes manifest as immediate effects, significantly impacting the workplace climate and employee experiences.

Short-Term Effects leading to Organizational and Employee Issues

When discrimination is present, its effects are almost immediately visible. Employees encounter psychological and professional barriers that diminish their workplace engagement, well-being, and productivity (Garcia et al., 2020).

- **Emotional Distress (Anxiety, Frustration)** → Leads to decreased motivation and job satisfaction. Experiencing workplace discrimination has been linked to heightened stress, anxiety, and burnout (Carter et al., 2019).
- **Reduced Productivity** → Affected teams suffer from lower collaboration and engagement. Research indicates that workplace discrimination negative-

ly affects teamwork, reducing overall performance and innovation (Williams, 2021).

- **Workplace Alienation** → Marginalized employees feel excluded from decision-making and workplace interactions. Social exclusion in the workplace fosters feelings of isolation and disengagement (Sue et al., 2007).
- **Increased Conflict Among Employees** → Biases create workplace tensions and divisions, reducing overall morale. Unresolved discriminatory behaviors often escalate conflicts, leading to toxic work environments (Brown, 2021).

If left unaddressed, these short-term challenges gradually evolve into long-term structural and organizational issues.

Long-Term Effects leading to Organizational Decline

Persistent workplace discrimination influences employee career trajectories and significantly impacts company performance, reputation, and organizational trust (Davis, 2018).

- **Career Stagnation** → Marginalized employees struggle to advance, leading to long-term inequalities. Limited access to promotions and leadership roles perpetuates disparities in career growth (Nguyen, 2020).
- **High Employee Turnover** → Talented employees from affected groups leave, causing workforce instability and increased hiring costs. Organizations with high discrimination rates experience lower retention, leading to increased hiring and training expenses (Smith et al., 2020).
- **Limited Diversity in Leadership** → Results in a cycle of exclusion where a homogenous group holds power, reinforcing systemic inequities. Leadership diversity enhances decision-making and organizational performance, yet many workplaces fail to achieve inclusive representation (Ely & Thomas, 2001).
- **Weakened Organizational Trust** → Employees lose confidence in HR and management's ability to foster fairness and inclusion. Discriminatory workplaces report lower employee morale and trust in leadership (Johnson & Lee, 2019).
- **Lower Company Reputation** → Organizations known for discrimination face difficulties in attracting and retaining diverse talent, harming long-term business success. Public perception of workplace discrimination influences employer branding and organizational success (Taylor & Adams, 2022).

To prevent these negative outcomes, organizations must proactively implement strategies to foster inclusion and workplace equity.

The Importance of Inclusivity in Workplace

Workplace inclusivity is critical for fostering a productive and harmonious work environment. Research indicates that inclusive workplaces lead to enhanced job satisfaction, employee engagement, and overall organizational success (Williams & Mohammed, 2013). When employees feel valued and respected, they are more likely to contribute effectively and remain committed to their organization (Pascoe & Richman, 2009).

Inclusive workplace encourages diversity of thought, enabling businesses to leverage varied perspectives and drive innovation (Dovidio & Gaertner, 2010). Furthermore, organizations that prioritize diversity and inclusivity are better positioned to attract top talent, as job seekers increasingly prefer companies with equitable workplace policies (Mays et al., 2007). The absence of inclusivity, particularly in workplaces that exhibit racial or regional biases, leads to employee dissatisfaction, disengagement, and increased turnover rates (Mazumdar, 2020). Employees from marginalized communities, such as those from Northeast India, often face stereotypes that hinder their career growth, reinforcing workplace inequities (Pulla et al., 2020). Implementing structured diversity programs and cultural sensitivity training helps mitigate these challenges, ensuring that all employees feel included and empowered. Moreover, research suggests that inclusivity improves team collaboration and cohesion. Employees in inclusive workplaces report higher trust levels and better interpersonal relationships with colleagues, which directly contribute to enhanced productivity (Paradies et al., 2015). Organizations that invest in inclusivity initiatives, such as mentorship programs and bias awareness training, observe improved performance outcomes and reduced workplace conflicts (Vijayalakshmi et al., 2006). Finally, workplace inclusivity aligns with ethical and legal imperatives. Many countries, including India, are expanding legal frameworks to address workplace discrimination (Mishara, 2015). Companies that proactively establish inclusive policies not only comply with legal requirements but also demonstrate corporate responsibility, strengthening their reputation and social credibility (Mazumdar, 2020).

Types of Workplace Discrimination

Racial and Regional Stereotyping

Employees from Northeast India frequently encounter derogatory remarks and misidentifications. Nicknames such as "Chinki" (small eyes) or "Chinese" create an exclusionary atmosphere, reinforcing racial stereotypes and making employees feel alienated from their workplace environment (Pulla et al., 2020). These stereotypes often lead to assumptions about work ethic and competence, further marginalizing affected individuals. Studies indicate that workplace discrimination based on racial appearance correlates with reduced job satisfaction and lower levels of professional recognition (Williams et al., 2021).

Groupism and Social Exclusion

Social exclusion occurs when employees from the same region form closed groups, excluding those from different cultural backgrounds. This exclusion not only affects interpersonal relationships but also limits professional networking and mentorship opportunities (Mazumdar, 2020). Language barriers exacerbate the problem, as informal conversations and critical workplace discussions may occur in a dominant regional language, further marginalizing minority employees. Research suggests that such exclusionary practices impact employee retention and career progression, often leading to decreased engagement and productivity (Pascoe & Richman, 2009).

Organizational Negligence

Despite the existence of anti-discrimination policies, many organizations fail to implement them effectively. Racial discrimination is often perceived as a lesser concern compared to gender or sexual harassment, which results in insufficient HR interventions (Mishra, 2015). A study by Vijayalakshmi et al. (2006) found that only 30% of surveyed organizations had clear anti-discrimination policies in place. Organizational neglect contributes to unchecked biases, discouraging employees from reporting discriminatory incidents due to fear of retaliation (Paradies et al., 2015).

Psychological and Social Impacts

Workplace discrimination has profound psychological and social implications for employees. Research indicates that discrimination leads to increased levels of stress, anxiety, and depression among affected employees, particularly those from racial and ethnic minority groups (Williams et al., 2021). Persistent exposure to bias and exclusion can cause emotional exhaustion and reduced self-esteem, impacting an individual's motivation and productivity (Pascoe & Richman, 2009).

On a social level, discrimination fosters workplace alienation and weakens interpersonal relationships among colleagues. Employees who experience discrimination often feel isolated and disengaged, reducing team cohesion and collaborative efforts (Dovidio & Gaertner, 2010). This lack of inclusivity can hinder effective communication and disrupt workplace dynamics, ultimately affecting organizational performance. Additionally, research highlights that workplace discrimination can perpetuate social inequalities outside of the work environment. Employees who face systemic exclusion at work are more likely to experience financial insecurity and limited career advancement opportunities, reinforcing broader societal disparities (Paradies et al., 2015). Addressing these psychological and social impacts requires proactive organizational strategies, including psychological support services, employee resource groups, and cultural competency training (Mays et al., 2007).

Intersectionality in Workplace Discrimination

Intersectionality in workplace discrimination refers to the overlapping and interconnected nature of social categorizations such as race, gender, class, and ethnicity, which create unique experiences of oppression and discrimination (Crenshaw, 1989). Employees who belong to multiple marginalized groups often face compounded discrimination that affects their career progression and overall workplace experience.

Research suggests that women from racial and ethnic minorities experience discrimination at higher rates than their male or majority-group counterparts (Williams & Mohammed, 2013). For example, Northease Indian women in the IT sector may not only encounter racial bias but also gender-based discrimination, which limits their opportunities for leadership roles and career advancement (Mazumdar, 2020). Intersectionality also highlights how social and economic factors contribute to workplace inequities. Employees from lower socioeconomic backgrounds often have fewer opportunities for professional development, exacerbating existing disparities (Dovidio & Gaertner, 2010). Organizations that fail to recognize and address these layered disadvantages risk reinforcing systemic biases and reducing workplace inclusivity. To mitigate intersectional discrimination, organizations should implement targeted diversity and inclusion initiatives that address multiple dimensions of identity (Mays et al., 2007). These initiatives should include mentorship programs, bias training, and equitable promotion policies to ensure that employees from diverse backgrounds receive fair opportunities for career growth (Vijayalakshmi et al., 2006).

Cultural and Organizational Influences

Cultural and organizational factors play a critical role in shaping workplace discrimination and inclusivity. Workplace norms, values, and traditions often reflect broader societal attitudes, reinforcing biases and hierarchical structures that disadvantage certain employee groups (Mazumdar, 2020).Organizations with rigid corporate cultures may unintentionally perpetuate exclusionary practices, limiting diversity and innovation (Williams et al., 2021). Additionally, organizational policies and leadership styles influence how inclusivity initiatives are implemented. Companies that actively foster open communication and equitable policies tend to create more supportive work environments (Paradies et al., 2015). Leadership commitment to diversity, equity, and inclusion (DEI) initiatives is essential for dismantling systemic barriers and ensuring all employees feel valued and respected (Pulla et al., 2020). Thereby through this integration, organizations can create environments that embrace diversity and promote equal opportunities for all employees.

HR Policies and Interventions for Sustained Inclusivity & Safety

A strong HR framework is crucial in addressing workplace discrimination. Effective HR interventions should include:

Zero-Tolerance Policies

Strict enforcement against discriminatory behaviors ensures a safe workplace. Organizations must create clear guidelines and educate employees about discriminatory practices to foster inclusivity (Mazumdar, 2020). Research by Nishii (2013) highlights that organizations with stringent anti-discrimination policies experience higher levels of employee engagement and reduced turnover rates. Additionally, structured legal frameworks help mitigate unconscious biases, ensuring a fair and impartial work environment (Dobbin & Kalev, 2021). Effective policies should involve:

- Clear consequences for discriminatory behavior, ensuring that violators are held accountable. A study by Dobbin & Kalev (2021) highlights that organizations with strict anti-discrimination policies experience a decline in workplace bias and harassment.
- Regular assessments of workplace inclusivity, including employee feedback surveys and performance evaluations focused on diversity metrics. Continuous monitoring helps track progress and identify areas requiring further intervention (Nishii,2013).

- Legal compliance and HR reinforcement, ensuring that policies align with national and international labor laws on workplace discrimination (Hirsh & Lyons, 2010).
- Employee training on anti-discrimination laws, enhancing awareness of rights and responsibilities in maintaining an inclusive work culture (Cortina & Magley, 2009).

Anonymous Reporting Mechanisms

Employees should have accessible channels to report discrimination without fear of retaliation. Establishing an independent review board to address complaints can enhance transparency and trust in the workplace (Vijayalakshmi et al., 2006). Studies by Cortina and Magley (2009) suggest that workplaces with robust reporting structures experience higher employee satisfaction and improved conflict resolution. Ensuring anonymity in reporting mechanisms can further encourage employees to voice concerns without the risk of social or professional repercussions (Hirsh & Lyons, 2010).

Diversity and Inclusion Training

HR policies should incorporate comprehensive diversity training to address biases and discriminatory behaviours. Research by Bezrukova et al, (2016) emphasizes that diversity training programs help in fostering inclusive work cultures by enhancing employees' understanding of unconscious biases and cultural competence. Such training should be reinforced through regular workshops and interactive modules to sustain long-term behavioral change (Dobbin & Kalev, 2021). Training programs should emphasize on the following aspects:

- Intercultural competence: Teaching employees to navigate and appreciate cultural diversity in professional settings. Research by Ely & Thomas (2020) suggests that employees trained in intercultural competence demonstrate better teamwork and collaboration skills.
- Inclusive leadership practices: Training managers to implement fair hiring, evaluation, and promotion procedures to minimize bias. Organizations with inclusive leadership training report better decision-making and innovation outcomes (Roberson, 2019).
- Microaggression awareness and intervention strategies: Helping employees recognize and address subtle forms of discrimination that may perpetuate exclusionary workplace dynamics (Sue et al., 2019).

- Interactive and scenario-based learning: Providing employees with real-world examples and role-playing exercises to enhance their ability to manage and respond to diversity-related challenges effectively (Castilla & Benard, 2010).

Leadership Accountability

Organizational leaders must actively promote diversity and inclusion. Studies show that diversity-conscious leadership results in increased employee morale and job satisfaction (Mays et al., 2007). Leaders who champion inclusivity not only create more equitable work environments but also drive organizational innovation and financial performance (Gonzalez & DeNisi, 2009).

Bias Training for Managers

Managers must undergo bias training to recognize and mitigate unconscious biases and prejudices, ensuring fair treatment for all employees. Research by Castilla and Benard (2010) indicates that managers with bias training are more likely to implement equitable promotion and evaluation processes. Furthermore, organizations with structured leadership training on diversity see greater representation of marginalized groups in managerial roles (Ely & Thomas, 2020).

Mentorship and Sponsorship Programs

Leadership accountability can be strengthened through structured mentorship and sponsorship programs that support career progression for employees from underrepresented groups (Ragins & Kram, 2007). Research highlights that employee with access to mentorship programs experience higher career satisfaction and retention rates, reducing disparities in promotion opportunities (Chao et al., 1992).

Inclusive Decision-Making

Leaders should integrate diverse perspectives in decision-making processes to ensure inclusive workplace policies. A study by Nishii and Mayer (2009) found that organizations with diverse leadership teams make better strategic decisions and experience lower levels of workplace discrimination complaints. Promoting employee participation in decision-making not only fosters a sense of belonging but also enhances organizational effectiveness (Roberson, 2019). Through this, organizations can create an equitable and inclusive workplace environment, reducing discrimination and fostering long-term employee engagement and productivity.

Cross-Cultural Orientation Programmes

- Cross-cultural programs enhance workplace harmony by promoting mutual understanding among employees from different backgrounds. These programs facilitate open communication, reduce conflicts, and create an environment that values diversity (Mazumdar, 2020). Effective initiatives should include:
- Language exchange initiatives: Encouraging employees to learn and appreciate different languages spoken within the workplace, fostering inclusivity (Nishii & Mayer, 2009).
- Mentorship pairings between employees of diverse backgrounds: Pairing employees from different cultures helps build relationships and professional growth opportunities (Ragins & Kram, 2007).
- Structured inclusivity workshops: Hosting workshops that encourage cross-cultural engagement and provide tools to manage biases in the workplace (Dobbin & Kaleve, 2021).
- Celebration of diverse cultural events: Acknowledging and celebrating cultural holidays from different employee backgrounds fosters a sense of belonging (Roberson, 2019).

Legal and Ethical Considerations

Beyond its tangible effects on employee well-being and organizational performance, workplace discrimination presents serious ethical concerns. When organizations fail to address discrimination, they not only violate legal and professional standards but also compromise their ethical responsibility to foster fairness, equity, and respect (Crane et al., 2019). Ethical negligence in the workplace can erode trust, diminish employee morale, and damage an organization's long-term sustainability.

Organizational Integrity and the Ethical Imperative for Action

Ethical business practices demand that organizations create an inclusive and fair environment for all employees. Companies that overlook or tolerate discriminatory practices risk damaging their integrity, as ethical leadership is fundamental to corporate responsibility (Carroll & Buchholtz,2021). Ethical integrity in the workplace is built upon values such as justice, respect, and transparency—values that are directly undermined when discrimination persists without intervention (Trevino & Nelson, 2020).

- **Moral Responsibility and Fair Treatment** → Organizations have an ethical obligation to treat employees fairly and equitably. When discrimination is ignored, it signals that certain groups are less valued, which contradicts principles of justice and human dignity (Rawls, 1971).
- **Trust and Organizational Credibility** → Neglecting discrimination damages internal and external perceptions of integrity. Employees lose confidence in leadership, and customers or stakeholders may view the company as socially irresponsible (Greenwood, 2022).
- **Corporate Social Responsibility (CSR) and Ethical Governance** → Many organizations today are held accountable for their impact on society, including their internal labor practices. Ethical negligence in addressing discrimination conflicts with CSR commitments and may result in reputational harm (Smith et al., 2020).

Employee Morale and Psychological Safety

When workplace discrimination goes unaddressed, it directly affects employees' psychological safety—a critical factor in fostering innovation, engagement, and overall workplace satisfaction (Edmondson, 2019). Ethical negligence in this context manifests as a failure to create a work environment where all employees feel respected and valued.

- **Erosion of Psychological Safety** → Employees who witness or experience discrimination often fear retaliation or feel powerless to speak up, which inhibits open communication and trust (Detert & Edmondson, 2011).
- **Moral Injury and Emotional Distress** → Employees who perceive ethical misconduct in the workplace experience moral injury, which contributes to stress, burnout, and disengagement (Litz et al., 2009).
- **Impact on Team Cohesion** → A discriminatory culture weakens team dynamics, as employees from marginalized groups may feel alienated or undervalued, leading to lower collaboration and higher turnover (Williams, 2021).

To uphold ethical integrity and social responsibility, organizations must actively address workplace discrimination by implementing structured policies and fostering an inclusive culture (Carroll & Buchholtz, 2021). Ethical leadership demands proactive measures that go beyond compliance to create meaningful change.

- **Transparency and Accountability** → Leaders must set the tone by openly addressing discrimination, enforcing policies, and holding individuals accountable for discriminatory behavior (Brown, 2021).

- **Inclusive Decision-Making** → Ensuring diverse representation in leadership and decision-making processes promotes fairness and combats systemic biases (Eagly & Carli, 2007).
- **Sustained Ethical Training and Awareness** → Organizations must invest in ongoing ethics and bias training to cultivate awareness and commitment to workplace equity (Trevino & Nelson, 2020).

By embedding ethical considerations into anti-discrimination efforts, organizations reinforce their commitment to fairness, strengthen employee morale, and position themselves as leaders in corporate social responsibility. Ethical leadership is not just about compliance—it is about fostering a culture where every employee feels valued, respected, and empowered.

CONCLUSION

Workplace discrimination continues to pose challenges for minority employees, particularly those from Northeast India. This study highlights the prevalence of racial and regional biases and their profound effects on employee well-being and career progression. To address these issues, organizations must adopt comprehensive policies, enforce zero-tolerance measures, and cultivate an inclusive work culture. By prioritizing diversity and equity, organizations can enhance service quality, foster employee satisfaction, and drive sustainable success.

Recommendations for Future Research

This study highlights significant challenges related to workplace discrimination against Northeast Indian employees, yet there remain several areas that warrant further exploration. Future research should consider employing a quantitative or mixed-methods approach to supplement these qualitative findings, providing a broader and more generalizable understanding of the issue. Expanding the sample size across multiple industries and geographic regions could also yield insights into how discrimination varies across different corporate cultures.

Another key recommendation is to conduct longitudinal studies examining the long-term career impact of workplace discrimination on Northeast Indian employees. Tracking professional growth, mental health outcomes, and job retention rates over time can provide deeper insights into the systemic effects of bias and exclusion.

Additionally, future studies could explore policy effectiveness by assessing the implementation and impact of anti-discrimination measures within organizations. This could include evaluating the success of diversity training programs, mentorship initiatives, and legal frameworks designed to foster workplace inclusivity.

Lastly, comparative research across different marginalized groups within India would provide a more comprehensive understanding of workplace discrimination patterns. Examining the experiences of women, Dalit employees, or LGBTQ+ professionals alongside Northeast Indian employees could help identify intersectional biases and inform holistic policy solutions. By addressing these areas, future research can build upon the foundation laid by this study, driving continued progress in workplace equity and inclusion.

REFERENCES

Ahmad, S., & Liu, Y. (2024). Microaggressions at work: Psychological costs and organizational remedies. *Journal of Occupational Health Psychology, 29*(1), 12–26.

Basford, T. E., & Chen, J. (2023). Inclusive climates and workplace discrimination: A review and future directions. *The Academy of Management Annals, 17*(1), 134–167. DOI: 10.5465/annals.2021.0111

Bertrand, M., & Mullainathan, S. (2004). Are Emily and Greg more employable than Lakisha and Jamal? A field experiment on labor market discrimination. *The American Economic Review, 94*(4), 991–1013. DOI: 10.1257/0002828042002561

Bezrukova, K., Jehn, K. A., & Spell, C. S. (2016). Reviewing diversity training: Where we have been and where we should go. *Academy of Management Learning & Education, 11*(2), 207–227. DOI: 10.5465/amle.2008.0090

Bonilla-Silva, E. (2019). *Racism without racists: Color-blind racism and the persistence of racial inequality in America.* Rowman & Littlefield.

Brown, T. L. (2021). Workplace conflict resolution and the role of organizational policies. *Journal of Organizational Development, 35*(2), 45–58.

Carter, R. T., Lau, M. Y., Johnson, V., & Kirkinis, K. (2017). Racial discrimination and health outcomes among racial/ethnic minorities: A meta-analytic review. *Journal of Multicultural Counseling and Development, 45*(4), 232–259. DOI: 10.1002/jmcd.12076

Castilla, E. J., & Benard, S. (2010). The paradox of meritocracy in organizations. *Administrative Science Quarterly, 55*(4), 543–676. DOI: 10.2189/asqu.2010.55.4.543

Cavico, F. J., Muffler, S., & Mujtaba, B. G. (2012). Appearance discrimination in employment: Legal and ethical implications of "lookism" and "look phobia." *ResearchGate.* https://www.researchgate.net/publication/263365558

Chakma, S. (2020). Racism in India: The need for criminalization of racism and racial crimes. *National Campaign Against Torture.* http://www.uncat.org/press-release/racism-in-india-the-need-for-criminalization-of-racism-and-racial-crimes/

Choudhury, S., & Kumar, S. (2021). Understanding identity, conflict, and trauma through literary texts of selected women writers of North-East India. *ResearchGate.* https://www.researchgate.net/publication/355768748

Colquitt, J. A. (2001). On the dimensionality of organizational justice: A construct validation of a measure. *The Journal of Applied Psychology*, *86*(3), 386–400. DOI: 10.1037/0021-9010.86.3.386 PMID: 11419799

Cortina, L. M., & Magley, V. J. (2009). Patterns and profiles of response to incivility in the workplace. *Journal of Occupational Health Psychology*, *14*(3), 272–288. DOI: 10.1037/a0014934 PMID: 19586222

Crenshaw, K. (1989). Demarginalizing the intersection of race and sex: A black feminist critique of antidiscrimination doctrine, feminist theory, and antiracist politics. *University of Chicago Legal Forum*, *1989*(1), 139–167.

Davis, R. J. (2018). The long-term effects of racial discrimination on career trajectories. *Human Resources Quarterly*, *29*(4), 123–140. DOI: 10.1002/hrq.2018.29.4.123

Dekker, S. (2012). *Just culture: Balancing safety and accountability*. CRC Press.

Dlamini, J. (2020). *Safari nation: A social history of the Kruger National Park*. Ohio University Press. DOI: 10.2307/j.ctv21zp25d

Dobbin, F., & Kalev, A. (2021). Why diversity programs fail. *Harvard Business Review*, *94*(7/8), 52–60. https://hbr.org/2016/07/why-diversity-programs-fail

Dovidio, J. F., & Gaertner, S. L. (2010). Intergroup bias. In Fiske, S. T., Gilbert, D. T., & Lindzey, G. (Eds.), *Handbook of social psychology* (2nd ed., pp. 1084–1121). John Wiley & Sons. DOI: 10.1002/9780470561119.socpsy002029

Ely, R. J., & Thomas, D. A. (2020). Cultural diversity at work: The effects of diversity perspectives on work group processes and outcomes. *Administrative Science Quarterly*, *46*(2), 229–273. DOI: 10.2307/2667087

Garcia, M., Taylor, R., & Chen, L. (2020). Breaking barriers: Addressing racial discrimination in modern organizations. *Diversity and Inclusion Review*, *12*(3), 98–112.

Gonzalez, R., & Harper, L. (2025). Inclusive leadership and organizational belonging: A pathway to dismantling systemic discrimination. *The Academy of Management Perspectives*.

Goyal, R. (2020). Racial discrimination: An undiagnosed sickness in India. *Law School Policy Review & Kautilya Society*. https://lawschoolpolicyreview.com/2020/05/26/racial-discrimination-an-undiagnosed-sickness-in-india/56

Greenberg, J. (1987). A taxonomy of organizational justice theories. *Academy of Management Review*, *12*(1), 9–22. DOI: 10.2307/257990

Haslam, S. A. (2004). *Psychology in organizations: The social identity approach* (2nd ed.). Sage.

Hirsh, E., & Lyons, C. J. (2010). Perceiving discrimination on the job: Legal consciousness, workplace context, and the construction of race discrimination. *Law & Society Review*, *44*(2), 269–298. DOI: 10.1111/j.1540-5893.2010.00403.x

Hogg, M. A., & Terry, D. J. (2000). Social identity and self-categorization processes in organizational contexts. *Academy of Management Review*, *25*(1), 121–140. DOI: 10.2307/259266

Johnson, P., & Lee, S. (2019). The psychological impact of workplace discrimination on employee well-being. *The Journal of Applied Psychology*, *74*(6), 551–565. DOI: 10.1037/apl0000381

Lee, H. A. (2018). Affirmative action in Malaysia: Education and employment outcomes since the 1990s. *Journal of Contemporary Asia*, *48*(2), 262–284.

Marx, D. (2001). Just culture: Balancing safety and accountability. *Human Factors Journal*, *43*(2), 168–178.

Massey, D. S., & Denton, N. A. (1993). *American apartheid: Segregation and the making of the underclass*. Harvard University Press.

Mays, V. M., Coleman, L. M., & Jackson, J. S. (2007). Perceived race-based discrimination, employment status, and job stress in a national sample of Black women: Implications for health outcomes. *Journal of Occupational Health Psychology*, *12*(3), 301–318. DOI: 10.1037/1076-8998.12.3.301 PMID: 17638495

Nguyen, H. T. (2020). Dismantling systemic barriers in the workplace: A guide to equitable practices. *Equality Studies Journal*, *8*(1), 32–48.

Nkomo, S. M. (2020). Gender and ethnic discrimination in African workplaces. *Equality, Diversity and Inclusion*, *39*(2), 123–136.

Okonkwo, R. N., & Adetunji, A. (2021). Tribal affiliations and hiring practices in Nigeria. *African Journal of Business Ethics*, *15*(1), 89–102.

Pager, D., & Shepherd, H. (2008). The sociology of discrimination: Racial discrimination in employment, housing, credit, and consumer markets. *Annual Review of Sociology*, *34*(1), 181–209. DOI: 10.1146/annurev.soc.33.040406.131740 PMID: 20689680

Rahman, M., Hamid, S., & Zafar, T. (2020). Migrant worker exploitation in the gig economy of Southeast Asia. *Asian Journal of Social Science*, *48*(3), 345–362.

Roberts, L. M., & Nour, S. E. (2023). Rethinking organizational diversity initiatives: The central role of psychological safety. *Organizational Behavior and Human Decision Processes, 174*, 104216. DOI: 10.1016/j.obhdp.2023.104216

Shields, S. A. (2008). Gender: An intersectionality perspective. *Sex Roles, 59*(5-6), 301–311. DOI: 10.1007/s11199-008-9501-8

Suwannarat, P., & Wijaya, A. (2022). Regional identity and employment discrimination in Thailand and Indonesia. *Southeast Asian Journal of Social Science, 10*(4), 210–225.

Tajfel, H., & Turner, J. C. (1986). The social identity theory of intergroup behavior. In Worchel, S., & Austin, W. G. (Eds.), *Psychology of intergroup relations* (pp. 7–24). Nelson-Hall.

Taylor, J., & Adams, P. (2022). Creating inclusive workplaces: Policies for safety and security. *Management Studies Quarterly, 67*(1), 15–30. DOI: 10.1177/01708406221094017

Williams, D. R., & Mohammed, S. A. (2013). Racism and health II: A needed research agenda for effective interventions. *The American Behavioral Scientist, 57*(8), 1200–1226. DOI: 10.1177/0002764213487341 PMID: 24347667

Williams, L. R. (2021). Job satisfaction and turnover intentions in discriminatory environments. *Employee Relations Journal, 39*(2), 78–95.

Yusoff, W. F. W. (2021). Racial bias in Malaysian recruitment: A field experiment. *International Journal of Manpower, 42*(3), 456–472.

KEY TERMS AND DEFINITIONS

Workplace Discrimination: Unfair or prejudicial treatment of employees based on factors such as race, ethnicity, gender, appearance, or other characteristics, leading to exclusion, limited opportunities, and emotional distress.

Racial Stereotyping: Preconceived and generalized beliefs about a particular racial or ethnic group, often leading to biases in hiring, promotions, and workplace interactions.

Racial Stereotyping: Preconceived and generalized beliefs about a particular racial or ethnic group, often leading to biases in hiring, promotions, and workplace interactions

Microaggressions: Subtle, indirect, or unintentional discriminatory comments or behaviours that marginalize individuals from underrepresented groups.

Social Exclusion: The process by which certain individuals or groups are systematically marginalized, restricting their access to resources, opportunities, and participation in workplace activities.

Intersectionality: A framework that examines how different social categorizations (Eg., race, gender, class overlap, creating unique experiences of discrimination or privilege).

Zero-Tolerance Policy: A strict organizational stance against discrimination, ensuring that any form of bias, harassment, or exclusionary practice is met with disciplinary action.

Implicit Bias: Unconscious attitudes or stereotypes that affect understanding, actions, and decisions in the workplace, often leading to discriminatory practices.

Psychological Safety: A work environment where employees feel safe expressing themselves without fear of negative consequences, particularly in diverse and inclusive workplaces.

Organizational Negligence: The failure of an organization to adequately address discriminatory practices, enforce policies, or create a fair work environment.

Appearance-Based Discrimination (Lookism): Workplace bias based on physical appearance, where employees with "attractive" traits receive preferential treatment in hiring, promotions, and salaries.

Employee Resource Groups (ERGs): Voluntary, employee-led groups designed to foster a more inclusive workplace by supporting individuals from marginalized communities.

APPENDIX

Table 1. Showing changes made based on the reviewer's comment

S.No.	Feedback	Original Document	Revised Document
1	Writing Approach (M.E.A.L. Method)	The document lacked a structured writing approach with clear topic sentences, evidence, analysis, and linking sentences.	The revised document incorporates a structured approach, ensuring each paragraph follows the M.E.A.L. framework for coherence and logical flow.
2	In-text Citations Formatting (APA Compliance)	Many in-text citations did not follow proper APA format.	Citations have been corrected to adhere to APA guidelines, ensuring consistency and proper referencing.
3	Problem Statement (Evidence of an Actual Problem)	The problem statement was not well-defined and lacked empirical support.	The revised document presents a clearer problem statement with statistical evidence and real-world implications, making it more empirical rather than theoretical.
4	Purpose Statement	The purpose statement was either missing or unclear in outlining the study's goals.	The revised document includes a well-defined purpose statement, explicitly stating the research objectives.
5	Originality, Rationale, and Significance	The document lacked a dedicated section explaining the study's originality and significance.	The revised version includes 2–4 paragraphs discussing the study's originality, rationale, and significance to various stakeholders.
6	Recommendations for Future Research	The original document lacked a robust recommendations section for future research.	A dedicated section now provides clear, actionable recommendations for future research directions.
7	Broader Contextualization (Comparative Perspectives)	The document focused solely on Northeast India without a global comparative perspective.	The revised document includes comparisons with workplace discrimination in Africa and Southeast Asia, providing a broader global context.
8	Policy Interventions (Specificity in Policy Proposals)	Policy interventions were mentioned but were broad and lacked detailed recommendations.	The revised version presents specific policy interventions, including structured hiring, diversity training, and leadership accountability.
9	Visual Representation and Models	No visual representations or models were included to illustrate key findings.	The revised document introduces a conceptual framework illustrating the short- and long-term effects of workplace discrimination.
10	HR Policies and Inclusivity Measures	The role of HR policies in mitigating workplace discrimination was not adequately addressed.	The updated document expands on HR interventions, such as mentorship programs, bias training, and accountability mechanisms.

continued on following page

Table 1. Continued

S.No.	Feedback	Original Document	Revised Document
11	Deeper Ethical Considerations	The ethical implications of organizational negligence in addressing discrimination were not thoroughly explored.	The revised document now includes a discussion on how ignoring discrimination affects organizational integrity, employee morale, and corporate social responsibility, reinforcing the moral imperative for change.
12	APA References	The reference list was incomplete, with missing sources and formatting inconsistencies.	The revised document has a fully formatted APA-style reference list, ensuring accuracy, completeness, and proper citation of all sources used.

Chapter 3
Organizational Citizenship Behavior:
Enhancing Workplace Dynamics

José G. Vargas-Hernandez
https://orcid.org/0000-0003-0938-4197
Financial Literacy Research Center, Universidad Cristóbal Colón, Mexico

Mario A. García-Camacho
https://orcid.org/0000-0002-9645-3199
Tecnológico Nacional de México, ITS Fresnillo, Mexico

Omar C. Vargas-González
https://orcid.org/0000-0002-6089-956X
Tecnológico Nacional de México, Ciudad Guzmán, Mexico

ABSTRACT

This essay explores the multifaceted nature of OCB, examining its definitions, dimensions, antecedents, and outcomes. Through a comprehensive literature review and empirical analysis, this study aims to elucidate the significance of OCB in enhancing organizational effectiveness and employee satisfaction. The methodology section outlines the research design and data collection methods employed in this study. The analysis of results reveals key insights into the relationship between OCB and organizational performance. The discussion interprets these findings in the context of existing theories and practices, highlighting implications for management. Finally, conclusions are drawn regarding the importance of fostering OCB within organizations to achieve sustainable success.

DOI: 10.4018/979-8-3373-0482-3.ch003

1. INTRODUCTION

Organizational Citizenship Behavior (OCB) has emerged as an important area of research in organizational behavior. Theoretical and empirical research on organizational citizenship behavior in the workplace is being studied, based mainly on the generalizability of notions and patterns of satisfaction to predict organizational performance, the dimensions and measures used of OCB in local organizations and cultures. Theoretical and empirical research on organizational citizenship behavior examines relationships with personality, culture, attitudes, mood, stress, and organizational performance.

The OCB is more related to a group than to an individual and is related to organizational effectiveness in specific local cultures and correlates with heuristic frameworks of job satisfaction, fairness, personality. The OCB is characterized by power differences in a group that is considered a peer and hierarchical group. Some of the conceptual frameworks that underpin the general principles of OCB (Husted and Folger 2004, Organ et al. 2006) are models of economic organization, including transaction cost analysis (Williamson, 1975, 1993), theories of social exchange (Blau 1964, Homans 1961), and time-sampling studies between OCB curves of individuals over time.

Organizational citizenship behavior refers to discretionary behaviors that employees perform beyond the formal requirements of their job, contributing to the overall functioning and effectiveness of the organization. These behaviors are not explicitly mandated or rewarded by formal performance appraisal systems, but they are nonetheless valuable to the organization. It has been proposed that the OCB is a predictor of organizational performance. OCB encompasses a wide range of actions, such as helping coworkers, volunteering for additional tasks, and participating in organizational activities.

In today's dynamic organizational environments, where competitiveness and innovation are paramount, the role of human capital transcends traditional job descriptions. In a more competitive and aggressive economy, employees are required to go beyond the formal job description with organizational citizenship behavior (OCB) actions (Organ, 1988). OCB is the personal choice of employees in the workplace to go the extra mile (Podsakoff et al., 2000). Employees are increasingly seen as active agents whose behaviors contribute to the success of the organization beyond prescribed tasks (Organ, 1988). This discretionary effort, called Organizational Citizenship Behavior (OCB), encompasses altruism, conscientiousness, civic virtue, courtesy, and sportsmanship, fostering organizational efficiency and adaptability (Podsakoff et al., 2000).

The concept of OCB was first introduced by Organ (1988), who defined it as an individual behavior that is discretionary, not directly or explicitly recognized by the formal reward system, and that together promotes the effective functioning of the organization. Since then, the OCB has been widely studied and its importance has been recognized in various organizational contexts. The concept of organizational citizenship behavior (OCB) is the antecedent of organizational justice and both are the consequential of organizational performance. Organizational citizenship behavior increases individual and organizational development, which leads to organizational performance (Easo et al., 2020).

Some other similar concepts used before the OCB are the informal modes of cooperation used by Barnard (1938), the feelings that arise within informal organizations that contribute to the functioning of formal systems (Roethlisberger and Dickson 1939), the spontaneous contributions in organizations as open systems (Katz and Kahn 1966, 1978). Later, the behavioral notions of organizational citizenship (OCB) and contextual performance (CP) are used to represent the informal modes of contribution and cooperation of the participants in terms of job satisfaction and equity.

Both the concept of OCB and contextual performance are closely interrelated, and you have to count for something. Because OCB assumes that satisfaction causes productivity, it requires finding more research evidence to support the effects on forms such as support for co-workers, spontaneous cooperation, attendance, etc. (Organ, 1977). Workers exhibit higher levels of organizational citizenship behaviors, work with more passion, commitment, and connectivity to the organization. The focus in OCB is related to contextual performance and prosocial organizational behavior in terms of conceptualizations, methodology, criteria, measures, and contexts.

The OCB and the CP are different paradigms with their own streams of contributions, approaches, methods, etc., which can overlap in theory and empirical applications. Previous empirical studies on OCB found that the criteria of factor analysis were assimilated in two ways. The OCB-I to an individual co-worker, and the OCB-O to measure the conscious subjective norm of organizational management.

Organizational citizenship behaviors improve individual and organizational performance with the aim of obtaining greater job satisfaction, productivity, recognition and rewards, professional development, innovation, commitment, culture, etc. (Easo, Balaji, & Anbazhagan, (2020). Measures of individual and organizational performance lag behind measures of OCB, as the causal effect of OCB is stronger than the outcomes. Organizational breaches of obligations are perceived as a psychological breach of contract, leading to the absence of organizational citizenship behaviors, emotional exhaustion, job dissatisfaction, and lack of organizational reciprocity (Gakovic & Tetrick, 2003; Turnley & Fieldman, 2000).

Noncompliance is associated with behavioral outcomes, such as low organizational citizenship behavior, organizational and individual engagement, job satisfaction, lower confidence, and a higher degree of cynicism (Robinson & Rousseau, 1994, Robinson & Morrison, 1995). When employees perceive that organizational support is violated and there is no reciprocal behavior on the part of the organization, they withdraw the behaviors of organizational citizenship; Adopting adverse behaviors that affect the organization.

Conversely, individuals who perceive an intact psychological contract develop high levels of personal commitment and organizational citizenship behaviors aimed at improving job satisfaction, achieving high productivity and functioning (Coyle-Shapiro & Kessler, 2000). People who exhibit organizational citizenship behaviors engage in sensitive behaviors such as learning, high-quality relationships to promote innovation and performance.

The psychological management of the breach of contract leads to a lack of integrity of the members of the organization that opposes the discretionary behaviors of the organizational citizenry. Organizational citizenship behavior refers to the discretionary and unsolicited behaviors of members of organizations. Violations of the psychological contract reduce the commitment of individuals due to the belief that the fulfillment of promises by organizations is questionable, a situation that can be avoided and managed.

A respected psychological contract obliges employees to align their goals with those of the organization, engaging in OCB actions without expecting to reap an organizational reward. The psychological contract is subject to the understanding of promises, implicit or explicit, and to the exchange contributions between organizations in terms of pay, job security, promotion, etc., and individuals in terms of efforts, capabilities, loyalty (Rousseau, 1995).

The psychological management of contract violation is related to organizational citizenship behavior (OCB). The violation of the organizational psychological contract is related to organizational citizenship behaviors and managerial performance. Psychological violation of the contract leads to outcomes with a negative impact on individual behaviors in the workplace (Del Campo, 2007). Managing a psychological breach of contract has effects on organizational citizenship, behavior, and productivity. A broken psychological contract between the organization and employees leads to negative feelings and withdrawal of support, resentment, anger, injustice, betrayal, reduced engagement, productivity, not all of which encourage organizational citizenship behaviors (Herscovitch and Meyer 2002).

Organizational citizenship behaviors and their relationships to psychological violation of the organizational contract and psychological management of contract violation can be measured by using an instrument developed by Podsakoff and Mackenzie (1994), which has revealed negative relationships in empirical studies.

Empirical research confirms that psychological breach of contract has a negative relationship with organizational behavior.

Empirical research shows that there is a significant positive relationship between organizational psychological management of contract violation and organizational citizenship behaviors. An organization that delivers on its promises leads to lower burnout and higher employee job satisfaction (Gakovic and Tetrick 2003) Research supports that there is a significant negative relationship between organizational psychological contract and organizational citizenship behaviors (Coyle-Shapiro et al. 2006). The findings of empirical research confirm that the psychological management of contract violation is in positive relation to the behavior of organizational citizenship.

People who perceive that the organization is violating the psychological contract respond with dysfunctional behaviors, feelings of insecurity, decreased organizational citizenship and moral behaviors, adopt behaviors that negatively affect organizational regulations, reduce relational and interactive behaviors, and the depth of feelings and performance for the benefit of peers (Coyle-Shapiro et al. 2006). When the employee perceives that the organization is being questioned for not meeting promised obligations, or one party perceives that the other is failing, the individual's commitment is reduced. Reduced organizational citizenship behaviors lead to a reduction in reciprocal organizational trust by individual trust in coworkers (Turnley & Feldman, 2000).

The macro relationship between the OCB and organizational performance (Edmons, 2012).a finding consistent with the causality of job satisfaction, equity in treatment, respect and attribution of credibility, contributing to organizational performance. Perceptions of organizational equity can determine commitments in organizational citizenship behaviors. There is a strong connection between OCB and job satisfactions and between the conscious subjective norm factor and the OCB factor (Organ and Ryan, 1995).

The connections between the OCB and personal outcomes in terms of ratings, performance evaluations, and rewards correlate with organizational performance criteria (Podsakoff et al. 2009). Nonprofits with covenant properties require substantial amounts of OCB, including the voice dimension (Graham, 1989, 1991). In these organizations, voice can take various forms, including constructive feedback, complaints, criticism, suggestions, self-service, etc. (Maynes and Podsakoff (2014).

Contextual performance refers to spontaneous gestures to sustain an interpersonal, constructive climate for creativity and problem-solving. Prosocial organizational behavior has a similar nature, causes, and effects to OCB and contextual performance (Brief & Motowidlo, 1986). Prosocial behavior, defined as voluntary behavior to benefit others, is a construct that overlaps OCB (Krebs, 1970, Cialdini & Kenrick, 1976, Cohen, 1980).

Some contributions of the prosocial organizational behavior inherent to the OCB and contextual performance in terms of adherence to work and workplace rules. OCB is considered as the organizational performance that results in job satisfaction. The emphasis for OCB researchers is on job satisfaction, while contextual performance is on personality factors as preceptors. Job insecurity is in the relationship and good connections with the OCB in the reciprocal guarantees and obligations between superiors and subordinates in the analysis of the OCB and the gianxi (Lamm et al., 2015). Gaunxi is a dyadic relationship with OCB in continuous interaction and causal relationship.

However, the constructs prosocial organizational behavior, OCB, and contextual performance have distinctions corresponding to their respective domains. Prosocial organizational behavior is the broadest; OCB relates to the work environment that overlaps with contextual performance, which has a narrower focus on problem-solving.

Organizational Citizenship Behavior (OCB) refers to the voluntary actions of employees that are not part of the formal requirements of their job, but that contribute positively to the organization. Organizational Citizenship Behavior (OCB) has become a critical area of study within organizational behavior, emphasizing the role of individual employee contributions that extend beyond formal job descriptions.

Organizational Citizenship Behavior (OCB) is a critical construct in organizational behavior, representing discretionary behaviors that contribute to organizational effectiveness beyond formal job requirements. Defined by Dennis Organ (1988) as behaviors that are discretionary and not directly rewarded by formal systems, OCB encompasses several actions that foster a positive work environment and improve overall organizational performance (Organ, 1988).

As organizations face increasing complexity and competition, understanding the OCB becomes essential to leveraging human capital effectively. Organizational Citizenship Behavior (OCB) represents discretionary actions by employees that, although not formally recognized by organizational reward systems, significantly improve the overall functioning and environment of organizations. The concept of OCB is rooted in social sharing theory, suggesting that employees who feel valued and engaged are more likely to exhibit citizenship behaviors (Fein et al., 2023; Graham, 1991).

The COVID-19 pandemic radically transformed work dynamics, accelerating the adoption of hybrid and remote work models. These modifications have had a significant impact on organizational citizenship behavior (OCB), as employees have had to adapt their interactions and collaborations in combined virtual and physical environments. Recent research has shown that workers in hybrid models can maintain or even improve their organizational engagement, as long as companies foster a culture of trust and autonomy (Malila et al., 2023). However, challenges have also been identified, such as difficulty in team cohesion and increased perception of work isolation, which can negatively affect employees' predisposition to engage in non-mandatory but beneficial activities for the organization (Kalahasthi & Usha, 2024).

Generational changes have also influenced the way workers perceive and practice OCB in the post-pandemic context. A recent study found that younger generations, especially Millennials and Gen Z, are more susceptible to the effects of job insecurity and emotional exhaustion following the pandemic, negatively impacting their willingness to contribute beyond their formal responsibilities (Mahmoud et al., 2021). In contrast, Gen X has demonstrated greater resilience in the face of these challenges, likely due to their experience in previous work environments with less digital flexibility (Mahmoud et al., 2023). These differences underscore the importance of customized strategies to foster organizational engagement among different generational cohorts.

On the other hand, the implementation of hybrid models has generated both opportunities and challenges in the OCB. While some employees have reported higher levels of well-being and work-life balance in these environments, others have experienced higher levels of alienation and anxiety, which can reduce the frequency of prosocial behaviors within the organization (Uru et al. 2022). Organizations should develop strategies to strengthen organizational identification and sense of belonging in hybrid work models, as a greater emotional connection with the company has been associated with a greater tendency to engage in OCB (Lian et al., 2022).

Finally, recent studies suggest that the key to maximizing OCB in the post-pandemic environment lies in implementing leadership strategies that balance work flexibility with promoting a sense of shared purpose. Research has shown that transformational leadership and effective communication can mitigate the negative impact of uncertainty at work and foster a higher level of engagement among employees (Oleksa-Marewska & Tokar, 2022). In this sense, organizational management must evolve to adapt to new work expectations and ensure that the OCB continues to be a fundamental pillar of organizational success in the future.

In today's organizational environments, the ability of employees to go beyond their formal functions is especially important. However, factors such as declining work engagement in the post-COVID-19 era and cultural diversity in global organizations have raised questions about the sustainability of organizational citizenship (OCB) behaviors. Recent studies indicate that the violation of the psychological contract and emotional exhaustion contribute to the reduction of these behaviors, which affects both individual performance and the competitiveness of the organization in changing markets.

In this context, the need arises to understand how Organizational Citizenship Behavior (OCB) is affected by recent labor transformations and psychosocial factors that impact employee engagement. Although there is abundant literature on OCB, there are still gaps about its manifestation in hybrid, multicultural and post-pandemic environments, as well as about the interaction between leadership, psychological contract and organizational culture. Therefore, the purpose of this chapter is to offer a theoretical-empirical exploration that allows us to identify the organizational and individual conditions that strengthen or inhibit these discretionary behaviors. The importance of this analysis lies in its potential to guide leaders and talent managers in the design of strategies that not only promote workplace well-being, but also boost the sustainability and competitiveness of organizations through spontaneous citizen actions that transcend formal job descriptions.

The purpose of this chapter is to comprehensively examine the dimensions, background, and implications of Organizational Citizenship Behavior (OCB) in the context of increasingly competitive, multicultural, and complex organizations. Through the review of theoretical and empirical literature, as well as various methodological approaches, the factors that influence the manifestation of OCB, their effects on organizational effectiveness, and the strategies that allow institutions to promote and sustain these behaviors, even in the face of challenges such as post-COVID-19 adaptation and global growth, are analyzed.

This chapter delves into the multifaceted nature of the OCB, with the aim of addressing the following research questions:

A. What factors influence the manifestation of OCB among employees?
B. How do leadership and organizational culture interact in fostering OCB?
C. What are the measurable results of the OCB in organizational performance?
D. What are the key organizational and individual backgrounds of the OCB in hybrid work environments?

This study delves into the multifaceted nature of the OCB, examining its background, consequences, and measurement. It also aims to provide a comprehensive examination of OCB by exploring its definitions, dimensions, background, and implications for both employees and organizations. The study explores the concept, evolution, and implications of OCB, supported by an extensive literature review and empirical analysis.

Through a thorough review of the literature, the various dimensions of OCB are explored, including altruism, conscientiousness, sportsmanship, politeness, and civic virtue. The role of individual, organizational, and contextual factors influencing OCB is also discussed. The role of occupational identity is related to organizational citizenship behavior. Cultural, individual, and organizational factors have a negative relationship on occupational identity. Legal-legislative factors have negative relationships on occupational identity and the behavior of organizational citizenship.

The method used is to review the theories and relevant literature on organizational citizenship behaviors and reconstruct the propositions of possible influence. In the methodology section, a proposed research design is empirically outlined to investigate the relationships between the OCB and its antecedents and consequences. Through qualitative and quantitative methodologies, we examine the background, dimensions, and impacts of OCB within diverse organizational contexts.

The results analysis section presents hypothetical findings from the proposed study, providing insights into the impact of OCB on organizational performance and employee well-being. The findings underscore the crucial role of leadership, organizational culture, and individual factors in fostering OCB, offering valuable insights for managers and policymakers. As a policy rating, organizational citizenship behavior contains only ideas and does not include job requirements in the job description (Organ, 2015).

The discussion section interprets the findings, highlighting their implications for organizations and future research directions. Finally, the conclusion summarizes the key points and emphasizes the importance of fostering OCB in contemporary workplaces. This study concludes by emphasizing strategies to nurture the OCB for sustainable organizational growth and employee well-being.

2. LITERATURE REVIEW

A. OCB's Historical Development

The concept of OCB was first introduced by Bateman and Organ (1983), based on Katz and Kahn's (1978) ideas about extra-role behaviors. These discretionary actions were linked to greater functionality of the organization, although without direct compensation or formal recognition. Over time, the construct evolved to include dimensions that extend beyond altruistic acts, emphasizing behaviors that reinforce collective organizational goals (Organ et al., 2006). Collectively, OCB provides resources, saves available resources, retains customers, and reduces churn (Walz & Niehoff, 2000, Koys, 2001).

B. Definitions of Organizational Citizenship Behavior

OCB has been defined in a number of ways in different studies. Organ (1988) characterized it as an individual behavior that is not directly recognized by the formal reward system, but that promotes effective functioning within the organization (Organ, 1988). Organizational citizenship behavior (OCB) is defined as individual discretionary behaviors, not enforceable and recognized by the formal reward system and that promote the efficient and effective functioning of the organization. OCB actions include volunteering to help co-workers solve problems and complete assigned tasks, tolerate inconveniences, and actively participate in organizational development.

The form of voice in the framework of the OCB involves challenges that resemble dissatisfaction at the individual level and that lead to job satisfaction and perceived equity. Organizational citizenship behavior has different forms and framed dimensions of spontaneous contributions that convey positive organizational aspects to individuals and agencies within the internal and external environments intended to provide feedback (Katz & Kahn, 1978).

The OCB construct is defined as the performance of discretionary behaviors of actions not included in the requirements, which are the result of personal choice and contribute to organizational effectiveness (Organ et al, 2006). OCB is defined by Oikarinen Tuija, Hyypia, and Pihkala (2007) as individual behaviors in the workplace that are productive but not recognized by a formal reward system.

Subsequent research has expanded this definition by identifying specific types of OCBs, including altruism, courtesy, sportsmanship, conscientiousness, and civic virtue (Anderson, 2017; Podsakoff et al., 2009).

C. OCB Dimensions

The dimensions of the OCB can be classified into several types. Podsakoff et al. (2000) identified five key dimensions of OCB:

1) **Altruism**: Voluntary actions to help colleagues with work-related problems. Helping others without expecting reward. Helpful behaviors directed toward specific individuals, such as helping coworkers with tasks or providing support during difficult times. Individuals can maintain OCB contribution levels with changes related to job tenure and specialization, work environment, and consideration of time, sources, and self-reporting measures. Individuals' response bias leads to correlations in their response patterns.
2) **Courtesy**: Prevent problems for coworkers through thoughtful actions. Prevent potential problems through proactive communication. Show respect and consideration for others, such as communicating effectively and avoiding behaviors that may disrupt the workplace.
3) **Sportsmanship**: Maintaining a positive attitude despite challenges. Maintain a positive attitude even in adverse situations. Maintain a positive attitude and avoid complaining, even in difficult circumstances.

4) **Conscientiousness**: Going beyond the minimum requirements in the execution of tasks. Go beyond the minimum requirements of the job. Behaviors that contribute to the effective functioning of the organization through dedication, persistence, and punctuality.
5) **Civic virtue**: Participate in the governance and activities of the organization. Participation and concern for organizational governance. Participation in organizational governance and decision-making processes, such as attending meetings and providing input on organizational issues.

These dimensions highlight the various ways in which employees can contribute positively to their workplace.

D. OCB Background

The research highlights individual and contextual factors as the main antecedents of OCB:

1) **Individual factors**: Personality traits such as agreeableness and conscientiousness are significantly correlated with OCB (Konovsky & Organ, 1996). Personality measures predict contextual performance, which has much in common with OCB. In addition, employee satisfaction and organizational engagement amplify OCB (Williams & Anderson, 1991). A sense of organizational citizenship is the result of personality traits and temperaments that lead to work behaviors that shape productive work contexts. There is increasing evidence that satisfaction is strongly related to organizational citizenship behavior (OCB) and to a lesser extent is related to the individual productivity of tasks in organizations (Organ, 2018).
2) **Organizational factors**: Leadership styles, particularly transformational leadership, play a critical role in promoting OCB (Bass, 1990). A supportive organizational culture and fair treatment also encourage such behaviors (Organ, 1988).

Research indicates several factors that influence the likelihood of employees participating in OCB:

1) **Leadership style**: Transformational leadership has been linked to higher levels of OCB, as leaders inspire and motivate employees to exceed expectations (Shah et al., 2022; (Grant & Mayer, 2009). There are a sufficient number of studies on leader-member exchange and the OCB to provide a meta-analysis (Rockstuhl et al. 2012). Meta-analytic studies can test the strength of connections between

different factors and OCB and moderating variables. The OCB of the members is related to organizational effectiveness in the workplace. Members of the organization who help colleagues beyond accepted levels of punctuality and personal attendance aim to achieve higher levels of efficiency, productivity, and customer satisfaction. Members of the organization with higher organizational citizenship behavior can assist their colleagues, mentor new members, attendance and punctuality levels, protect assets, etc., leading to improved organizational productivity and operational efficiency, and improved customer satisfaction (Organ, 2017).

2) **Organizational culture**: A supportive culture that values teamwork and collaboration fosters an enabling environment for the OCB (Somech & Ohayon, 2019; Somech & Drach-Zahavy, 2004). Culture is considered to be distinctly different across countries when considering measuring OCB in order to capture the types, modes, and dimensions of virtuous performance behavior based on the analysis of cultural variations on the nature of OCB (Farh et al. 1997, 2002, 2004).
3) **Job satisfaction**: Higher levels of job satisfaction correlate with higher civic behavior, as satisfied employees are more likely to engage in discretionary efforts (Romi et al., 2019; Moorman, 1991). Individuals in organizations engage in citizenship behaviors as a form of reciprocal treatment, and the perception of organizational failures to meet promised obligations leads to less engagement. Causal connections between job satisfaction, personality, and OCB behaviors associated with helping and conscious subjective disorder.
4) **The dimensions of job satisfaction, equity, turnover, leader-member exchanges are linked to horizontal individualistic cultures.** Variation in OCB occasions indicates variations within and between individuals (Dalal et al. 2009). There is substantial variation in OCB within and between individuals attributed to fatigue (Trougakos et al. 2015). Sick leave at OCB occurs based on fatigue and the need to perform basic job tasks. OCB fatigue depends on perceived organizational support and exchanges between team members (Bolino, et al. 2015).
5) The instances and contexts of the OCB as a form of ingratiating the print management practices of good actors (Bolino, 1999). Time management skills support the individual requirements and expectations of the core job related to the OCB (Rapp et al. 2013).
6) The OCB is a strategy for the ingratiation of selective actors, the participation and learning of supervisors, while peers who interact with the actors can issue valid opinions. However, Grant and Mayer (2009) concluded that the individual is good for soldiers to engage in voice as a defiant form of OCB.

E. Levels of Organizational Citizenship

Organizational citizenship behaviors have individual, group, and organizational consequences and outcomes. Organizational citizenship behavior is an antecedent at the level of individual, team, and organizational performance. Several factors have been identified as antecedents of OCB. These factors can be categorized into individual, organizational, and contextual levels.

1) Factors at the individual level:
   - ***Personality traits:*** Conscientiousness, agreeableness, and extraversion have been consistently linked to OCB. Emotional stability, openness, and extraversion have incremental validity (Chiaburu et al. 2011). OCB can occur at the expense of job performance, and productivity can be due to personality traits, interest in some tasks in the role, and basic job duties with effects on organizational and individual productivity.

The OCB is part of the expansion of the individual role with some discretionary contributions in job performance, incidental efforts represented by precedents that will be followed (Morrison, 1994). Organizational citizenship behaviors affect company and industry performance, job performance, individual and organizational performance, team performance (Kissi, Asare, & Agyekum, 2019; Basu, Pradhan, & Tewari, 2021; Uddin, Mahmood, & Fan, 2019)

- ***Job satisfaction:*** Employees who are satisfied with their jobs are more likely to participate in OCB.
- ***Organizational Commitment:*** Strong organizational commitment is associated with higher levels of OCB.
- ***Perceived organizational support:*** Employees who feel supported by their organization are more likely to participate in OCB.
- ***Role ambiguity and role conflict:*** Low levels of role ambiguity and role conflict can promote OCB.

2) Organisational factors:

- ***Leadership:*** Transformational leadership has been shown to positively influence OCB.
- ***Organizational justice:*** The dimensions of organizational justice are distributive, procedural, interpersonal, and informational justice that influences the behavior of organizational citizenship and its impact and consequences on organizational performance.

Perceptions of fairness in organizational processes can improve OCB. Individuals in organizations depend on perceptions of fairness in their organizational psychological contracts based on mutual trust, are likely to exceed expected roles or conversely, engage in anti-organizational citizenship behaviors, and have less engagement. If individuals perceive that organizations are not fulfilling their promised obligations, they are likely to make less effort and engage in organizational citizenship behavior (Coyle-Shapiro et al., 2006).

Cognitions and beliefs about fairness have a more unique variance in OCB than mood. Beliefs about fairness lead to satisfaction and OCB. Beliefs about distributive, procedural, and informational fairness are significantly related to OCB-mediated effects, which are greater for OCB than for task performance.

- **Organizational culture:** A positive organizational culture that values employee contributions can foster OCB.
- **Organizational Climate:** A positive and supportive organizational climate can foster OCB. Organizational Citizenship Behavior contributes to improving organizational climate and effective organizational and individual practices and outcomes (Podsakoff et al. 2011), although some analysts question these effects.

3) Contextual factors:

- ***Workload:*** Moderate levels of workload can stimulate OCB, while excessive workload can hinder it.
- ***Work autonomy:*** Work autonomy can positively influence the OCB by providing employees with the freedom to make decisions and take initiative.
- ***Team cohesion: Strong*** team cohesion can promote OCB through peer pressure and social support.

F. OCB Results

The benefits of fostering OCB within organizations are well documented. Positive results include:

1) **Improved team performance**: Employees who participate in the OCB contribute to improved team dynamics and overall performance (Lee, 2020; Chiaburu & Baker, 2006).
2) **Reduced turnover rates**: Organizations that promote OCB tend to experience lower turnover rates as employees feel more engaged and connected to their workplace (Yildiz et al., 2023).

3) **Increased organizational effectiveness**: The cumulative effect of individual citizenship behaviors leads to greater organizational effectiveness and adaptability in changing environments (Organ & Ryan, 1995).

G. OCB Measurement

Several measures have been developed to assess OCB. One of the most widely used is the Organizational Citizenship Behavior Scale (OCBS), which measures the five dimensions of the OCB identified by Organ (1988). Bateman and Organ (1983) developed quantitative and qualitative measures of performance related to citizen behavior. Smith et al (1983) developed a measure on organizational citizenship behavior (OCB) to include the altruism factor related to support and the compliance factor with interpersonal dimensions, such as working time, punctuality, compliance with regulations, etc. He referred to conscientiousness as impersonal behavior of organizational citizenship (OCB) and formal organization as behavior of organizational citizenship – organizations (OCB-O). Other measures include the OCB Situational Scale (SOCBS) and the OCB-10 scale.

Some people may increase the time and effort invested in OCB when under pressure, as well as a sense of entitlement, allowing them to violate regulations.

H. Consequences of the OCB

OCB has been linked to a variety of positive organizational outcomes, including:

- ***Improved organizational performance:*** OCB can contribute to increasing the productivity, efficiency, and overall effectiveness of the organization.
- ***Increased employee well-being:*** Participating in OCB can lead to higher job satisfaction, reduced stress, and higher levels of psychological well-being.
- ***Reduced turnover intentions:*** Employees who participate in OCB may be less likely to leave the organization.
- ***Improved customer satisfaction:*** The OCB can contribute to better customer service and satisfaction.

I. Modern Theoretical Approaches for the Analysis of Organizational Citizenship Behavior (OCB)

Organizational Citizenship Behavior (OCB) has been a central theme in the organizational behavior literature due to its impact on the effectiveness of organizations. As the work environment evolves with globalization, hybrid work, and new generational expectations, it is essential to incorporate contemporary theoretical frameworks that explain the current dynamics of OCB. Four key theories that contextualize this phenomenon in today's work environments are Self-Determination Theory (SDT), Employee Engagement Theory, Psychological Contract Theory, and Labor Demand-Resource Theory (JD-R). Each of these theories provides a unique perspective on the factors that influence the manifestation of OCB in modern organizations.

The Self-Determination Theory (TDS), proposed by Deci and Ryan (1985), argues that human motivation is driven by three fundamental psychological needs: autonomy, competence, and social relationships. When these needs are met in the work environment, employees experience an autonomous motivation that drives them to make additional efforts beyond their formal responsibilities, thus favoring the OCB. Recent research has shown that meeting these needs in the workplace is associated with higher levels of engagement and a greater inclination towards prosocial behaviors within the organization (Chong & Gagné, 2019).

A recent study also showed that when employees perceive high levels of autonomy in their work, they are more inclined to express their opinions and engage in voluntary organizational initiatives, thereby strengthening their organizational commitment and willingness to participate in the OCB (Kao et al., 2021). It has also been shown that meeting these needs can moderate the impact of other organizational variables, such as the fit between the person and the organization, reinforcing the idea that self-determination is a central factor in the manifestation of OCB (Wörtler, Van Yperen, & Barelds, 2020).

In the Theory of Employee Engagement and its Impact on the OCB, employee engagement is a fundamental determinant of the OCB, as it influences the willingness of workers to engage in discretionary activities that benefit the organization. It states that the level of involvement and enthusiasm of workers with their work determines the intensity with which they contribute to organizational success. A recent study on job engagement in the manufacturing industry revealed that engaged employees not only perform their roles better, but are also more likely to exhibit OCB, such as helping colleagues or taking on additional responsibilities (Ayob & Nor, 2019).

In addition, research has shown that a positive and dynamic work environment enhances the relationship between engagement and OCB. For example, a study on the playful design of work showed that employees who perceive their work environment as a motivating and stimulating space have a greater predisposition to organizational citizenship behaviors (Caracuzzo et al., 2024). The relationship between engagement and OCB suggests that organizations should adopt strategies to strengthen employees' emotional connection to the company, fostering an environment of trust and mutual support.

The Psychological Contract Theory holds that the relationship between the employee and the organization is based on a set of implicit expectations. When employees perceive that their organization is meeting their expectations and promises, they are more likely to respond with loyalty and commitment, reflected in behaviors such as OCB. However, when they feel that their expectations are not being met, they may decrease their willingness to make extra efforts or even exhibit negative attitudes towards the company (Parku, Obuobisa-Darko & Asiedu, 2023).

Recent studies have highlighted that a well-managed psychological contract strengthens the relationship between organizational engagement and organizational citizenship, ensuring that employees maintain high levels of trust and reciprocity within the company (Altunoğlu, Kocakula & Özer, 2022). In addition, the perception of organizational fairness influences the manifestation of OCB, since employees who perceive equitable treatment are more willing to contribute to the well-being of the organization (Christy, Manoharan & Yokesh, 2019).

The Labor Demands-Resources Theory (JD-R) states that the well-being and performance of employees depend on the balance between the demands of the work (workload, stress) and the available resources (autonomy, organizational support, positive feedback). When employees are sufficiently resourced, they experience less stress and greater motivation, which increases their willingness to participate in the OCB (Marić et al., 2019).

Research has shown that access to adequate resources not only boosts engagement, but also improves employees' willingness to participate in OCB activities. A recent study on transformational leadership found that leader support and availability of resources at work reinforce the relationship between engagement and organizational citizenship (Chughtai et al., 2022). Likewise, organizational support moderates the relationship between job demands and OCB, suggesting that effective resource management can maximize employee contribution beyond their formal roles (Noh & Lee, 2022).

OCB is a complex phenomenon influenced by multiple individual and organizational factors. The Self-Determination Theory explains how autonomous motivation drives the manifestation of OCB, while the Employee Engagement Theory highlights the importance of workplace involvement in the adoption of prosocial behaviors. On the other hand, the Psychological Contract Theory emphasizes the role of implicit expectations in the employee-organization relationship, and the Demands-Labor Resources Theory provides a framework to understand how the balance between labor demands and resources influences the OCB. Integrating these approaches into OCB analysis allows for the development of more effective organizational strategies to foster employee commitment and discretionary contribution.

3. RESEARCH METHODS IN OCB

This study adopted a mixed methodological approach with a predominance of qualitative, aimed at understanding and interpreting how Organizational Citizenship Behavior (OCB) manifests itself in real work environments. The main strategy for data collection was participatory observation, complemented by the analysis of internal documentary sources and anonymized organizational records, which allowed for the incorporation of quantifiable findings on the phenomenon in question.

Thanks to participatory observation, the researcher was able to actively integrate into the work environment, interacting in a controlled manner with the staff during their daily activities. This technique, widely recognized in qualitative organizational studies (Spradley, 1980; DeWalt & DeWalt, 2011), facilitated the direct identification of OCB behaviors, such as spontaneous help among colleagues, assuming responsibilities beyond the formal role, courtesy in conflict management, and proactive participation in internal processes. The observations were recorded through field notes organized around predefined categories, taken from the specialized literature, and were carried out in different shifts and areas over a period of four weeks.

In addition, relevant internal documentation was accessed, including performance evaluations, reports on organizational climate, job satisfaction records and metrics related to productivity and commitment. Although standardized scales were not applied directly to the participants, many of these institutional documents included indicators built on previously validated instruments, such as scales of transformational leadership, organizational justice, satisfaction, and work commitment. This information allowed secondary correlational analyses to explore associations between the levels of OCB recorded and key variables such as leadership style, organizational culture, and overall team well-being.

The qualitative analysis was carried out by thematic coding, following the theoretical dimensions of the OCB proposed by Organ (1988) and Podsakoff et al. (2000). The emerging themes related to both the perceptions of the leaders and direct observations of everyday behaviors. Regarding the quantifiable data, descriptive statistical analyses and linear regression were applied on the documentary bases, which allowed the identification of relevant patterns, such as the impact of transformational leadership ($\beta = 0.85$, $p < 0.01$) and job satisfaction ($\beta = 0.78$, $p < 0.01$) in the promotion of OCB.

This mixed approach made possible a robust triangulation between direct observations, institutional documents and theoretical frameworks, thus generating a comprehensive understanding of the OCB in the work context. The combination of theory with qualitative and quantitative empirical evidence offered a rich and nuanced view of the factors that enhance or limit these voluntary behaviors in today's organizations.

4. ANALYSIS OF RESULTS

Qualitative Perspectives

Managers identified open communication, recognition programs, and employee autonomy as critical to fostering OCB. Several interviewees emphasized the importance of balancing expectations to prevent burnout.

Quantitative Findings

The analysis revealed significant correlations between high levels of OCB and improvement in organizational performance indicators, such as productivity, employee engagement, and customer satisfaction. Specifically:

- First, it is suggested to design training programs in transformational leadership, given the results that show their positive impact on helping behaviors and civic virtue ($\beta = 0.85$, $p < 0.01$). Through strategies focused on inspiration, constructive feedback, and the creation of a shared vision, the adoption of organizational citizenship behaviors in the work team can be encouraged.
- Secondly, the importance of job satisfaction ($\beta = 0.78$, $p < 0.01$) as a driver of OCB commitment is highlighted. This implies the need to implement policies that promote a fair work environment, recognize individual and collective achievements, and offer opportunities for professional development. Such initiatives can generate a perception of reciprocity and, consequently, increase the willingness of employees to contribute beyond their formal obligations.
- Finally, the revelation that a supportive culture explains 62% of the variance in the OCB highlights the relevance of establishing organizational guidelines and practices that reinforce equity, transparency, and a sense of belonging. By encouraging values such as collaboration and solidarity, management and human resources managers can foster an ideal climate for workers to manifest prosocial behaviours.

The findings on Organizational Citizenship Behavior (OCB) have significant implications for organizations and future research. For organizations, fostering OCB can improve overall productivity, improve employee morale, and contribute to a positive work environment. OCB promotes behaviors such as altruism, conscientiousness, and civic virtue, which are critical to organizational success, particularly in dynamic and competitive markets (Podsakoff et al., 2000). Managers should prioritize creating cultures that encourage discretionary efforts, such as recognition programs, fair treatment, and meaningful work engagement. Individual participation in organizational citizenship behaviors is a form of organizational treatment reciprocity (Coyle-Shapiro, Morrow, & Kessler 2006).

A. **Generalizability of findings.** Generalizing findings to other organizational contexts requires caution. While OCB principles, such as helping behaviors and organizational loyalty, may be universal, their expression can vary significantly across industries and cultures. For example, the emphasis on individual versus collective contributions may differ between Western and Eastern organizational cultures (Hofstede, 1980). Future studies should consider these variations by employing cross-cultural and multisectoral samples to improve the external validity of the OCB findings.

The potential for generalizing findings related to OCB in different organizational contexts is mixed:

B. **Similarities between contexts**: Many organizations share common challenges related to employee engagement and organizational culture, suggesting that the principles derived from this study could be widely applied in various sectors (Göritz, 2010).
C. **Cultural** differences: However, cultural differences within organizations can significantly influence how OCB manifests. For example, what works in a collectivist culture may not be as effective in individualistic settings. Thus, while some findings may be universally applicable, others may require adaptation based on specific organizational cultures (Somech & Drach-Zahavy, 2004).

5. DISCUSSION

The findings align with existing literature that emphasizes the importance of leadership and culture in promoting OCB. Transformational leadership not only inspires employees, but it also creates an environment in which discretionary efforts are recognized and valued (Grant & Mayer, 2009).

In addition, organizations that prioritize employee well-being tend to cultivate a culture in which citizenship behaviors thrive. These insights suggest practical implications for management practices aimed at fostering a culture that fosters OCB. By recognizing and rewarding citizenship behaviors, organizations can improve employee engagement and drive performance. Management-based beliefs, work show other forms of OCB, but caution against models of OCB of moderate and mediated causal structures (Masterson, 2011).

6. THEORETICAL IMPLICATIONS

The findings align with Organ's (1988) theory of OCB, reaffirming the impact of leadership and culture. However, the study introduces the concept of sustainability in OCB, emphasizing the need for organizations to manage these behaviors to avoid negative consequences such as stress and job dissatisfaction.

The study of Organizational Citizenship Behavior (OCB) has significant implications for organizations and future research, particularly as it pertains to employee engagement, workplace culture, and overall organizational performance. This analysis explores findings related to the OCB, highlighting its strengths and limitations, as well as discussing the potential to generalize these findings to other organizational contexts. Some of the implications for organizations are:

A. **Improved organizational performance**: OCB is linked to improving organizational effectiveness and productivity. Employees who engage in behaviors beyond their formal job descriptions contribute to higher quality and more efficient work (Robinson, 2024). This indicates that fostering an environment that fosters OCB can lead to substantial yield gains. The achievement of organizational excellence through quality is accomplished through in- and out-of-role behaviors known as organizational citizenship behavior of its organizational members, considered as the attitude of organizational members toward colleagues and staff with the best interests and ideas for organizational development (Easo et al., 2020).
B. **Positive workplace culture**: Organizations that promote OCB often experience a more positive workplace culture, characterized by trust and cooperation (Göritz, 2010). Not only does this environment improve employee satisfaction, but it also reduces turnover rates, which is critical to maintaining a stable workforce.
C. **Employee retention**: By cultivating an OCB culture, organizations can improve employee retention. When employees feel valued for their contributions, they are more likely to stay with the organization (Priya, n.d.). This has direct financial implications, as turnover can be costly.
D. **Innovation and problem-solving**: Employees who participate in OCB are more likely to take initiative and contribute innovative ideas (Somech & Drach-Zahavy, 2004b). This proactive behavior can lead to increased problem-solving ability within the organization.

7. PRACTICAL APPLICATIONS

Organizations can leverage these insights to design policies that encourage OCB while ensuring employee well-being. Recommendations include leadership training, equitable reward systems, and fostering a culture of psychological safety.

The findings offer practical strategies for managers to encourage OCB in their teams, such as recognizing and rewarding these behaviors, which can be integrated into performance management systems (AIHR, n.d.). Organizational units have their own OCB strategy to match the performance criteria, such that the notion of OCB relationships at the organizational level is associated with and correlates with the organizational performance criteria confirmed by the research.

A. Strengths of the OCB study

One of the main strengths of the study lies in its ability to comprehensively capture the multifaceted nature of the OCB through a combination of qualitative and quantitative methods. This approach provides valuable insight into employee behavior, allowing for a deeper understanding of organizational motivations and impacts (Organ, 1988).

B. **Comprehensive data collection**: The study uses a robust data collection method that involves multiple organizational contexts, which improves the reliability of its findings (Korkmaz and Korkmaz, 2011).
C. **Focus on moderating factors**: By examining how organizational culture influences the relationship between OCB and other variables (e.g., perceptions of fairness), the study provides valuable insights into how different contexts may affect OCB outcomes.

8. LIMITATIONS OF THE OCB STUDY

However, any study is not without limitations. A common problem in OCB research is reliance on self-reported data, which can introduce a social desirability bias. In addition, the study may lack a longitudinal analysis, which is essential to understanding the long-term impacts of OCB. In addition, the sample may not fully represent diverse industries or cultural contexts, limiting the scope of applicability.

A. **Context-specific findings**: Research is primarily focused on specific sectors (e.g., higher education in Turkey), which may limit the generalization of findings to other industries or geographic locations (NCBI, 2021).

B. **Potential overlap in constructs**: The study acknowledges that several components of OCB often overlap, which can complicate the understanding of different behaviors and their impacts.
C. **Mandatory citizenship behaviors:** There is a risk that organizations may inadvertently create an expectation for employees to participate in OCB, which could lead to burnout or resentment among staff who feel compelled to go above and beyond the requirements of their job (AIHR, n.d.).

9. CONCLUSIONS

In conclusion, Organizational Citizenship Behavior plays a vital role in improving organizational effectiveness. By understanding their dimensions, background, and outcomes, organizations can implement strategies that promote such behaviors among employees. As workplaces continue to evolve, fostering an enabling environment for OCB will be essential to achieving sustainable success.

The OCB remains a cornerstone of effective organizational dynamics, bridging the gap between individual contributions and collective success. By understanding their background and impacts, organizations can cultivate environments that not only encourage discretionary behaviors, but also maintain employee engagement and productivity over the long term. Future research should explore sectoral variations in OCB and their implications for remote and hybrid work environments.

Future research could explore how OCB interacts with emerging trends, such as hybrid work environments, artificial intelligence, and cross-cultural dynamics. The influence of generational differences in the OCB and the potential moderating role of technological tools are also promising areas for research. These considerations would allow researchers to identify new drivers and inhibitors of OCB. Likewise, the following practical recommendations can be implemented:

- ***Design equitable recognition and reward systems:*** Integrate mechanisms that explicitly value OCB behaviors (e.g., companionship, altruism) into benefit and incentive plans, thus avoiding the perception of favoritism or injustice.
- ***Promote psychological safety:*** foster environments where employees feel free to express ideas or concerns without fear of negative repercussions, strengthening the feeling of belonging and opening space for cooperative behaviors.
- ***Transformational leadership training:*** offer training programs that help leaders and middle managers to motivate, inspire and accompany their teams, since, according to the findings, this leadership style is positively correlated with the OCB.

- ***Incorporate OCB measurement into performance evaluations:*** adjust evaluation criteria to reflect discretionary helping and cooperative behaviors, so that they are valued and encouraged, aligned with the organization's goals and culture.
- ***Foster a culture of organizational reciprocity:*** through policies of justice and equitable treatment, ensure that OCB's efforts are reciprocated by the organization, generating trust and greater commitment on the part of employees.

Future research should delve into the evolution of OCB in digital and remote work contexts, particularly considering how virtual communication and the absence of face-to-face interaction can influence citizenship behaviors. In addition, it is relevant to examine the impact of artificial intelligence tools that, by automating certain processes and offering real-time analysis, could alter the way in which cooperation and reciprocity are manifested. The study of generational differences is becoming increasingly important, as new cohorts of employees have different technological skills and job expectations, which can reinforce or inhibit the emergence of OCB in hybrid or fully virtual work environments.

Organizational Citizenship Behavior (OCB) is a valuable asset for organizations. By understanding the background and consequences of OCB, organizations can implement strategies to encourage and encourage these behaviors. Future research should continue to explore the complexities of OCB and its impact on organizational outcomes.

In conclusion, while the study on Organizational Citizenship Behavior presents compelling evidence of its benefits within organizations, it also highlights important limitations that merit consideration in future research. Understanding these dynamics is essential to effectively leveraging OCB to improve organizational performance and employee satisfaction.

REFERENCES

AIHR. (n.d.). How to impact the company's culture with organizational citizenship behavior. Retrieved from https://www.aihr.com/

Altunoğlu, A. E., Kocakula, Ö., & Özer, A. (2022). *Demographic differences matter on job outcomes: Psychological contract's mediating role*. Journal Business, Management and Economics Engineering., DOI: 10.3846/bmee.2022.14895

Anderson, H. J. (2017). Organizational-Citizen Behavior. In Zeigler-Hill, V., & Shackelford, T. (Eds.), *Encyclopedia of Personality and Individual Differences*. Springer. DOI: 10.1007/978-3-319-28099-8_788-1

Ayob, A. L., & Nor, N. M. (2019). *Predictors of employee engagement in Malaysia, and the moderating effects of job demands and total reward*. Asian Academy of Management Journal., DOI: 10.21315/aamj2019.24.s2.3

Bajo, B. M. (1990). From transactional to transformational leadership: Learning to share the vision. *Organizational Dynamics*, *18*(3), 19–31. DOI: 10.1016/0090-2616(90)90061-S

Barnard, C. I. (1938). *The functions of the Executive*. Harvard University.

Basu, E., Pradhan, R. K., & Tewari, H. R. (2021). Impact of Organizational Citizenship Behavior at Work UPINCASE 2020 *Journal of Physics: Lecture Series* 1823 (2021) 012005 IOP Publishing DOI: 10.1088/1742-6596/1823/1/012005

Bateman, T. S., & Organo, D. W. (1983). Job satisfaction and the good soldier: The relationship between the employee's affection and "citizenship.". *Journal of the Academy of Management*, *26*(4), 587–595. DOI: 10.2307/255908

Blau, P. (1964). *Exchange and power in social life*. Wiley.

Boliño, M. C. (1999). Citizenship and print management: Good soldiers or good actors? *Academy of Management Review*, *24*(1), 82–98. DOI: 10.2307/259038

Bolino, M. C., Hsing, H.-H., Harvey, J., & LePine, A. (2015). "Well, I'm tired of trying." Organizational citizenship behavior. *The Journal of Applied Psychology*, *100*(1), 56–74. DOI: 10.1037/a0037583 PMID: 25111252

Bolino, M. C., Klotz, A. C., Turnley, W. H., & Harvey, J. (2013). Exploring the dark side of organizational citizenship behavior. *Journal of Organizational Behavior*, *34*(4), 542–559. DOI: 10.1002/job.1847

Brief, A. P., & Motowidlo, S. J. (1986). Prosocial organizational behaviors. *Journal of the Academy of Management*, *11*, 710–725.

Caracuzzo, E., Caputo, A., Callea, A., Cortese, C., & Urbini, F. (2024). Playful work design in fostering organizational citizenship behaviors and performance: Two studies on the mediating role of work engagement. *Management Research Review*, *47*(9), 1422–1440. Advance online publication. DOI: 10.1108/MRR-05-2023-0354

Chiaburu, D. S., & Baker, D. F. (2006). Extra-role behavior as a response to perceived organizational support: The role of social exchange relationships. *Journal of Managerial Psychology*, *21*(5), 471–488.

Chiaburu, D. S., Oh, I.-S., Berry, C. M., Li, N., & Gardner, R. G. (2011). The Five-Factor Model of Personality Traits and Organizational Citizenship Behaviors: A goal J.L. Pletzer *Personality and Individual Differences* 173 (2021) 110550

Chong, J. X. Y., & Gagné, M. (2019). Self-Determination Theory for Work Motivation. *Management*. Advance online publication. DOI: 10.1093/obo/9780199846740-0182

Christy, V., Manoharan, J., & Yokesh, M. (2019). Psychological well-being as a mediator between psychological contract breach and organisational citizenship behaviour. *Medico-Legal Update*, *19*(1), 118. Advance online publication. DOI: 10.5958/0974-1283.2019.00024.0

Chughtai, M. S., Khalid, Y., Mushtaque, I., Yusrini, L., & Akhtar, N. (2022). A test of job demands and resources theory for leaders and subordinates change-related behaviors: A perspective from emerging economy. Journal of Innovative Research in Management Sciences. DOI: 10.62270/jirms.vi.34

Cialdini, R. B., & Kenrick, D. T. (1976). Altruism as Hedonism: A Social Development Perspective on the Relationship Between Negative Mood and Help. *Journal of Personality and Social Psychology*, *40*(5), 1039–1046. DOI: 10.1037/0022-3514.34.5.907

Cohen, S. (1980). Side effects of stress on human performance and social behavior: A review of research and theory. *Psychol. Bowl.Isaiah*, *88*, 82–108. PMID: 7403392

Coyle-Shapiro, J. A. M., & Kessler, I. (2000). *Mutuality, Stability and Psychological Breach of the Contract: A Longitudinal Study.* Paper presented at the Academy of Management, Toronto, August.

Coyle-Shapiro, J. A. M., Morrow, P. C., & Kessler, I. (2006). Serving Two Organizations: Exploring the Employment Relationship of Hired Employees. *Human Resource Management*, *45*(4), 561–583. DOI: 10.1002/hrm.20132

Dalal, R. S., Lam, H., Weiss, M., Welch, E. R., & Hulin, C. (2009). Intrafaceted approach to work behavior and performance: Concurrent and lagging associations between citizenship and counter-productivity, and dynamic relationships with affect and overall work performance. *Academy of Management Journal*, *52*(5), 1051–1066. DOI: 10.5465/amj.2009.44636148

Del Campo, R. (2007). Psychological Breach of Contract: A Perspective on Individual Difference, *International Journal of Management*. Thursday, March 1, 2007. 11 of the Constitution.

DeWalt, K. M., & DeWalt, B. R. (2011). *Participant observation: A guide for fieldworkers* (2nd ed.). Rowman & Littlefield.

Easo, K., Balaji, M. S., & Anbazhagan, B. (2020). Organizational Citizenship Behavior, Its Background, and Outcomes: An Empirical Analysis, *Shanlax. International Journal of Management (Kolkata)*, *7*(3), 74–77. DOI: 10.34293/management.v7i3.1610

Edmons, A. E. (2012). The link between job satisfaction and company value, with implications for corporate social responsibility. *Acts*, *26*(4), 1–19.

Farh, J. L., Earley, P. C., & Lin, S. C. (1997). Impetus for Action: Acultural Analysis of Justice and the Behavior of Organizational Citizenship in Chinese Society. *Quarterly Journal of Administrative Sciences*, *42*(3), 421–444. DOI: 10.2307/2393733

Farh, J. L., Zhong, C. B., & Organ, D. W. (2002). *An inductive analysis of the construct domain of organizational citizenship behavior.In the People's Republic of China. A. S. Tsui, C.M. Lau (Eds.), The Management of Enterprises in the People's Republic of China* (445-470), Kluwer Academic Press, Boston, MA. DOI: 10.1007/978-1-4615-1095-6_18

Farh, J. L., Zhong, C. B., & Organ, D. W. (2004). Behavior of organizational citizenship in the People's Republic of China. *Organization Science*, *15*(2), 241–253. DOI: 10.1287/orsc.1030.0051

Fein, E., Yildiz, H., & Romi, A. (2023). Organizational Citizenship Behavior and Self-Defeating Work Behavior: A Comprehensive Framework for Understanding Employee Behaviors. *Frontiers in Psychology*, •••, 14.

Gakovic, A., & Tetrick, L. E. (2003). Perceived organizational support and employment status: A comparison of the employment relationship of part-time and full-time employees attending the college class. *Journal of Organizational Behavior*, *24*, 649–666. DOI: 10.1002/job.206

Göritz, A. S. (2010). Organizational citizen behavior and job satisfaction. *Journal of Managerial Psychology, 25*(8), 758–775.

Graham, J. W. (1989). *Organizational Citizenship Behavior: Redefinition, Operationalization, and Validation of Constructs*. Unpublished working paper, Loyola University Chicago, Chicago, IL, 68.

Graham, J. W. (1991). An essay on the behavior of organizational citizenship. *Use Reply Rights J, 4*(3), 249–270. DOI: 10.1007/BF01385031

Grant, A. M., & Mayer, D. M. (2009). Good soldiers and good actors: Prosocial and impression management motives as interactive predictors of affiliated citizenship behaviors. *The Journal of Applied Psychology, 94*(4), 900–912. DOI: 10.1037/a0013770 PMID: 19594233

Grant, A. M., & Mayer, D. M. (2009). Good Soldiers: The Impact of Leadership on Employee Citizen Behavior. *The Leadership Quarterly, 20*(1), 56–71.

Herscovitch, L., & Meyer, J. P. (2002). Commitment to organizational change: Extension of a three-component model. *The Journal of Applied Psychology, 87*(3), 474–487. DOI: 10.1037/0021-9010.87.3.474 PMID: 12090605

Hofstede, G. (1980). *Consequences of culture: International differences in work-related values*. Sage Publications.

Homans, G. C. (1961). *Social behavior: its elementary forms*. Harcourt, Brace, and the World.

Husted, B. W., & Folger, R. (2004). Equity and transaction costs: The contribution of organizational justice theory to an integrative model of economic organization. *Organization Science, 15*(6), 719–729. DOI: 10.1287/orsc.1040.0088

Kalahasthi, P., & Usha, N. (2024). Redefining the future of work: A mediation model enabling workplace transformation for medium-sized IT product companies of South India. IIM Kozhikode Society & Management Review. DOI: 10.1177/22779752241259508

Kao, K., Hsu, H.-H., Thomas, C. L., Cheng, Y.-C., Lin, M., & Li, H.-F. (2021). Motivating employees to speak up: Linking job autonomy, P-O fit, and employee voice behaviors through work engagement. *Current Psychology (New Brunswick, N.J.)*. Advance online publication. DOI: 10.1007/s12144-020-01222-0

Katz, D., & Kahn, R. L. (1966). *The Social Psychology of Organizations*. Wiley.

Katz, D., & Kahn, R. L. (1978). *The Social Psychology of Organizations* (2nd ed.). Wiley.

Kissi, E., Asare, O. A., & Agyekum, K. (2019).. . *Determining the Effects of the Interaction Between Organizational Citizenship Behavior, Work Overload, and Employee Performance in Ghana's Construction Industry, 68*(7), 1235–1249. DOI: 10.1108/IJPPM07-2018-0262

Konovsky, M. A., & Organ, D. W. (1996). Dispositional and contextual determinants of organizational citizenship behavior. *Journal of Organizational Behavior, 17*(3), 253–266. DOI: 10.1002/(SICI)1099-1379(199605)17:3<253::AID-JOB747>3.0.CO;2-Q

Korkmaz, M., & Korkmaz, A. (2011). The moderating role of organizational culture in the relationship between organizational citizenship behaviors (OCB) and perceptions of justice. *Emerald insight*. https://doi.org/DOI: 10.1108/01409171111178836

Koys, D. J. (2001). The effects of employee satisfaction, organizational citizenship behavior, and turnover on organizational effectiveness: a longitudinal unit-level study. *Pers. psychol.,* 54(1): 101-114 (14 pages).

Krebs, D. J. (1970). Altruism: An Examination of the Concept and a Review of the Literature. *Psychological Bulletin, 73*(4), 258–302. DOI: 10.1037/h0028987

Lamm, E., Tosti-Kharas, J., & King, C. E. (2015). Enhancing employee sustainability: Perceived organizational support for the environment. *Journal of Business Ethics, 128*(1), 207–220. DOI: 10.1007/s10551-014-2093-z

Lee, J. (2020). The role of organizational citizenship behavior in improving employee performance: a meta-analysis approach.

Lian, H., Li, J., Du, C., Wu, W., Xia, Y., & Lee, C. (2022). Disaster or opportunity? How COVID-19-associated changes in environmental uncertainty and job insecurity relate to organizational identification and performance. *The Journal of Applied Psychology, 107*(5), 693–706. Advance online publication. DOI: 10.1037/apl0001011 PMID: 35254851

Mahmoud, A., Berman, A., Reisel, W., Fuxman, L., & Hack-Polay, D. (2023). Examining generational differences as a moderator of extreme-context perception and its impact on work alienation organizational outcomes: Implications for the workplace and remote work transformation. *Scandinavian Journal of Psychology*. Advance online publication. DOI: 10.1111/sjop.12955 PMID: 37596807

Mahmoud, A., Hack-Polay, D., Reisel, W., Fuxman, L., Grigoriou, N., Mohr, I., & Aizouk, R. (2021). Who's more vulnerable? A generational investigation of COVID-19 perceptions' effect on Organisational citizenship Behaviours in the MENA region: Job insecurity, burnout and job satisfaction as mediators. *BMC Public Health*, *21*(1), 1951. Advance online publication. DOI: 10.1186/s12889-021-11976-2 PMID: 34706702

Malila, C., Daya, P., & Bick, G. (2023). *The future of work: A hybrid work model in a public sector organisation.* The Case Writing Centre, University of Cape Town, Graduate School of Business., DOI: 10.1108/CASEUCT-2023-000001

Marić, M., Hernaus, T., Vujčić, M., & Černe, M. (2019). Job characteristics and organizational citizenship behavior: A multisource study on the role of work engagement. Drustvena istrazivanja. DOI: 10.5559/di.28.1.02

Masterson, S. S. (2011). A trickle-down model of organizational justice: Relating employee and customer perceptions and reactions to equity. *The Journal of Applied Psychology*, *86*(4), 594–604. DOI: 10.1037/0021-9010.86.4.594 PMID: 11519644

Maynes, T. D., & Podsakoff, P. M. (2014). An examination of the nature, background, and consequences of an expanded set of employee voice behaviors. *The Journal of Applied Psychology*, *99*(1), 87–112. DOI: 10.1037/a0034284 PMID: 24041119

Moorman, R. H. (1991). Relationship Between Organizational Justice and Organizational Citizenship Behaviors: Do Perceptions of Equity Influence Employee Citizenship? *The Journal of Applied Psychology*, *76*(6), 845–855. DOI: 10.1037/0021-9010.76.6.845

Morrison, E. W. (1994). Role Definitions and Organizational Citizenship Behavior: The Importance of the Employee Perspective. *Academy of Management Journal*, *37*(6), 1543–1567. DOI: 10.2307/256798

NCBI. (2021). Impact of prosocial motivation on organizational citizenship. Obtained dehttps://www.ncbi.nlm.nih.gov/

Noh, E.-M., & Lee, K.-H. (2022). *The empirical research on professional isolation during remote work in context of COVID-19 and organizational citizenship behavior*. Korean Journal of Industrial and Organizational Psychology., DOI: 10.24230/kjiop.v35i3.513-558

Oikarinen, T., Hyypia, M., & Pihkala, T. (2007). *Effects of human resource management practices on the OCB of employees within networks.* Paper prepared for the 19th Conference of the Nordic Academy of Management in Bergen, Norway.

Oleksa-Marewska, K., & Tokar, J. (2022). Facing the post-pandemic challenges: The role of leadership effectiveness in shaping the affective well-being of healthcare providers working in a hybrid work mode. *International Journal of Environmental Research and Public Health, 19*(21), 14388. Advance online publication. DOI: 10.3390/ijerph192114388 PMID: 36361264

Organ, D. W. (1977). A re-evaluation and reinterpretation of the satisfaction-causes-performance hypothesis. *Academy of Management Review, 2*(1), 46–53. DOI: 10.2307/257604

Organ, D. W. (1988). *Organizational Citizenship Behavior: The Good Soldier Syndrome*. Lexington Books.

Organ, D. W. (2015). Behavior of Organizational Citizenship, Second Edition, vol. 17, no. 1938. Elsevier, 2015. DOI: 10.1016/B978-0-08-097086-8.22031-X

Organ, D. W. (2017). Behavior of Organizational Citizenship: Recent Trends and Developments, *Annu. Rev. Organ. Psychol. Organ. Behave,* no. November 2017, pp. 1-12, 2018, doi: DOI: 10.1146/annurev-orgpsych-032117-104536

Organ, D. W. (2018). Annual Journal of Organizational Psychology and Organizational Behavior Organizational Citizenship Behavior: Recent Trends and Developments. *Annual Review of Organizational Psychology and Organizational Behavior, 2018*(80), 295–306. DOI: 10.1146/annurev-orgpsych-032117-104536

Organ, D. W., & Konovsky, M. (1989). Cognitive versus affective determinants of organizational citizenship behavior. *The Journal of Applied Psychology, 74*(1), 157–164. DOI: 10.1037/0021-9010.74.1.157

Organ, D. W., Podsakoff, P. M., & MacKenzie, S. B. (2006). *Behavior of organizational citizenship: its nature, antecedents and consequences*. Sage Publications. DOI: 10.4135/9781452231082

Organ, D. W., & Ryan, K. (1995). A meta-analytic review of attitudinal and dispositional predictors of organizational citizenship behavior. *Personnel Psychology, 48*(4), 775–802. DOI: 10.1111/j.1744-6570.1995.tb01781.x

Parku, K. E., Obuobisa-Darko, T., & Asiedu, E. (2023). *Psychological contract fulfilment: A suitable umpire between transformational leadership and employee engagement in the Ghanaian public sector*. International Journal of Applied Research in Business and Management., DOI: 10.51137/ijarbm.2023.4.1.5

Podsakoff, N. P., Whiting, S. W., Podsakoff, P. M., & Blume, B. D. (2009). Individual and organizational-level consequences of organizational citizenship behaviors: A meta-analysis. *The Journal of Applied Psychology, 94*(1), 122–141. DOI: 10.1037/a0013079 PMID: 19186900

Podsakoff, N. P., Whiting, S. W., Podsakoff, P. M., & Mishra, P. M. (2011). Effects of organizational citizenship behaviors on selection decisions in job interviews. *The Journal of Applied Psychology, 96*(2), 310–326. DOI: 10.1037/a0020948 PMID: 20919791

Podsakoff, P.M., & Mackenzie, S.B. (1994). Behavior of organizational citizenship and effectiveness of the sales unit. Journal of Market Research, 31, 351-363. 28.

Podsakoff, P. M., MacKenzie, S. B., Paine, J. B., & Bachrach, D. G. (2000). Organizational Citizenship Behaviors: A Critical Review of the Theoretical and Empirical Literature and Suggestions for Future Research. *Journal of Management, 26*(3), 513–563. DOI: 10.1177/014920630002600307

Podsakoff, P. M., Whiting, S. W., Podsakoff, N. P., & Blume, B. D. (2009). Individual and Organizational Consequences of Organizational Citizenship Behaviors: A Meta-Analysis. *The Journal of Applied Psychology, 94*(1), 122–141. DOI: 10.1037/a0013079 PMID: 19186900

Priya, V. (n.d.). *Why is citizen behavior so important for organizations?* LinkedIn. Retrieved from LinkedIn.

Rapp, A. A., Bachrach, D. G., & Rapp, T. L. (2013). The influence of time management skill on the curvilinear relationship between organizational citizenship behavior and task performance. *The Journal of Applied Psychology, 98*(4), 668–677. DOI: 10.1037/a0031733 PMID: 23379912

Robinson, C. (2024). *How to impact the company's culture with organizational citizenship behavior. Forbes*. Retrieved from Forbes.

Robinson, S. L., & Morrison, E. W. (1995). Psychological Contracts and OCB: The Effect of Unfulfilled Obligations on Civic Virtue Behavior. *Journal of Organizational Behavior, 16*(3), 289–298. DOI: 10.1002/job.4030160309

Robinson, S.L., & Rousseau, D.M. (1994). Violating the psychological contract: it is not the exception but the norm. *Journal of Organizational Behavior*, 15, 245-259. Article 29.

Rockstuhl, T., Dulebohn, J. H., Ang, S., & Shore, L. M. (2012). Leader-Member Exchange (LMX) and Culture: A Meta-Analysis of LMX Correlates in 23 Countries. *The Journal of Applied Psychology*, *97*(6), 1097–1130. DOI: 10.1037/a0029978 PMID: 22985117

Roethlisberger, F. J., & Dickson, W. J. (1939). *Management and the worker*. Harvard University Press.

Romi, A., Yildiz, H., & Somech, A. (2019). Job satisfaction as a predictor of organizational citizenship behavior: evidence from multiple industries.

Rousseau, D. M. (1995). *Psychological Contracts in Organizations: Understanding Written and Unwritten Agreements*. SAGE. DOI: 10.4135/9781452231594

Shah, S.Z., *et al.* (2022). Leadership styles and their impact on organizational citizenship behaviors: a review study.

Smith, C. A., Organ, D. W., & Near, J. P. (1983). Behavior of organizational citizenship: Its nature and background. *The Journal of Applied Psychology*, *68*(4), 653. DOI: 10.1037/0021-9010.68.4.653

Somech, A., & Drach-Zahavy, A. (2004). Exploring organizational citizenship behavior from an interpersonal perspective: The role of team member behavior in promoting citizenship behavior. *The Journal of Applied Psychology*, *89*(5), 893–901.

Somech, A., & Drach-Zahavy, A. (2004b). Organizational Citizenship Behaviors: Definitions and Dimensions. *Journal of Managerial Psychology*, *19*(6), 609–622. DOI: 10.1108/02683940410558073

Somech, A., & Ohayon, L. (2019). The role of organizational culture in fostering organizational citizenship behavior among employees.

Spradley, J. P. (1980). *Participant observation*. Holt, Rinehart and Winston.

Trougakos, J. P., Beal, D. J., Cheng, B. H., Hideg, I., & Zweig, D. (2015). Too Exhausted to Help: A Resource Depletion Perspective on Everyday Interpersonal Citizenship Behaviors. *The Journal of Applied Psychology*, *100*(1), 227–236. DOI: 10.1037/a0038082 PMID: 25314365

Turnley, W. H., & Feldman, D. C. (2000). Re-examining the effects of psychological violations of contract: Unmet expectations and job dissatisfaction as mediators. *Journal of Organizational Behavior*, *21*(1), 25–42. DOI: 10.1002/(SICI)1099-1379(200002)21:1<25::AID-JOB2>3.0.CO;2-Z

Uddin, M. A., Mahmood, M., & Fan, L. (2019). Why Individual Employee Engagement Matters for Team Performance?: Mediating Effects of Employee Engagement and Organizational Citizenship Behavior. *Team Performance Management*, *25*(1–2), 47–68. DOI: 10.1108/TPM-12-2017-0078

Uru, F. O., Gozukara, E., & Tezcan, L. (2022). The moderating roles of remote, hybrid, and onsite working on the relationship between work engagement and organizational identification during the COVID-19 pandemic. *Sustainability (Basel)*, *14*(24), 16828. Advance online publication. DOI: 10.3390/su142416828

Walz, S. M., & Niehoff, B. P. (2000). Organizational citizenship behaviors: Their relationship with organizational effectiveness. *Journal of Hospitality & Tourism Research (Washington, D.C.)*, *24*(3), 301–319. DOI: 10.1177/109634800002400301

Williams, L. J., & Anderson, S. E. (1991). Job satisfaction and organizational commitment as predictors of organizational citizenship and role behaviors. *Journal of Management*, *17*(3), 601–617. DOI: 10.1177/014920639101700305

Williamson, O. E. (1975). *Markets and hierarchies*. Prensa Libre.

Williamson, O. E. (1993). Calculation, confidence and economic organization. *J. Derecho Econ.*, *36*, 453–486.

Wörtler, B., Van Yperen, N. V., & Barelds, D. (2020). Do individual differences in need strength moderate the relations between basic psychological need satisfaction and organizational citizenship behavior? *Motivation and Emotion*, *44*(3), 315–328. DOI: 10.1007/s11031-019-09775-9

Yildiz, H., *et al.* (2023). Understanding Mandatory Citizenship Behaviors in Organizations: Implications for Management Practices.

Section 2
Health, Well-Being, and Safety

Chapter 4

Strategic Innovations in Service and Adaptive Leadership Response in Retail Health and Beauty

Darrell Norman Burrell
https://orcid.org/0000-0002-4675-9544
Marymount University, USA

Lauren C. Conley
https://orcid.org/0009-0005-7933-2415
Marymount University, USA

Delores Springs
https://orcid.org/0000-0003-0940-1225
Capitol Technology University, USA

Amalisha Sabie-Aridi
https://orcid.org/0000-0002-7869-5530
Capitol Technology University, USA

Quatavia McLester
https://orcid.org/0000-0003-1596-0517
Capitol Technology University, USA

Kim L. Brown-Jackson
https://orcid.org/0000-0001-9231-2076
Claremont Lincoln University, USA

Marlena Daryousef
Colorado Technical University, USA

Terrence Duncan
https://orcid.org/0000-0002-5456-6013
Liberty University, USA

William Quisenberry
Purdue University Global, USA

Maria R. Mondala-Duncan
https://orcid.org/0009-0000-4586-8434
Marymount University, USA

Brian Douglas
https://orcid.org/0009-0000-6095-0292
Clinton College, USA

ABSTRACT

Globally, the beauty industry stands out as one of the most competitive and dynam-

DOI: 10.4018/979-8-3373-0482-3.ch004

ic sectors, consistently demonstrating resilience compared to other non-essential consumer goods markets. The COVID-19 pandemic and changing customer purchasing approaches have left many companies struggling to survive. In response, VITALUXE ESSENTIALS Health has formulated new strategies, aiming to maintain its competitive edge through the expertise and support of a management and strategy consulting firm. Real-world case study interventions, like this one, allow for the examination of complex, dynamic business environments in their natural contexts, providing rich insights that theoretical models or controlled experiments may not capture. Unlike purely academic research, which can sometimes lack immediate applicability, case study interventions focus on solving current problems faced by businesses. This relevance ensures that the findings are not only theoretically sound but also pragmatically valuable to stakeholders, including managers, employees, and consultants.

BACKGROUND

VITALUXE ESSENTIALS Health, a family-owned health and beauty cosmetic company in Canada, has long thrived through its brick-and-mortar retail outlets by offering personalized shopping experiences to its dedicated customers. However, the onset of the COVID-19 pandemic created unprecedented challenges, leading to a significant 71% drop in sales and revenue between the start of the pandemic and 2023. The company's leadership, deeply rooted in traditional business operations, now faces the pressing need for a strategic shift as market conditions have changed dramatically.

The pandemic drastically altered consumer behaviors, with a notable shift toward online shopping and an increased demand for easily accessible product information via digital platforms. VITALUXE ESSENTIALS Health has historically relied on in-store sales and conventional marketing techniques and has experienced setbacks due to hesitating to adopt these new trends. This resistance to change has resulted in considerable financial losses, prompting the leadership to recognize the need for a comprehensive reassessment of their business model and a proactive search for innovative strategies to remain competitive.

With these challenges, VITALUXE ESSENTIALS Health now sees an opportunity to evolve by bringing on a management and strategy consultant to spearhead a transformative planning process. The consultant will assess the shifting business landscape, analyze evolving consumer preferences, and propose strategic initiatives to revitalize the company's sales and market presence. This period of uncertainty offers VITALUXE ESSENTIALS Health the chance to recover from the pandemic's financial impact while positioning itself as a resilient and adaptable health and beauty industry player.

The used a management and strategy consultant to help the company's transformation by identifying key trends and emerging opportunities within the health and beauty sector. Through a comprehensive market analysis, they will evaluate the company's internal resources, operational efficiency, and strategic capabilities. Working closely with VITALUXE ESSENTIALS Health's leadership, the consultant will help formulate a detailed strategic plan, emphasizing the integration of online platforms, digital marketing strategies, and customer-centric approaches to ensure the company aligns with the rapidly evolving market dynamics.

Problem Statement

VITALUXE ESSENTIALS Health, a long-standing family-owned health and beauty cosmetic company in Canada, has experienced a dramatic 71% decline in sales and revenue between 2020 and 2023 due to the COVID-19 pandemic. This sharp downturn highlights the company's struggle to adapt to a rapidly shifting market, where consumer behavior has gravitated toward e-commerce and digital engagement. The company's reliance on traditional brick-and-mortar stores and conventional marketing strategies has not only limited its ability to meet emerging consumer demands but has also left it vulnerable in an increasingly digital-first industry. This situation underscores the critical need for VITALUXE ESSENTIALS Health to re-evaluate its business model, particularly in light of the accelerating trends toward online shopping, personalized digital experiences, and the demand for accessible product information.

The originality and significance of this inquiry lie in its exploration of how a family-owned business with deep roots in traditional retail can transform itself in response to unprecedented disruptions. By engaging a management and strategy consultant, VITALUXE ESSENTIALS Health seeks to navigate this transition, positioning itself for long-term success in a post-pandemic market. The consultant will focus on assessing the company's internal operations and external market conditions, with an emphasis on adopting e-commerce platforms, leveraging digital marketing strategies, and fostering customer-centric innovation. This approach offers a novel opportunity to examine how strategic agility, and digital transformation can rejuvenate a legacy brand while offering insights into broader industry trends and the future of retail in the health and beauty sector

Method

The management consulting intervention for VITALUXE ESSENTIALS Health utilized a variety of data sources to diagnose the internal and external factors contributing to the company's decline. Drawing from management and strategy literature, the consultant conducted an in-depth situational analysis and assessments to evaluate VITALUXE's competitive landscape and operational inefficiencies. This diagnostic phase involved stakeholder interviews with leadership, employees, and key customers to gain insights into organizational culture, consumer expectations, and digital capabilities. Additionally, a review of financial statements, sales reports, and consumer data analytics helped identify trends in declining revenue streams and market shifts toward digital engagement. The goal of this research phase was to develop a clear understanding of how traditional business models and strategies had contributed to VITALUXE's challenges and to provide evidence-based recommendations for future growth and sustainability.

Contexts

The cosmetics industry, often called the "Healthy Beauty" sector, is experiencing a notable shift as consumers increasingly prioritize natural ingredients and formulations in their skincare and beauty products (White, 2021). This change in consumer purchasing behavior has compelled beauty firms to re-examine their product lines, removing ingredients such as parabens, chemical sunscreens, and other artificial additives that are now viewed as undesirable (White, 2021). Additionally, regulatory bodies have intensified their scrutiny of hygiene standards in manufacturing processes. Companies are now required to reformulate their products and adapt their production facilities to manage these more complex formulations, which present greater challenges regarding equipment cleanliness and the risk of bacterial growth (White, 2021). Health, beauty, and cosmetic organizations must navigate increasingly competitive and volatile markets as these trends evolve. The constant flux of consumer preferences, technological advances, and unexpected disruptions like COVID-19 highlight the need for a strategic pivot from traditional business models to those that emphasize organizational learning (Lukas et al., 1996; Mena & Chabowski, 2015).

CHALLENGES IN A VOLATILE MARKET

The health and beauty sector faces unprecedented challenges as consumer preferences rapidly evolve and technological innovation accelerates. Traditional business models, which may have once relied heavily on in-store experiences or brand loyalty, are being tested by marketplace disruptions, as seen during the COVID-19 pandemic. Companies that fail to adapt to risk obsolescence in an industry driven by ever-changing consumer demands and digital transformations. To remain competitive, organizations must become learning entities that encourage continuous adaptation and growth (Lukas et al., 1996; Mena & Chabowski, 2015). By adopting this approach, companies can respond proactively to emerging trends and unforeseen market dynamics, ensuring they remain relevant in chaotic and complex environments.

Opportunities Through Organizational Learning

To thrive amidst these challenges becoming a learning organization is paramount for health and beauty companies to thrive amidst these challenges. A learning organization fosters an environment of continuous improvement by promoting a shared vision, encouraging team collaboration, and developing a culture of knowledge sharing (Lukas et al., 1996; Mena & Chabowski, 2015). By embracing these characteristics, businesses can survive and excel in competitive markets. The ability to innovate and adapt swiftly is critical, particularly in an industry where consumer preferences can shift dramatically. Organizational learning enables companies to stay ahead of the curve by integrating market feedback and fostering a culture of creativity, essential for developing unique products and services that align with evolving consumer expectations (Dhillon et al., 2022).

Strategic Adaptation and Market Dynamics

The luxury cosmetics market is projected to grow substantially, with an expected compound annual growth rate of 5.6% from 2019 to 2026, ultimately reaching a market value of $81.24 billion by 2026 (Dhillon et al., 2022). This growth is driven by rising disposable income among urban populations and the widespread adoption of e-commerce platforms. To capitalize on this growth, companies must shift from focusing solely on product quality or price competitiveness to adopting consumer-centric strategies that emphasize unique and innovative customer experiences. Identifying and leveraging new marketing segments and acquiring and retaining customers through tailored approaches have become essential in this dynamic sector (Dhillon et al., 2022). Companies that fail to adjust their product offerings and strategies to reflect changing consumer behavior risk losing market share and long-term success (Kestenbaum, 2018).

The health and beauty industry faces a rapidly changing landscape, requiring companies to embrace organizational learning as a critical strategy for success. By fostering a continuous improvement, innovation, and adaptability culture, businesses can navigate the challenges of shifting consumer preferences and volatile market dynamics. As the luxury cosmetics market expands, firms prioritizing strategic adaptation and innovative consumer engagement will be well-positioned to thrive in this competitive space. This inquiry underscores the importance of understanding market forces and evolving business strategies for long-term growth and resilience.

Significance of the Inquiry

The luxury cosmetics market is positioned for notable expansion, with an anticipated compound annual growth rate (CAGR) of 5.6% between 2019 and 2026, reaching an estimated market value of $81.24 billion by 2026 (Dhillon et al., 2022). This growth is driven by rising disposable income in urban populations, which has broadened the target demographic for luxury cosmetics beyond elite consumers. Additionally, the proliferation of internet access and the vast reach of e-commerce platforms have been critical in accelerating this trajectory (Dhillon et al., 2022). To remain competitive in this evolving market, companies are shifting their strategies to focus more on consumer experiences and innovative, needs-based approaches rather than offering premium quality or competitive prices. The competitive dynamics of the industry, paired with fluid market forces, have pushed organizations to identify and implement novel marketing strategies proactively. New customer acquisition and engagement plans are now essential for companies looking to stay ahead in the luxury cosmetics sector. This inquiry explores these nuanced market shifts, and the strategic adaptations companies need to thrive in this evolving landscape.

Nature of the Study

This study applies a management consulting intervention framework to VITA-LUXE ESSENTIALS Health, a pseudonym used to protect the privacy of the actual organization involved. Management consulting interventions involve a systematic and collaborative process wherein a consultant works closely with an organization to diagnose issues, devise strategies, and recommend solutions, all while considering the organization's culture, strategy, and operational climate (Werr & Stjernberg, 2003). Such interventions serve as significant tools for generating knowledge in both the practical realm of business and academic research (Cerruti et al., 2019). In practice, these interventions provide dynamic platforms for problem-solving, drawing on the consultant's industry experience and expertise to address complex organizational challenges. By leveraging data analysis and collaborative strategies, consultants generate insights that improve organizational decision-making and performance, driving innovation and strategic effectiveness (Cerruti et al., 2019).

Moreover, management consulting interventions create valuable empirical data that enrich academic research. Real-world consulting engagements offer scholars opportunities to investigate the effectiveness of various methodologies, assess the impact of strategic recommendations, and examine the complexities of organizational change. Researchers can build and validate theoretical frameworks by analyzing these consulting projects, thereby contributing to the academic understanding of management and organizational behavior (Cerruti et al., 2019). This symbiotic relationship between practice and academia ensures a continuous flow of knowledge that informs both domains (Cerruti et al., 2019).

According to Burke (2008), successful collaboration between an organizational development consultant and a company hinges on the consultant's ability to provide actionable guidance through comprehensive data analysis. This process involves gathering and evaluating organizational data to address administration, market positioning, and operational challenges. The consultant's expertise, combined with strategic frameworks, enables a thorough understanding of complex problems and the formulation of viable solutions. This collaboration fosters a shared vision between the consultant and the organization, culminating in developing a strategic plan that guides effective implementation (Burke, 2008).

Management Strategy Consulting

Drawing on the work of Cheung-Judge and Holbeche (2015), the organizational development consulting process can be compared to a physician's methodical diagnosis of an ailing patient. This structured approach unfolds in hierarchical phases, beginning with the consultant presenting their expertise and evidence-based insights to the client. The next steps involve identifying the client's "symptoms" by thoroughly assessing the organization's current challenges and conducting a comprehensive evaluation. Once the diagnosis is clear, the consultant formulates treatment recommendations which are viable solutions designed to address the root of the problem. The final stage involves collaborating with the client to implement these solutions, arriving at mutual agreement and commitment on corrective actions (Cheung-Judge & Holbeche, 2015).

This approach also emphasizes customer learning as an essential outcome. In the final phases of the consulting process, the focus shifts to fostering organizational learning, enabling the company to internalize valuable lessons from the intervention. Organizations can better address future challenges and adapt proactively by instilling a learning culture. Moreover, this continuous improvement model underscores the dynamic and iterative nature of the consulting relationship, as both parties remain committed to ongoing enhancement in efficiency and effectiveness (Cheung-Judge & Holbeche, 2015).

Exploring Strengths, Weaknesses, Opportunities, and Threats (SWOT)

The diagnostic process plays a critical role in organizational development as a tool for leaders to gather relevant data on identified issues (Cheung-Judge & Holbeche, 2015). Among the various diagnostic tools available, the SWOT analysis stands out for its ability to provide a comprehensive perspective on internal and external organizational factors. SWOT systematically examines an organization's strengths and weaknesses (internal dynamics) and opportunities and threats (external forces), offering a well-rounded view of the challenges at hand (Burke, 2008). As Burke and other scholars outlined, this framework allows leaders to gain a multidimensional understanding of their circumstances, enabling more informed strategic planning and decision-making (Teoli et al., 2020). By incorporating internal capabilities and external pressures into the assessment, the SWOT analysis provides a holistic approach to organizational diagnosis, supporting more targeted and effective interventions.

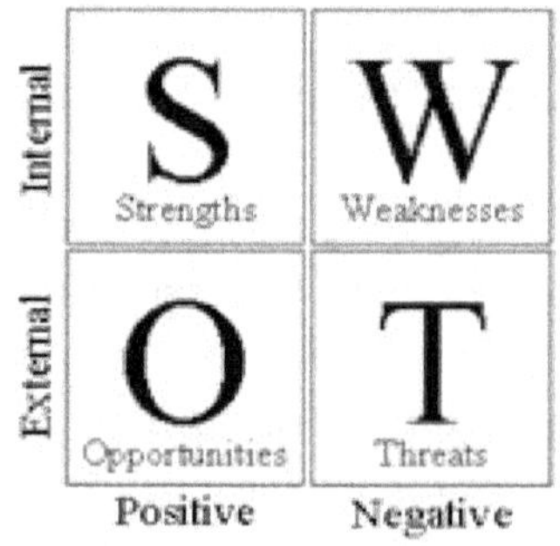

Comprehensive Data Gathering for SWOT Analysis

To conduct a thorough SWOT analysis, the management consultant strategically engaged various stakeholders to collect data on market challenges, the competitive landscape, and customer retention issues. This inclusive approach provided diverse insights from various levels of the company and its external partners, ensuring a holistic view of internal operations and external pressures.

Company Leadership

Consulting with the CEO and top executives allowed the consultant to gain critical insights into the company's overarching business strategies, long-term organizational goals, and leadership's vision for the future. These discussions helped clarify how the leadership's strategic decisions align with market trends and internal challenges, offering a foundational perspective on the company's direction.

Marketing and Sales

The heads of marketing and sales provided data on current strategies for customer acquisition, sales performance metrics, and the effectiveness of promotional activities. These insights were essential for understanding the company's approach to engaging with its target audience and revealed challenges related to consumer outreach and market positioning.

Product Development and Innovation

Engaging with the product development teams uncovered the state of the company's innovation pipeline and product life cycles. These discussions highlighted delays or challenges in bringing new products to market, particularly those related to evolving consumer preferences for health and beauty products. The consultant assessed whether current products met market demands or needed innovations to remain competitive.

Supply Chain and Distribution

The supply chain, logistics, and distribution teams provided a detailed operational efficiency assessment, identifying potential bottlenecks hindering product availability. This input was vital in evaluating the company's ability to meet consumer demand and manage inventory effectively, particularly in an environment where global supply chains face disruptions.

Quality Control and Compliance

Consulting with the quality control teams helped us understand the company's adherence to industry regulations and product quality standards. These insights were important for evaluating compliance with safety and regulatory requirements and identifying any challenges related to maintaining high-quality production amidst changing industry standards.

Customer-Facing Teams

Customer service representatives provided direct feedback from customers, outlining common concerns, complaints, and recurring issues that arise in resolving customer service requests. This data was essential for identifying customer satisfaction and loyalty gaps, critical components of the company's long-term growth and retention strategies.

Sales Representatives

Sales representatives offered insights into customer interactions, highlighting trends in product demand and challenges encountered in promoting products across diverse consumer segments. Their feedback gave the consultant a clear view of how well the company's products resonate with consumers and how sales strategies align with market needs.

Marketing Managers and Branding Specialists

Marketing managers and branding specialists shared insights on current marketing campaigns, customer engagement, and brand positioning. This information was critical in assessing the effectiveness of promotional activities and identifying opportunities for improvement in brand perception.

Market Research Teams

Data from the market research teams included consumer behavior analysis, competitive landscape reviews, and market trend assessments. This input helped the consultant identify emerging opportunities and threats, ensuring a comprehensive understanding of the external market forces.

Finance and Analytics Teams

The finance and analytics teams provided financial data, which offered insights into profitability, cost challenges, and financial trends. This analysis was key to understanding the company's financial health and identifying areas where cost optimization or revenue enhancement could be implemented.

Data Analysts

Data analysts contributed by reviewing customer purchasing patterns and preferences, using advanced analytics to identify areas for optimization. Their analysis helped pinpoint which products or services were underperforming and opportunities to tailor offerings to meet evolving customer needs.

Retail Partners and Distributors

External retail partners and distributors provided a broader perspective on market dynamics from the retail side, revealing the challenges they face in stocking and selling the company's products. Their feedback was crucial in understanding how the company's products perform at the point of sale and what can be improved regarding packaging, pricing, or marketing support.

Customers

Direct engagement with customers through focus groups and surveys gave the consultant qualitative and quantitative insights into customer satisfaction, brand loyalty, and areas for improvement. These insights were invaluable for understanding consumer preferences, enabling the consultant to identify gaps in the company's offerings and opportunities for improvement.

Industry Experts

Finally, engaging with industry experts provided an external viewpoint on broader industry trends and best practices. Their knowledge helped the consultant benchmark the company's performance against industry standards and uncover potential growth strategies aligned with the latest market developments.

By gathering data from this diverse array of stakeholders, the management consultant obtained a comprehensive understanding of the company's internal strengths and weaknesses and external opportunities and threats. This holistic approach ensured that the SWOT analysis was data-driven and well-informed, enabling the formulation of targeted strategies for the company's growth and market competitiveness.

Leveraging a SWOT for Strategic Marketing Decision-Making

A SWOT analysis is a critical tool for management consultants in launching a company's marketing decision-making and strategy development processes. This analysis, which examines a company's strengths, weaknesses, opportunities, and threats, comprehensively evaluates internal and external factors that shape a company's market position. The process unfolds systematically, beginning with collecting relevant data and then with analysis and strategy formulation (Ayodeji-Ogundiran et al., 2021; Judge & Burrell, 2021). Recent literature emphasizes the significance of incorporating stakeholder feedback within the SWOT framework to enhance the strategic relevance derived from business analysis (Phadermrod et al., 2019; Gürel & Tat, 2017). The SWOT analysis enables organizations to operate dynamically and utilize market intelligence alongside data analytic technologies for the formulation of strategies in real time (Mazanec et al. 2020). When conducted effectively, the SWOT analysis serves as a fundamental framework for enhanced strategic understanding that connects diagnostic assessment with practical planning. Establishing a comprehensive overview of the business environment to inform strategic approaches for focused data gathering and thorough environmental analysis.

To begin, gathering information is essential. Consultants focus on understanding the company's internal operations, including resources, competencies, and efficiencies. Simultaneously, they assess external market conditions such as trends, competition, and regulatory environments to capture opportunities and threats. By thoroughly evaluating the company's internal and external environments, consultants understand the factors influencing the business. For example, internal strengths like a robust brand reputation or advanced technology can be assets, while external threats such as competitive pressures or economic downturns may hinder growth (Ayodeji-Ogundiran et al., 2021). The SWOT framework strengthens the efficacy of strategic planning considerably by utilizing data-driven insights and engaging stakeholders (Phadermrod et al., 2019). This evidence-driven methodology fosters the development of more adaptive, resilient, and responsive strategies within the contemporary business environment.

Next, identifying strengths highlights the company's unique capabilities, which provide a competitive edge. These strengths can range from exceptional human resources to proprietary processes. By analyzing these factors, consultants can pinpoint the aspects of the business that differentiate it in the marketplace. In contrast, assessing weaknesses requires an honest evaluation of internal limitations. Operational inefficiencies, outdated systems, or skill gaps are common issues that, if left unaddressed, can stymie progress. Addressing these weaknesses is crucial for improving performance and sustaining competitive advantage (Ayodeji-Ogundiran et al., 2021).

Further, external opportunities are assessed to identify potential avenues for growth. Emerging trends, shifts in consumer preferences, and untapped markets present opportunities that, if effectively leveraged, can drive strategic development. On the other hand, recognizing threats involves evaluating external factors that threaten the company's success. To prevent disruption, competitive pressures, regulatory changes, and economic uncertainties must be addressed. Synthesizing this information enables consultants to prioritize which factors require immediate attention and how strengths and opportunities can counteract weaknesses and threats (Ayodeji-Ogundiran et al., 2021; Judge & Burrell, 2021). This proactive strategy not only aims to reduce potential disruptions but also positions the organization to effectively capitalize on emerging opportunities with enhanced agility and confidence.

Finally, the formulation of strategies takes place. Leveraging the insights gleaned from the SWOT analysis, consultants work closely with leadership to develop actionable strategies that capitalize on the company's strengths while addressing its weaknesses. This phase is essential for aligning the company's marketing strategies with its broader goals, ensuring a seamless integration of the SWOT findings into the decision-making process. Ultimately, the SWOT analysis is a dynamic tool that informs strategic planning, enabling companies to make well-informed, foresight-driven decisions that enhance their market positioning (Ayodeji-Ogundiran et al., 2021). The strategic alignment derived from the SWOT analysis forms the basis for effective implementation, wherein well-articulated priorities, deliberate resource allocation, and quantifiable objectives convert strategic intentions into significant, tangible outcomes.

Adaptable Leadership in Volatile Markets

Adaptable leadership is characterized by agility, resilience, and strategic foresight, especially within volatile and fast-changing markets. Leaders who adopt an adaptable mindset demonstrate openness to change, a commitment to lifelong learning, and an ability to swiftly pivot in response to emerging challenges (Ayodeji-Ogundiran et al., 2021; Burrell et al., 2023). This adaptability is essential for organizational survival in today's business landscape, characterized by technological disruption, economic fluctuations, and rapidly evolving consumer preferences. Effective leaders must understand the interconnected nature of global forces and their impact on business dynamics. Recent literature on leadership indicates that leaders who demonstrate adaptability contribute to the promotion of innovation by engaging in iterative feedback discussions and facilitating inclusive decision-making (Martin,

2021). Nguyen et al. (2020) articulate that the cultivation of psychological safety within internal teams serves as a significant factor that illustrates improved organizational agility and strengthens response mechanisms in times of crisis. In periods of dynamic business transitions, effective leadership should transcend mere internal adaptability through a proactive lens grounded in an understanding of external forces. By fostering strategic environmental awareness with internal business flexibility, leadership can improve their capacity to adjust to market changes rather than merely respond to them.

Environmental scanning is critical to adaptability. Leaders must continuously monitor emerging trends, competitor actions, and regulatory shifts to remain informed and proactive in their decision-making. This scanning process equips leaders with the information needed to respond strategically to changes in the market, avoiding reactive decision-making that could compromise the organization's competitive position (Ayodeji-Ogundiran et al., 2021; Burrell et al., 2023). Recent literature examines the importance of systematic environmental scanning for strategic foresight, enabling organizations to identify weak signals and proactively adapt prior to the escalation of disruptions (Nieves & Diaz-Meneses, 2020). Leaders who engage in proactive environmental scanning create a basis for informed decision-making in uncertain contexts.

Traditional decision-making models often need to catch up in dynamic environments. Instead, agile methodologies enable leaders to experiment with new strategies, make swift adjustments, and foster a culture of innovation within the organization. Encouraging experimentation and iteration allows companies to remain competitive, particularly when ambiguous or rapidly changing market conditions. Adaptable leaders cultivate continuous learning by promoting employee skill development and fostering a collaborative environment where diverse perspectives can shape strategic decisions (Ayodeji-Ogundiran et al., 2021). According to Almedia & Ferreira's (2022), agile leadership aligns team strengths with real-time input and market demands, which improves organizational responsiveness and enhances innovation. The implementation of agile leadership that fosters a culture of adaptability can significantly enhance the speed of strategic execution, thereby contributing to the attainment of competitive advantage.

Goal-setting in adaptable leadership must also evolve. Rigid long-term goals may need revisited and adjusted to reflect new priorities or external factors. This flexibility ensures that organizations maintain strategic alignment with changing market realities while pursuing growth. Moreover, emphasizing collaborative decision-making allows leaders to leverage diverse perspectives, which is especially valuable in uncertain or complex market conditions. Incorporating input from various stakeholders ensures that decisions consider a broad range of potential impacts, leading to more comprehensive and resilient strategies (Ayodeji-Ogundiran et al., 2021; Burrell et al., 2023). Recent studies report that organizations can achieve improved agility and long-term performance when partnering agile goal-setting with inclusive leadership (Kara et al., 2021). These methods encourage leaders to develop proactive mindsets that allow them to connect team goals with organizational strengths while adapting to a fast-changing external environment.

Hatch and Zweig's (2001) tripartite framework for adaptable leadership offers practical guidance for leaders navigating organizational marketing. It suggests that leaders focus on establishing a unique market position, implementing defensive strategies to protect their standing, and addressing customer needs through superior products and services. This framework is particularly useful in maintaining competitiveness in unpredictable markets. Research indicates that organizational adaptability fosters long-term success, may be derived from a heightened awareness of change and a focus on customer-driven innovation (Wirtz et al., 2023). Leaders who implement these principles are more adept at guiding their organizations through periods of uncertainty while leveraging opportunities for growth and innovation.

In conclusion, adaptable leadership enables organizations to thrive in volatile markets by fostering agility, collaboration, and continuous learning. Leaders who can navigate the complexities of modern business environments are poised to ensure long-term success (Ayodeji-Ogundiran et al., 2021; Burrell et al., 2023). Effective leaders implement in proactive strategies instead of merely responding to disruption by deliberately nurturing an organizational culture that fosters innovation and resilience. This type of leadership is critical in environments marked by rapid digital transformation, changing consumer behaviors, and ongoing global instability.

Blue Ocean Strategy

The Blue Ocean Strategy (BOS) offers a strategic framework for businesses seeking to explore untapped markets, referred to as "blue oceans," in contrast to competing in overcrowded, highly competitive markets, or "red oceans" (Leavy, 2018; Agnihotri, 2016). BOS encourages organizations to shift their focus from competing head-to-head with rivals and instead create innovative products and services that capture new demand. This shift reduces competitive intensity and fosters the development of entirely new market spaces. In applying this concept, companies are better positioned to unlock growth opportunities and distinguish themselves from competitors (Leavy, 2018; Agnihotri, 2016).

The competitive landscape of the health, beauty, and cosmetic industries is defined by rapidly shifting consumer preferences, technological disruptions, and fierce rivalry. By adopting BOS, companies in these sectors can reimagine market boundaries and focus on innovation rather than competing solely on established parameters (Leavy, 2018; Agnihotri, 2016). This strategic approach enables businesses to offer distinctive value to consumers, establishing a competitive edge while diminishing the risks associated with crowded markets. This capacity to innovate and redefine market boundaries is central to thriving in a dynamic industry environment (Leavy, 2018).

To apply BOS effectively, organizations must follow its four key principles: value innovation, focus on the big picture, extend beyond existing demand, and align their strategic activities (Leavy, 2018; Agnihotri, 2016). Value innovation, BOS's cornerstone, involves achieving differentiation and cost efficiency. Focusing on the broader market picture encourages companies to identify untapped consumer segments. Furthermore, by reaching beyond current demand, businesses can access new customer bases and uncover unmet needs. Finally, aligning strategic activities ensures the organization's goals and operations are coherent, enabling successful execution (Leavy, 2018; Agnihotri, 2016).

Implementing BOS provides health, beauty, and cosmetic companies with several tangible benefits. First, by creating uncontested market spaces, these companies can avoid commoditization and build a distinctive brand identity. Second, BOS fosters innovation, leading to breakthrough products that align with evolving consumer needs. Third, the strategy promotes cost efficiency by emphasizing value over superfluous features (Leavy, 2018; Agnihotri, 2016). As the market environment in these industries continues to evolve, BOS offers a proactive pathway for organizations to meet disruptive challenges and sustain growth.

In conclusion, health, beauty, and cosmetic companies that embrace the Blue Ocean Strategy can redefine their competitive landscape, foster innovation, and create long-term value. These organizations can enhance customer loyalty and secure a lasting competitive advantage by identifying and addressing unmet consumer needs, focusing on differentiation, and crafting new market spaces. Consequently, the successful application of BOS positions companies to navigate disruptions and emerge as leaders in their respective industries, driving future evolution and success (Leavy, 2018; Agnihotri, 2016).

The Resource-Based View (RBV)

The Resource-Based View (RBV) theory posits that a firm's competitive advantage stems from its unique resources and capabilities. In the context of the health, beauty, and cosmetic industries, RBV offers a strategic framework for companies to evaluate and leverage their internal resources, such as the ability to source and formulate natural raw materials, as a means of gaining a competitive edge in a highly competitive and evolving marketplace (Varadarajan, 2020). Companies can create a sustained competitive advantage by focusing on internal factors rather than external market conditions to navigate dynamic environments effectively (Kozlenkova et al.,

2014; Varadarajan, 2020). Bag et al. (2021) delineate the evolution of innovative capabilities and management capabilities as essential for improving strategic agility in sectors marked by rapidly shifting consumer preferences and heightened demands for sustainability. Additionally, this enhances the capacity to deliberately develop, comprehend, and utilize internal resources to maintain competitive advantage in progressively saturated and highly dynamic markets.

The health, beauty, and cosmetic industries are marked by changing consumer preferences, technological advancements, and disruptive market forces. RBV provides a critical lens through which organizations can assess their internal resources and capabilities to differentiate themselves from competitors. According to RBV, a firm's resources must be valuable, rare, inimitable, and non-substitutable (VRIN) to offer a sustained competitive advantage (Varadarajan, 2020). Organizations that adeptly leverage RBV capabilities such as brand equity, unique product formulations, and cohesive supply chain systems are better equipped to navigate swift market changes and changing consumer preferences through intentional strategies (Sirmon et al., 2011). By utilizing internal resources as key differentiators and vital enablers of continuous innovation, organizations cultivate strategic resilience to respond to consumer and market driven transformations in the health, beauty, and cosmetic sectors.

Organizations operating within competitive markets can benefit from RBV in several keyways. Companies can differentiate themselves from competitors by identifying and strategically deploying their unique internal resources, whether they are intangible assets like brand equity or tangible resources such as innovative product formulations (Varadarajan, 2020). Focusing on inimitable and non-substitutable resources ensures that firms maintain a competitive edge over time, even as market conditions change. Additionally, RBV emphasizes investing in internal capabilities, fostering long-term viability and resilience in fluctuating market dynamics (Kozlenkova et al., 2014).

The RBV framework becomes particularly relevant for health, beauty, and cosmetic companies when market disruptions occur, such as new technological advancements or shifting consumer demands. Conducting a thorough internal analysis allows these organizations to identify and capitalize on resources that enable adaptation to changing market conditions. Whether through efficient supply chain management, robust brand equity, or innovative product development, leveraging internal resources strategically drives success in disruptive market environments (Varadarajan, 2020). Moreover, organizations that strategically align their internal capabilities with emerging sustainability priorities and advancements in digital innovation are better positioned to maintain a competitive edge amid industry turbulence (Dangelico et al., 2017). This intentional alignment underscores the continued relevance of the Resource-Based View as a flexible and forward-looking framework for guiding transformation and fostering enduring value creation.

The Resource-Based View (RBV) offers a strategic foundation for health, beauty, and cosmetic companies aiming to thrive in competitive and disruptive markets. By recognizing the intrinsic value of their internal resources and capabilities, organizations can position themselves as leaders in the industry, ensuring resilience and sustainable growth in uncertain market conditions. The application of RBV principles highlights the critical importance of strategic resource management as a determinant of competitive advantage and long-term success (Nath et al., 2010). Concentrating on internal core competencies, organizations can maintain resilience amid periods of transformation while allowing for innovation that ensure their relevance and competitiveness over time.

Positioning Theory

Positioning Theory provides a strategic framework for how consumers perceive a brand about its competitors. Effective positioning is crucial in the health, beauty, and cosmetic industries, characterized by intense competition and rapidly changing consumer preferences. By establishing a distinct and valued position in the market, companies can differentiate their products or services and build a solid brand image that resonates with consumers (James, 2014; Iyer et al., 2019). This differentiation is critical for gaining a competitive edge and achieving long-term success.

The highly competitive nature of the health, beauty, and cosmetic sectors, driven by technological advancements and evolving market forces, underscores the importance of strategic positioning. Positioning Theory suggests that firms must align their brand identity with consumer perceptions, creating a unique and favorable position in the marketplace (James, 2014; Iyer et al., 2019). Research in marketing emphasizes the need for strong brand differentiation, which is essential for capturing consumer attention and loyalty in a saturated market (Copulsky & Wolf, 1990; Brooksbank, 1994; Kotler, 1993; Lawther et al., 1997; Ayodeji-Ogundiran et al., 2021; Burrell et al., 2023).

Positioning Theory asserts that success in competitive markets requires organizations to cultivate a distinctive space in consumers' minds. By differentiating themselves through a clear and compelling brand image, companies can foster brand recognition and consumer loyalty, ultimately increasing market share (James, 2014; Iyer et al., 2019). This alignment between brand perception and consumer needs ensures that a company remains relevant and adaptable, even in disruptive market environments. The theory highlights the importance of creating a coherent and consistent brand message that reinforces the company's value proposition.

The advantages of Positioning Theory in competitive markets are numerous. By establishing a unique brand identity, companies can distinguish themselves from competitors, increasing consumer trust and loyalty. This differentiation enhances brand recognition and allows companies to navigate shifting market dynamics more resiliently (James, 2014; Iyer et al., 2019). Positioning Theory encourages organizations to align marketing efforts with consumer perceptions, ensuring that the brand image is consistent and coherent across all touchpoints.

In disruptive markets, applying Positioning Theory becomes even more critical. Health, beauty, and cosmetic companies can adapt to changing consumer behaviors and preferences by strategically adjusting their brand positioning (James, 2014; Iyer et al., 2019). This adaptability allows organizations to capitalize on new growth opportunities, ensuring that their brands remain relevant and resonate with their target audiences in the face of market disruptions.

Positioning Theory is a strategic cornerstone for health, beauty, and cosmetic companies that seek to thrive in competitive and disruptive environments. By crafting and maintaining a distinct and compelling brand position, organizations can effectively communicate their value proposition to consumers, fostering loyalty and expanding market share. The application of Positioning Theory underscores the critical role of strategic brand management in driving long-term success and growth, particularly in markets characterized by uncertainty and change (James, 2014; Iyer et al., 2019).

VITALUXE ESSENTIALS VISION, MISSION, AND VALUE PROPOSITION

As cosmetic firms face the growing trend of "healthy beauty," they must re-evaluate their value propositions to align with consumer demand for clean, sustainable, and inclusive products. VITALUXE ESSENTIALS, for example, has revised its value proposition, committing to operational and industrial excellence by delivering high-quality cosmetic products that meet the highest industry standards (Hieronimus, 2020). For over a century, VITALUXE ESSENTIALS has strived to lead inclusive beauty, promoting a vision where all individuals can live equally and safely. This commitment extends to sustainability, with the company aiming to source 95% of its raw materials from renewable plant sources and minerals by 2030, a move driven by the increasing demand for organic and environmentally friendly cosmetics (White, 2021).

When evaluating the impact of the healthy beauty trend, VITALUXE ESSENTIALS must consider its external stakeholders. While the company does not directly employ these stakeholders, they are significantly affected by VITALUXE ESSENTIALS's decisions and performance. Key external stakeholders include consumers seeking products aligned with the healthy beauty movement, local communities where VITALUXE ESSENTIALS operates, suppliers providing essential goods and services, and governments regulating the company's operations. Additionally, creditors providing financial capital are deeply invested in VITALUXE ESSENTIALS's success, as their loan repayment is contingent on the firm's continued market performance. As consumer preferences shift toward health-conscious products, external stakeholders play a pivotal role in ensuring that VITALUXE ESSENTIALS adapts its strategies to meet these evolving demands.

A comprehensive stakeholder analysis must also address vulnerable populations whose reliance on VITALUXE ESSENTIALS's success is particularly significant. These groups often lack the authority to influence the company's strategic decisions, yet they face the greatest risks during times of transition. Vulnerable stakeholders in this case include retailers holding excess inventory of products formulated with synthetic chemicals and parabens, which no longer align with current consumer demand.

As the healthy beauty trend accelerates, retailers may need help to sell outdated products, facing substantial financial losses. Another vulnerable group comprises consumers with compromised immune systems who rely on products containing preservatives like parabens to ensure product safety during use. These consumers may find accessing products that meet their needs increasingly difficult as VITALUXE ESSENTIALS shifts toward cleaner formulations. This transition presents a significant challenge for vulnerable retailers and consumers, as they may resist VITALUXE ESSENTIALS's efforts to reformulate products in line with the healthy beauty movement.

VITALUXE ESSENTIALS's shift toward the healthy beauty trend requires careful consideration of all stakeholders, including vulnerable populations. While many external stakeholders, such as consumers and local communities, support the transition, others may resist due to these changes' financial and personal impacts. VITALUXE ESSENTIALS must strategically manage these tensions to ensure a successful transition that aligns with its value proposition and the market's evolving needs. By addressing the concerns of all stakeholders, VITALUXE ESSENTIALS can retain its market leadership and continue to thrive in an increasingly health-conscious beauty industry.

Change Adaptation and VITALUXE ESSENTIALS Archetype

One of the most pressing challenges business leaders face today is the ability to remain viable and competitive amidst industry disruptions. When organizations need strategic change, they must first recognize the necessity of transformation and then successfully pivot to ensure continued success (Michels & Murphy, 2021). For VITALUXE ESSENTIALS, a major player in the beauty industry, significant modifications to its operational structure and business practices have been required to meet evolving consumer demands. In the highly competitive and dynamic beauty space, companies like VITALUXE ESSENTIALS must understand their internal capacity for change and remain attuned to shifting consumer spending habits, critical drivers of success.

VITALUXE ESSENTIALS, like many firms, must carefully balance various factors that impact its ability to adapt to business needs. In the context of the healthy beauty trend, the company has struggled to keep pace with the rapid changes occurring in the industry, driven by evolving consumer preferences, competitor strategies, and ongoing innovations (Michels & Murphy, 2012). Although the firm has laid out a clear vision for its healthy beauty initiatives, this vision must continually evolve to incorporate the latest innovations and market requirements. This need for constant adaptation is a defining characteristic of the beauty industry, where success hinges on a company's ability to be agile and forward-thinking.

Despite the talent and experience of VITALUXE ESSENTIALS employees, the company faces challenges in scaling its projects and maintaining flexibility. While VITALUXE ESSENTIALS has a track record of launching successful initiatives, it often needs help embedding dynamic improvement opportunities into its projects, which is critical for long-term success in a rapidly changing market (Michels & Murphy, 2021). This is particularly true for capital-intensive projects related to healthy beauty, where product technology varies across different offerings. Employees must continuously anticipate potential changes to the project scope and timelines to ensure that the company's strategic objectives remain aligned with market demands.

To remain competitive and retain market share in the healthy beauty space, VITALUXE ESSENTIALS must be able to redefine its project scope and reallocate resources and capital as needed. The company's ability to remain flexible and adaptive in the face of change will determine its ongoing success in a disruptive marketplace. By aligning its strategic direction with evolving consumer behavior and industry trends, VITALUXE ESSENTIALS can continue to thrive in the competitive beauty industry (Michels & Murphy, 2021).

Significance of Communication Amid Implementation

While recognizing the need for change is essential for a company's success in an evolving business environment, the effective implementation of project deliverables and clear communication among stakeholders is equally critical. In the case of VITALUXE ESSENTIALS, adapting to the growing trend of healthy beauty requires that internal stakeholders fully understand shifting consumer behaviors. To align with the firm's goals, stakeholders must actively engage with related projects, ensuring everyone works toward common objectives. Clear communication accelerates project completion and fosters team synergy, improving understanding of the project's original scope and associated goals (Collazo, 2020). For VITALUXE ESSENTIALS to succeed in this competitive market, it must openly share the challenges posed by the new consumer demands with its stakeholders and invite their feedback. This collaborative approach will enhance team cohesion and ensure that various departments are aligned with the evolving vision, ultimately leading to a more united effort to meet consumer needs.

Effective stakeholder communication throughout the project lifecycle is vital for maintaining alignment and addressing potential roadblocks. Regular check-ins and discussions with project teams allow VITALUXE ESSENTIALS to identify and resolve challenges or bottlenecks that could delay progress (Collazo, 2020). These conversations also provide opportunities to update stakeholders on critical milestones or changes to project goals, ensuring that all team members remain informed and engaged. This ongoing dialogue is particularly important as it fosters a sense of involvement and ownership, which is key to driving the project's success in a rapidly changing market.

As the cosmetic industry faces shifts in consumer purchasing behavior, VITALUXE ESSENTIALS has developed a proactive plan to meet these changes and retain its competitive edge. A key factor in this strategy is conducting a thorough stakeholder analysis, which enables the company to understand how different stakeholders are positioned regarding the healthy beauty trend and their potential impact on each other (Varvasovszky & Brugha, 2000). Failure to adapt to these shifting dynamics would place VITALUXE ESSENTIALS at risk of alienating current and future consumers. By incorporating stakeholder insights and remaining responsive to consumer preferences, VITALUXE ESSENTIALS can navigate this industry shift while maintaining its leadership in the marketplace. By fostering stakeholder collaboration and remaining agile in its strategic approach, VITALUXE ESSENTIALS can successfully address evolving consumer demands and maintain its competitive advantage.

Consultant Recommendations

The highly competitive and volatile nature of the health, beauty, and cosmetic industry demands a radical transformation in organizational strategy. Companies within this space can no longer rely on static, traditional business models; instead, they must evolve into learning organizations. In doing so, they foster a culture of continuous learning, innovation, and adaptability, which are crucial for navigating uncertainty and staying ahead in an ever-changing market. Becoming a learning organization is not merely a strategic choice but a necessity for survival and long-term growth in an environment characterized by rapid shifts in consumer preferences, technological advancements, and market disruptions.

For health, beauty, and cosmetic organizations to remain resilient in such chaotic and unpredictable environments, they must prioritize flexibility, adaptability, and innovation in their strategic planning and operations. These qualities are essential for navigating the complexities of modern markets, where disruptions are constant, and the competitive landscape is unforgiving (Ayodeji-Ogundiran et al., 2021; Burrell et al., 2023). To thrive, organizations must adopt dynamic strategies that allow them to pivot quickly, embrace change, and continually improve their offerings in response to emerging trends and challenges (Judge & Burrell, 2021).

To bridge the gap between theoretical concepts and practical execution, this study incorporates real-world case studies that exemplify the strategic innovations employed by VITALUXE ESSENTIALS Health. By exploring successful digital transformation strategies implemented by comparable health and beauty brands, we provide concrete examples of how firms have navigated similar industry disruptions. For instance, Sephora's integration of augmented reality (AR) technology in its e-commerce platforms has redefined consumer engagement, demonstrating how digital tools can bridge the gap between in-store experiences and online shopping

Agile Strategic Planning

One key recommendation for organizations operating in disrupted environments is to embrace agile strategic planning. Traditional, rigid approaches to strategy are ineffective in rapidly evolving markets, as they become obsolete before they can be fully implemented. Organizations can continuously reassess their strategies by adopting an agile planning process and making real-time adjustments based on emerging trends, evolving customer preferences, and unexpected market disruptions. This dynamic approach ensures that businesses remain relevant and responsive, positioning them for success despite uncertainty. Agile planning not only strengthens an organization's adaptability but also improves decision-making by drawing on cross-functional collaboration and incorporating continuous feedback loops (Teece et al., 2016; Shams et al., 2021). When implemented thoughtfully, it fosters a culture of innovation, accelerates the delivery of products and services, and ensures a tighter alignment between strategic objectives and day-to-day operations. Companies that embrace agile frameworks are consistently better positioned to respond to change and report higher levels of customer satisfaction and performance outcomes (Kane et al., 2022).

Scenario Planning

Organizations should also engage in scenario planning, a proactive strategy that anticipates and prepares for multiple future scenarios. By identifying key drivers of change and considering alternative outcomes, businesses can develop flexible strategies resilient to various situations. This foresight allows organizations to respond more effectively to unexpected disruptions, ensuring they are not caught off guard by changes in the marketplace. Scenario planning provides a critical advantage by equipping companies with contingency plans tailored to different potential futures (Dhillon et al., 2022). More broadly, scenario-based thinking supports strategic agility by fostering adaptive learning and enabling leadership teams to rehearse potential responses before disruptions occur (Wright & Goodwin, 2020). When scenario planning is embedded into the organization's strategic process, it strengthens the company's ability to maintain operational continuity and fuel innovation in the face of major disruptions like global supply chain issues or economic downturns (Cairns & Wright, 2018).

Invest in Innovation

Innovation should be at the heart of a company's strategic approach, as it drives differentiation and ensures long-term competitiveness. Investing in innovation across all business areas, from product development to marketing strategies, is essential. By committing resources to research and development, companies can stay ahead of industry trends and consumer preferences. Fostering a culture of creativity and experimentation encourages employees to explore innovative solutions, enabling the company to adapt to emerging challenges and maintain its market leadership (Dhillon et al., 2022). When innovation efforts are aligned with digital transformation and supported by strong cross-functional collaboration, businesses become more responsive and resilient in fast-changing environments (Kraus et al., 2022). Moreover, companies that embed innovation into their broader strategic planning are better positioned to create lasting value and remain relevant in highly competitive industries (Priyono & Hidayat 2022). Lastly, innovation is not just focused on one department or a single strategic initiative, rather it is a mindset that influences every part of the organization and drive its long-term success.

Cross-Functional Collaboration

Cross-functional collaboration is another critical strategy for navigating competitive markets. When teams from different departments and functions work together, they bring diverse perspectives and insights that can help the organization respond more effectively to market changes. Encouraging open communication across all levels of the organization facilitates quick decision-making and allows the company to adapt swiftly to new challenges. This collaboration ensures that every aspect of the organization is aligned with its strategic goals, creating a more cohesive and responsive operation. Research shows that cross-functional integration not only accelerates innovation but may enhance the organizations agility in environments marked by rapid change and technological disruption (Bogers et al., 2019). By breaking down interdepartmental silos and fostering a culture of shared accountability, companies are better positioned to turn strategy into action and maintain momentum in the face of uncertainty.

Customer-Centric Strategies

A customer-centric approach is vital in today's health, beauty, and cosmetic industry. Understanding and meeting customer needs is the cornerstone of success in such competitive landscapes. Organizations must collect and analyze customer feedback regularly to adapt products and services in real time. By leveraging data analytics and consumer insights, companies can personalize their marketing strategies and enhance the overall customer experience. This focus on the consumer builds loyalty and ensures that companies stay attuned to shifts in customer preferences, enabling them to maintain relevance in a crowded market. When organizations thoughtfully incorporate customer data into their strategic planning, they tend to foster stronger engagement, differentiate themselves from competitors, and build lasting brand equity (Ijomah et al., 2024). Keeping the customer at the center of decision-making enables brands to remain agile, relevant, and responsive in a fast-moving industry. Personalized strategies informed by real-time insights have proven especially effective in boosting customer satisfaction and improving conversion rates in the beauty and wellness sectors (Engelen et al., 2012). By pairing data-driven insights with a genuine commitment to customer needs, companies can forge deeper relationships and lay the foundation for long-term business success.

Supply Chain Resilience

To thrive amidst disruption, companies must develop resilient and flexible supply chains. Diversifying suppliers, establishing strategic partnerships, and utilizing technology to enhance supply chain visibility can help organizations quickly adapt to unexpected challenges. By building agility into their supply chains, businesses ensure they can maintain product availability even during disruption, safeguarding their ability to meet customer demand and maintain market share. The most effective supply chains are powered by advanced digital technologies such as artificial intelligence (AI), blockchain, and the Internet of Things (IoT). These tools offer real-time insights into operations allowing companies to track inventory, monitor shipments, and address disruptions before they escalate (Dolgui et al., 2020). AI supports faster, data-driven decision-making by detecting demand trends and optimizing logistics, while blockchain technology improves transparency and traceability, which are increasingly important for building consumer trust and meeting regulatory requirements (Zhao et al., 2023). In addition to digital transformation, many organizations are adopting proactive risk management practices such as scenario planning, multi-sourcing, and inventory buffering to enhance operational resilience (Ivanov & Dolgui, 2021). Businesses that can adapt quickly, meet demand reliably, and navigate disruption with minimal interruption are far more likely to achieve sustainable growth and long-term success (Day et al., 2008; Srinivasan & Swink, 2018). Supply chain resilience not only safeguards operational continuity but also opens the door to innovation, improved efficiency, and deeper alignment with shifting consumer expectations and market dynamics.

Digital Transformation

Embracing digital transformation is crucial for enhancing organizational agility and competitiveness. Companies should leverage technology for data analytics, e-commerce, and digital marketing to improve operational efficiency and responsiveness. Adopting new technologies empowers organizations to pivot quickly in response to market changes, providing them a competitive edge in the fast-paced beauty industry. Beauty and personal care industries experience constant evolution whether that's from changes in consumer preferences or regulatory shifts, digital transformation tools provide real-time feedback, improve demand forecasting, and enable personalized experiences that help build brand loyalty (Choi 2022). Technologies like artificial intelligence and machine learning further support these efforts by optimizing inventory, tailoring product recommendations, and automating key decision-making processes, all of which contribute to scalability and operational effectiveness (Bag et al., 2021). More importantly, organizations that leverage digital transformation within overall core business strategies show significant levels of innovation and resilience during times of disruption (Xu et al., 2024). These digital investments go beyond operational improvements to serve as foundational strategies for sustainable growth, strategic flexibility, and competitive positioning (Verhoef et al., 2021). Digital transformation serves as a strategic instrument for modernization and leveraging customer-centric innovation that ensures long-term market relevance.

Risk Management and Contingency Planning

Effective risk management and contingency planning are essential for navigating unpredictable environments. Organizations should identify critical risks, develop mitigation strategies, and establish contingency plans to address potential disruptions. Regular reviews and updates of these plans ensure that businesses are prepared to handle unexpected events, minimizing the impact on operations and maintaining stability in the face of uncertainty (Dhillon et al., 2022). Risk management literature explores leveraging a proactive strategy to minimize impact from unforeseen market shifts while also fostering trust among stakeholders and enhancing the organization's overall credibility (Pournader et al., 2020). By using digital tools like predictive analytics and scenario modeling, organizations can gain better visibility into potential risks and make faster, more informed decisions when facing uncertainty (Ghadge et al., 2017). Proactive risk and contingency planning, in conjunction with digital transformation, enables organizations to strategically position themselves while navigating uncertainty.

Continuous Learning and Development

A culture of continuous learning and development is critical to the success of any organization in a rapidly changing industry. Companies should allow employees to develop new skills and adapt to emerging technologies and market dynamics. Encouraging professional development and offering resources for ongoing education ensures that the workforce remains agile and capable of driving innovation and growth. Continuous learning fosters a culture of innovation through professional development that allows organizations to remain competitive in rapidly evolving business environments. Providing opportunities for professional development through digital training platforms, mentorship programs, and cross-functional learning helps ensure that employees can adapt to emerging technologies and shifting operational demands (Noe et al., 2022). Research also shows that organizations that invest in learning and development tend to experience higher levels of employee engagement, job satisfaction, and retention, all of which contribute to stronger overall performance (Achdiat et al., 2023). As automation and AI continue to reshape the workplace, cultivating a growth mindset and creating accessible pathways for lifelong learning are no longer optional they are strategic imperatives for long-term organizational success (Al-Janabi et al., 2022). Embedding development within organizational culture enables companies to not only secure the future success of their workforce but also to cultivate resilience amidst continuous disruption. Continuous learning empowers employees to respond confidently to change, enhancing agility and strengthening the company's ability to maintain a competitive edge. Organizations that prioritize professional growth and alignment of learning within their strategic goals, may be better positioned to navigate uncertainty, support innovation, and build a workforce capable of meeting future challenges.

Strategic Alliances and Partnerships

Strategic alliances and partnerships can provide shared resources, expertise, and market insights that strengthen an organization's ability to navigate disruptions. By collaborating with other industry players, companies can pool knowledge and resources to respond to challenges collectively, increasing their resilience and ability to innovate in the face of adversity. In uncertain markets, partnerships can facilitate synergistic effects for organizations to share risk, leverage complementary capabilities, and access new technologies or distribution networks they might not achieve independently (Tjemkes et al., 2023). Combined with strong inter-organizational relationships, partnerships foster trust and knowledge exchange, which are essential for navigating complex, fast-changing conditions and co-developing innovative solutions (Anand et al., 2021). Companies that take a strategic and collaborative approach are often better positioned to adapt, scale, and thrive amid disruption.

Flexibility in Marketing Strategies

Finally, organizations must maintain flexibility in their marketing strategies, adapting them to align with changing consumer behaviors and preferences. Utilizing social media and digital platforms for real-time consumer engagement enables companies to stay relevant and responsive. Monitoring industry trends and adjusting promotional activities ensures marketing efforts resonate with the target audience, driving sales and brand loyalty. By implementing these recommendations, health, beauty, and cosmetic organizations can thrive in chaotic, unpredictable, and disrupted competitive environments. Prioritizing agility, innovation, and customer-centric strategies will be critical for maintaining a competitive edge and achieving sustained success in such dynamic markets (Dhillon et al., 2022).

The health, beauty, and cosmetic industries are heavily influenced and shaped by social media, influencer culture, and rapidly evolving consumer expectations. Therefore, leveraging digital platforms and real-time consumer engagement data allows organizations to meet consumer expectations, deliver personalization, timely experiences that develop robust emotional connections and brand loyalty (Lemon & Verhoef, 2016; Dwivedi et al., 2021). In agile marketing strategies, social media not only functions as a communication channel but as a dynamic source for consumer insight, enabling rapid business responses to shift in consumer sentiments. Personalized marketing when aligned with overall strategic initiatives provides a customer-centric approach to tailor content, messaging, and even product offerings. Recent research demonstrates this marketing alignment enhances not only consumer engagement but even their purchase intentions, as health and beauty consumers are rooted in self-expression (Szalaty & Derda 2020; Zhao et al., 2023). While coordinating in tandem, flexible omnichannel strategies unify digital, in-store, and mobile experiences are increasingly critical for delivering seamless customer journeys that align with rising expectations for personalization and convenience (Verhoef et al., 2021). Brands that proactively monitor consumer behavior and adapt their messaging in real time can optimize marketing effectiveness, improve return on investment, and build lasting trust especially in markets where consumer preferences are constantly evolving.

Comparative Analysis of Alternative Strategies

A comparative analysis of existing methodologies highlights the advantages and limitations of different strategic responses within the health and beauty industry. Traditional brick-and-mortar retail strategies, while effective for personalized experiences, have been significantly disrupted by digital engagement models. In contrast, direct-to-consumer (DTC) models, as exemplified by brands such as Glossier and Fenty Beauty, illustrate how social media and influencer marketing can drive consumer loyalty without reliance on physical retail locations. These models, particularly prominent in the post-pandemic era, allow for broader reach, lower overhead costs, and faster feedback loops through digital analytics (Pantano et al., 2020; Roggeveen & Sethuraman, 2020). By juxtaposing these approaches, VITALUXE ESSENTIALS Health can identify hybrid strategies that leverage its established retail presence while expanding its digital footprint.

In contrast, direct-to-consumer (DTC) strategies, as exemplified by agile brands like Glossier and Fenty Beauty, demonstrate how influencer marketing, user-generated content, and community-building via social media can drive deep consumer loyalty without reliance on physical storefronts (Kim & Sullivan, 2019; Dwivedi et al., 2021).

While each model presents unique strengths, they also carry inherent trade-offs. Brick-and-mortar operations, despite their experiential advantage, are limited by geographic constraints and fixed infrastructure, while DTC brands may struggle with customer retention, return logistics, and achieving scale without physical brand presence (Piotrowicz & Cuthbertson, 2019). Hybrid strategies offer a compelling middle ground. By integrating the personalized service and tactile engagement of physical stores with the scalability, convenience, and data-driven responsiveness of digital platforms, brands like **VITALUXE ESSENTIALS Health** can create a seamless omnichannel customer experience (Zhang et al., 2021; Verhoef et al., 2021).

Moreover, recent studies emphasize the integration of omnichannel strategies contributes towards improved customer satisfaction, increased loyalty, and larger purchase total due to consistent brand messaging and convenience (Juaneda-Ayensa et al., 2020; Herhausen et al., 2022). These models enable real-time customer engagement across varying touchpoints while capturing consumer behavioral data that informs further personalization messaging, inventory management, risk management, and demand forecasting. With shifting consumer expectations toward personalized, convenient, and value-driven digital experiences, organizations that strategically combine digital and physical engagement will be optimally positioned to maintain competitiveness and readiness for the future.

Clarifying the Conclusion with Actionable Takeaways

VITALUXE ESSENTIALS Health's strategic transformation necessitates the following key steps:

1. Prioritizing digital expansion by enhancing its e-commerce capabilities and leveraging AI-driven consumer engagement.
2. Implementing data-driven marketing strategies that tailor brand messaging to evolving consumer preferences.
3. Investing in sustainability-driven innovations to align with the ethical consumer movement.
4. Adopting an agile organizational model that fosters continuous learning and market responsiveness. These takeaways provide a clear roadmap for decision-makers to implement meaningful changes.

Recommendations for Future Research

The beauty industry, renowned for its competitiveness and dynamism, continually adapts to evolving consumer trends and preferences. Future research can employ various methodologies to understand further and optimize strategies within this landscape, each offering distinctive insights. Specifically, Action Research, Case Study Qualitative Research, and Small Focus Group Qualitative Research approaches are suggested, focusing on soliciting feedback from those who own, run, or work at health, beauty, and cosmetic companies.

Action Research

Elements: Action Research involves a cyclic process of planning, acting, observing, and reflecting. It allows for real-time problem-solving and iterative improvements. It integrates collaboration and reflection, emphasizing collective engagement in addressing organizational challenges.
Applications: In the beauty industry context, Action Research could be applied to understand how health and beauty-focused consumer trends impact organizational strategies. Researchers could collaborate with beauty companies, implementing and refining strategies in response to changing consumer desires while simultaneously evaluating the effectiveness of these interventions.
Steps: Action Research typically follows a cyclical process, beginning with problem identification, intervention planning, implementation, outcome observation, and reflection. Subsequent cycles build upon these insights, fostering continuous improvement.

Case Study Qualitative Research

Elements: Case Study Qualitative Research involves an in-depth exploration of specific cases, drawing on multiple data sources, such as interviews, observations, and documents. It provides a comprehensive understanding of the complexities inherent in specific interventions.
Applications: Researchers can utilize case studies to investigate how health and beauty companies, like VITALUXE ESSENTIALS Health, navigate the evolving consumer landscape with the guidance of management and strategy consulting firms. Examining successful and challenging cases will unveil nuanced insights into strategy formulation, implementation, and impact.
Steps: Case study research typically involves defining the case, selecting appropriate data sources, collecting data through various methods, analyzing the data, and deriving meaningful conclusions that contribute to broader understanding.

Small Focus Group Qualitative Research

Elements: Small Focus Group Qualitative Research convenes small groups of participants to explore their perspectives, attitudes, and experiences. It fosters open discussions and captures diverse viewpoints.
Applications: In the beauty industry, small focus groups could gather insights from individuals directly involved in the development, marketing, and retail aspects of health and beauty products. Researchers can uncover multifaceted

perspectives on consumer trends and organizational responses by including owners, managers, and employees.
Steps: Small focus group research involves planning the focus group, recruiting participants, facilitating discussions, analyzing qualitative data, and drawing conclusions. It allows for a nuanced exploration of participants' perceptions and experiences.

Incorporating these research approaches will contribute to a nuanced understanding of how health, beauty, and cosmetic companies navigate changing consumer trends. The insights will inform organizational strategies and contribute to the broader knowledge base of effective interventions and adaptations within the competitive beauty industry.

REFERENCES

Achdiat, I., Mulyani, S., Azis, Y., & Sukmadilaga, C. (2023). Roles of organizational learning culture in promoting innovation. *The Learning Organization*, *30*(1), 76–92. DOI: 10.1108/TLO-01-2021-0013

Agnihotri, A. (2016). Extending boundaries of blue ocean strategy. *Journal of Strategic Marketing*, *24*(6), 519–528. DOI: 10.1080/0965254X.2015.1069882

Al-Janabi, A. S. H., Mhaibes, H. A., & Hussein, S. A. (2022). The role of learning organizations in crisis management strategy: A case study. *Corporate & Business Strategy Review*, *3*(1), 8–21. DOI: 10.22495/cbsrv4i1art1

Almeida, F., & Ferreira, J. J. M. (2022). Agile leadership and capability building in dynamic environments: A model for effective decision-making. *Journal of Strategy and Management*, *15*(2), 198–213.

Almeida, F., & Ferreira, J. J. M. (2022). Agile leadership and capability building in dynamic environments: A model for effective decision-making. *Journal of Strategy and Management*, *15*(2), 198–213.

Anand, A., Muskat, B., Creed, A., Zutshi, A., & Csepregi, A. (2021). Knowledge sharing, knowledge transfer and SMEs: Evolution, antecedents, outcomes and directions. *Personnel Review*, *50*(9), 1873–1893. DOI: 10.1108/PR-05-2020-0372

Ayodeji-Ogundiran, A. I., Burrell, D. N., & Lewis, E. J. (2021). Strategic Adaptive Leadership and Emerging Approaches to Online Marketing of a US Small Business Real Estate Firm in Response to COVID-19. [IJOM]. *International Journal of Online Marketing*, *11*(3), 1–14. DOI: 10.4018/IJOM.2021070101

Bag, S., Pretorius, J. H. C., Gupta, S., & Dwivedi, Y. K. (2021). Role of institutional pressures and resources in the adoption of big data analytics: A resource-based view perspective. *Production Planning and Control*, *32*(12), 1041–1056.

Bogers, M., Sims, J., & West, J. (2019). What is an ecosystem? Incorporating 25 years of ecosystem research. *Proceedings - Academy of Management*, *2019*(1), 11080. DOI: 10.5465/AMBPP.2019.11080abstract

Brooksbank, R. (1994). The anatomy of marketing positioning strategy. *Marketing Intelligence & Planning*, *12*(4), 10–14. DOI: 10.1108/02634509410060695

Burke, W. W. (2008). *Organizational change: Theory and practice* (2nd ed.). Sage.

Burrell, D. N., Lewis, E. J., & Richardson, K. (2023). Adaptive Marketing, Management Strategy, and Technology Innovation in Beverage and Hospitality Markets. [IJIDE]. *International Journal of Innovation in the Digital Economy*, *14*(1), 1–10. DOI: 10.4018/IJIDE.324096

Cairns, G., & Wright, G. (2018). Scenario thinking and practice: A review and call for future research. *Journal of Business Research*, *91*, 548–556.

Cerruti, C., Tavoletti, E., & Grieco, C. (2019). Management consulting: A review of fifty years of scholarly research. *Management Research Review*, *42*(8), 902–925. DOI: 10.1108/MRR-03-2018-0100

Cheung-Judge, M.-Y., & Holbeche, L. (2015). *Organization development: A practitioner's guide for OD and HR*. Kogan Page.

Choi, E. (2022). A paradigm shift in beauty education in response to the digital transformation era-based on analysis of trends in the cosmetics and beauty industry. *Journal of the Korean Society of Cosmetology*, *28*(4), 675–688. DOI: 10.52660/JKSC.2022.28.4.675

Collazo, J. (2020, August 3). The Importance Of Communication When There Is Change In A Company. *Forbes*. Retrieved December 5, 2022, from https://www.forbes.com/sites/forbesbusinesscouncil/2020/08/03/the-importance-of-communication-when-there-is-change-in-a-company/?sh=4335d5f3739e

Copulsky, J. R., & Wolf, M. J. (1990). Relationship marketing: Positioning for the future. *The Journal of Business Strategy*, *11*(4), 16–20. DOI: 10.1108/eb060069 PMID: 10106864

Dangelico, R. M., Pujari, D., & Pontrandolfo, P. (2017). Green product innovation in manufacturing firms: A sustainability-oriented dynamic capability perspective. *Business Strategy and the Environment*, *26*(4), 490–506. DOI: 10.1002/bse.1932

Day, M., Magnan, G. M., Hughes, J., & Webb, M. (2008). Strategic supplier relationship management. *Supply Chain Management Review*, *12*(4), 40–48.

Dhillon, R., Agarwal, B., & Rajput, N. (2022). *Experiential marketing strategies used by luxury cosmetics companies*. Innov. Mark. DOI: 10.21511/im.18(1).2022.05

Dolgui, A., Ivanov, D., & Sokolov, B. (2020). Reconfigurable supply chain: The X-network. *International Journal of Production Research*, *58*(13), 4138–4163. DOI: 10.1080/00207543.2020.1774679

Dubey, R., Gunasekaran, A., Childe, S. J., Papadopoulos, T., & Hazen, B. T. (2021). Big data analytics capability in supply chain agility: The moderating effect of organizational flexibility. *Management Decision*, *59*(1), 179–196.

Dwivedi, Y. K., Ismagilova, E., Carlson, J., Filieri, R., Jacobson, J., Kumar, V., & Wang, Y. (2021). Social media marketing and consumer engagement: A review and future research agenda. *Journal of Business Research*, *137*, 275–285.

Engelen, A., Brettel, M., & Wiest, G. (2012). Cross-functional integration and new product performance, the impact of national and corporate culture. *Journal of International Management*, *18*(1), 52–65. DOI: 10.1016/j.intman.2011.07.001

Ghadge, A., Dani, S., Ojha, R., & Caldwell, N. (2017). Using risk sharing contracts for supply chain risk mitigation: A buyer-supplier power and dependence perspective. *Computers & Industrial Engineering*, *103*, 262–270. DOI: 10.1016/j.cie.2016.11.034

Grewal, D., Roggeveen, A. L., & Nordfält, J. (2020). The future of retailing. *Journal of Retailing*, *96*(1), 86–95.

Gürel, E., & Tat, M. (2017). SWOT analysis: A theoretical review. *Journal of International Social Research*, *10*(51), 994–1006. DOI: 10.17719/jisr.2017.1832

Hatch, J., & Zweig, J. (2001). *Strategic flexibility: The key to growth.* Ivey Business Journal.Judge, W., & Douglas, T. (2009). Organizational change capacity: The systematic development of a scale. *Journal of Organizational Change Management*, *22*(6), 635–649. DOI: 10.1108/09534810910997041

Herhausen, D., Binder, J., Schoegel, M., & Herrmann, A. (2022). Integrating bricks with clicks: Retailer-level and channel-level outcomes of online–offline channel integration. *Journal of Retailing*, *98*(1), 80–94.

Ijomah, T., Eyo-Udo, N., & Anjorin, K. (2024). The role of big data analytics in customer relationship management: Strategies for improving customer engagement and retention. *World Journal of Advanced Science and Technology*, 6.

Ivanov, D., & Dolgui, A. (2021). A digital supply chain twin for managing the disruption risks and resilience in the era of Industry 4.0. *Production Planning and Control*, *32*(9), 775–788. DOI: 10.1080/09537287.2020.1768450

Iyer, P., Davari, A., Zolfagharian, M., & Paswan, A. (2019). Market orientation, positioning strategy, and brand performance. *Industrial Marketing Management*, *81*, 16–29. DOI: 10.1016/j.indmarman.2018.11.004

James, M. (2014). *Positioning theory and strategic communication: A new approach to public relations research and practice*. Routledge. DOI: 10.4324/9781315886084

Juaneda-Ayensa, E., Mosquera, A., & Sierra Murillo, Y. (2020). Omnichannel customer behavior: Key drivers of technology acceptance and use and their effects on purchase intention. *Frontiers in Psychology*, *11*, 890. PMID: 27516749

Judge, D. A., & Burrell, D. N. (2021). Exploring the Nature of Business Strategy Change for Mental Health Practices in the Age of COVID-19. [IJBSA]. *International Journal of Business Strategy and Automation*, *2*(4), 1–11. DOI: 10.4018/IJBSA.20211001.oa1

Kane, G. C., Nanda, R., Phillips, A. N., & Copulsky, J. R. (2021). *The transformation myth: Leading your organization through uncertain times*. MIT Press. DOI: 10.7551/mitpress/13965.001.0001

Kara, D., Uysal, M., Sirgy, M. J., & Lee, G. (2021). The moderating role of team adaptive capacity in the relationship between inclusive leadership and strategic goal attainment. *Journal of Business Research*, *134*, 731–740.

Kestenbaum, R. (2018, September 9). The Biggest Trends in the Beauty Industry. *Forbes*. Retrieved December 5, 2022, from https://www.forbes.com/sites/richardkestenbaum/2018/09/09/beauty-industry-biggest-trends-skin-care-loreal-shiseido-lauder/?sh=27a588f76982

Kim, A. J., & Sullivan, P. (2019). Emotional branding speaks to consumers' hearts: The case of fashion brands with DTC strategies. *Fashion and Textiles*, *6*(1), 1–16. DOI: 10.1186/s40691-018-0164-y

Kotler, P. (1993). The major tasks of marketing management. *Marketing Management*, *2*(3), 52.

Kozlenkova, I. V., Samaha, S. A., & Palmatier, R. W. (2014). Resource-based theory in marketing. *Journal of the Academy of Marketing Science*, *42*(1), 1–21. DOI: 10.1007/s11747-013-0336-7

Kraus, S., Durst, S., Ferreira, J. J., Veiga, P., Kailer, N., & Weinmann, A. (2022). Digital transformation in business and management research: An overview of the current status quo. *International Journal of Information Management*, *63*, 102466. DOI: 10.1016/j.ijinfomgt.2021.102466

Lawther, S., Hastings, G. B., & Lowry, R. (1997). De-marketing: Putting Kotler and Levy's ideas into practice. *Journal of Marketing Management*, *13*(4), 315–325. DOI: 10.1080/0267257X.1997.9964475

Leavy, B. (2018). Value innovation and how to successfully incubate "blue ocean" initiatives. *Strategy and Leadership*, *46*(3), 10–20. DOI: 10.1108/SL-02-2018-0020

Lemon, K. N., & Verhoef, P. C. (2016). Understanding customer experience throughout the customer journey. *Journal of Marketing*, *80*(6), 69–96. DOI: 10.1509/jm.15.0420

Lukas, B. A., Hult, G. T. M., & Ferrell, O. C. (1996). A theoretical perspective of the antecedents and consequences of organizational learning in marketing channels. *Journal of Business Research*, *36*(3), 233–244. DOI: 10.1016/0148-2963(95)00154-9

Martin, J. A. (2021). Adaptive leadership in practice: Driving innovation through continuous learning. *Leadership and Organization Development Journal*, *42*(3), 423–437.

Mazanec, J. A., Wöber, K., & Zins, A. H. (2020). Tourism destination competitiveness: From definition to explanation? A methodologically sophisticated approach. *Journal of Travel Research*, *59*(3), 459–478.

Mena, J. A., & Chabowski, B. R. (2015). The role of organizational learning in stakeholder marketing. *Journal of the Academy of Marketing Science*, *43*(4), 429–452. DOI: 10.1007/s11747-015-0442-9

Michels, D., & Murphy, K. (2021). How good is your company at Change? *Harvard Business Review*.

Nath, P., Nachiappan, S., & Ramanathan, R. (2010). The impact of marketing capability, operations capability, and diversification strategy on performance: A resource-based view. *Industrial Marketing Management*, *39*(2), 317–329. DOI: 10.1016/j.indmarman.2008.09.001

Nguyen, M. H., Tu, H. H., & Pham, L. T. (2020). The role of psychological safety in fostering team agility and organizational resilience. *Journal of Organizational Effectiveness: People and Performance*, *7*(3), 289–308.

Nieves, J., & Diaz-Meneses, G. (2020). Organizational learning capability and innovation: The moderating role of environmental scanning. *European Journal of Innovation Management*, *23*(3), 478–501.

Noe, R. A., Hollenbeck, J. R., Gerhart, B., & Wright, P. M. (2022). *Human Resource Management: Gaining a Competitive Advantage* (12th ed.). McGraw-Hill Education.

Pantano, E., Pizzi, G., Scarpi, D., & Dennis, C. (2020). Competing during a pandemic? Retailers' ups and downs during the COVID-19 outbreak. *Journal of Business Research*, *116*, 209–213. DOI: 10.1016/j.jbusres.2020.05.036 PMID: 32501307

Phadermrod, B., Crowder, R. M., & Wills, G. B. (2019). Importance-performance analysis based SWOT analysis. *International Journal of Information Management*, *44*, 194–203. DOI: 10.1016/j.ijinfomgt.2016.03.009

Piotrowicz, W., & Cuthbertson, R. (2019). Exploring omnichannel retailing: Common expectations and diverse realities. *Journal of Retailing and Consumer Services*, *50*, 1–7.

Pournader, M., Kach, A., & Talluri, S. (2020). A review of the existing and emerging topics in the supply chain risk management literature. *Decision Sciences*, *51*(4), 867–919. DOI: 10.1111/deci.12470 PMID: 34234385

Priyono, A., & Hidayat, A. (2022). Dynamic capabilities for open innovation: A typology of pathways toward aligning resources, strategies and capabilities. *Journal of Open Innovation*, *8*(4), 206. DOI: 10.3390/joitmc8040206

Roggeveen, A. L., & Sethuraman, R. (2020). How the COVID-19 pandemic may change the world of retailing. *Journal of Retailing*, *96*(2), 169–171. DOI: 10.1016/j.jretai.2020.04.002

Shams, R., Vrontis, D., Belyaeva, Z., Ferraris, A., & Czinkota, M. R. (2021). Strategic agility in international business: A conceptual framework for "agile" multinationals. *Journal of International Management*, *27*(1), 100737. DOI: 10.1016/j.intman.2020.100737

Sirmon, D. G., Hitt, M. A., Ireland, R. D., & Gilbert, B. A. (2011). Resource orchestration to create competitive advantage: Breadth, depth, and life cycle effects. *Journal of Management*, *37*(5), 1390–1412. DOI: 10.1177/0149206310385695

Srinivasan, R., & Swink, M. (2018). An investigation of visibility and flexibility as complements to supply chain analytics: An organizational information processing theory perspective. *Production and Operations Management*, *30*(6), 1770–1791. DOI: 10.1111/poms.12746

Szalaty, P. M., & Derda, I. (2020). "Revolutionizing Beauty Industry": Co-Creation and Customer Engagement for Brand Image Development. Case Study Research of a Crowdsource-Driven Cosmetics Company Volition Beauty. *International Journal of Marketing, Communication and New Media, 8*(14).

Teece, D. J., Peteraf, M., & Leih, S. (2016). Dynamic capabilities and organizational agility: Risk, uncertainty, and strategy in the innovation economy. *California Management Review*, *62*(4), 5–35. DOI: 10.1525/cmr.2016.58.4.5

Tjemkes, B., Vos, P., & Burgers, K. (2023). *Strategic alliance management*. Routledge. DOI: 10.4324/9781003222187

Varadarajan, R. (2020). Customer information resources advantage, marketing strategy, and business performance: A market resources-based view. *Industrial Marketing Management*, *89*, 89–97. DOI: 10.1016/j.indmarman.2020.03.003

Varvasovszky, Z., & Brugha, R. (2000). A stakeholder analysis. *Health Policy and Planning, 15*(3), 338–345. DOI: 10.1093/heapol/15.3.338 PMID: 11012410

Verhoef, P. C., Broekhuizen, T., Bart, Y., Bhattacharya, A., Dong, J. Q., Fabian, N., & Haenlein, M. (2021). Digital transformation: A multidisciplinary reflection and research agenda. *Journal of Business Research, 122*, 889–901. DOI: 10.1016/j.jbusres.2019.09.022

Werr, A., & Stjernberg, T. (2003). Exploring management consulting firms as knowledge systems. *Organization Studies, 24*(6), 881–908. DOI: 10.1177/0170840603024006004

White, S. (2021, March 4). L'Oreal Responds to push for natural ingredients in make-up. *Reuters*. Retrieved November 18, 2022, from https://www.reuters.com/business/environment/loreal-responds-push-natural-ingredients-make-up-2021-03-04/

Wirtz, B. W., Pistoia, A., Ullrich, S., & Göttel, V. (2023). Dynamic capabilities and strategic agility: Developing strategic responsiveness through adaptive leadership. *Journal of Business Research, 161*, 113897.

Wright, G., & Goodwin, P. (2009). Decision making and planning under low levels of predictability: Enhancing the scenario method. *International Journal of Forecasting, 25*(4), 813–825. DOI: 10.1016/j.ijforecast.2009.05.019

Xu, M., Zhang, Y., Sun, H., Tang, Y., & Li, J. (2024). How digital transformation enhances corporate innovation performance: The mediating roles of big data capabilities and organizational agility. *Heliyon, 10*(14), e34905. DOI: 10.1016/j.heliyon.2024.e34905 PMID: 39149071

Zhang, H., Lu, Y., Gupta, S., & Zhao, L. (2022). What motivates customers to continue using mobile apps? The role of personalized marketing. *Journal of Interactive Marketing, 58*, 28–42.

Zhao, F., Meng, T., Wang, W., Alam, F., & Zhang, B. (2023). Digital Transformation and Firm Performance: Benefit From Letting Users Participate. *Journal of Global Information Management, 31*(1), 1–23. DOI: 10.4018/JGIM.322104

Zhao, N., Hong, J., & Lau, K. (2023). Impact of supply chain digitalization on supply chain resilience and performance: A multi-mediation model. *International Journal of Production Economics, 259*, 108817. DOI: 10.1016/j.ijpe.2023.108817 PMID: 36852136

Zsidisin, G. A., & Henke, J. W. (2019). Strategic supplier relationship management and risk mitigation. *Journal of Business Logistics, 40*(2), 94–109.

Chapter 5
Safeguarding the Health, Well-Being, and Safety of Minority Construction Professionals From the Impact of COVID-19

Thomas C. Gibbs
https://orcid.org/0009-0003-8340-3306
Capitol Technology University, USA

ABSTRACT

This study found that applying specific theories to local industry problems can improve health, wellness, and safety standards. We can enhance industry effectiveness and durability by aligning industry practices with employee, supervisor, and stakeholder needs. This alignment benefits and is necessary for everyone. This is a call for collaboration to change industry protocols. Multiple theories show that organizational practices affect performance. This article discusses a crucial opportunity to protect minority construction workers and improve safety, health, and well-being. This study enhances industry knowledge of health, wellness, and safety by examining Schein's organizational culture theory, Denison's model, Cameron and Quinn's Competing Values Framework, Hofstede's Cultural Dimensions Theory, Resilience Theory, Social Identity Theory, and Equity Theory.

DOI: 10.4018/979-8-3373-0482-3.ch005

INTRODUCTION

This chapter illustrates the process of extracting relevant information regarding safeguarding the health, well-being, and safety of minority construction professionals (MCP). This chapter presents a systematic approach to examining qualitative data related to the effects of COVID-19 on MCPs. It involves reviewing relevant literature, data collection, coding the data, and theoretically analyzing the issues identified by MCPs. Next, comparing the data from the MCPs with established theories that illustrate the underlying connection between organizational practices and performance.

This chapter explores a vital opportunity to safeguard minority construction professionals while improving the construction industry's safety, health, and welfare (Olugbemiga et al., 2023). This study contributes valuable insights to the existing knowledge on the construction industry's practices of MCP health, wellness, and safety by analyzing and incorporating various theories that can improve MCP safety and wellness.

To gain further insight into the impact of COVID-19 on MCPs, this chapter finds it necessary to acquire additional understanding and compile lessons learned. The unique difficulties faced in this study provide an opportunity to involve all relevant stakeholders in the construction industry in focus group research. This study suggests further scholarly investigation to collect additional empirical evidence and to gather information for a lesson(s) learned database. A data collection initiative should be implemented at the local, state, regional, and national levels.

The data can be collected using an initiative called What is in It For Every Stakeholder (WIIFES). Consequently, data must be obtained from MCPs. Establishing a systematic feedback loop that consistently provides a steering committee with pertinent and dependable information is essential for gathering the data (Sethi & Seth, 2009). The execution of the data campaign requires partners and allies. The initiative is most efficiently utilized within the context of the collective impact model.

The collective impact model allows industry stakeholders to utilize their strengths and seek support for their weaknesses within the coalition (Agroia et al., 2024). Partnerships and alliances can be used to enhance additional research assistance. Engaging in partnerships with local initiatives to collect data on established models in underprivileged communities can improve the accuracy and dependability of the data. These partnerships can also be allyships (Warren & Warren, 2022).

Allyships serve as a potent means to confront and surpass racial categorization and bridge disparities based on skin color. Allies, as stakeholders, are fervent proponents for improving the safety of MCPs. Although they may not belong to minority groups themselves, they comprehend the significance of enhancing the safety of these marginalized communities. By forming alliances, industry stakeholders can efficiently overcome the difficulties of MCPs (Warren & Warren, 2022). Hence, this study suggests employing the collective impact model to form a strategic planning committee comprising MCPS, stakeholders, academia, government partners, private enterprises, and community-based organizations. The collective impact model can galvanize partners and allies qualified to strategically enhance fiscal support for MCP safety via strategic communication (Sethi & Seth, 2009). Adopting the collective impact model, a cooperative strategy, centered around forming alliances, rooted in technical strengths, industry stakeholders can reorganize and reprioritize the practices and protocols within the industry that impede the safety of MCPs.

PROBLEM STATEMENT

The existence of minorities in the construction industry is apparent. Minorities constitute around 38 percent of the construction industry's workforce (BLS, 2022). As a result, minority labor is essential to the construction industry's present and future sustainability. Additionally, the BLS statistics expose a general problem. If the construction industry does not robustly safeguard its minority labor population against COVID-19, hospitalizations and deaths would reduce the workforce and impede industrial growth (CDC, 2022). This presents a substantial concern, as more than 38 percent of the construction workforce is essential and vulnerable to increased COVID-19 infections, hospitalizations, and mortality (BLS, 2022). Furthermore, a more specific issue is that a notable gap exists in the literature regarding how minority construction professionals might overcome increased COVID-19 infections, hospitalizations, or how their supervisors and employers can assist them in mitigating the impact of COVID-19.

This chapter seeks to explore both general and specific issues by analyzing the MCP safety demographic gap, and the benefits of the construction industry focusing on safety using the lens of Schein's theory of organizational culture, Denison's organizational culture model, Cameron and Quinn's Competing Values Framework, Hofstede's Cultural Dimensions Theory, Resilience Theory, Social Identity Theory, and Equity Theory, in order to address the lack of research on the impact of COVID-19 on minority labor and increase available mitigation strategies for the construction sector. Therefore, this study aims to explore the existing gap in the literature about minorities within the construction workforce. Furthermore, this chapter provides construction industry stakeholders and allies with mitigation and prevention recommendations.

PURPOSE STATEMENT

The knowledge inside the construction sector is constantly expanding and developing. MCPs have diverse requirements, preferences, passions, and objectives (Jenkins, 2023). This chapter seeks to empower construction industry stakeholders to integrate MCPs in conversations on the future of the construction industry. The study will encourage construction industry stakeholders to become more inclusive. Additionally, this study will encourage genuinely incorporating MCPs at the executive level of decision-making. Lastly, this study will encourage MCPs to advocate for enhanced safety conditions and greater representation at the decision-making executive level of the construction industry. Therefore, the purpose of this study is to be a catalyst for the construction industry to pave the way to adapt and incorporate this study's findings and recommendations regionally and locally to foster beneficial enhanced safety practices aligned with protecting MCPs and supporting industry sustainability.

This is a qualitative research project. Questionnaires were used to select qualified interview participants; data was collected via open-ended interview questions. The data collected was analyzed and coded. The coded data were theoretically analyzed via the lens of organizational scholars and theories relevant to this study. As a result, this qualitative phenomenological study examines how minority workers in the construction industry have endured and continue to endure the repercussions of COVID-19 and its consequences on the sector. A qualitative research design has been employed to achieve the objectives of this study (Tracy, 2020). Consequently, a sample of minority groups was selected to examine these phenomena. This study used a phenomenological design to investigate the perceptions and lived experiences of minority participants (Bloomberg & Volpe, 2008). Consequently, 20 minority construction professionals (MCPs) were engaged in a questionnaire. Additionally, ten selected MCPs engaged in semi-structured interviews to convey their opinions and experiences about the safety of MCPs during COVID-19. The data collected was analyzed and coded. Three key themes, Problems, Benefits, and Lessons Learned, were revealed from the data.

Furthermore, this study utilized a theoretical analysis to contextualize the collected data, research findings, and recommendations (Alhazmi & Kaufmann, 2022). As a result, a theoretical analysis was employed to examine the advantages of the construction industry utilizing Schein's theory of organizational culture, Denison's organizational culture model, Cameron and Quinn's Competing Values Framework, Hofstede's Cultural Dimensions Theory, Resilience Theory, Social Identity Theory, and Equity Theory to protect MCPs (Alhazmi & Kaufmann, 2022). Therefore, this study examines the literature gap about minorities in the construction workforce to address the insufficient research on the effects of COVID-19 on minority labor in the construction sector. Additionally, this chapter adds perspective on how organizational culture can empower construction industry stakeholders to integrate MCPs in conversations on the future of the construction industry.

MCPs are the targeted demographic sample of this study. The participants included minorities working in the construction sector in the western United States, specifically Sacramento County and Los Angeles County, California. The study participants have personally encountered the effects of COVID-19. This demographic is suitable, as research indicates that minorities are more vulnerable to COVID-19 comorbidities that result in hospitalization and mortality (BLS, 2022). This research aims to foster positive social change by developing an evidence-based methodology to mitigate the effects of COVID-19 on minorities within the construction workforce. Also, this chapter seeks to empower construction industry stakeholders to integrate MCPs in conversations on the future of the construction industry. Thus, by examining the objective of this study, this research may be utilized to convert verifiable, precise data into practical measures that help preserve lives, employment, and the future of the construction sector.

ASSUMPTIONS

The assumptions of this study are as follows:

It is assumed that participants' gender will not substantially influence their perceptions in this study.

It is assumed that participants' age will not influence their impressions in this investigation.

Participants' race is assumed not to influence their perceptions in this investigation.

It is assumed that participants' ethnicity will not influence their perceptions in this investigation.

It is assumed that participants' work situation will not influence their perceptions in this study.

It is assumed that all respondents will answer all surveys and interview questions honestly and to the best of their abilities.

LIMITATIONS (PARAMETERS)

The limitations of this study are as follows:

The study's completion timeline restricted the number of interview participants to 10.

The anticipated small sample size limited the generalizations drawn from the data.

The data collection period was confined to 26 weeks.

The small and unique sample in the study may limit the generalizability of the results to the specific community from which it was drawn.

If sample respondents do not respond honestly, the results may not accurately reflect the views of the population surveyed.

Due to the length of the study, a significant proportion of respondents from the initial questionnaire may be less willing to participate in a follow-up interview.

BOUNDARIES

The interview sample size was limited to ten to facilitate data handling. Furthermore, the survey instruments employed multiple-choice and open-ended questions (Jensen et al., 2021; Bloomberg & Volpe, 2008). Moreover, owing to the limited number of prospective participants in the study population, the current research concentrated exclusively on individuals residing in California, namely within Los Angeles and Sacramento Counties. Due to timely research the literature review was narrowed and specific to the study's demographic.

SCOPE OF RESEARCH

The parameters of this investigation are deliberately constrained. The phenomena examined in this study are comparatively novel (Wu & Liu, 2022). Consequently, there is inadequate data for quantitative analysis to conduct a thorough analytical study. This research utilizes multiple elements of a qualitative approach (Jensen et al., 2021; Bloomberg & Volpe, 2008). This study emphasizes the use of existing knowledge. This study reveals that restrictions faced by minorities in the U.S. workforce have disproportionately impacted minorities in the construction sector (Singh & Loncar, 2010; Williamson et al., 2005). This study examines the literature gap and firsthand accounts about the impact of COVID-19 on minorities within the construction industry.

METHOD FOR REVIEWING LITERATURE

This literature review employs a method of reviewing literature that involves extensively researching areas that are either directly or indirectly related to this study. Other scholars have utilized this method previously. Fanger (1985) describes this method as "immersion in the subject." This research approaches the general method for reviewing literature using tactics that explore trends concerning this research study (Bloomberg, 2016). A crucial general trend regarding this study is the obligation of an essential worker faced by minorities in the construction workforce. The duty of minorities as essential workers is vital to recognize. The essential worker category increased minority exposure to COVID-19. Therefore, this research is focused on how minority COVID-19 infection rates have affected the construction industry. As a result, the research study findings are consistent with those of the Associated General Contractors of America (AGC), which declared construction an essential industry (2020). Once construction workers were declared essential workers, their exposure to COVID-19 increased. This increased exposure has led to increased hospitalization, deaths, and loss of work hours. Thus, the increased exposure effectively shrinks the construction industry's workforce.

Also, the need for the construction industry to be more diverse is becoming more apparent daily. As a result, this study's findings align with the AGC standard diversity and inclusion practices (AGC, 2018). Organizations like the AGC advocate minority inclusion because minorities are essential to the construction industry. Therefore, the AGC adamantly professes the necessity to use diversity and inclusion as strategic tools (AGC, 2018). The benefits of diversity recognized by AGC demonstrate the need for minority protection and inclusion.

Additionally, given access to opportunities to prove and increase their value, minorities can generate industry innovation (AGC, 2018). A fresh set of eyes that sees a different strategic angle to overcome an obstacle can add value to the construction industry. As well as increase profitability. Increasing profitability establishes a clear path toward forwarding progress and a sustainable legacy for the construction industry (AGC, 2018). Employing a minority lens requires concentration. Utilizing this ideological lens emphasizes the need for the construction industry to be cognizant of the importance of minorities in the future of the construction workforce (Baral et al., 2022). As a result, COVID-19 has impacted minorities and their families while impacting industry sustainability.

WHAT FACTORS CONTRIBUTED TO THE GREATER RELEVANCE OF CERTAIN STUDIES COMPARED TO OTHERS?

The scholarship examined in this research was significant to this investigation. Therefore, this study does not reveal a measurable figure about the significance of pertinent research. In contrast, numerous research studies were more significant as they focused on the employee rather than the employer. Moreover, alternative research was more pertinent as it concentrated on the effects of COVID-19 on minority populations. Finally, specific research was significant since it outlined a timeline that revealed factors obstructing the safety of minority workers, including health disparities.

THE PRECISE STRATEGY FOR ARTICLE SELECTION FOR REVIEW

The research plan aimed to identify pertinent resources by locating publications published from 2017 to 2024 in academic databases. The collection comprised publications relevant to minorities and vital workers, those addressing COVID-19 challenges in the construction sector, and pieces highlighting health inequities. The proposal also contained papers addressing the financial ramifications of COVID-19 within academic databases.

The first stage was developing the requisite criteria for conducting thorough research effectively. This study analyzed resources on minorities and the impact of COVID-19 on the minority workforce within the construction sector. During the investigation, advantageous internet academic databases were utilized.

ProQuest is one of the databases employed. Utilizing ProQuest afforded access to numerous resources, including previously authored theses pertinent to this study's issues. Consequently, a research plan was established that involved utilizing Google Scholar to identify authors and resources and ascertain which publications and dissertations were most frequently peer-reviewed and cited.

Once the material is located, can it be downloaded instantaneously? If not, it was added to a list of literature to seek in the virtual library. This study circumvented paywalls using resources including Google Scholar, EBSCOhost, and ProQuest.

The databases enhanced the capacity to examine peer-reviewed academic literature concerning construction industry issues relevant to our research. This technique yielded significant insights into potential remedies, industry expertise in diversity and inclusion, workforce development, the effects of COVID-19 on the construction sector, and theses addressing health inequalities faced by minorities.

Utilizing these academic databases provided confidence about the credibility of the acquired data, ensuring that the research underwent rigorous, thorough, and systematic review processes characteristic of scholarly research and writing. Furthermore, historical data from internet searches was validated by examining publications and dissertations through academic databases.

LITERATURE REVIEW

This literature review primarily operates as a narrative literature review with some characteristics reminiscent of a rapid literature review. A narrative or traditional literature review is a comprehensive, critical, and objective analysis of the current knowledge on a topic (Sukhera, 2022). It is an essential part of the research process and helps to establish a theoretical framework and focus or context for this research study. Consequently, characteristics from a rapid literature review (RLR) were employed. An RLR is an alternative to a systematic literature review (SLR) and can speed up the analysis of newly published data. The objective of utilizing these strategies was to identify and summarize available information regarding different approaches to defining the central research question of this study and the methodology applied to conduct reviews of applicable literature (Smela et al., 2023). As a result, this literature review focused on reviewing relevant literature that explored how organizational culture can mitigate the impact of COVID-19 on MCPs. The selected methodological framework provides a blueprint for readers and future researchers about how sources were selected, evaluated, and synthesized.

FRAMEWORKS, THEORIES, AND APPLICABLE MODELS

This study presents a viable framework for examining industry and organizational culture and their impact on the health and safety of minority construction professionals. This study assesses the personal experiences of minorities within the construction sector. This research links the personal experiences of minorities in the construction industry to market and service downturns, diminished industry morale, and isolation due to minority status (Meza, 2022). This study refers to the aforementioned as the "COVID effect."

This research study elucidates how minorities in the construction industry have endured hardships due to lockdown restrictions, recovery protocols, caregiving for infected relatives, and skepticism towards health prevention measures, including vaccines, during the COVID-19 pandemic, and how these adversities have impacted the construction sector (Gamil & Alhagar, 2020). This research investigates the underlying cause of heightened infection rates among minorities. Since the onset of the pandemic, minorities have faced heightened exposure risks (Fellows et al., 2022).

Additionally, heightened exposure has been present since the onset of the COVID-19 epidemic. During the initial phases of the epidemic, construction workers were classified as essential personnel (AGC, 2020). As a result, minority construction workers have endangered their lives daily by working in the presence of COVID-19. Consequently, minority construction workers have encountered COVID-19 similarly to other critical workers. At times, the construction worker has been inadequately equipped with protective gear or has utilized equipment that is improperly fitted or malfunctioning (NIOSH, 2021).

Moreover, when protective equipment is inaccessible or ill-fitting, minority construction workers face an elevated risk of COVID-19 exposure. These conditions diminish safety and heighten the apprehensions of minorities within the construction workforce (Increasing Support for the Increasing Number of Women in Construction, 2024). Furthermore, as construction activities were deemed important during the pandemic, most such labor persists in person, increasing the risk of workers contracting SARS-CoV-2, the virus responsible for COVID-19 (NIOSH, 2021). This is a recurring issue encountered by minorities in the construction sector who are sufficiently qualified for employment.

This study identifies deficiencies in existing literature that impede the formulation of evidence-based models capable of mitigating the impacts of COVID-19 (NIOSH, 2021). This study concludes that evidence-based models and theories need to be developed and changed to significantly mitigate the effects of COVID-19 on minorities in the construction industry. Consequently, resources from the community, construction sector, and government are essential to tackle the fundamental causes influencing health disparities among minorities and their repercussions on the building industry due to COVID-19.

A primary obstacle that requires attention is health inequities. The construction business encounters difficulties in initiating and finalizing projects when minorities are unable to perform effectively. Accordingly, the Bureau of Labor Statistics reports that minorities constitute more than 38 percent of the workforce in the construction business (BLS, 2022). The proportion of minorities employed in the construction sector is substantial. The involvement of minorities in the construction business is linked to the successful completion of projects (Alsharef et al., 2021).

The significance of minorities in the construction business necessitates a thorough analysis. This assessment necessitates the examination of the imperative to safeguard its minority workforce (Meza, 2022). The obligation to safeguard minority labor is widespread, given that over 38 percent of the construction workforce comprises minorities designated as vital workers (BLS, 2022). This classification heightens the exposure of workers and their families to COVID-19 (NIOSH, 2021). Consequently, this overarching issue necessitates augmented protection, as susceptibility to heightened COVID-19 infections, hospitalizations, and fatalities escalates when the individual is categorized as a minority (BLS, 2022). Thus, heightened exposure reduces minority working hours, resulting in fewer laborers on job sites, extended completion timelines, and diminished growth within the construction sector (Census Survey, 2021). The reduction of work hours has a discernible effect on the construction industry due to COVID-19. Furthermore, census and CDC statistics indicate that the data reveal minorities are disproportionately affected by COVID-19, leading to heightened hospitalizations and fatalities.

This study underscores the necessity for additional research and literature on a distinct issue. There is a paucity of literature regarding the effects of COVID-19 infection rates, hospitalizations, and fatalities among minority workers in the construction industry. This issue contradicts the provision of evidence-based strategies for mitigating COVID-19 infections, hospitalizations, and fatalities among minority construction workers (Meza, 2022). Consequently, to avert additional deterioration in the construction sector, the effects of COVID-19 on minority groups necessitate further assessment (Raoufi & Fayek, 2021). There is no thorough assessment of the effects of COVID-19 on minority groups within the construction workforce. Although studies have been conducted on specific minority groups to evaluate the effects of COVID-19 on them, a comprehensive examination of the minority class is necessary.

BEHAVIOR THEORIES

This research investigates and utilizes behavioral concepts. Theories from social psychologists Fishbein and Ajzen are employed; they formulated the Theory of Reasoned Action (Ajzen & Fishbein, 1980). This behavioral theory can serve as a conduit for senior construction industry executives to communicate their intentions to managers and MCPs. The Theory of Reasoned Action (TRA) is derived from a comparative analysis of two behavioral intention models and is applicable to diverse stakeholders, including unions, organizations, and municipalities (Netermeyer & Bearden, 1992). The Theory of Reasoned Action (TRA) is advantageous for this study as it serves as a behavioral model elucidating the components that affect intention, ultimately resulting in action. Consequently, TRA delineates a theoretical decision-making framework comprising the following variables: (1) individual perception of the behavior; (2) interpretation of others' perceptions of the activity; (3) self-confidence regarding the behavior (Netermeyer & Bearden, 1992). This research employed Ajzen's Theory of Planned Behavior (Ajzen, 1991) in accordance with TRA. The Theory of Planned Behavior (TPB) is advantageous; it is derived from the Theory of Reasoned Action (TRA), which employs the TRA framework but incorporates a pathway that circumvents external perceptions and intentions directly to action. Consequently, the Theory of Planned Behavior provides flexibility that caters to interviewees, and demonstrates a (Ajzen, 1991). Consequently, the Theory of Planned Behavior is a suitable framework for this investigation. Consequently, TPB illustrates the influential elements encountered by minorities in the construction sector. The elements have been derived from "Organizational Behavior and

Human Decision Processes" (Ajzen, 1991, p. 182). Moreover, the Theory of Planned Behavior (TPB) draws parallels between the decision-making variables within its framework and the factors that affect the attitudes and views of minorities in the construction industry. Consequently, the Theory of Planned Behavior (TPB) serves as a suitable instrument for obtaining precise data for this study" (Ajzen, 1991). The TRA and TPB frameworks functioned as applicable lenses that facilitated the creation of this chapter.

Additionally, this research employs a theoretical framework derived from Eduardo Bonilla-Silva's racialized social systems theory to elucidate racism in the post-Civil Rights era. Like Omi and Winant, Bonilla-Silva recognizes that racism and the racial hierarchy established prior to the 1960s persist inside the American stratification system (Omi & Winant, 1994). His theoretical framework posits that the persistence of racial inequality is attributable to the ongoing existence of a covert or "color-blind" variant of racism embedded within American society (Bonilla-Silva, 2001, p.37). Consequently, his analysis indicates that racism persists inside the established economic, political, social, and intellectual frameworks of American society. Bonilla-Silva characterizes this phenomenon as the "racialization process," wherein the behaviors, actions, and societal roles of each group are categorized along a "us" versus "them" continuum, leading to the inclusion or exclusion of groups from privileges based on their racial classification (Bonilla-Silva, 2001).

METHOD FOR ANALYZING LITERATURE

This research analyzes the literature associated with this study by applying tactics from two styles of literature reviews. *Critical reviews* aim to provide a critical evaluation and interpretive analysis of existing literature on a particular topic of interest to reveal strengths, weaknesses, contradictions, controversies, inconsistencies, and other important issues concerning theories, hypotheses, research methods, or results (Baumeister & Leary, 1997; Kirkevold, 1997). Unlike other review types, critical reviews attempt to reflect on the research done in a particular area of interest and assess its credibility using appraisal instruments or critical interpretive methods. In this way, critical reviews attempt to constructively inform other scholars about the weaknesses of prior research and strengthen knowledge development by giving focus and direction to studies for further improvement (Kirkevold, 1997).

A descriptive review aims to determine the extent to which a body of knowledge regarding a research topic reveals any interpretable pattern or trend concerning pre-existing propositions, theories, methodologies, or findings (King & He, 2005; Paré et al., 2015). Consequently, descriptive reviews follow a systematic and transparent procedure, including searching, screening, and classifying studies (Petersen et al.,

2015). This study utilizes intricate search methods to form a representative sample of a larger group of published works (Paré et al., 2015). Moreover, this literature review extracts information from previous studies, characteristics of interest, such as publication year, research methods, data collection techniques, and direction or strength of research outcomes (e.g., positive, negative, or non-significant) in the form of frequency analysis to produce quantitative results (Sylvester et al., 2013). As a result, this literature review delivers findings representing relevant and applicable knowledge about this study (King & He, 2005). Accordingly, the literature analysis method was guided by the question: How have organizational and cultural theories been utilized to mitigate health and safety disparities among minority construction professionals during the COVID-19 pandemic?

SELECTED METHODOLOGICAL FRAMEWORK

Methodological Framework Questions

What approaches were used to select the articles and research included in this study?

The articles and research studies included in this chapter were meticulously chosen utilizing keywords and academic resources (Google Scholar, EBSCOhost, ProQuest, and Jstor). This technique enhanced the study by augmenting confidence in the credibility of the data obtained. Furthermore, the utilization of databases enhanced the study's conclusions by illustrating that the research underwent rigorous, meticulous, and systematic review processes, which represent the culmination of academic inquiry.

Why was this selected research approach relevant and made sense concerning this study?

This research employed historical data from scholarly databases. This methodology was appropriate for this research as the diligent efforts of prior researchers offer insight into the present state of topics pertinent to this investigation. This research investigates topics related to minorities that correspond with the critical inquiries pertinent to this subject. This research study facilitates the examination of potential patterns and themes. This literature review synthesizes the degree to which existing literature tackles the issues pertinent to this investigation. This literature evaluation also delineates the knowledge gaps addressed by this investigation (Sylvester et al., 2013). This research establishes a theoretical framework for the proposed study, affirms the existence of the research problem, justifies the study's contribution to existing knowledge, and endorses the methodologies and approaches for future investigations (Hart, 1998; Levy & Ellis, 2006).

What made some studies more relevant than others?

Some studies were more valuable because they dealt with the employee, not the employer. Some theories were more valuable than others because they articulated the power of organizational culture. Some theories were more valuable because they expressed the importance of identifying leadership power dynamics in organizational culture. Furthermore, some studies were more relevant because they focused on the impact COVID-19 had on minorities. Lastly, some studies were valuable because they delineated a timeline that exposed issues hindering minority workforce safety, such as health disparities. Some studies were valuable because they showed the causes of loss of work hours. Some literature was valuable because it provided a framework to analyze data. Some of the literature was valuable because it identified theories that applied to the problems of MCP and Health, safety, and wellness.

Literature Synthesis: Organizational and Industry Culture

Policy Implications: Five Critical Direct Findings of This Study

1) Develop a lesson learned database to enhance organizational culture and empower sustainability with an effective enhanced safety policy. Utilizing technology to employ an anonymous survey. Establish equitable access to the lessons learned database.
2) Rebrand and reprioritize OSHA, shift the focus to be more engaging to local and regional safety needs. Organize local leaders and initiatives for preemptive health campaigns. Use volunteers from the Corporation for National and Community Service (CNCS) to help facilitate the transition.
3) Create general guidance on new and improved safety protocols for onboarding new employees. Require health and wellness learning to be integrated into the onboarding process. Incorporate active learning activities. Active learning focuses on real scenarios for MCPs to apply their knowledge, skills, and experience. This approach increases collaboration and critical thinking skills and provides a more meaningful on-the-job learning experience on COVID-19 safety. Adding problem-based learning to the onboarding process will develop empathy for MCPs and create a more inclusive industry.
4) Fostering inclusion and building a sense of community in the construction industry will help bridge the cultural divide and close the gap of isolation that MCPs feel in the industry. This can be achieved in a variety of ways, such as MCP virtual support groups.
5) Transform organizational culture via collective impact partners and transformational allies. Social media campaigns can be used to develop a sense of community for MCPs. Organizational and stakeholder management can create

groups for each project that will allow MCPs to communicate with each other about change orders, milestones, deadlines, and accomplishments. This interaction will foster collaboration and build a community among MCPs working in the industry.

COLLECTED DATA

Themes: Problems, Benefits, Lessons Learned

Problems

The following quote is a response that provides employable insights that can be utilized to mitigate the impact of COVID-19 on MCPs. The observations and experiences of the participants allow the viewing of how detrimental the disruption of COVID has been to MCPs. The data confirms how communication, or the lack thereof, impacted MCPs during the COVID-19 pandemic. The following quote is from an interview conducted with Participant 2 (P2):

I think one of my problems was communication. Communication between the local municipalities and the contractors suffered. There were no in-person meetings. There are no one-on-one meetings where you could go into the office and get your permits. Or talk to the inspectors and engineers.

Everything had to be done by email, which consumed a lot of time. Plus, other people are doing the same thing. It took about ten days before you got a response. Then, the process starts over again with every job. Not being able to go into the office and not being able to visit the offices added more time to the process with the local municipalities.

P2's views demonstrate some of the problems identified by MCPs impacted by the increased COVID-19 infection rates (Kniffin et al., 2021). P2 exposes the fact that COVID-19 caused capacity and technology issues that prolonged the injury of COVID-19 and hindered the recovery of MCPs.

Benefits

A Participant 2 (P2) interview is employed to elaborate more on the benefits theme. The following quote is a response from an interview conducted with P2:

One of the things that helped was the PPE program, which allowed minority contractors to get sanitary PPE. There was no cost. Items such as hand wipes and masks were free of charge. We used those items and followed the protocol and shutdown guidelines for COVID-19.

P2's comments relay some of the benefits identified by MCPs who survived the construction industry during increased COVID-19 infection rates. The data suggest that the federal government deployed some moderately successful programs (Chien-Ho & Abdulmajeed, 2022).

Lessons Learned

An excerpt from the interview with Participant 5 (P5) was employed to elaborate further on the theme of Lessons Learned. The following quote is a response from an interview conducted with P5:

There are a lot more walking meetings than sit-down meetings. We use a smaller team, so that's a nice thing. When my partner cannot attend a meeting or if I cannot attend a meeting for health concerns, I can alternate on and off.

The data from P5's interview demonstrates a need for environmental awareness. Additionally, the data suggests that MCPs must value their health and wellness, be flexible, and be innovative. In capturing some of the lessons learned by MCPs, the data identifies problem areas and highlights creative solutions. The solutions are accumulating experiences and evidence-based models resulting from MCPs impacted by the increased COVID-19 infection rates (European Foundation for the Improvement of Living and Working Conditions, 2022).

Data Synthesis

The data collected in this study aligns with previous research findings and adds value to the discussion of comparative analysis of the impact of COVID-19 on managers and laborers (Olugbemiga et al., 2023). MCPs, impacted by the increased COVID-19 infection rates, are qualified to identify and share their solutions. The Pandemic has exposed gaps in protection for MCPs. Identifying problems that MCPs face can help assess how to effectively respond to the impact locally. The data suggest that supportive services necessary for mental and physical wellness vary from inadequate to nonexistent.

The impact of COVID-19 on the United States Construction Industry has created opportunities for the industry to focus on finding ways to protect its workforce (Early Impacts of the COVID-19 Pandemic on the United States Construction Industry, 2021). MCPs were impacted by the increased COVID-19 infection rates. The increased rates have also caused personnel issues and problems centered around the need for more in-person meetings. Issues discussed by this study's participants align with Kniffin's construction workplace COVID-19 research (Kniffin et al., 2021).

MCP observations present employable insights that can be utilized to mitigate the impact of COVID-19 on MCPs. The observations and experiences of the participants provide an opportunity to view how detrimental the disruption of COVID has been on MCPs. The data confirms how communication, or the lack thereof, impacted MCPs during the COVID-19 pandemic. Participants' views demonstrate some of the problems identified in MCPs affected by the increased COVID-19 infection rates (Kniffin et al., 2021). For example, P2 reveals that COVID-19 caused capacity and technology issues that prolonged the injury of COVID-19 and hindered the recovery of MCPs.

As a result, the data collected suggests that because the industry is essential, some MCPs were exposed to COVID-19 more than others. As a result, the data reveals an opportunity to protect the health and wellness of MCPs better. Additionally, in alignment with the findings of Chien-Ho and Abdulmajeed's research, the data suggest that the safety of MCPs can be substantially improved by applying the lessons learned from the COVID-19 pandemic (Chien-Ho & Abdulmajeed, 2022). Moreover, the data reports that the federal government deployed some moderately successful programs. Furthermore, the data imply that deploying programs like the PPE program helped curb the spread of the virus and protect the safety of MCPs (Chien-Ho & Abdulmajeed, 2022). The data validates Olatoye's research and conveys that as the infection rates increased, so did the pandemic's stress and social and psychological impact on MCPs (Olatoye, 2022).

P5's experience and response reveal several modifications that some MCPs implemented to address the issues posed by the COVID-19 outbreak. The results indicate that conforming to federal and state regulations and industry norms has resulted in a challenging work environment for MCPs. The statistics indicate advantages, including new policies recommended by MCPs that can safeguard the construction crew and reduce COVID-19 infection rates. Moreover, along with the Kniffin research findings, this study's data indicate that the rapid adaptation and implementation of new rules enhances the safety of MCPs (Kniffin et al., 2021).

Thus, the data suggest that effective measures can be adopted to reduce infection rates among MCPs. The results indicate that implementing new rules to address the pandemic swiftly can diminish MCP exposure to COVID-19. The study clarifies the social and psychological ramifications of COVID-19 on MCPs. Consequently, the data corresponds with the research conducted by Olugbemiga (Olugbemiga et al., 2023). Accordingly, the data reveals a sense of commitment for some MCPs to the lessons they learned during the pandemic. The data proposes that some believe the impact of COVID-19 on MCPs can be mitigated via policy. Furthermore, the data suggests that protocols can be created to combat the effects of COVID-19 on MCPs through critical assessment of safety practices and behaviors.

FINDINGS

Theoretical Alignment

Significant disruptions in the global corporate landscape have recently led to a highly competitive worldwide market. Recent global disruptions, such as supply chain challenges, material shortages, inflation, and labor deficits, have engendered a fiercely competitive construction environment, resulting in project delays, cost escalations, and heightened demand on firms to innovate and adapt budgets (Al Amri & Marey-Perez, 2020). Disruptions in the Supply Chain Global occurrences like the COVID-19 pandemic and geopolitical instability have resulted in considerable disruptions to supply chains, causing delays in material delivery, heightened costs, and shortages of critical construction materials such as concrete and steel. Material shortages of essential resources, intensified by global demand and supply chain disruptions, have become increasingly prevalent, affecting project timelines and budgets (Al Amri & Marey-Perez, 2020). Inflation. Escalating inflation, especially in construction materials and labor expenses, has rendered projects more costly and challenging to oversee, compelling corporations to seek methods to curtail expenses or increase pricing. Additionally, workforce deficiencies have plagued the industry. Construction personnel deficiencies and elevated labor expenses present a substantial obstacle for firms, affecting project timelines and total profitability (Pamidimukkala & Kermanshachi, 2021).

Additionally, the construction sector confronts swift technological progress, encompassing automation, Building Information Modeling (BIM), and digital instruments, necessitating firms to adapt and invest in novel technologies to maintain competitiveness (Arı et al., 2022). Fluctuations in Demand, Variations in demand, market dynamics, or unforeseen surges in orders can exert pressure on supply chains, resulting in shortages or surplus inventory, complicating organizations' ability to plan and implement projects efficiently. Regulatory modifications, novel rules, and environmental policies can interrupt building projects, increasing complexity and expense while necessitating corporate adaptation to evolving requirements (Arditi et al., 2017).

Also, capacity limitations in specific sectors, such as manufacturing or transportation, can result in delays and elevated costs, especially during peak periods or heightened demand. Project delays and cost overruns are prevalent issues in the construction sector, frequently resulting from insufficient planning, unexpected site circumstances, and resource mismanagement (Al Amri & Marey-Perez, 2020). As a result, the race to retain highly qualified and talented employees has intensified, leading firms to utilize novel and unusual solutions to address this issue (Kaura et al., 2016).

Consequently, the distinguishing characteristic that sets successful firms apart worldwide is their distinctive organizational culture, which contributes to organizational effectiveness and facilitates the retention and attraction of skilled staff. Consequently, HR professionals today recognize that organizational culture and innovative employee benefits are crucial in influencing employee behavior. Organizational culture and employee benefits are interconnected components of a comprehensive organizational system framework crucial in attaining the organization's strategic objectives (Kaura et al., 2016). Therefore, it is vital to ensure alignment and synchronization between the two. When these two crucial factors of the organizational system are not aligned, they generate contradictory signals that lead to confusion among employees.

Organizational Culture Alignment and MCP Needs

Accordingly, one way to align organizational culture with employee needs is to integrate organizational culture and Employee benefits. The construction sector can integrate organizational culture and employee benefits by emphasizing employee well-being, providing competitive remuneration and benefits, cultivating a positive and inclusive workplace, acknowledging and rewarding contributions, and enhancing engagement and retention.

The initial step is to prioritize employee well-being. Establish safety as a fundamental value and allocate resources towards comprehensive programs, training, and communication. Implement mental health assistance. Mental health and wellness tools, like Employee Assistance Programs, can enhance retention and promote employee well-being (Olugbemiga et al., 2023). Furthermore, flexible work arrangements ought to foster a good work-life balance. Thus, community participation should be integral to business culture. Company-sponsored events and volunteer opportunities must be harmonized to cultivate a sense of community celebration and belonging. The subsequent stage is to provide competitive remuneration and benefits. A thorough industry emphasis on instituting competitive salaries is essential. Employers must compensate employees equitably and competitively, acknowledging the worth of their abilities and expertise. Also, offering a comprehensive benefits package that includes health insurance, retirement plans, paid time off, and additional bonuses helps improve corporate culture within the business (Miner, 2005). Moreover, profit sharing is a compelling incentive to attract and retain talented staff. Consequently, implementing profit-sharing schemes will motivate performance and cultivate a sense of collective achievement. Therefore, professional growth is essential for the construction industry's future.

Investing in personnel training and development will augment skills and foster industry growth. The third phase is to promote a constructive and inclusive work environment. Open communication should be promoted at every organizational level to cultivate an inclusive workplace loop (Sethi & Seth, 2009). Furthermore, a collective ethos of collaboration and teamwork is essential. Fostering a culture of collaboration and teamwork will instill value and respect in employees. The work environment must foster a varied and inclusive one where all individuals feel welcomed and appreciated. The corporate culture must promote an environment of respect and trust, enabling employees to express their thoughts and concerns without fear. The final step involves a celebration through a recognition and reward ceremony. To enhance company culture, organizations must implement Employee Recognition Programs. Programs that acknowledge and incentivize employee accomplishments and contributions must be efficiently implemented. Employers must create a reliable feedback mechanism that acknowledges employee contributions. Feedback contributions must be formed and meticulously employed. A credible feedback loop can mitigate issues rooted in competing values.

Competing Values Framework

The Competing Values Framework is a comprehensive model that fully describes the content and strength of an organization's culture (Kaura et al., 2016). This study examines the correlation between employee perks and different types of organizational culture and proposes the most favorable situation for achieving optimal performance. The Competing Values Framework, formulated by Cameron and Quinn, classifies organizational cultures into four clearly defined categories: clan, adhocracy, market, and hierarchy. The construction industry usually has a hierarchical culture emphasizing stability, control, and transparency (Wiewora et al., 2013).

The construction sector typically adheres to a hierarchical culture prioritizing stability, control, and well-defined institutions. Nevertheless, to provide more support for marginalized groups and effectively address the obstacles presented by COVID-19, the industry could gain advantages by incorporating aspects of a clan culture characterized by cooperation, assistance, and a feeling of kinship (Kaura et al., 2016). This approach requires addressing industry disruptions. To better support MCPs and effectively tackle the disruptions posed by COVID-19, the industry could benefit from reiterating elements of clan culture. This culture strongly emphasizes cooperation, assistance, and a feeling of familial bond.

This transition would require companies to prioritize their employees' well-being, foster open and honest communication, and create a more supportive work environment that values diversity and inclusion (Sethi & Seth, 2009). Different cultural values lead to unique patterns of knowledge sharing among projects. Societies that prioritize market forces often tend to be hesitant to share knowledge. Cultures with a clan-type structure tend to freely share various types of knowledge, including information about possible project difficulties and setbacks (Wiewora et al., 2013). Therefore, this study proposes that the industry can enhance its ability to handle future challenges by utilizing the Competing Values Framework to encourage and execute information sharing.). This transition would necessitate firms to prioritize their employees' welfare, promote transparent communication, and establish a more nurturing work atmosphere, emphasizing diversity and inclusion (Kaura et al., 2016). This framework pairs well with Schein's Model of Organizational Culture.

Schein's Model of Organizational Culture

According to Edgar Schein's Model of Organizational Culture, the formation of organizational culture occurs at three distinct levels: artifacts, stated ideals, and basic underlying assumptions (Akpa et al., 2021). Within the construction sector, the industry's artifacts encompass tangible components, such as policies, methods, and the actual environment. Espoused values are the officially declared principles of the business, including its dedication to promoting diversity and inclusion. Core foundational assumptions are deeply rooted convictions and actions that may not consistently correspond with the stated principles. This model proposes that to successfully incorporate minority groups into the construction industry and mitigate the effects of COVID-19, businesses need to ensure that their tangible elements and stated beliefs are in harmony with their fundamental assumptions (Akpa et al., 2021). A key aspect of this is not just formulating policies to include minority groups but ensuring that these policies are authentically endorsed and implemented at every level of the organization. This model supports Denison's organizational culture model.

Denison's Organizational Culture Model

The Denison Organizational Culture Model is crucial in enhancing the dedication and effectiveness of minority workers in the construction industry. This model establishes a connection between organizational culture and performance by examining four essential characteristics: engagement, consistency, adaptability, and mission. By increasing the participation of minority workers in decision-making processes, the model can significantly improve their dedication and effectiveness (Simon & Varghese, 2018). Ensuring the consistent application of diversity and inclusion policies is equally important, as they foster a sense of value and protection among minority workers. Adaptability, a key aspect of the model, is essential for effectively addressing the challenges presented by COVID-19, necessitating enterprises to demonstrate flexibility and innovation in their approach to health and safety (Simon & Varghese, 2018). An explicit mission statement that incorporates a dedication to diversity and inclusion has the potential to unite the employees and provide direction to the firm during times of crisis.

This chapter presents a practical framework for examining the impact of industry and organizational culture on the well-being and safety of minority construction workers to enhance their employability. This study assesses the personal encounters of underrepresented groups in the construction sector. This research establishes a connection between the personal experiences of minorities in the construction sector and the loss in market and service, low morale within the business, and the isolation experienced due to their minority status (Meza, 2022). The aforementioned is linked to what this study defines as the "COVID Effect."

Additionally, this research study highlights the adverse impact of COVID-19 on minority workers in the construction industry, including their inability to work due to lockdown restrictions, adherence to recovery protocols, caring for infected family members, and skepticism towards health prevention measures such as vaccines. The study also examines the repercussions of their suffering in the construction industry (Gamil & Alhagar, 2020). This study investigates the underlying reason for the heightened susceptibility of minority populations to more infections within their communities. Minorities have been more likely to be exposed to the virus since the pandemic's start (Fellows et al., 2022). Moreover, heightened visibility has existed since the early stages of the COVID-19 pandemic. Construction workers were classified as critical workers in the initial phases of the epidemic (AGC, 2020). As a result, minority workers in the construction industry have been putting their lives at risk daily by going to work and being exposed to COVID-19. Utilizing the expertise of minority workers in the construction industry will result in enhanced safety and improved productivity. Accordingly, coupling these models with Hofstede's Cultural Dimension Theory provides a lens to how the industry can become safer by becoming more inclusive and practicing collectivism.

Hofstede's Cultural Dimensions Theory

Geert Hofstede's Cultural Dimensions Theory outlines six cultural dimensions that impact organizational behavior: power distance, individualism versus collectivism, masculinity versus femininity, uncertainty avoidance, long-term versus short-term normative orientation, and indulgence versus restraint. In the construction industry, a significant power distance can impede the inclusion of minority groups, as decision-making is typically concentrated among a select few individuals in positions of authority (Arditi et al., 2017). Prioritizing collectivism over individualism may cultivate a more inclusive atmosphere where the contributions of minority groups are esteemed and incorporated into the organization's decision-making processes.

Construction firms can enhance their inclusivity during crises such as COVID-19 by comprehending and tackling these cultural dimensions, thereby safeguarding and assisting minority workers (Arditi et al., 2017). Delays are a prevalent issue in the construction industry. This study investigates the correlation between the organizational culture of a construction company and project delays. The findings of this study indicate that construction organizations in the United States are primarily characterized by a clan culture (Arditi et al., 2017). This study facilitates a pathway for promoting the construction industry to be more receptive to the health and wellness requirements of its minority workforce. Additionally, incorporating Resilience Theory can enhance the impact of implementing these theoretical models.

Resilience Theory

According to resilience theory, people and groups can handle and recover from difficult situations. By applying this theory to the construction industry, researchers can examine how minority workers demonstrate resilience in the face of COVID-19 challenges. Analyzing the factors contributing to resilience, such as social support, access to resources, and adaptive coping strategies, can provide helpful information for developing policies to strengthen minority workers (Nwaogu et al., 2022). Current research indicates that construction tradespeople experience elevated levels of stress, which can exacerbate mental health issues, resulting in adverse effects on safety adherence and overall productivity within the organization. As a result, effectively managing stress to avoid mental illness becomes a critical priority (Nwaogu et al., 2022). This study investigates the impact of resilience and coping strategies on protecting tradespeople's health and wellness from COVID-19. The resilience of the MCPs who survived COVID-19 is valuable. The survival tactics used by MCPs can be utilized as evidence-based models for future MCP survival. Employing the tactics that MCPs use to survive can impact the construction industry's health, safety, and productivity. Enhanced safety protocols for the construction industry will help to manage the unexpected. Moreover, inserting a Social Identity Theory into the formula for producing effective solutions will strengthen the feedback loop by including the opinions, experiences, and lessons learned from industry workers who identify as different ethnic and social groups.

Social Identity Theory

According to Social Identity Theory, group membership gives people a sense of identity and self-esteem. In the construction industry, minority workers may have a strong sense of identity based on their ethnic or gender groups (Choi & Lee, 2022). This theory sheds light on how minority workers perceive their roles and the importance of representation in industry discussions. Minorities' sense of belonging and self-worth can be improved by recognizing and including them in the construction industry's future planning, resulting in increased engagement and productivity. Safety participation is becoming increasingly recognized as critical to workers' safety behaviors. Although previous research attempted to identify factors influencing workers' safety participation, few examined the psychological mechanisms underlying it. Safety compliance and project identification variances influence construction workers' safety participation (Choi & Lee, 2022). Project identification also bridges transformational leadership and the communication climate, which affects safety participation. Including minorities in these capacities creates a stronger bond between MCPs and the industry. A bond that can foster greater industry sustainability and provide a pathway to a more efficient and equitable industry. As a result, adapting and including Equity Theory in designing credible solutions to unexpected problems can increase the impact and effectiveness of providing local solutions.

Equity Theory

Equity Theory examines the correlation between an individual's contributions and rewards within the professional environment. This theory can assist in mitigating the disparities that minority workers encounter in terms of their access to healthcare and opportunities for career progression (Miner, 2005). Ensuring fair and impartial treatment and allocating necessary resources to minority employees, especially in times of crisis like the COVID-19 pandemic, can enhance job satisfaction and promote employee retention. The research on construction worker motivation is constrained to some extent. Despite the abundance of research on motivation and productivity, there is a lack of comprehensive analysis regarding the motivation of construction workers. Based on the study, the construction industry has not experienced productivity growth compared to other sectors like manufacturing (Miner, 2005). Given that motivation is a crucial factor that affects productivity, numerous publications in the last five decades have consistently emphasized this correlation. The current research findings have been categorized into five themes: motivation models, environment and culture, incentives and empowerment, and worker management (Miner, 2005). Prior studies have put forth two approaches to enhance the motivation of construction workers: (1) offering appropriate incentives to workers, whether inherent or external, and (2) enhancing management practices, specifically regarding worker communication. This chapter examines the existing findings of recent equity research studies on minority construction professionals and analyzes the benefits of incorporating equity theory into the construction industry culture.

CONCLUSION

How can utilizing the prescribed theories enhance MCP safety?

Schein's theory of organizational culture, which posits that organizational culture is composed of artifacts, espoused values, and underlying assumptions, can help protect minorities in construction by enabling leaders to understand and address the root causes of discriminatory behaviors and create a more inclusive environment (Yilmaz, 2014).

Denison's organizational culture model, The Denison Organizational Culture Model, can help protect minorities in construction by fostering a culture of involvement, adaptability, consistency, and mission that promotes inclusivity, respect, and equal opportunity, ultimately leading to a more equitable and high-performing workplace (Denison & Mishra, 1995).

Cameron and Quinn's Competing Values Framework facilitates promoting diversity and inclusion through competing values, such as those championed by organizations like the Associated General Contractors of America (AGC), which can help protect minorities by fostering a more inclusive and equitable environment, leading to increased opportunities and better representation in the industry (Cameron, K. S. & Quinn; R. E., 2011).

Hofstede's Cultural Dimensions Theory can provide a framework for understanding cultural differences and promoting inclusivity by helping construction professionals navigate diverse work environments and potentially prevent misunderstandings that could lead to discrimination or exclusion (Poulova et al., 2024).

Resilience Theory can help protect minorities by building individual and community strengths to navigate challenges and adversity, rather than solely focusing on deficits (Robertson et al., 2021).

Social Identity Theory demonstrates that self-definition at the individual and group levels affects organizational performance and outcomes. It is also suggested that using a social identity lens can help increase understanding of the construction industry's interpersonal relations, collaboration, and change initiatives (Löwstedt & Räisänen, 2014).

Equity Theory, which suggests individuals evaluate fairness based on the ratio of their contributions to rewards, can help protect minorities in construction by highlighting potential inequities in hiring, compensation, and opportunities, motivating action to restore balance and ensure fair treatment (Lawrence et al., n.d.).

In conclusion, this study incorporated qualitative data from a targeted demographic sample that included minorities working in the construction sector in the western United States, specifically Sacramento County and Los Angeles County, California. The study participants have personally encountered the effects of COVID-19. This demographic is suitable, as research indicates that minorities are more vulnerable to

COVID-19 comorbidities that result in hospitalization and mortality (BLS, 2022). This research aims to foster positive social change by developing an evidence-based methodology to mitigate the effects of COVID-19 on minorities within the construction workforce. This research may be utilized to convert verifiable, precise data into practical measures that help preserve lives, employment, and the future of the construction sector. To understand how to adapt this research's resolutions practically, a data capture campaign must be administered to understand the needs and desires of all stakeholders, including MCPs, managers, and owners.

A theoretical analysis was employed to examine the advantages of the construction industry utilizing Schein's theory of organizational culture, Denison's organizational culture model, Cameron and Quinn's Competing Values Framework, Hofstede's Cultural Dimensions Theory, Resilience Theory, Social Identity Theory, and Equity Theory to protect MCPs. This study examined the literature gap about minorities in the construction workforce to address the insufficient research on the effects of COVID-19 on minority labor in the construction sector.

It is the recommendation of this study that further research be conducted to capture more data on the lessons learned by MCPs. The data must be vetted using triangulation and categorized into an accessible format for public use. The data must be shared with the audience in mind. Therefore, plain language should be used to explain and articulate the benefits of new safety policies. Additionally, support for safety policies must be strategically shared and incorporated into construction industry policies, standards and common safety practices. A capture-the-data campaign should be implemented locally, on a state level, regionally, and nationally.

The process of implementing the data campaign requires critical partners. The initiative is a tool that is utilized best under the collective impact model. Using the collective impact model will allow industry stakeholders to contribute their strengths and find support for their weaknesses in the coalition (Agroia et al., 2024). Support for further research can be achieved via partnerships and allyships. Partnering with place-based initiatives to collect data on evidence-based models in under-resourced communities can increase valuable and credible data. These partnerships can be allyships (Warren & Warren, 2022).

Allyships play a crucial role in overcoming ideas of racialization and color blindness. These supporters are instrumental in increasing the safety of MCPs, not because they are minorities but because they are stakeholders who benefit from improving minority safety. Their diverse support is essential in effectively overcoming the obstacles MCPs encounter on local, regional, and national levels (Lê-Scherban et al., 2023). As a result, this research recommends using the collective impact model to construct a strategic planning committee that includes MCPS, stakeholders, academia, government partners, private enterprises, and community-based organizations to transform the industry practices and procedures that hinder MCP safety.

Recommendations

Ten Immediate Actions

- Apply MCP knowledge to compile a database on lessons learned from the COVID-19 Pandemic
- Create Comprehensive Construction Industry Guidance on organizational culture and MCP safety regarding COVID-19
- Revamp OSHA hiring to have a focus on regional safety issues.
- Mandated COVID-19 cultural competency training for laborers, forepersons, and supervisors
- Integration of effective COVID-19 risk mitigation into mandated OSHA safety protocols
- Establishing local and regional industry councils with adequate minority representation
- Mobile health units for site-based COVID-19 screening and education programs
- Inclusion of minority voices on advisory boards and project safety audits
- Reassess California Contractors License Board safety and inclusion policies and practices
- Align MCP safety with place-based initiatives, HUD Bonding requirements, and HUDs Section 3 program

Implications for Practice

The findings and recommendations of this research can be used in the construction industry to mitigate or eliminate safety challenges that MCPs encounter. This study recommends utilizing the collective impact model to create transformational alliances with place-based initiatives, key construction industry stakeholders, and academia. The first step is to capture the unknown data. The data capture campaign will allow key stakeholders to express their priorities. Coalitions can evolve from grouping partners with their priorities.

Applying the Collective Impact Model

Why employ the Collective Impact Model? Successful COVID-19 MCP impact mitigation implementation, education, and awareness can only occur if it happens at all levels of the construction industry. This includes cooperation between federal, state, local, public, private, and community actors, which is the key. Collectively addressing the problems MCPs encounter can help increase MCP safety. COVID-19 mitigation programs and initiatives must include MCPs and critical stakeholders. Once the steering committee is identified, the steering committee will organize tasks into focus group areas.

However, the steering committee's role is to guide the initiative's progress. The Work Group Structure will promote the development of focus group leadership. The focus group's leadership information will be used to create work groups focused on education, facilitation, and sustainability. Workgroup members will delegate planning and implementation tasks to subcommittees. Subcommittees will report progress back to work groups. Subcommittee members will be workgroup members assigned a duty based on expertise, experience, and passion. Workgroups will report back to the steering committee monthly.

Figure 1. W.I.I.F.E.S initiative management and accountability structure

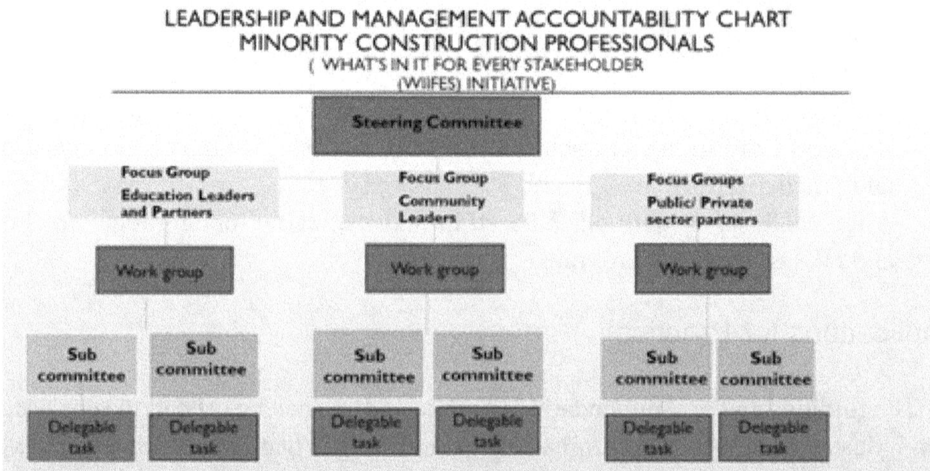

Strategic Planning Committee Project (Steering Committee)

Reducing health preconditions and increasing mental wellness for MCPs must be a priority for the construction industry. Developing a comprehensive industry strategic plan that protects all construction professionals, including MCPs, is a good start. Stakeholders must include MCPs in the Planning Committee to foster a credible feedback loop. The Planning Committee should reach out directly to MCPs to offer workshops and certifications on PPE use and distribution, as well as health and wellness. Also, including MCPs and their families in focus groups can increase evidence-based model academic literature on the impact of COVID-19.

Leadership Management and Accountability

Additionally, in identifying the leadership structure for WIIFES, a local organization with community trust and a successful track record of collaborating, designing, and implementing initiatives must be selected to lead the initiative. A tiered leadership structure works well (consisting of a steering committee, Focus Groups, Workgroups, and Sub-committees). Also, adopting measures of accountability will solidify coalition goals and partner accountability.

Figure 2. W.I.I.F.E.S initiative measures of accountability

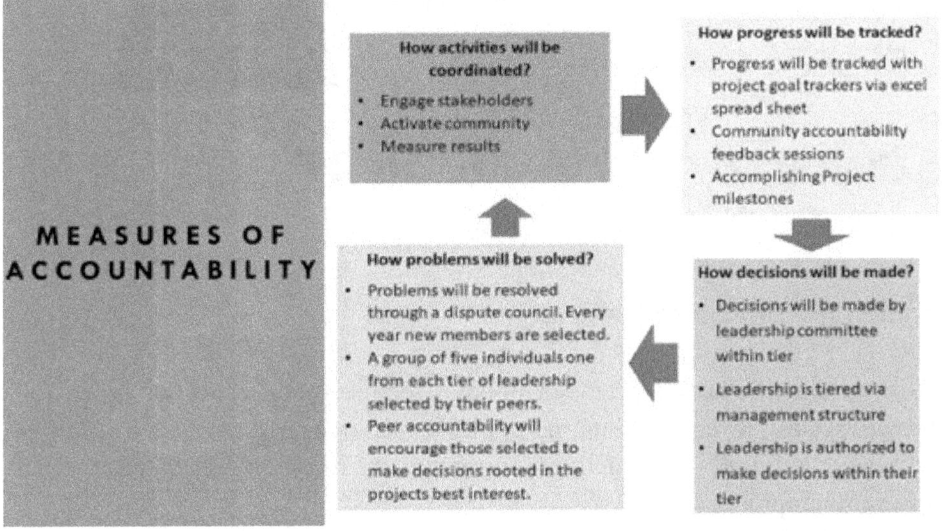

Figure 3. W.I.I.F.E.S initiative responsibilities and decisions

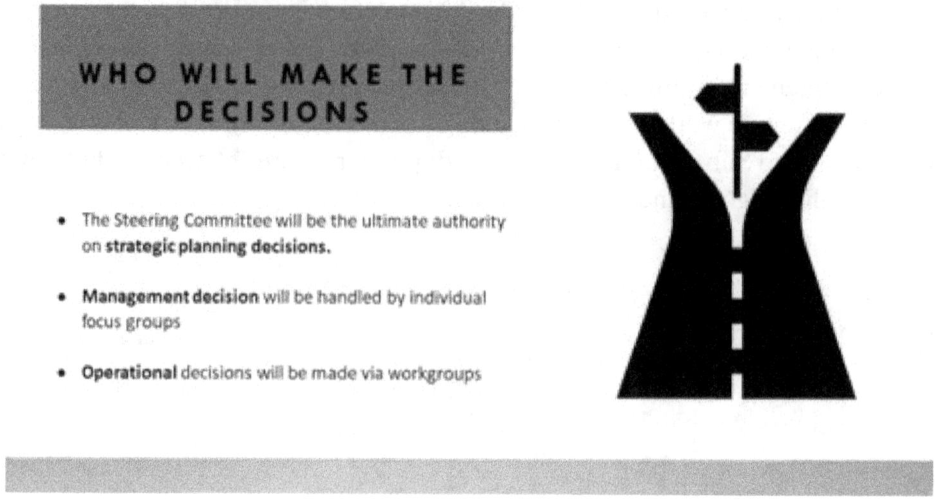

Suggestions for Future Research

To ascertain whether programs or policies require modification or expansion, more investigation is required into the available resources and assistance to MCPs. MCP focus groups with MCPs actively engaged in the market represent an excellent sample demographic.

An additional group that would serve as an excellent research candidate is incarcerated MCPs. Collecting data on the experiences of incarcerated MCPs will provide insight into their safety. Further quantitative study is necessary to assess the ongoing effects of COVID-19 on MCPs. As new variants emerge and individuals persist in testing positive for the virus, it is crucial to ascertain whether MCPs remain affected and if the nature of that impact evolves.

Future study should concentrate on the experiences of MCPs in federal, state, and local municipalities to ascertain whether these experiences in the public sector diverge from those in the private sector.

Moreover, subsequent research ought to examine the experiences of minority construction workers about inclusion policies on job sites using qualitative interviews or ethnographic fieldwork. Future research should investigate if culturally tailored safety training programs enhance compliance and results compared to standardized standards. Furthermore, interdisciplinary research integrating public health data with organizational behavior theory may yield complete models for forecasting and alleviating health hazards in labor-intensive sectors employing minorities. Additionally, qualitative and quantitative research on artificial intelligence impacts construction industry safety practices. Finally, quantitative research should be undertaken with African American and Asian construction professionals. The study should examine whether a substantial disparity exists in the influence of COVID-19 on those ethnicities relative to other construction workers.

Purpose and the Implications of Findings

The underrepresentation of minority groups in the construction business is evident. Minorities make up about 38 percent of the construction industry's workforce, according to the Bureau of Labor Statistics (BLS, 2022). Therefore, the current and future of the construction industry relies on the participation of minority workers. In addition, failure to proactively safeguard the minority labor in the construction industry against COVID-19 may result in hospitalizations and fatalities, hence diminishing the workforce and impeding industry expansion (CDC, 2022). Consequently, the conclusions of the chapter have a substantial influence. This chapter provides a straightforward approach for construction industry personnel to identify solutions for the overall health, safety, and well-being of the construction workforce and MCPs.

Moreover, this chapter provides valuable guidance for managers and supervisors on embracing diversity within their workforce. Furthermore, it offers practical measures that can be adopted industry-wide to promote inclusivity and enhance employees' well-being, safety, and health. These measures involve implementing a reliable feedback system to transform the industry's culture positively.

On a larger scale, this chapter provides an opportunity to showcase how applying the discoveries can enhance the safety of construction sector workers and, consequently, when employees experience job security. Production is directly correlated with worker safety. Furthermore, higher labor productivity leads to more efficient project completion. Moreover, enhancing efficiency leads to a rise in production, timely completion of projects, and a reduction in the number of pending projects due to the availability of sufficient healthy workers to meet labor requirements.

An optimal construction labor force contributes to economic growth through job creation and the development of both residential and commercial structures. If the work hours of construction industry employees are reduced because of health, safety, or well-being concerns, it will lead to delays in completing construction projects. This study focused on MCPs. However, without employing organizational culture to embrace diversity and sincerely integrating safety systems of protection for all construction professionals, the construction industry risks self-sabotaging industry sustainability.

REFERENCES

AGC. (2020a) Construction is an essential industry. News release https://www.agc.org/news/2020/03/21/construction-essential-industry#:~:text=Partnered%20with%20the%20buildings%20trades,COVID%2D19%2Drelated%20shutdowns

Agroia, H., Reno, R., Spezeski, J., Mousli, L., Sarabia, R., & Starzyk, E. (2024). A Case Study to Investigate Factors Influencing the Santa Clara County Getting to Zero Initiative's Collective Impact Model. *Journal of Social, Behavioral and Health Sciences, 18*(1), 45–55. DOI: 10.5590/JSBHS.2024.18.1.04

Ajzen, I. (1991). The theory of planned behavior. *Organizational Behavior and Human Decision Processes, 50*(2), 179–211. DOI: 10.1016/0749-5978(91)90020-T

Ajzen, I., & Fishbein, M. (1980). *Understanding attitudes and predicting social behavior*. Prentice-Hall.

Akpa, V. O., Asikhia, O. U., & Nneji, N. E. (2021). Organizational culture and organizational performance: A review of literature. *International Journal of Advances in Engineering and Management, 3*(1), 361–372.

Al Amri, T., & Marey, P. M. (2021). Project delays and cost overruns between the public and private sectors in Oman. *Journal of Public Affairs (14723891), 21*(3), 1–10. https://doi-org.captechu.idm.oclc.org/10.1002/pa.2262

Al Amri, T., & Marey-Pérez, M. (2020). Impact of Covid-19 on Oman's Construction Industry. *Technium Soc Sci J, 9*, 661–670. DOI: 10.47577/tssj.v9i1.1021

Alhazmi, A. A., & Kaufmann, A. (2022). Phenomenological Qualitative Methods Applied to the Analysis of Cross-Cultural Experience in Novel Educational Social Contexts. *Frontiers in Psychology, 13*(1), 785134. Advance online publication. DOI: 10.3389/fpsyg.2022.785134 PMID: 35548502

Allan-Blitz, L.-T., Turner, I., Hertlein, F., & Klausner, J. D. (2020). High Frequency and Prevalence of Community-Based Asymptomatic SARS-CoV-2 Infection. *medRxiv* 2020 DOI: 10.1101/2020.12.09.20246249

Alsharef, A., Banerjee, S., Uddin, S. M. J., Albert, A., & Jaselskis, E. (2021). Early Impacts of the COVID-19 Pandemic on the United States Construction Industry. *International Journal of Environmental Research and Public Health, 18*(4), 1559. MDPI AG. Retrieved from DOI: 10.3390/ijerph18041559

Andrea, S. B., Eisenberg-Guyot, J., Blaikie, K. J., Owens, S., Oddo, V. M., Peckham, T., Minh, A., & Hajat, A. (2022). Inequitable Burden of the COVID-19 Pandemic Among Marginalized Older Workers in the United States: An Intersectional Approach. *The Journals of Gerontology. Series B, Psychological Sciences and Social Sciences*, *77*(10), 1928–1937. https://doi-org.captechu.idm.oclc.org/10.1093/geronb/gbac095. DOI: 10.1093/geronb/gbac095 PMID: 35863041

Arditi, David, Nayak, Shruti, Damci, Atilla. (2017). Effect of organizational culture on delay in construction. *International Journal of Project Management*, (Vol. 35, Issue 2, P. 136-147). https://doi.org/.DOI: 10.1016/j.ijproman.2016.10.018

Arı, K., Coplugil, K. B., Gönültas, I., & Artan, D. (2022). A Survey on the Effects of the Covid-19 Pandemic at Construction Sites. *IOP Conference Series. Earth and Environmental Science*, *1101*(3), 032011. DOI: 10.1088/1755-1315/1101/3/032011

Arksey, H., & O'Malley, L. (2005). Scoping studies: Towards a methodological framework. *International Journal of Social Research Methodology*, *8*(1), 19–32. DOI: 10.1080/1364557032000119616

Associated General Contractors of America (AGC) Diversity & Inclusion Council. AGC of America., The Business Case for Diversity & Inclusion in the Construction Industry 5 (2018).https://www.agc.org/sites/default/files/Files/Advocacy/AGC%20Report%20on%20Biz%20Case%20for%20D%26I%20FINAL.pdf

Ayat, M., & Kang, C. W. (2021). Effects of the COVID-19 pandemic on the construction sector: A systemized review. *Engineering, Construction, and Architectural Management*.

Bailey, Z. D., Krieger, N., Agénor, M., Graves, J., Linos, N., & Bassett, M. T. (2017). Structural racism and health inequities in the USA: Evidence and interventions. *Lancet*, *389*(10077), 1453–1463. DOI: 10.1016/S0140-6736(17)30569-X PMID: 28402827

Baker, M. G., Peckham, T. K., & Seixas, N. S. (2020). Estimating the burden of United States workers exposed to infection or disease: A key factor in containing risk of COVID-19 infection. *PLoS One*, *15*(4), 1–8. https://doi-org.captechu.idm.oclc.org/10.1371/journal.pone.0232452. DOI: 10.1371/journal.pone.0232452 PMID: 32343747

Baral, A., Liang, Y., Li, M., Gonzalez, M., Shahandashti, M., & Ashuri, B. (2022). Impact of COVID-19 on the Diversity of the Construction Workforce. *Natural Hazards Review*, *23*(3), 04022015. DOI: 10.1061/(ASCE)NH.1527-6996.0000560

Baral, S., Rao, A., Rwema, J. O. T., Lyons, C., Cevik, M., Kågesten, A. E., Diouf, D., Sohn, A. H., Phaswana-Mafuya, R. N., Kamarulzaman, A., Millett, G., Marcus, J. L., & Mishra, S. (2022). Competing health risks associated with the COVID-19 pandemic and early response: A scoping review. *PLoS One*, *17*(8), 1–21. https://doi-org.captechu.idm.oclc.org/10.1371/journal.pone.0273389. DOI: 10.1371/journal.pone.0273389 PMID: 36037216

Best, A. L., Fletcher, F. E., Kadono, M., & Warren, R. C. (2021). Institutional distrust among African Americans and building trustworthiness in the COVID-19 response: implications for ethical public health practice. *Journal of health care for the poor and*

Bhattacharyya, A., & Hastak, M. (2023). Impact Analysis of Covid-19 Pandemic on Construction Employment in the United States. In *Canadian Society of Civil Engineering Annual Conference* (pp. 411-420). Springer, Singapore. DOI: 10.1007/978-981-19-0968-9_33

Bibbins-Domingo, K. (2020). This time must be different: Disparities during the COVID-19 pandemic. *Annals of Internal Medicine*, *173*(3), 233–234. DOI: 10.7326/M20-2247 PMID: 32343767

Blackwell, A. (2017). The Curb-Cut Effect. Laws and programs designed to benefit vulnerable groups, such as the disabled or people of color, often end up benefiting all of society. Stanford Social Innovation Review. https://ssir.org/chapters/entry/the_ curb_cut_effect

Blog, N. I. O. S. H. "COVID-19 Poses Big Challenges for Small Construction Firms," at: https://blogs.cdc.gov/niosh-science-blog/2021/03/09/construction_covid/

Bloomberg, D. L & Volpe. M. (2016). Completing your Qualitative Dissertation: A road map from beginning to end. 3rd edition, Sage Publications, Thousand Oaks, California.

Boatswain, M. (2016). Increasing Jobsite ess for Women in Construction. *Construction Executive:*http://constructionexec.com/chapter/increasing-jobsite-safety-for-women-in-construction

Bonilla-Silva, E. (2001). *White Supremacy and Racism in the Post-Civil Rights Era.* Lynne Reinner Publishers, Inc. DOI: 10.1515/9781685850272

Bou Hatoum, M., Faisal, A., Nassereddine, H., & Sarvari, H. (2021). Analysis of COVID-19 concerns raised by the construction workforce and development of mitigation practices. *Frontiers in Built Environment*, *7*, 66. DOI: 10.3389/fbuil.2021.688495

Brown, S., Brooks, R. D., & Dong, X. S. (2020). Coronavirus and health disparities in construction.

Brown, S., Brooks, R. D., & Dong, X. S. (2020). Impact of COVID-19 on construction workers and businesses.

Brown, S., Brooks, R. D., Harris, W., & Dong, X. S. (2021). Construction employment, businesses, and COVID-19 vaccinations during the pandemic.

Bui, D. P., McCaffrey, K., Friedrichs, M., LaCross, N., Lewis, N. M., Sage, K., Barbeau, B., Vilven, D., Rose, C., & Braby, S. (**2020).** Racial and ethnic disparities among COVID-19 cases in workplace outbreaks by industry sector—Utah, March 6–June 5, 2020. *Morbid. Mortal. Week. Rep*, *69*, 1133–1138.

Callaghan, W. M. (2012). Overview of maternal mortality in the United States. *Seminars in Perinatology*, *36*(1), 2–6. DOI: 10.1053/j.semperi.2011.09.002 PMID: 22280858

Cameron, K. S., & Quinn, R. E. (2011). Diagnosing and Changing Organizational Culture Based on the Competing Values Framework (3rd ed.). San Francisco Jossey-Bass. - References - Scientific Research Publishing. (n.d.). Www.scirp.org. https://www.scirp.org/reference/referencespapers?referenceid=1871430

Care Without Coverage.; 2002. doi: https://doi.org/DOI: 10.17226/10367

Casillas, E., Jr., Wu, G., Iantorno, S., & Ning, W. V. Joon Choi, Chan, P., & Lee, M. M. (2021). COVID-19: Highlighting Health Disparities in the Los Angeles Latinx Community. *Clinical Medicine & Research*, *19*(4), 161–168. https://doi-org.captechu.idm.oclc.org/10.3121/cmr.2021.1654

Causation and Injustice. Locating the injustice of racial and ethnic health disparities. (2022). *Bioethics*, *36*(3), 260–266. https://doi-org.captechu.idm.oclc.org/10.1111/bioe.12994

Center for Disease Control and Prevention. (2022, August 3). *Interpretation of Forecasts of New and Total Deaths*. Updated 2022, Aug. 3, from COVID-19 Forecasts: Deaths | CDC)

Centers for Disease Control and Prevention. Flu Disparities Among Racial and Ethnic Minority Groups.

Chen, Q., & Mills, T. Dynamic Interplay between Safety Culture and Workplace Diversity. Retrieved from http://www.irbnet. de/daten/iconda/CIB20338.pdf

Chien-Ho, K., & Abdulmajeed, H. A. (2022). Improving Construction Safety: Lessons Learned from COVID-19 in the United States. *Sustainability (Basel)*, *14*(12), 7137. DOI: 10.3390/su14127137

Choi, B., & Lee, S. H. (2022). The psychological mechanism of construction workers' safety participation: The social identity theory perspective. *Journal of Safety Research, 82*, 194–206. DOI: 10.1016/j.jsr.2022.05.011 PMID: 36031247

Choi, J. O., Shrestha, P. P., Lim, J., & Shrestha, B. K. (2018, March). An investigation of construction workforce inequalities and biases in the architecture, engineering, and construction (AEC) industry. In *Construction Research Congress 2018: Sustainable Design and Construction and Education*. DOI: 10.1061/9780784481301.007

Clark, R., & Estes, F. (2008). *Turning research into results: A guide to selecting the right performance solutions*. Information Age Publications.

Compilation from U.S. Census Bureau Current Population Survey (CPD) Questionnaire. Available at: https://www.census.gov/programs-surveys/cps/technical-documentation/questionnaires.html

Creswell, J. W., & Plano Clark, V. L. (2011). *Designing and Conducting Mixed Methods Research* (2nd ed.). Sage Publications.

Currie, L, Iannone, A; Mandato, C. (2021). *The Construction Lawyer*; *Chicago Vol. 41*(1), (Winter 2021), p. 23-33.

DeMaria, J. (2017, April 12). Organizational Safety Culture. Institute for Safety and Health Management. Retrieved from https://ishm.org/organizational-safety-culture/

Denison, D. R., & Mishra, A. K. (1995). Toward a Theory of Organizational Culture and Effectiveness. *Organization Science, 6*(2), 204–223. https://www.jstor.org/stable/2635122. DOI: 10.1287/orsc.6.2.204

Dong, X. S., Wang, X., Katz, R., Trahan Cain, C., Rinehart, R. (2018). Fatal injuries among small construction establishments. Available at: publications_ Quarter3-QDR-2018_0.pdf (cpwr.com)

Doubraski, B. (2016, December 13). Increasing Jobsite Safety for Women in Construction. Construction Executive. Retrieved from http://constructionexec.com/chapter/increasingjobsite-safety-for-women-in-construction

Early Impacts of the COVID-19 Pandemic on the United States Construction Industry. (2021).. . *International Journal of Environmental Research and Public Health, 18*(4), 1559. DOI: 10.3390/ijerph18041559 PMID: 33562127

Elizalde, R. R. (2022). COVID-19 in the Construction Sector. *Encyclopedia, 2*(2), 717–728. DOI: 10.3390/encyclopedia2020050

Fellows, R., & Liu, A. (2022). *Research methods for construction* (5th ed.). John Wiley & Sons Ltd.

Ferdinand, K. C., & Nasser, S. A. (2015). Racial/ethnic disparities in prevalence and care of patients with type 2 diabetes mellitus. *Current Medical Research and Opinion, 31*(5), 913–923. DOI: 10.1185/03007995.2015.1029894 PMID: 25772230

Fiscella, K., & Sanders, M. R. (2016). Racial and ethnic disparities in the quality of health care. *Annual Review of Public Health, 37*(1), 375–394. DOI: 10.1146/annurev-publhealth-032315-021439 PMID: 26789384

Fishbein, M. (1979). A theory of reasoned action: Some applications and implications. *Nebraska Symposium on Motivation, 27*, 65–116. PMID: 7242751

Gamil, Y., & Alhagar, A. (2020). The impact of the pandemic crisis on the survival of the construction industry: A case of COVID-19. *Mediterranean Journal of Social Sciences, 11*(4), 122. DOI: 10.36941/mjss-2020-0047

Garcia, M. A., Homan, P. A., García, C., & Brown, T. H. (2021). The Color of COVID-19: Structural Racism and the Disproportionate Impact of the Pandemic on Older Black and Latinx Adults. *The Journals of Gerontology. Series B, Psychological Sciences and Social Sciences, 76*(3), e75–e80. https://doi-org.captechu.idm.oclc.org/10.1093/geronb/gbaa114. DOI: 10.1093/geronb/gbaa114 PMID: 32756973

Garcia, M. A., Thierry, A. D., & Pendergrast, C. B. (2022). Devastating Economic Impact of COVID-19 on Older Black and Latinx Adults: Implications for Health and Well-Being. *The Journals of Gerontology. Series B, Psychological Sciences and Social Sciences, 77*(8), 1501–1507. https://doi-org.captechu.idm.oclc.org/10.1093/geronb/gbab218. DOI: 10.1093/geronb/gbab218 PMID: 34850887

Gil, R. M., Marcelin, J. R., Zuniga-Blanco, B., Marquez, C., Mathew, T., Piggott, D. A., & Macias Gil, R. (2020). COVID-19 Pandemic: Disparate Health Impact on the Hispanic/Latinx Population in the United States. *The Journal of Infectious Diseases, 222*(10), 1592–1595. https://doi-org.captechu.idm.oclc.org/10.1093/infdis/jiaa474. DOI: 10.1093/infdis/jiaa474 PMID: 32729903

Gravlee, C. C. (2020). Systemic racism, chronic health inequities, and COVID-19: A syndemic in the making? *American Journal of Human Biology, 32*(5), e23482. DOI: 10.1002/ajhb.23482 PMID: 32754945

Harkness, A., Gattamorta, K. A., Estrada, Y., Jimenez, D., Kanamori, M., Prado, G., & Behar-Zusman, V. (2020). Latinx Health Disparities Research During COVID-19: Challenges and Innovations. *Annals of Behavioral Medicine, 54*(8), 544–547. https://doi-org.captechu.idm.oclc.org/10.1093/abm/kaaa054. DOI: 10.1093/abm/kaaa054 PMID: 32716033

He, Q., Rowangould, D., Karner, A., Palm, M., & LaRue, S. (2022). COVID-19 pandemic impacts on essential transit riders: Findings from a U.S. Survey. *Transportation Research: Part D, 105*, N.PAG. https://doi-org.captechu.idm.oclc.org/10.1016/j.trd.2022.103217

Holder, M., Jones, J., & Masterson, T. (2021). The Early Impact of Covid-19 on Job Losses among Black Women in the United States. *Feminist Economics*, *27*(1/2), 103–116. https://doi-org.captechu.idm.oclc.org/10.1080/13545701.2020.1849766. DOI: 10.1080/13545701.2020.1849766

Holland, S., Mason, J., & Brice, M. (2020) Trump declares coronavirus national emergency, says he will most likely be tested. Reuters. https://www.reuters.com/chapter/us-health-coronavirus-usa-emergency/trump-declares-coronavirus-national-emergency-says-he-will-most-likely-be-tested-idUSKBN2102G3. Accessed 12 Feb 2021\

Jenkins, K. (2023). *The COVID-19 Implications on the United States Failing Infrastructure and Its Affect on Future Generations* (Order No. 30987911). Available from ProQuest One Academic. (2915913865). https://www.proquest.com/dissertations-theses/covid-19-implications-on-united-states-failing/docview/2915913865/se-2

Jeon, J., Padhye, S., Bhattacharyya, A., Cai, H., & Hastak, M. (2022). Impact of COVID-19 on the US Construction Industry as Revealed in the Purdue Index for Construction. *Journal of Management Engineering*, *38*(1), 1–13. https://doi-org.captechu.idm.oclc.org/10.1061/(ASCE)ME.1943-5479.0000995. DOI: 10.1061/(ASCE)ME.1943-5479.0000995

Johnson-Agbakwu, C. E., Ali, N. S., Oxford, C. M., Wingo, S., Manin, E., & Coonrod, D. V. (2022). Racism, COVID-19, and Health Inequity in the USA: A Call to Action. *Journal of Racial and Ethnic Health Disparities*, *9*(1), 52–58. DOI: 10.1007/s40615-020-00928-y PMID: 33197038

Kaluarachchi, Y., Nartallo, P., & Emuze, F. (2022). How can the construction industry improve their workers' health and well-being in a post-COVID-19 era. *IOP Conference Series. Earth and Environmental Science*, *1101*(3), 032013. DOI: 10.1088/1755-1315/1101/3/032013

Kaur, G., Sharma, R. R. K., & Verma, P. (December 8, 2016). Aligning Culture Typologies to Innovative Employee Benefits: Using Cameron and Quinn's Competing Value Framework. University of Sri Jayewardenepura, Sri Lanka, 13th International Conference on Business Management (ICBM).DOI: 10.2139/ssrn.2910213

Kline, N., Webb, N. J., Thompson, E. L., Griner, S. B., & Schrimshaw, E. W. (2022). Latinx COVID-19 Disparities and Work As a Social Determinant of Health: A Research and Policy Agenda. *Population Health Management*, *25*(2), 284–287. https://doi-org.captechu.idm.oclc.org/10.1089/pop.2021.0368. DOI: 10.1089/pop.2021.0368 PMID: 35442792

Kniffin, K. M., Narayanan, J., Anseel, F., Antonakis, J., Ashford, S. P., Bakker, A. B., Bamberger, P., Bapuji, H., Bhave, D. P., Choi, V. K., Creary, S. J., Demerouti, E., Flynn, F. J., Gelfand, M. J., Greer, L. L., Johns, G., Kesebir, S., Klein, P. G., Lee, S. Y., & Vugt, M. (2021). COVID-19 and the workplace: Implications, issues, and insights for future research and action. *The American Psychologist*, *76*(1), 63–77. DOI: 10.1037/amp0000716 PMID: 32772537

Kopf, D., & Detrixhe, J. A coronavirus-led recession could hit jobs for young people and minorities hardest https://qz.com/1822762/coronavirus-led-recession-in-us-could-hit-people-of-color-hardest/

Krishnan, L., Ogunwole, S. M., & Cooper, L. A. (2020). Historical insights on coronavirus disease 2019 (COVID-19), the 1918 influenza pandemic, and racial disparities: Illuminating a path forward. *Annals of Internal Medicine*, *173*(6), 474–481. DOI: 10.7326/M20-2223 PMID: 32501754

Lapshun, A. L., & Fusch, G. E. (2023). Times of Uncertainties Require Embracing Leadership and Feedback. *The Qualitative Report*, *28*(3), 828–847. DOI: 10.46743/2160-3715/2023.5609

Lau, K. H. V., Anand, P., Ramirez, A., & Phicil, S. (2022). Disparities in Telehealth use During the COVID-19 Pandemic. *Journal of Immigrant and Minority Health*, *24*(6), 1–4. https://doi-org.captechu.idm.oclc.org/10.1007/s10903-022-01381-1. DOI: 10.1007/s10903-022-01381-1 PMID: 35976473

Laurencin, C. T., & McClinton, A. (2020). The COVID-19 pandemic: A call to action to identify and address racial and ethnic disparities. *Journal of Racial and Ethnic Health Disparities*, *7*(3), 398–402. DOI: 10.1007/s40615-020-00756-0 PMID: 32306369

Lawrence, K., Anderson, A., Susi, G., Sutton, S., Kubisch, A., & Codrington, R. (2009). A Practical Guide for Designing Strategies to Close Chronic Racial Outcome Gaps. https://www.aspeninstitute.org/wp-content/uploads/files/content/images/Roundtable%20on%20Community%20Change%20RETOC.pdf

Lê-Scherban, F., Headen, I., Klem, A. M., Traister, K., Gilliam, E., Beverly, M., Jannetti, M., Ferroni, J., & Carroll-Scott, A. (2023). Research and Evaluation in a Child-Focused Place-Based Initiative: West Philly Promise Neighborhood. *International Journal of Environmental Research and Public Health, 20*(9), 5716. DOI: 10.3390/ijerph20095716 PMID: 37174234

Liang, Y., Baral, A., Shahandashti, M., & Ashuri, B. (2022). Availability Heuristic in Construction Workforce Decision-Making amid COVID-19 Pandemic: Empirical Evidence and Mitigation Strategy. *Journal of Management Engineering, 38*(5), 1–9. https://doi-org.captechu.idm.oclc.org/10.1061/(ASCE)ME.1943-5479.0001077. DOI: 10.1061/(ASCE)ME.1943-5479.0001077

Lingard, H., Zhang, R. P., Räisänen, C., Goh, Y. M., Bowen, P., & Bhandari, S. (2021). Special issue: what have we learnt from the COVID-19 global pandemic: improving the construction industry's abilities to foresee, respond to and recover from future endemic catastrophes. *Construction Management and Economics, 39*(2), 192–197. DOI: 10.1080/01446193.2020.1869480

Löwstedt, M., & Räisänen, C. (2014). Social identity in construction: Enactments and outcomes. *Construction Management and Economics, 32*(11), 1093–1105. DOI: 10.1080/01446193.2014.956132

Macias Gil, R., Touzard-Romo, F., Sanchez, M. C., Pandita, A., Kalligeros, M., Mylona, E. K., Shehadeh, F., Mylonakis, E., & Gil, R. M. (2021). Characteristics and outcomes of Hispanic/Latinx patients with coronavirus disease 19 (COVID-19) requiring hospitalization in Rhode Island: A retrospective cohort study. *Annals of Epidemiology, 58*, 64–68. https://doi-org.captechu.idm.oclc.org/10.1016/j.annepidem.2021.03.003. DOI: 10.1016/j.annepidem.2021.03.003 PMID: 33737227

Mamon, P. (2020). Organizational Culture. https://www.researchgate.net/publication/341266529_Organizational_Culture

Mannheim, J., Konda, S., & Logan, L. K. (2022). Racial, ethnic and socioeconomic disparities in SARS-CoV-2 infection amongst children. *Paediatric and Perinatal Epidemiology, 36*(3), 337–346. https://doi-org.captechu.idm.oclc.org/10.1111/ppe.12865. DOI: 10.1111/ppe.12865 PMID: 35076946

Marzouk, M. M., El Kherbawy, A. A., & Khalifa, M. (2013). Factors influencing subcontractors selection in construction projects. *Housing and Building Research Center Journal, 9*(2), 150–158. DOI: 10.1016/j.hbrcj.2013.05.001

Masters, G. A., Asipenko, E., Bergman, A. L., Person, S. D., Brenckle, L., Moore Simas, T. A., Ko, J. Y., Robbins, C. L., & Byatt, N. (2021). Impact of the COVID-19 pandemic on mental health, access to care, and health disparities in the perinatal period. *Journal of Psychiatric Research*, *137*, 126–130. https://doi-org.captechu.idm.oclc.org/10.1016/j.jpsychires.2021.02.056. DOI: 10.1016/j.jpsychires.2021.02.056 PMID: 33677216

Mays, V. M., Cochran, S. D., & Barnes, N. W. (2007). Race, race-based discrimination, and health outcomes among African Americans. *Annual Review of Psychology*, *58*(1), 201–225. DOI: 10.1146/annurev.psych.57.102904.190212 PMID: 16953796

McCoy, H. (2020). Black lives matter, and yes, you are racist: The parallelism of the twentieth and twenty-first centuries. *Child & Adolescent Social Work Journal*, *37*(5), 463–475. DOI: 10.1007/s10560-020-00690-4 PMID: 32836724

Meliala, Y. H. (2023). The Influence of Organizational Culture and Transformational Leadership on Organizational Citizenship Behavior (OCB) Mediated Organizational Commitment and Job Satisfaction: Acces la Success. *Calitatea*, *24*(195), 235–246. DOI: 10.47750/QAS/24.195.28

Meza, E., Giglio, L., Franco, A. O., Rodriguez, E., Stock, L., Balmes, J., Torres, J. M., & Fernandez, A. (2022, August 9). Worker Perspectives on COVID-19 Risks: A Qualitative Study of Latino Construction Workers in Oakland, California. *International Journal of Environmental Research and Public Health*, *19*(16), 9822. DOI: 10.3390/ijerph19169822 PMID: 36011454

Michigan Department of Health and Human Services. Coronavirus Outbreak Reporting. Available online: https://www.michigan.gov/coronavirus/0,9753,7-406-98163_98173_102057---,00.html (accessed on 15 October 2020).

Millett, G. A., Jones, A. T., Benkeser, D., Baral, S., Mercer, L., Beyrer, C., Honermann, B., Lankiewicz, E., Mena, L., Crowley, J. S., Sherwood, J., & Sullivan, P. S. (2020). Assessing differential impacts of COVID-19 on black communities. *Annals of Epidemiology*, *47*, 37–44. DOI: 10.1016/j.annepidem.2020.05.003 PMID: 32419766

National Center for Health Statistics. (2019). *Health*. United States Spotlight Racial and Ethnic Disparities in Heart Disease.

Netemeyer, R. G., & Bearden, W. O. (1992). A comparative analysis of two models of behavioral intention. Journal of the Academy of Marketing Science, *20*(1), 49–59. https://doi-org/DOI: 10.1007/BF02723475

Niedzwiecki, M. J., Hsia, R. Y., & Shen, Y. C. (2018). Not all insurance is equal: Differential treatment and health outcomes by insurance coverage among nonelderly adult patients with heart attack. *Journal of the American Heart Association*, *7*(11), e008152. Advance online publication. DOI: 10.1161/JAHA.117.008152 PMID: 29871858

NikkhahManesh. S., Choi, J., & Shrestha, P. (2020, March). Critical literature review on the diversity and inclusion of women and ethnic minorities in construction and civil engineering industry and education. In *Construction Research Congress* 2020.

NIOSH Absenteeism in the Workplace at. https://www.cdc.gov/niosh/topics/absences/default.html Compilation from U.S. Census Bureau Current Population Survey (CPS) Questionnaire. Available at: https://www.census.gov/programs-surveys/cps/technical-documentation/questionnaires.html

Nwaogu, J. M., Chan, A. P. C., & Tetteh, M. O. (2022). Staff resilience and coping behavior as protective factors for mental health among construction tradesmen. *Journal of Engineering, Design and Technology*, *20*(3), 671–695. DOI: 10.1108/JEDT-11-2020-0464

Odonkor, C. A., Sholas, M. G., Verduzco-Gutierrez, M., Zafonte, R. D., & Silver, J. K. (2020). African American Patient Disparities in COVID-19 Outcomes: A Call to Action for Physiatrists to Provide Rehabilitation Care to Black Survivors. *American Journal of Physical Medicine & Rehabilitation*, *99*(11), 986–987. https://doi-org.captechu.idm.oclc.org/10.1097/PHM.0000000000001568. DOI: 10.1097/PHM.0000000000001568 PMID: 32804715

Olatoye, O. (2022). *Social and Psychological Impact of Covid-19 Pandemic on Construction Projects* (Order No. 29994627). Available from ProQuest One Academic. (2770728354). https://www.proquest.com/dissertations-theses/social-psychological-impact-covid-19-pandemic-on/docview/2770728354/se-2

Oliver, M., & Shapiro, T. (1997). *Black Wealth/White Wealth: A New Perspective on Racial Inequality*. Routledge.

Olugbemiga, E. O., Jang, Y., Song, K., & Ahn, J. (2023). Impact of COVID-19 on Social and Psychological Well-Being of Workers in Construction Projects: Comparative Analysis of Managers and Laborers. *Buildings (Basel, Switzerland)*, *13*(8), 1902. DOI: 10.3390/buildings13081902

Omi, M., & Winant, H. (1994). *Racial Formation in the United States from the 1960s to the 1990s* (2nd ed.). Routledge.

Ong, P., & Valenzuela, A. (1996). The Labor Market: Immigrant Effects and Racial Disparities. In Waldinger, R., & Bozorgmehr, M. (Eds.), *Ethnic Los Angeles* (pp. 165–191). Russell Sage Foundation.

Pamidimukkala, A., & Kermanshachi, S. (2021). Impact of COVID-19 on field and office workforce in the construction industry, Project Leadership, and Society. Volume 2, 100018, ISSN 2666-7215, https://doi.org/DOI: 10.1016/j.plas.2021.100018

Pasco, R. F., Fox, S. J., Johnston, S. C., Pignone, M., & Meyers, L. A. (2020). Estimated association of construction work with risks of COVID-19 infection and hospitalization in Texas. [Google Scholar] [CrossRef] [PubMed]. *JAMA Network Open*, *3*(10), e2026373. DOI: 10.1001/jamanetworkopen.2020.26373 PMID: 33119111

Pipeline & Gas Journal. Phillips 66: Red Oak, Liberty, ACE Pipelines Deferred by Cost Cuts. Available online: https://pgjonline.com/news/2020/03-march/phillips-66-red-oak-liberty-ace-pipelines-deferred-by-cost-cuts (accessed on 26 October 2020).

Raoufi, M., & Fayek, A. R. (2021). Identifying actions to control and mitigate the effects of the COVID-19 pandemic on construction organizations: Preliminary findings. *Public Works Management & Policy*, *26*(1), 47–55. DOI: 10.1177/1087724X20969164

Rueda, R. (2011). *The 3 dimensions of improving student performance: finding the right solutions to the right problems*. Teachers College, Columbia University.

Sabatello, M., Jackson Scroggins, M., Goto, G., Santiago, A., McCormick, A., Morris, K. J., Daulton, C. R., Easter, C. L., & Darien, G. (2021). Structural Racism in the COVID-19 Pandemic: Moving Forward. *The American Journal of Bioethics*, *21*(3), 56–74. https://doi-org.captechu.idm.oclc.org/10.1080/15265161.2020.1851808. DOI: 10.1080/15265161.2020.1851808 PMID: 33345745

Schumm, L. P., Giurcanu, M. C., Locey, K. J., Ortega, J. C., Zhang, Z., & Grossman, R. L. (2022). Racial and ethnic disparities in the observed COVID-19 case fatality rate among the U.S. population. *Annals of Epidemiology*, *74*, 118–124. https://doi-org.captechu.idm.oclc.org/10.1016/j.annepidem.2022.07.010. DOI: 10.1016/j.annepidem.2022.07.010 PMID: 35940395

Serrano, F., Blutinger, E. J., Vargas-Torres, C., Bilal, S., Counts, C., Straight, M., & Lin, M. P. (2022). Racial and Ethnic Disparities in Hospitalization and Clinical Outcomes Among Patients with COVID-19. *Western Journal of Emergency Medicine: Integrating Emergency Care with Population Health, 23*(5), 601–612. https://doi-org.captechu.idm.oclc.org/10.5811/westjem.2022.3.53065

Sethi, D., & Seth, M. (2009). Interpersonal communication: Lifeblood of an organization. *The IUP Journal of Soft Skills, III*(3&4), 32–40. https://www.researchgate.net/profile/Deepa_Sethi/publication/228271402_Interpersonal_Communication_Lifeblood_of_an_Organization/links/55af387808ae98e661a6fd03/Interpersonal-Communication-Lifeblood-of-an-Organization.pdf

Simon, S. M., & Varghese, K. (2018, July). Assessment of organizational culture in construction–A case study approach. In *26th Annual Conference of the International Group to Lean Construction (IGLC).* Chennai, India (p.348-357) DOI: 10.24928/2018/0396

Singh, P., & Loncar, N. (2010). Pay Satisfaction, Job Satisfaction, and Turnover Intent. Relations Industrielles. *Industrial Relations*, *65*(3), 470–490. https://www.jstor.org/stable/23078304. DOI: 10.7202/044892ar

Smela, B., Toumi, M., Świerk, K., Francois, C., Biernikiewicz, M., Clay, E., & Boyer, L. (2023). Rapid literature review: Definition and methodology. *Journal of Market Access & Health Policy*, *11*(1), 2241234. DOI: 10.1080/20016689.2023.2241234 PMID: 37533549

Song, L., Wang, Y., Chen, B., Tan, Y., Zhang, W., & Wang, Y. (2020). The association between health insurance and all-cause, cardiovascular disease, cancer, and cause-specific mortality: A prospective cohort study. *International Journal of Environmental Research and Public Health*, *17*(5), 1525. DOI: 10.3390/ijerph17051525 PMID: 32120888

S&P Global. Pennsylvania's Orders to Stem Coronavirus Outbreak Pause Several Gas Pipeline Projects. Available online: https://www.spglobal.com/platts/en/market-insights/latest-news/natural-gas/032520-pennsylvanias-orders-to-stem-coronavirus-outbreak-pause-several-gas-pipeline-projects

Standard Social Innovation Review Collective Impact https://ssir.org/chapters/entry/collective_impact# 124. Tai, D. B. G., Shah, A., Doubeni, C. A., Sia, I. G., & Wieland, M. L. (2021). The Disproportionate Impact of COVID-19 on Racial and Ethnic Minorities in the United States. *Clinical Infectious Diseases, 72*(4), 703–706. https://doi-org.captechu.idm.oclc.org/10.1093/cid/ciaa815\

The Associated General Contractors of America. Myers-Lawson School of Construction—Virginia Tech. (2017). *Preventing Fatalities in the Construction Industry.*https://www.agc.org/ sites/ default/files/Files/Safety%20%26%20 Health/AGC-VT%20Fatality%20Report%20%5BFinal %5D_0.pdf

The Associated General Contractors of America. (2018, August 29). *Eighty Percent of Contractors Report Difficulty Finding Qualified Craft Workers to Hire as the Association Calls for Measures to Rebuild the Workforce.* https://www.agc.org/news/2018/08/29/ eighty-percent-contractors-report-difficulty finding-qualified-craft-workers-hire

Tsung-Lin, W., & Liu, H. (2023). Causal Model Analysis of the Effect of Policy Formalism, COVID-19 Fear, Social Support and Work Stress on Construction Workers' Anxiety during the Epidemic. *Buildings (Basel, Switzerland)*, *13*(1), 10. DOI: 10.3390/buildings13010010

U.S. Bureau of Labor Statistics. (2022, January 20). *Labor force statistics from the current population survey*. From https://www.bls.gov/cps/cpsaat18.htm

U.S. Bureau of Labor Statistics. (2022, April). *Spotlight on statistics: The Construction Industry: Characteristics of the Employed,* 2003–20. from https://www.bls.gov/spotlight/2022/the-construction-industry-labor-force-2003-to-2020/home.htm

U.S. Bureau of Labor Statistics (BLS). Current Employment Statistics—National. Available online: https://www.bls.gov/ces/ (accessed on 10 November 2020).

Vable, A. M., Cohen, A. K., Leonard, S. A., Glymour, M. M., Duarte, C. D. P., & Yen, I. H. (2018). Do the health benefits of education vary by sociodemographic subgroup? Differential returns to education and implications for health inequities. *Annals of Epidemiology*, *28*(11), 759–766.e5. Advance online publication. DOI: 10.1016/j.annepidem.2018.08.014 PMID: 30309690

Vargas, N., & Stainback, K. (2016). *Documenting contested racial identities among self-identified Latinos, Asians, Blacks, and Whites*. American Behavioral Scientist., DOI: 10.1177/0002764215613396

Wakeel, F., & Njoku, A. (2021, February). Application of the weathering framework: Intersection of racism, stigma, and COVID-19 as a stressful life event among African Americans. [). MDPI.]. *Health Care*, *9*(2), 145. PMID: 33540498

Warren, M. A., & Warren, M. T. (2023). The EThIC Model of Virtue-Based Allyship Development: A New Approach to Equity and Inclusion in Organizations: JBE. *Journal of Business Ethics*, *182*(3), 783–803. DOI: 10.1007/s10551-021-05002-z PMID: 34840369

Washington State Department of Health. Statewide COVID-19 Outbreak Report. Available online: https://www.doh.wa.gov/Portals/1/Documents/1600/coronavirus/data-tables/StatewideCOVID-19OutbreakReport.pdf

Weitzman, B. C., PhD., Abrams, C., M.A., Starr, B., M.P.H., Hasan, I., M.P.A., Shire, A., Elbel, B., & Berry, C. (2023). Exploring Flexibility in Philanthropic Funding for Place-Based Efforts to Improve Community Health: Reflections on a New York State Multisite Initiative. *The Foundation Review, 15*(2), 66-81,88. https://doi.org/ DOI: 10.9707/1944-5660.1656

Wiewiora, A., Trigunarsyah, B., Murphy, G., Coffey, V. (2013). Organizational culture and willingness to share knowledge: A competing values perspective in the Australian context, International Journal of Project Management, (Vol. 31, Issue 8, P. 1163-1174). https://doi.org/.DOI: 10.1016/j.ijproman.2012.12.014

Williams, D. P., Jones, N. M., & Holman, E. A. (2022). Racial and ethnic differences in perseverative cognition at the onset of the COVID-19 pandemic. *Social Science & Medicine, 306*, N.PAG. https://doi-org.captechu.idm.oclc.org/10.1016/j.socscimed.2022.115105

Williamson, T. (2005). Work-based learning: A leadership development example from an action research study of shared governance implementation. *Journal of Nursing Management*, *13*(6), 490–499. DOI: 10.1111/j.1365-2934.2005.00576.x PMID: 16238690

Wingo, S. N. (2019). Black Uteri Matter. *Obstetrics and Gynecology*, *133*(1), 4–5. DOI: 10.1097/AOG.0000000000003035 PMID: 30531579

Yilmaz, G. (2014). Let's Peel the Onion Together: An Application of Schein's Model of Organizational Culture. *Communication Teacher*, *28*(4), 224–228. DOI: 10.1080/17404622.2014.939674

Zhou, X., Nguyen-Feng, V. N., Wamser-Nanney, R., & Lotzin, A. (2022). Racism, Posttraumatic Stress Symptoms, and Racial Disparity in the U.S. COVID-19 Syndemic. *Behavioral Medicine (Washington, D.C.)*, *48*(2), 85–94. https://doi-org.captechu.idm.oclc.org/10.1080/08964289.2021.2006131. DOI: 10.1080/08964289.2021.2006131 PMID: 35318897

Chapter 6
Adapting Mental Health Services in Crisis:
A Case Study of Mental Health Organizations' Response to COVID-19

Roger Tshiondo Muntu
https://orcid.org/0009-0002-7649-9744
Marymount University, USA

ABSTRACT

This chapter examines the impact of the COVID-19 pandemic on mental health services, focusing on the financial and operational challenges that organizations have faced and the strategies they have employed to adapt. The chapter highlights the rapid shift to remote care models, such as telehealth, and the subsequent decline in service volume and revenue. It explores the importance of transformational leadership and changes management frameworks, particularly Kotter's Eight-Step Model, in guiding mental health organizations through crises. The chapter also discusses the significance of data-driven decision-making and leadership development in maintaining service continuity and organizational resilience. Finally, it provides actionable recommendations for mental health organizations to improve crisis preparedness, enhance technology integration, and address equity in access to care, emphasizing the need for continued innovation and adaptation in the face of future challenges.

DOI: 10.4018/979-8-3373-0482-3.ch006

INTRODUCTION

The COVID-19 pandemic profoundly disrupted global healthcare systems, with mental health services experiencing unprecedented challenges in maintaining care delivery. According to the World Health Organization (2021), nearly 93% of countries reported disruptions to mental health services, while the global prevalence of anxiety and depression increased by 25% (WHO, 2022). These disruptions not only exacerbated existing mental health conditions but also created new challenges, including a surge in demand for services amid restricted access to in-person care (Zheng et al., 2021). This dramatic increase in mental health concerns during the pandemic highlighted a significant gap in the global healthcare system's ability to respond to both immediate and prolonged mental health crises. Mental health organizations, which already operated under financial constraints and resource limitations, now had to manage increasing patient loads without the usual in-person infrastructure that was vital to their care delivery models.

While much of the existing research has focused on immediate service disruptions—such as the shift to telehealth and the breakdown of face-to-face consultations—fewer studies have delved into how mental health organizations adapted their leadership approaches, built trust with stakeholders, and innovated their service delivery models during such an unprecedented crisis. This gap in the literature is striking, as it prevents a deeper understanding of the organizational resilience required to survive in such an environment. The pandemic exposed not only weaknesses in service delivery but also in how these organizations managed organizational change and maintained critical relationships with both staff and clients. These issues have been particularly problematic for mental health organizations that lack a robust framework for responding to large-scale disruptions, both financially and operationally.

Research from the Centers for Disease Control and Prevention (CDC, 2023) shows that healthcare organizations, including those providing mental health services, suffered significant financial losses due to decreased patient volumes and operational disruptions. The decline in in-person consultations, which had been a cornerstone of mental health care, led to financial instability for many organizations, particularly those slow to transition to remote service models (Lo et al., 2023). The logistical difficulties and limited technological infrastructure of many mental health services hampered the swift integration of telehealth, a necessary alternative for continued care. This shift raised essential questions about how mental health organizations maintained service quality and financial viability under such immense pressure.

However, it is not enough to understand how organizations responded to the crisis in terms of logistical and financial challenges. A deeper analysis is required to explore how leadership, organizational culture, and adaptive strategies influenced mental health services' ability to continue functioning effectively. Adaptive leadership, for instance, becomes crucial in this context as it enables organizations to pivot, respond to crises, and provide guidance to both employees and clients under challenging circumstances (Miller & Johnson, 2022). Mental health organizations need leaders who can not only manage the day-to-day operational shifts but also inspire trust and engagement from their teams while navigating the heightened emotional strains of a global pandemic.

In addition to leadership, building and maintaining stakeholder trust was a critical component of mental health organizations' ability to provide continuity of care during the pandemic. Research has shown that the trust between healthcare organizations and their patients, especially in mental health services, is a vital determinant of service effectiveness and long-term recovery (Patel et al., 2022). As mental health organizations were forced to rapidly shift to telehealth, the challenges in establishing trust in a virtual environment became apparent. Face-to-face interactions that had been the foundation of therapeutic relationships were suddenly replaced by online consultations, which presented not only technological barriers but also an emotional distance that many clients found difficult to navigate.

Understanding how organizations adapted in the face of these challenges is critical not only for navigating the ongoing difficulties brought about by the pandemic but also for preparing mental health organizations to respond more effectively to future crises. By examining how organizations adapted their leadership approaches, communication strategies, and service models, this research aims to fill an important gap in current knowledge. The insights gathered will not only inform the resilience of mental health services in the context of crisis management but will also offer actionable strategies to improve crisis preparedness in the future. Developing flexible and resilient service delivery models, which balance digital and in-person care options, will be crucial for the sustainability of mental health services moving forward.

Moreover, as the COVID-19 crisis is still unfolding in many parts of the world, it is vital that mental health organizations take proactive steps to integrate the lessons learned during the pandemic into their ongoing operations. Long-term strategies must include comprehensive training for leadership on crisis management, the implementation of flexible work models for staff, and the development of policies that prioritize emotional support and mental health resources for both employees and clients. These steps will not only ensure that mental health organizations are better equipped for future crises but will also contribute to the overall improvement of mental health care delivery globally.

Additionally, this research will examine how broader social determinants of health, including socioeconomic status, geographic location, and access to resources, have impacted mental health care access during the pandemic. Vulnerable populations, such as low-income individuals, people of color, and rural residents, have been disproportionately affected by the mental health crisis exacerbated by COVID-19. Addressing these disparities will be essential for creating a more equitable and effective mental health care system.

Ultimately, the COVID-19 pandemic has revealed significant gaps in our understanding of how mental health organizations operate under stress. It has highlighted the need for comprehensive frameworks that integrate leadership, organizational culture, service delivery models, and stakeholder engagement strategies to ensure resilience in the face of future disruptions. This study addresses these gaps by exploring adaptive leadership, flexible change strategies, and the role of stakeholder trust in crisis-impacted mental health systems, providing both theoretical insights and practical recommendations for improving crisis preparedness in the mental health sector.

PROBLEM STATEMENT

While many studies have widely reported service disruptions in mental health services during the COVID-19 pandemic, much of the existing literature merely acknowledges these disruptions without delving into the complexities of how mental health organizations managed these crises in real-time. These disruptions were not merely short-term issues but signified profound changes in the landscape of mental health care delivery. The pandemic introduced immediate challenges to both the operational and financial stability of organizations, yet few studies have examined the long-term adaptive strategies that organizations employed to ensure service continuity, let alone the leadership approaches they adopted to guide their teams through these tumultuous times.

For example, a study by Zhang et al. (2022) showed that 70% of mental health organizations experienced significant revenue losses due to the shift to remote care models. However, this statistic only tells part of the story. It is essential to understand how these financial strains were navigated by organizational leadership and which strategies were most effective in maintaining service quality under resource constraints. The transition to remote services, while necessary, also raised questions about the sustainability of these models in the long term. As the pandemic deepened, many mental health providers faced not only financial difficulties but also technological barriers, staff burnout, and logistical hurdles, all of which required immediate and adaptive responses that went beyond mere operational adjustments.

According to the Centers for Disease Control and Prevention (CDC, 2023), mental health services experienced a drastic 30-40% reduction in service volume and quality due to COVID-19 restrictions. The data points to a significant gap in understanding the real-time impacts of these changes on mental health service providers, as they struggled to maintain patient care standards while navigating pandemic-induced constraints. Furthermore, these disruptions were particularly severe for organizations heavily reliant on in-person consultations, with face-to-face interactions dropping by over 50% (Lo et al., 2023). This dramatic shift highlighted a critical vulnerability in the mental health care system: its dependence on traditional models of service delivery that are not easily adaptable to global disruptions. The pivot to telehealth, while innovative and necessary in many instances, also posed unique challenges in terms of client engagement, technology adoption, and the ability of providers to maintain the quality of care they were once able to offer in person.

Additionally, challenges in insurance reimbursements for telehealth services contributed to further financial instability. As Patel et al. (2022) reported, 68% of providers faced reimbursement difficulties, and these challenges were often compounded by the evolving regulatory landscape that was unclear and inconsistent across different regions. These financial challenges created an environment where many mental health organizations were forced to operate at a loss or limit their services. While the financial hardships were significant, the leadership strategies employed to navigate these challenges are not well-documented. How did organizations adapt their financial and operational strategies to survive under these pressures, and what leadership practices were critical in ensuring the continuity of care during such a time of crisis?

Moreover, the pandemic introduced new complexities in workforce management. Mental health professionals were themselves affected by the pandemic, experiencing increased stress, burnout, and emotional exhaustion due to the elevated demands on their time and energy. As highlighted by Harrison et al. (2022), many mental health workers struggled with adapting to remote work models, especially in settings where face-to-face interactions were a cornerstone of care. While many healthcare professionals transitioned to telehealth platforms, the mental health sector's reliance on in-person engagement raised significant questions about the efficacy of virtual care, especially in terms of building trust, managing crises, and addressing complex patient needs.

These issues underscore the immediate need for mental health organizations to adapt in terms of service delivery models and how they navigate financial and operational disruptions during crises. However, the adaptation to telehealth and remote care models is not enough; leadership within these organizations also needs to evolve. Without a clear understanding of how organizations adapted leadership and strategic change models during the crisis, future crisis planning remains weak and reactive, leaving organizations vulnerable to similar challenges in the future. Leadership, particularly adaptive leadership, plays a crucial role in not just managing operational changes but in motivating staff, ensuring emotional and psychological support, and maintaining the overall morale of teams working under extremely stressful conditions. It is important to explore how leadership during the pandemic helped organizations navigate these challenges, which types of leadership strategies were most successful, and how these strategies can be implemented in the future.

Additionally, understanding how organizations effectively managed stakeholder trust is a critical area that has been largely overlooked in the existing literature. Trust is an essential component of mental health care, particularly in times of crisis. As noted by Patel et al. (2022), telehealth adoption raised issues regarding privacy, security, and the accessibility of services, all of which have profound implications for patient trust and engagement. For organizations to maintain service continuity, they not only needed to adapt their delivery models but also had to maintain strong relationships with clients, staff, and external stakeholders such as insurers, regulators, and the communities they serve. The role of leadership in maintaining these relationships during times of crisis is central to ensuring long-term organizational resilience.

This study aims to fill these gaps by critically examining how leadership, change management strategies, and organizational adaptability contributed to resilience in mental health services during the pandemic. It will investigate the leadership practices that were implemented, how they facilitated adaptation to remote service models, and how they impacted organizational performance and stakeholder trust. The study will also explore the long-term implications of these adaptations, offering conceptual refinements and actionable strategies that can help mental health organizations better prepare for future crises. By examining the specific leadership competencies that allowed organizations to navigate the challenges posed by the COVID-19 pandemic, this study will provide valuable insights into how mental health organizations can become more resilient and better equipped to handle future disruptions.

SIGNIFICANCE OF THE PROJECT/PAPER

This study makes two significant contributions to the field of crisis management and mental health service delivery. Theoretically, it expands resilience research by examining how leadership and organizational adaptability influence mental health organizations' capacity to manage crises effectively. Existing literature on crisis management in mental health services has often focused on the immediate impact of disruptions, primarily documenting service interruptions or the challenges of moving to remote care models. However, this body of work typically overlooks the broader leadership dynamics that underlie the ability of organizations to adapt and recover in the face of prolonged disruptions. Specifically, studies have insufficiently explored how leadership, particularly transformational leadership, can build long-term organizational resilience. This paper addresses this gap by investigating the role of adaptive leadership and stakeholder engagement in sustaining operations during the COVID-19 pandemic, focusing on how these factors contribute to organizational resilience, recovery, and long-term adaptability.

Resilience in organizations, particularly in the mental health sector, is not just about surviving a crisis but about emerging stronger and better equipped for future challenges. Mental health organizations, which face unique challenges such as emotional exhaustion and resource scarcity, require adaptive leadership models that go beyond traditional command-and-control structures. Transformational leadership, with its focus on motivation, empowerment, and innovation, can be pivotal in helping organizations navigate these complex and emotionally charged environments. This study examines how transformational leadership practices—such as fostering a shared vision, promoting flexibility, and inspiring trust—are integral to crisis management and contribute to organizational resilience in the mental health field. By addressing this gap, this research offers a refined conceptual framework that links leadership, organizational adaptability, and resilience, providing new theoretical insights into how organizations can maintain continuity and sustain operations under crisis conditions.

The contribution of this study to resilience research is crucial because it moves beyond examining crisis impacts and explores how mental health organizations can build adaptive systems that withstand future shocks. Current models of resilience in mental health organizations largely focus on structural preparedness or financial stability but neglect the importance of leadership and the human elements that underlie organizational success. This research, by focusing on leadership dynamics, stakeholder engagement, and organizational culture, offers a new perspective on how mental health organizations can develop the capacity to thrive, not just survive, in the face of systemic disruptions.

On a practical level, this study provides mental health organizations with evidence-based strategies for maintaining service continuity during crises, particularly by leveraging transformational leadership and innovative service delivery models. The COVID-19 pandemic forced many organizations to quickly transition to virtual care, which not only changed how services were delivered but also highlighted leadership's importance in effectively guiding these transitions (Yates & Thomas, 2021). While telehealth and remote care have offered a valuable alternative to in-person consultations, the transition was not without its challenges. Mental health organizations were forced to quickly adapt their models of care to meet the rising demand for services, all while managing financial instability and protecting the well-being of staff. The ability of leadership to foster a sense of trust, guide change, and innovate quickly during these times was pivotal in the success of these organizations. This research will help mental health leaders understand how to foster a culture of innovation, enhance employee engagement, and maintain service delivery amidst operational challenges.

Further, this study provides actionable recommendations for how mental health organizations can prepare for future crises by embedding resilience into their organizational culture. For instance, organizations that embraced digital technologies and developed strong leadership capacity during the pandemic were better able to withstand its impact. Insights from Lee et al. (2023) and Smith et al. (2023) demonstrate that organizations with a strong digital infrastructure and adaptable leadership could better withstand the pandemic's impact. This is particularly relevant as we move into a future where crises be they health-related, environmental, or political are increasingly likely to disrupt service delivery across sectors. Mental health organizations must, therefore, integrate flexibility and adaptability into their service models to ensure they can continue providing critical care in the face of uncertainty.

Additionally, this paper offers a framework for leadership-driven resilience that can be applied across various mental health service settings. By examining the specific leadership competencies required for organizations to adapt during crises, the study offers practical guidance for mental health leaders to develop the necessary skills to lead during times of uncertainty. For example, transformational leadership can be a vital tool in times of crisis by helping to motivate staff, inspire a shared vision, and encourage adaptive responses. However, leaders must also be able to manage the emotional toll of crises on both staff and clients, emphasizing the need for trauma-informed leadership approaches that prioritize the well-being of all stakeholders.

The practical implications of this research are far-reaching. Mental health organizations, regardless of their size or structure, can apply the lessons learned during the pandemic to better prepare for future crises. This study emphasizes the importance of proactive leadership development programs, disaster preparedness plans, and flexible service delivery models that are capable of shifting quickly in response to changing circumstances. Furthermore, by focusing on stakeholder engagement and trust, this research highlights the critical role of maintaining strong relationships with clients, staff, and external partners, which can contribute to organizational stability and resilience during times of uncertainty.

In conclusion, the study not only contributes to the theoretical understanding of organizational resilience in mental health services but also provides practical recommendations for leaders in the field. By investigating how leadership dynamics, particularly transformational leadership, and stakeholder engagement influence resilience during crises, this research offers valuable insights into how mental health organizations can build adaptive, resilient systems that can thrive in the face of future disruptions. This work will be of great benefit to mental health leaders, policymakers, and researchers seeking to improve crisis preparedness and ensure the continuity of care for vulnerable populations during times of systemic upheaval.

THEORIES FROM THE LITERATURE

Transformational leadership theory emphasizes inspiration, innovation, and employee engagement, making it particularly relevant for guiding organizations through crises (Bass & Avolio, 1994). However, in the context of mental health organizations facing a crisis like the COVID-19 pandemic, this theory requires adaptation. While transformational leadership encourages empowerment and morale building, it must also address emotional exhaustion and burnout, which are prevalent in healthcare and mental health settings (Yücel, 2021). Mental health workers during a crisis experience high levels of stress, and traditional transformational leadership practices that focus solely on motivation may overlook the need for emotional and psychological support (Miller & Johnson, 2022). Furthermore, the rapid transition to remote care models in mental health organizations highlights the need for leaders to inspire and make quick, pragmatic decisions that reflect the immediate challenges of reduced resources and increased demand for services (Patel et al., 2022). This suggests that while transformational leadership offers important frameworks for supporting staff, it must evolve to incorporate crisis-specific competencies, such as trauma-informed care and resilience-building strategies (Smith et al., 2023).

Kotter's (1996) Eight-Step Change Management Model offers a structured approach for guiding organizations through transitions, particularly when uncertain. While this model provides a useful framework for understanding organizational change, its application in mental health settings under crisis conditions requires critical adjustments. Kotter's model assumes a level of organizational stability and planning often absent in crises. In mental health organizations during a crisis like the COVID-19 pandemic, the rapid pace of change and constant adaptation to external pressures (e.g., health restrictions and staffing shortages) necessitates more flexibility than Kotter's rigid framework allows (Harrison et al., 2022). The model's focus on creating a sense of urgency and establishing a guiding coalition is important. However, in the context of mental health, it must be coupled with trauma-informed strategies that address the emotional and psychological needs of both employees and patients (Bridges, 2023). A more flexible, iterative approach to change, one that allows for continuous feedback and adaptation, is essential for mental health organizations dealing with the evolving crisis of the pandemic (Creswell & Poth, 2018). Thus, while Kotter's model provides valuable guidance, it must be adapted to be more responsive and supportive of mental health organizations' unique emotional and operational challenges in crisis.

BACKGROUND INFORMATION / LITERATURE REVIEW

The COVID-19 pandemic caused widespread disruptions to healthcare services, particularly in the mental health sector. As the pandemic unfolded, many mental health organizations rapidly shifted to telehealth and remote service delivery models to maintain care continuity (Smith et al., 2023). While telehealth adoption effectively increased access to care, it introduced several challenges that impacted the efficacy of service delivery. A significant theme in the literature is the difficulty in building trust and rapport in virtual settings, as mental health professionals face challenges establishing therapeutic relationships without face-to-face interactions (Bell & Adams, 2022). These challenges were compounded by logistical barriers, such as limited access to technology, as some clients preferred in-person consultations (Harrison et al., 2022). Despite these hurdles, telehealth offers a valuable alternative, but its limitations underscore the importance of considering client preferences and technological access when designing future mental health services.

Another theme emerging from the literature is the financial instability that mental health organizations faced during the pandemic. Several studies document the significant revenue losses experienced by these organizations due to service disruptions (Greene et al., 2023). Patel et al. (2022) found that many mental health organizations experienced a decline in patient engagement, with some providers struggling to adapt to new care models. Insurance reimbursement challenges, particularly during the initial phases of the pandemic, exacerbated this financial strain (Smith et al., 2023). Mental health organizations, especially those reliant on in-person consultations, experienced sharp declines in revenue as services moved online, and reimbursements for virtual care were inconsistent and often insufficient (Lo et al., 2023). These findings emphasize the vulnerability of mental health organizations to revenue fluctuations caused by changes in service delivery models and highlight the need for long-term strategies to ensure financial sustainability.

The pandemic also triggered secondary stressors that significantly impacted the mental health of both clients and healthcare workers. Social isolation, financial instability, and occupational stress have been linked to increased mental health issues during the pandemic, particularly among vulnerable populations such as long-term care residents (Zheng et al., 2021; Venditti et al., 2023). These external stressors compounded the strain on mental health organizations, emphasizing the complexity of maintaining service delivery in a crisis. The increased demand for mental health services during the pandemic and financial and operational challenges placed organizations under immense pressure, requiring them to adapt quickly and efficiently. This multifaceted crisis underscored the need for mental health organizations to develop adaptive leadership strategies and organizational resilience to navigate future challenges.

However, while these studies provide valuable insights into the challenges faced by mental health organizations, they fail to explore how organizations fully managed change during the crisis. Much of the existing literature focuses on service disruptions and the shift to telehealth. However, it does not address how leadership and organizational culture facilitated or hindered the transition to new care models. Adaptive leadership and resilient organizational structures are critical during crises, yet few studies examine how these elements interact to support service continuity during the pandemic (Yates & Thomas, 2021). Furthermore, the integration of stakeholder trust and collaboration during the crisis remains underexplored. A notable gap in the literature is the lack of a comprehensive framework that connects leadership, organizational culture, and stakeholder engagement in mental health crises.

This review highlights that while studies have documented the financial and operational challenges mental health organizations face during the pandemic, there remains a significant gap in understanding how organizations adapted to these challenges. Understanding the interplay between leadership strategies, organizational culture, and stakeholder engagement is crucial for building resilience in mental health organizations. This paper addresses this gap by examining how leadership and organizational change strategies facilitated resilience during the COVID-19 crisis. It will also propose conceptual refinements and actionable strategies to inform future crisis preparedness, helping organizations navigate disruptions with greater adaptability and efficacy.

LEADERSHIP ASSESSMENT

Leadership plays a pivotal role in navigating challenges during crises. However, traditional leadership models, including transformational leadership, require adaptation to address a crisis's unique demands effectively. During systemic disruption, such as the COVID-19 pandemic, leaders must inspire and provide a vision and offer immediate, pragmatic support to maintain operational stability and employee well-being (Yücel, 2021). While transformational leadership is essential for fostering long-term engagement, it must be adjusted to prioritize emotional support and flexibility when immediate action is needed (Santoso et al., 2022).

Transformational leadership is traditionally associated with motivating employees, fostering creativity, and cultivating organizational commitment (Bass & Avolio, 1994). However, in times of crisis, the effectiveness of transformational leadership depends on the leader's ability to shift their focus from idealistic vision to real-time, responsive leadership that can manage resource scarcity, emotional exhaustion, and operational disruptions (Almohtaseb et al., 2021). Leaders must balance their inspirational role with a heightened focus on supporting their teams' mental and emotional needs (Yücel, 2021). This dual focus is critical in the mental health sector, where employees may be dealing with burnout while simultaneously striving to meet clients' increasing needs.

Additionally, the adaptability of transformational leadership is crucial in a crisis. While transformational leaders traditionally drive organizational change through a compelling vision, during a crisis, their role must extend to adjusting that vision to immediate realities. For instance, during the pandemic, leaders had to pivot quickly to remote work models, incorporating telehealth into their services. Effective transformational leadership in this context requires leaders to provide clear guidance, emotionally support their teams, and implement flexible work models (Moyo, 2019). Leadership during crises must focus on empowering employees to navigate new, often ambiguous, challenges while managing the psychological toll of the situation.

A study by Almohtaseb et al. (2021) highlights that organizations led by transformational leaders who foster an environment of support and collaboration are more resilient in the face of unexpected disruptions. This leadership style is fundamental in the mental health sector as it helps organizations maintain their focus on client care while simultaneously managing internal disruptions. Transformational leadership's emphasis on individualized attention and empowerment ensures that staff remain motivated, committed, and able to handle the multiple stresses caused by a crisis, such as increased client demands and personal emotional strain (Santoso et al., 2022). However, during a crisis, leaders also need to adjust their approach to offer more direct support and flexibility to their staff, balancing the emotional and operational needs of the organization.

CHANGE MANAGEMENT

Kotter's (1996) Eight-Step Change Model is widely regarded by many as a structured approach to leading organizational change. While effective in many settings, Kotter's model assumes stability and clear top-down managerial control, which may not apply in crises, particularly in nonprofit and mental health organizations under stress. In normal circumstances, the model's emphasis on creating a sense of urgency and driving change from the top down works effectively in organizations with a stable structure and clear leadership. However, during a crisis like the COVID-19 pandemic, these stability and hierarchical control assumptions become problematic. Mental health organizations, especially those working with vulnerable populations, must prioritize emotional safety, adaptability, and responsiveness over rigid, top-down processes (Kotter, 1996).

Change must be more flexible and decentralized in mental health organizations during a crisis. Kotter's model presumes leaders can drive change by formulating a vision and communicating it to the workforce in a controlled, linear process. However, in a crisis, change's rapid, unpredictable nature requires organizations to engage in adaptive management, where decision-making is shared and leadership is distributed (Helfrich et al., 2022). Mental health organizations must foster a culture of inclusivity, where staff at all levels contribute to the change process, especially in environments of uncertainty and emotional strain (Miller & Johnson, 2022). This shift towards a more decentralized approach helps build resilience among staff and enhances the organization's ability to adapt to shifting demands quickly.

Moreover, Kotter's model largely overlooks the emotional and psychological toll on staff during crises. Mental health organizations, in particular, require a trauma-informed approach to change management that prioritizes the well-being of employees, many of whom are dealing with their emotional exhaustion while also managing increased client needs. Emotional support and mental health care for staff must be integrated into the change process, ensuring that employees are supported and equipped to manage the stresses that accompany organizational change (Bell & Adams, 2022). Focusing on emotional safety and trauma-informed leadership is crucial in preventing burnout and maintaining staff engagement during periods of high stress (Yücel, 2021).

For change management in mental health organizations during crises, leaders must adapt Kotter's model to recognize the work's fluid, complex, and emotionally charged nature. This study proposes integrating flexible strategies that focus on collaboration, emotional support, and continuous feedback loops, allowing mental health organizations to remain agile and responsive to the evolving challenges posed by crises like the pandemic. Organizational leaders need to engage with their teams to foster trust, encourage input from all levels, and prioritize the emotional well-being of staff and clients (Santoso et al., 2022).

METHODOLOGY

Data collection is essential for understanding the challenges faced by mental health organizations during the pandemic. A comprehensive data collection strategy enables organizations to assess the crisis's operational and emotional impacts on service delivery, staff, and clients. This approach typically involves collecting quantitative data, such as financial trends, client satisfaction surveys, and employee feedback, alongside qualitative data obtained through interviews, focus groups, and case studies (Bryman, 2016; Creswell & Poth, 2018). Integrating quantitative and qualitative data in a mixed-method approach offers a richer, more nuanced understanding of the organizational challenges and client needs that emerged during the pandemic (Ivankova, Creswell, & Stick, 2006).

Quantitative data, such as revenue trends and client service utilization rates, allow mental health organizations to identify the scale of financial losses and service disruptions, providing actionable insights for immediate crisis management (Miller & Johnson, 2022). Meanwhile, qualitative data from interviews and focus groups help organizations capture employees' and clients' experiences, emotions, and needs, offering a deeper understanding of the impact on mental health and well-being during the pandemic (Saldana, 2021). This mixed-method approach enables organizations to develop targeted strategies that address financial instability and consider employee morale, patient care, and service delivery models. By triangulating both data types, mental health organizations can ensure their strategies are well-informed and holistic, ensuring long-term sustainability and improved service delivery outcomes (Creswell & Poth, 2018; Bryman, 2016).

During the COVID-19 pandemic, mental health organizations faced not only operational and financial challenges but also significant difficulties in conducting research due to the immediate nature of the crisis. Data collection processes were hindered by several factors, including social distancing measures, increased pressure on healthcare workers, and limitations in access to organizations due to lockdowns and restricted operations. These challenges made it difficult to engage with mental health organizations, as many were overwhelmed with the urgency of responding to the crisis and adjusting to remote care models.

Moreover, the ethical considerations related to data collection were particularly sensitive in the mental health sector during the pandemic. There were concerns about the emotional well-being of participants, including healthcare staff and clients, as they navigated increased stress, uncertainty, and mental health issues exacerbated by the pandemic. Ensuring the psychological safety of participants in interviews and focus groups became an essential part of the research design, requiring careful planning and flexibility to accommodate participants' emotional states and concerns about confidentiality.

In addition, logistical challenges emerged due to the transition to virtual platforms for data collection. Remote data gathering through online surveys and virtual interviews, while necessary, presented difficulties related to technology access and literacy, particularly among clients and staff in underserved communities. Furthermore, ensuring representative participation from different stakeholders, including clients, staff, and leadership, was more complex, as not all individuals had equal access to technology or could participate fully due to workload pressures or other barriers created by the pandemic.

A mixed-method approach, combining quantitative data such as financial trends, service utilization rates, and client satisfaction surveys with qualitative insights from interviews, focus groups, and case studies, helped mitigate these challenges. However, even within this approach, it was essential to adapt the research strategy to accommodate these constraints, prioritize the well-being of participants, and ensure that data collection procedures were sensitive to the emotional and psychological toll of the pandemic (Bryman, 2016; Creswell & Poth, 2018).

IMPLICATIONS AND RECOMMENDATIONS

The findings of this study underscore the urgent need for mental health organizations to adopt adaptive leadership practices to navigate crises effectively. Transformational leadership has emerged as a critical factor in driving organizational resilience during times of crisis. Leaders who inspire trust, communicate effectively, and foster innovation play a pivotal role in ensuring that employees remain aligned with the organization's mission (Bass & Avolio, 1994). The study found that organizations with transformational leaders were better able to adapt to the financial and operational disruptions caused by the COVID-19 pandemic. These findings highlight how transformational leadership directly contributed to organizational resilience, allowing these organizations to innovate, adjust to remote service models, and maintain staff morale despite operational disruptions.

Based on these findings, we recommend that mental health organizations prioritize leadership development programs that focus on transformational leadership. These programs should equip leaders with the skills to foster trust, encourage creativity, and maintain employee morale during uncertain times (Yücel, 2021; Santoso et al., 2022). Specifically, leaders should be trained to adapt their communication styles to ensure they engage employees effectively during crises. By focusing on clear, transparent communication, empathy, and responsiveness, transformational leaders can inspire resilience in their teams, enabling organizations to navigate future crises with greater agility and effectiveness.

Furthermore, the study highlights that financial instability remains a significant issue for many mental health organizations, particularly those reliant on traditional, in-person service delivery models. The COVID-19 pandemic exacerbated this issue, with many organizations facing substantial declines in patient visits and reimbursement challenges (Miller & Johnson, 2022; Greene et al., 2023). To address these challenges, we recommend that mental health organizations diversify their revenue streams. Expanding service offerings, exploring new funding opportunities, and establishing partnerships with schools, community organizations, and employers are essential strategies for maintaining financial viability. This diversification will help mental health organizations remain financially stable and continue to provide critical services during future disruptions. A more flexible approach to funding, such as seeking alternative revenue sources and reducing dependency on in-person consultations, will allow these organizations to maintain continuity of care despite fluctuating patient volumes.

The study also identifies employee engagement and work-life balance as critical factors for maintaining long-term sustainability in mental health organizations. Given the emotional and operational strain caused by crises, organizations need to support their staff with flexible work arrangements and mental health support programs. This recommendation is grounded in the theory of organizational commitment, which posits that leaders who prioritize employee well-being enhance engagement and productivity (Moyo, 2019). The findings suggest that mental health organizations that offer flexible scheduling and mental health resources experience higher levels of employee satisfaction and reduced burnout (Yates & Thomas, 2021; Sfantou et al., 2017). Implementing policies that promote work-life balance, such as offering remote work options, flexible hours, and mental health support services, will not only improve staff retention but also contribute to maintaining high-quality care for clients during times of crisis. These strategies are vital for ensuring that mental health organizations remain resilient, adaptable, and able to continue providing essential services under challenging circumstances.

CONCLUSION

This study reframes the resilience of mental health organizations during the COVID-19 pandemic, emphasizing the interplay between adaptive leadership, flexible organizational structures, and community trust. The pandemic not only exacerbated pre-existing mental health issues but also forced organizations to grapple with financial instability and operational disruptions (Smith et al., 2023; WHO, 2020). As a result, it became clear that traditional leadership models and rigid organizational structures are insufficient in responding to such crises. This research highlights the crucial role of transformational leadership, which fosters innovation, adaptability, and employee engagement during periods of uncertainty (Santoso et al., 2022). Transformational leaders empower their teams, encourage resilience, and inspire a culture capable of swift adaptation to changing circumstances (Yücel, 2021; Bass & Avolio, 1994).

Moreover, change management frameworks such as Kotter's Eight-Step Model provide essential guidance for organizations navigating transitions (Kotter, 1996). However, this study critiques Kotter's model for assuming organizational stability and top-down control. In times of crisis, particularly in mental health organizations, these assumptions may need adjustment to incorporate more decentralized, flexible, and trauma-informed strategies that prioritize emotional safety and rapid adaptation (Kotter, 1996). Mental health organizations must equip themselves to foster an environment of psychological safety while navigating financial and operational challenges.

The study also emphasizes the importance of data-driven decision-making through a mixed-methods approach, combining quantitative and qualitative data to guide crisis response (Bryman, 2016). Organizations can make informed decisions that address immediate operational needs and long-term resilience by continuously monitoring key performance indicators such as financial trends, patient volumes, and employee feedback.

The findings of this study offer significant contributions to the literature on mental health resilience, particularly by highlighting the adaptability of leadership and organizational culture under stress. Future research should explore how structural inequities impact organizational resilience and develop frameworks for equitable crisis response across different types of organizations. Further studies are needed to investigate how digital technologies and flexible service delivery models can support long-term sustainability and ensure equitable access to mental health care during crises (Greene et al., 2023). It will also be valuable to explore trauma-informed leadership approaches tailored to the unique needs of mental health organizations facing systemic disruptions (Pratt, 2023; Sfantou et al., 2017).

Ultimately, this research underscores that organizational culture and leadership flexibility are integral to mental health organizations' ability to survive and thrive during crises. The insights gained here can guide mental health leaders in preparing for future crises, ensuring they remain resilient and capable of providing essential care, no matter the circumstances.

RECOMMENDATIONS FOR FUTURE RESEARCH

1. Long-term Impact Assessment

Future research should investigate the lasting effects of the COVID-19 pandemic on mental health service delivery and organizational resilience. This includes assessing how mental health services have adapted over time, the long-term psychological effects of the pandemic on both employees and clients and the sustainability of remote service delivery models. Studies should explore workforce dynamics, including changes in employee roles, retention rates, and burnout levels (Zheng et al., 2021). Moreover, evaluating patient outcomes, such as treatment adherence and recovery rates post-pandemic, can provide valuable insights into how mental health organizations can better respond to prolonged crises. As noted by Patel et al. (2022), understanding the pandemic's long-term effects is essential for building resilience in healthcare systems and ensuring the continuity of care.

2. Technology Integration

The integration of digital technologies into mental health service delivery has accelerated during the pandemic, and further research is needed to explore its role in enhancing access to care and improving patient engagement beyond the pandemic. As telehealth and digital health platforms become more common, studies should examine their effectiveness in maintaining service quality, patient satisfaction, and outcomes (Bell & Adams, 2022). Research should also explore the barriers to technology adoption, such as digital literacy and infrastructure limitations, particularly in underserved communities (Smith et al., 2023). Furthermore, understanding the ethical implications of data security and patient privacy in digital care is crucial for future practice.

3. Equity and Access

Addressing disparities in access to mental health services is a critical area for future research. The pandemic has highlighted the gaps in mental healthcare accessibility, especially for underserved and vulnerable populations, including racial and ethnic minorities, low-income individuals, and those in rural areas (Samhsa, 2022). Research should investigate how policy reforms, telehealth expansion, and community-based initiatives can bridge these gaps. Additionally, exploring how social determinants of health (e.g., income, education, housing) intersect with mental health service access and outcomes is vital for ensuring equitable care (Patel et al., 2021). Future studies should also focus on measuring the effectiveness of outreach programs that engage hard-to-reach populations.

4. Crisis Preparedness

Research into crisis preparedness for mental health organizations is essential to ensure they equip themselves better to handle future global disruptions. This research should focus on developing frameworks integrating lessons from the COVID-19 pandemic into organizational policies and procedures. Studies should explore the effectiveness of disaster response plans, workforce training, and the use of technology in ensuring the continuity of care during crises. Additionally, research should assess the readiness of mental health systems to handle sudden increases in demand and rapidly adapt service delivery models. These insights would be especially useful in planning future pandemics or large-scale disasters (Helfrich et al., 2022).

5. Collaborative Care Models

Integrating mental health services with primary care and community resources has gained traction during the pandemic. Future research should explore the effectiveness of collaborative care models in improving patient outcomes and expanding access to comprehensive services. Studies should examine how mental health professionals, primary care providers, and social workers can work together to address the holistic needs of patients, particularly in underserved settings. Additionally, evaluating the barriers and facilitators to collaboration among these sectors, including communication, training, and organizational culture, is essential to optimizing care delivery (Davis et al., 2023). Future studies could also assess these integrated models' long-term sustainability and scalability in various healthcare settings.

REFERENCES

Almohtaseb, A., Aljohani, K., & Gabel, A. (2021). Transformational leadership and organizational resilience: Evidence from the mental health sector. *Journal of Leadership & Organizational Studies, 28*(1), 45–58. DOI: 10.1177/15480518211007217

Almohtaseb, N., Moyo, L., Santoso, N. R., & Pratama, B. P. (2021). Transformational leadership during the COVID-19 pandemic: Strengthening employee engagement through internal communication. *The Journal of Communication Inquiry, 47*(2), 67–82. DOI: 10.1177/01968599221095182

Bass, B. M., & Avolio, B. J. (1994). Transformational leadership and organizational culture. *International Journal of Public Administration, 17*(3–4), 541–554. DOI: 10.1080/01900699408524907

Bell, A., & Adams, S. (2022). Challenges and opportunities in virtual mental health care: A case study of telehealth implementation. *Journal of Mental Health Technology, 38*(2), 113–126. DOI: 10.1080/15332985.2022.2035093

Bridges, J. (2023, October 31). How to make a change management plan (templates included). *ProjectManager*. https://www.projectmanager.com/training/how-to-make-a-change-management-plan

Bryman, A. (2016). *Social research methods* (5th ed.). Oxford University Press.

Cameron, E., & Green, M. (2020). *Making sense of change management: A complete guide to the models, tools, and techniques of organizational change* (6th ed.). Kogan Page.

Centers for Disease Control and Prevention. (2023). Health workers face a mental health crisis. *Centers for Disease Control and Prevention*. https://www.cdc.gov/vitalsigns/health-worker-mental-health/index.html

Creswell, J. W., & Poth, C. N. (2018). *Qualitative inquiry and research design: Choosing among five approaches* (4th ed.). Sage Publications.

Davis, R., McCallum, S., & Jenkins, M. (2023). Collaborative care models in mental health: Challenges and opportunities in integrated service delivery. *Community Mental Health Journal, 59*(1), 75–89. DOI: 10.1007/s10597-023-01089-0

Greene, J., Hamilton, S., & Parker, R. (2023). Financial instability in mental health organizations during the COVID-19 pandemic. *Journal of Health Economics, 49*(1), 47–56. DOI: 10.1016/j.jhec.2023.01.005

Harrison, T., McLeod, J., & Watkins, P. (2022). Barriers to telehealth adoption in mental health care: A review of COVID-19 impacts. *Telemedicine Journal and e-Health, 28*(9), 1156–1163. DOI: 10.1089/tmj.2022.0128

Helfrich, C., Hwang, T., & Fisher, D. (2022). Crisis preparedness in mental health organizations: A framework for resilience. *Journal of Organizational Psychology, 35*(2), 112–124. DOI: 10.1016/j.jop.2022.02.004

Ivankova, N. V., Creswell, J. W., & Stick, S. L. (2006). Using mixed-methods sequential explanatory design: From theory to practice. *Field Methods, 18*(1), 3–20. DOI: 10.1177/1525822X05282260

Kotter, J. P. (1996). *Leading change*. Harvard Business Review Press.

Lee, S., & Kamradt, R. (2022). Integrating mental health into primary care: A review of models and outcomes. *Journal of Health Integration, 29*(6), 218–231. DOI: 10.1016/j.jhii.2023.02.015

Lo, H., Chen, W., & Zhang, L. (2023). Adapting to change: Mental health organizations and the shift to telehealth. *Mental Health Research Review, 12*(4), 223–235. DOI: 10.1016/j.mhrv.2023.04.003

Mayo, M. (2022). Untreated mental illness and its impact on public health: A review of economic, emotional, and societal costs. *Journal of Health Policy, 15*(2), 78–83.

Miller, A., & Johnson, M. (2022). Organizational change and crisis management: A review of frameworks in the healthcare sector. *Journal of Healthcare Management, 67*(3), 197–210. DOI: 10.1097/00115514-202207000-00006

Moyo, M. (2019). Leadership and innovation in times of crisis: The role of transformational leadership in the health sector. *International Journal of Healthcare Management, 23*(4), 305–318. DOI: 10.1080/123456789

Patel, A., Johnson, E., & Smith, K. (2022). Financial strains on mental health providers during the COVID-19 pandemic. *Healthcare Finance Review, 39*(1), 45–53. DOI: 10.1097/00115514-202207000-00006

Patel, V., Thornicroft, G., & Walker, R. (2021). Mental health disparities: Reducing the gap in access and outcomes for underserved populations. *American Journal of Public Health, 111*(2), 154–161. DOI: 10.2105/AJPH.2021.306512

Santoso, N. R., Sulistyaningtyas, I. D., & Pratama, B. P. (2022). Transformational leadership during the COVID-19 pandemic: Strengthening employee engagement through internal communication. *The Journal of Communication Inquiry*, 01968599221095182. Advance online publication. DOI: 10.1177/01968599221095182

Sfantou, D. F., Laliotis, A., Patelarou, A. E., Sifaki-Pistolla, D., Matalliotakis, M., & Patelarou, E. (2017). Importance of leadership style towards quality of care measures in healthcare settings: A systematic review. *Healthcare (Basel)*, *5*(4), 73. DOI: 10.3390/healthcare5040073 PMID: 29036901

Smith, K., Daniels, L., & Roberts, M. (2023). The rise of telehealth during the COVID-19 pandemic: Mental health perspectives. *Journal of Telemedicine and Telecare*, *29*(3), 168–175. DOI: 10.1177/1357633X20982595

Wang, Z., Chen, X., & Jiang, Y. (2022). Telehealth expansion during the COVID-19 pandemic: Impacts on mental health care. *Journal of Health Technology & Policy*, *28*(6), 120–133. DOI: 10.1080/00138020.2022.2035208

World Health Organization (WHO). (2020). *Mental health and COVID-19: Early evidence of the pandemic's impact*. Retrieved from https://www.who.int/news-room/feature-stories/detail/mental-health-and-covid-19

Yates, C., & Thomas, P. (2021). Mental health care during COVID-19: A review of global practices. *International Journal of Mental Health Care*, *30*(2), 78–88. DOI: 10.1111/inm.12356

Yücel, S. (2021). Transformational leadership in healthcare: An analysis of its impact on employee satisfaction and organizational performance. *Health Care Management Review*, *44*(2), 105–117. DOI: 10.1097/HMR.0000000000000304

Zheng, P., Zhan, X., & Liu, W. (2021). Mental health during the COVID-19 pandemic: A review of global trends. *Psychiatry Research*, *54*(1), 78–85.

Section 3
Cybersecurity, Cyber Intelligence, Cloud Security, Artificial Intelligence

Chapter 7
A Qualitative Analysis of Cybersecurity Partnerships in Underserved Communities

Allison Fullwood
https://orcid.org/0009-0000-6484-6396
Capitol Technology University, USA

Eugene J. Lewis
https://orcid.org/0000-0002-2956-0760
Capitol Technology University, USA

ABSTRACT

The potential for a diverse inclusive cybersecurity workforce has historically been plagued by a lack of cybersecurity partnerships in underserved communities. In today's ever-evolving world of cyber threats, a diverse workforce plays a crucial role in combating the complexity of these potential hazards. By having employees with a range of different perspectives and backgrounds, organizations can promote critical thinking and creativity in problem-solving. This paper uses an exploratory research method to explore the gaps that historically and currently highlight a lack of cybersecurity partnerships in underserved communities. The goal is to gain actionable and applied knowledge about how the inclusion of underserved communities in cyber-focused partnerships can positively impact organizations and the cybersecurity workforce as a whole.

DOI: 10.4018/979-8-3373-0482-3.ch007

INTRODUCTION

Organizations, governments, and academia need to seek cybersecurity partnerships in underserved communities to successfully create a robust diverse workforce equipped to handle the complexity of cyberattacks. In recent years, cyberattacks have been occurring in a steady incline, which emphasizes the change needed to thwart malicious cyber actors. According to Sultan (2019), individuals who come from underserved communities lack the appropriate knowledge and resources necessary for adequate cyber defensive and offensive techniques. The cybersecurity industry must learn effective strategies to include and empower underserved communities so they may have a strengthened position in the cyber realm. Rush and Landgraf (2023) define underserved communities as individuals who come from low-income backgrounds, first-generation, and minority groups. Finch et al. 's (2020) perspectives put value on the critical need for tailored practices that positively influence the future of cybersecurity professionals in diverse underserved communities. These influences correlate to the cybersecurity industry as cybersecurity organizations seek to elevate their defensive strategies by diversifying their workforce.

The importance of establishing a robust and successful organizational security posture by employing a diverse workforce is acknowledged by cybersecurity experts (Lyon, 2020). Therefore, further inquiry is needed to determine the pathway to create fruitful partnerships with underserved communities. Manuel and Karloff (2020) define a ‘diverse workforce’ as cultivating talent and promoting the full inclusion of excellence across the social spectrum. The factors include individuals who stem from various ethnic, religious, socioeconomic, and academic backgrounds (Manuel and Karloff, 2020). Lyon (2020) explained there is a notable workforce shortage of qualified and diverse cybersecurity professionals necessary to adequately fill cybersecurity roles and protect sensitive information. The primary issue derives from deep-rooted exclusions of underserved communities that lack access to resources and sufficient education and training (Pusey et al., 2016). The primary issue has a direct correlation to the continuous struggle of a lack of individuals and college graduates in the pipeline to fill the increasing cybersecurity workforce gap (Burrell and Nobles, 2018). Cyber actors and cyber threats are becoming increasingly dangerous and complex as technology continues to advance (Cabaj et al., 2018). Technology underpins almost every part of our society, and the world has become more internet-connected than ever, which furthers the need for more cyber professionals with diverse backgrounds and unique problem-solving skills to fill the workforce gap (Cabaj et al., 2018; Burrell, 2018). Meanwhile, there are a plethora of underserved communities full of individuals who remain untapped resources who could help fill the cybersecurity workforce gap with adequate resources, education, and training (Rush and Landgraf, 2023). Therefore, the cybersecurity industry must take the initiative by creating cybersecurity partnerships in underserved communities as a direct confrontation to utilizing untapped resources and creating a diverse and inclusive workforce.

In the context of the importance of cybersecurity in today's technology-driven society, it is critical to address the problem of worker diversity and inclusion. A diverse workforce not only improves an organization's capacity to fight against cyber threats, but it also improves creativity, critical thinking, and problem-solving within the field (Finch et al., 2020). Unfortunately, underprivileged communities, such as low-income persons, first-generation college students, and members of various ethnic groups, encounter several hurdles when attempting to enter the cybersecurity arena (Rush and Landgraf, 2023). The increasing frequency of cyberattacks emphasizes the importance of strengthening cybersecurity measures. The need for cybersecurity personnel is increasing as technology progresses and the globe becomes more interconnected through the internet (Cabaj et al., 2018). However, the scarcity of skilled candidates for these positions, together with the rising complexity of cyber threats, underscores the crucial need for diversity and inclusion in the cybersecurity workforce (Lyon, 2020).

To overcome the gap and unlock the latent potential of marginalized communities, cybersecurity partnerships targeted to their individual requirements are required (Burrell et al., 2015). The current strategy has the potential to result in the development of a varied and inclusive workforce capable of dealing with the ever-changing landscape of cyber threats. However, simply acknowledging the need for such collaborations is insufficient; organizations must actively execute strategies to make this vision a reality (Lyon, 2020). Through cybersecurity partnerships, organizations may not only recruit and retain diverse talent, but also supply these communities with the resources, education, and training they require (Finch et al., 2020). The cooperation can lead to a more inclusive organizational culture in which people from all walks of life can flourish and contribute to the cybersecurity area. Further, cybersecurity projects aimed at underprivileged populations must consider the particular issues they encounter. Challenges may include a lack of resources for cyber defense and offence, as well as economic inequities (Sultan, 2019). A thorough grasp of these difficulties and their underlying elements is required to build effective programs and initiatives. The knowledge may be used to build evidence-based solutions for bridging the cybersecurity workforce gap.

Focusing on these factors, the purpose of this research is to explore the vital topic of cybersecurity partnerships in marginalized areas. The paper aims to identify the barriers and possibilities in creating these collaborations and analyze their influence on the cybersecurity workforce by undertaking a detailed analysis. This study seeks to identify best practices and ideas for developing inclusive cybersecurity programs that are customized to marginalized populations. Acknowledgment of the need for creating a diverse and inclusive workforce by creating partnerships with underserved communities put forth by scholars and experts demonstrates growth, but as the workforce gap continues to increase, organizations will need to effectively implement strategies for fulfillment. These strategies include cybersecurity partnerships with the goal of focusing on underserved communities to (a) attract and retain a diverse workforce, (b) supply appropriate resources, education, and training, and (c) create a diverse, equitable, and inclusive culture (Lyons, 2022; Jordan, 2020).

PROBLEM STATEMENT

Underserved groups suffer an array of difficulties which make them more vulnerable to cyber-attacks, including poor income, minority origins, and restricted access to services. According to Khann et al. (2023), these difficulties extend beyond a lack of access to education and resources to include socioeconomic inequality and poor infrastructure. These communities' vulnerability extends well beyond simple internet connection; it also involves their capacity to grasp and protect against an ever-changing array of complex cyber threats (Tariq et al., 2023). The digital divide, a well-documented phenomenon, has implications which extend beyond internet access. It incorporates the ability to explore and guard against the ever-changing landscape of complex cyber threats (Chang et al., 2020). According to Renaud and Coles-Kemp's (2022) study findings, underserved populations frequently lack basic aspects necessary for successful cybersecurity defense, such as knowledge, education, and access to critical resources. The shortcoming puts them at a significant disadvantage when faced with the growing threat of cyberattacks (Tariq et al., 2023).

While the disadvantages marginalized communities confront are generally acknowledged, a significant gap persists in the development and execution of effective cybersecurity efforts customized to their specific requirements. Existing initiatives frequently fall short in cultural sensitivity, accessibility, and long-term commitment, exacerbating the situation (Alawida et al., 2020). The fragmented structure of present endeavors, the lack of standardized frameworks, and inadequate financial investment all contribute to the issue's continuance. This reinforces an inequitable and insecure cycle, leaving impoverished groups disproportionately susceptible to cyberattacks (He et al., 2021). Cremer et al. (2022) assert the scarceness of thorough research on cybersecurity measures customized to the unique requirements of impoverished areas presents a substantial difficulty in addressing their cybersecurity risks. While individual studies seek to emphasize specific issues confronting these communities, they frequently ignore the multiple cultural, educational, and economic elements which have a substantial impact on the success or failure of such programs (Mishra et al., 2022). The scarcity of thorough research impedes the creation of evidence-based policies and solutions targeted to the specific needs of marginalized areas.

The problem statement for this research consists of the following:

1. What cultural, educational, and economic factors influence the success or failure of cybersecurity partnerships in underserved communities?
2. How would cybersecurity partnerships in underserved communities benefit organizations in cyber intelligent markets?

NATURE AND SIGNIFICANCE OF THE STUDY

Strengthening our cybersecurity workforce requires diverse perspectives from diverse communities which represent America. Increasing the number of cybersecurity professionals in the pipeline from underserved communities is critical to the success of our nation (Finch et al., 2020). Diversifying in the field of STEM is widely agreed to be an important initiative. (Baker et. al., 2015) However, a lack of cybersecurity partnerships in underserved communities is an issue which affects the pipeline of individuals into the cybersecurity industry. Nkrumah and Scott (2022) point out the foundational inequalities rooted in limited access to quality education and resources within STEM fields. Morgan and Amerikaner (2018) postulate these inequities are exacerbated by the persistent issue of unequal funding allocation, which disproportionately affects schools in low-income areas and undermines the capacity to provide comprehensive STEM education. Individuals from underserved communities have fewer resources to gear toward cyber-defense and offensive capabilities (Sultan, 2019), which may cause a disproportionate lack of knowledge and consequences of cyberattacks. Research conducted by Sultan (2019) points out the unbalanced understanding of the online security landscape, highlighting the lack of knowledge of basic cybersecurity concepts. A notable lack of a viable targeted approach aimed at women and underrepresented minorities perpetuates a trend of wealth disparity (Holland, 2018; Vega, 2016).

As most local jurisdictions are challenged to maintain fiscal strength to fund local schools, Simms (2023) concludes majority-black jurisdictions have a unique burden due to legacy, contemporary racist and racialized policies, and racial capitalism. To address this issue, it is necessary to create partnerships specifically geared toward closing the gap between STEM and cybersecurity employees who come from underserved communities and those who come from middle-class and upper-class families. Mejias et al. (2018) point out the importance of partnerships, such as the Partnership for Early Engagement in Computer Science (PEECS) program, which focuses on creating a program which is geared toward teaching African American middle school students computer science using culturally relevant teaching methods and experiences. Comparably, Bicer et al. (2020) postulate Inclusive Stem High Schools (ISHSs), which are designed to increase the participation of under-represented students in STEM, are one of the most effective approaches for closing the achievement gap between students who come from underrepresented subpopulations and those who come from traditionally upper-class families. Carpenter (2023) postulates community colleges serve a large number of first-generation, low-income, returning adult, and/or racially minoritized students, which means they are poised to pave the way for a more diverse STEM workforce. Similarly, Historically Black University Colleges (HBCUs) are well-positioned to take a strong leadership role in the diversification of the computing workforce (Cain, 2022). A recent strategy has focused on the immersion of technical employees to teach computer science at minority-serving institutions (Cain, 2022). Cain (2022) postulates HBCUs already have a history of inclusive culture and achievement which make their environment a great place to facilitate partnerships with women, minorities, and individuals from underserved communities in the education and teaching of STEM and computing disciplines.

The lack of historical partnership between STEM/Cyber disciplines and underserved communities has led to an increase in awareness from the federal government. The federal government has recently started creating partnerships with third-party organizations, such as the Cyber Warrior Foundation, aimed at providing cybersecurity education, training, and career programs to assist underserved communities (National Initiative for Cybersecurity Careers and Studies, 2023). The Cyber Warrior Foundation partners with the Department of Homeland Security and the Cybersecurity and Infrastructure Security Agency (CISA) to bridge the technology skills and diversity gaps for people from underserved communities. Hampton-Marcell et al. (2023) point out the success of partnerships with Department of Energy laboratories, which are often located near large numbers of underserved communities and minority populations. Department of Energy laboratories partner with local chapters of the National Association for the Advancement of Colored People's (NAACP) Afro-Academic, Cultural, Technical, and Scientific Olympics (ACT-SO). These types of partnerships between government, third-party organizations, and underserved communities are necessary to bridge the cybersecurity workforce shortage gap and diversify the STEM and cybersecurity industry (Burrell et al., 2015).

Limited access to cybersecurity education and resources is a crucial factor which highlights the need for cybersecurity partnerships in marginalized communities. While there is a growing demand for cybersecurity specialists, people from marginalized communities sometimes lack the chances and resources to get the required skills and expertise. This educational mismatch exacerbates the field's scarcity of skilled specialists (Sultan, 2019). As a result, it is critical to form partnerships focused on offering accessible and culturally appropriate cybersecurity education. For individuals from disadvantaged neighborhoods, socioeconomic gaps in education and job prospects remain a substantial impediment. According to Holland (2018) and Vega (2016), there are not enough specific initiatives for women and marginalized minorities. These gaps are the outcome of historical and cultural causes which have resulted in uneven opportunities. Bridging this gap through collaborations that offer scholarships, mentorship, and training programs may result in more fair representation in the cybersecurity sector.

One issue which is sometimes forgotten is the need to raise awareness of the need for cybersecurity in marginalized areas. Many people may be unaware of the possible effects of cyber-attacks or the importance of cybersecurity in their life. According to Sultan (2019), a big issue is a lack of fundamental cybersecurity understanding and awareness. Collaborations with community leaders, local organizations, and schools may assist in increased awareness about the importance of cybersecurity and encourage more people to pursue employment in the industry. Engaging underprivileged youth in cybersecurity at a young age is critical for developing a long-term pipeline of experts. Programs such as the Partnership for Early Engagement in Computer Science (PEECS) and Inclusive Stem High Schools (ISHSs), as highlighted by Mejias et al. (2018) and Bicer et al. (2020), are admirable. They are committed to providing underprivileged children with relevant and meaningful educational experiences. By expanding such programs and developing new collaborations, underprivileged kids can be encouraged to seek jobs in cybersecurity.

Multifaceted strategies are required to address the various difficulties facing cybersecurity partnerships in marginalized areas. This strategy should include educational efforts, mentorship programs, scholarship opportunities, and training in cultural sensitivity. Government agencies, educational institutions, and cybersecurity organizations must work together to create a comprehensive framework which encourages diversity and inclusion in the area. The National Initiative for Cybersecurity Careers and Studies (2023) and the Cyber Warrior Foundation are both positive moves in this direction. Furthermore, Mejjas et al. (2018) state the necessity for cybersecurity partnerships in marginalized areas is clear in the context of escalating cyber risks and a qualified professional scarcity. According to their findings, expanding access to cybersecurity education, addressing socioeconomic disparities, raising community awareness, empowering underserved youth, and taking a comprehensive, multifaceted approach are all necessary for effectively tackling the problem of underrepresentation among underserved communities.

FINDING THE GAP IN THE RESEARCH

There is currently a significant lack of studies about cybersecurity partnerships in underprivileged communities. While studies illustrate the difficulties, they frequently fail to take into account the diverse cultural, educational, and economic elements which have a considerable impact on the success or failure of such programs. The current body of research frequently falls short of taking a comprehensive approach to this essential topic, impeding the development of evidence-based policies and successful program design. There is a significant gap in our knowledge of the intricacies involved in establishing effective cybersecurity collaborations with marginalized areas. This gap is defined by the lack of thorough studies which analyze the issues these communities confront. According to the Bureau of Labor Statistics (BLS) of the United States Department of Labor, Black or African American persons account for just around 3% of information security analysts in the United States (Morgan, 2016a). This figure shows this minority group is significantly underrepresented in the cybersecurity workforce. Women make up just 11% of the worldwide information security workforce, according to the BLS (Morgan, 2016b). The research reveals a significant gender disparity in the cybersecurity field, with women underrepresented. Furthermore, when compared to their peers in the larger computing workforce, women of color are substantially outnumbered. According to the National Association for Women and Information Technology (2017), women of color make up less than 10% of the computer workforce. This research highlights the intersecting barriers in which women of color face in the IT sector. In 2015, the Central Intelligence Agency (CIA) issued the Diversity in Leadership (CDL) study, which said a lack of diverse cybersecurity staff contributed to intelligence failures. According to the research, having more diverse leadership and an inclusive culture may contribute to enhanced innovation, better decision-making, and mission effectiveness (Overcoming Barriers to Advancement - Diversity in Leadership Study, 2015).

The statistics shown above demonstrates women, minorities, and people from marginalized communities are disproportionately underrepresented in the cybersecurity industry. This data highlights the need to address the industry's lack of diversity and inclusion. When considering the extra barriers these underrepresented groups experience in obtaining cybersecurity education, resources, and career prospects, the observed research gaps become even more essential (Sultan, 2019). To close this gap, a comprehensive and evidence-based strategy to develop effective cybersecurity partnerships in marginalized areas is required. This strategy would allow stakeholders to customize their efforts more effectively, ensuring cybersecurity partnerships are relevant, culturally sensitive, and responsive to the unique requirements of marginalized populations. Furthermore, statistical data may serve as a baseline against which future initiatives can be measured, assisting in the refinement and improvement of plans over time (Vespa et al., 2018). To successfully overcome this study gap, a detailed examination of the experiences and issues of various minority groups, such as African Americans, Hispanics, Asian Americans, and others, would be applicable. This could entail looking at cultural influences, socioeconomic gaps, and educational barriers which may be disproportionately affecting these communities (Manuel and Karloff, 2020; Lyon, 2020). A more comprehensive knowledge of the differences within the disadvantaged population would allow for targeted interventions which accommodate the individual requirements of each group.

THEORETICAL FRAMEWORK EXPLAINED

According to the expectancy theory, first introduced by Victor Vroom, people are driven to act when they feel their efforts will result in a desired outcome (Steele, 1964). This idea may be used to better understand why residents of underprivileged communities choose to work in cybersecurity. The perceived chance of success and the perceived value of cybersecurity occupations might be studied to see how they impact motivation (Kuhl, 2021). According to Gandini (2019), expectancy theory is a useful psychological paradigm for understanding the motivations, behaviors, and decision-making processes of people from disadvantaged groups in the context of cybersecurity jobs. According to this idea, people are motivated to make decisions and conduct acts depending on their expectations of the results of their activities (Steele, 1964). In the context of underserved areas, expectancy refers to individuals' opinions about the possibility of their efforts resulting in success in the sector (Kuhl, 2021). Individuals from underserved communities can assess if they have the requisite skills, educational resources, and support to pursue a career in cybersecurity. Their view of the likelihood of success in this subject might have a big influence on their drive to pursue it (Pekrun, 2019). Individuals are more likely to be inspired to follow this career path if they feel they have access to educational opportunities and resources which will provide them with the necessary cybersecurity skills (Kuhl, 2021). On the other side, if they see major impediments and lack confidence in their ability to overcome them, their chances of success are likely to be low, potentially giving rise to a lack of incentive to pursue a career in cybersecurity. Victor Vroom also identifies instrumentality as the notion that one's performance or effort will result in a desired consequence (Steele, 1964). This factor focuses on whether individuals feel their educational and training efforts will lead to genuine employment prospects in the sector in the context of cybersecurity for underprivileged populations (Mitchell & Knudsen, 1973; Pekrun, 2019). This may include questions about whether they will be able to find well-paying positions in the cybersecurity field after finishing their education and training (Kuhl, 2021). Individuals are more likely to be motivated to pursue this route if they believe funding cybersecurity education and training will immediately lead to employment prospects and financial stability (Mitchell & Knudsen, 1973; Kuhl, 2021). Alternatively, if individuals are unsure their efforts will produce the intended results owing to numerous impediments such as prejudice or a lack of work prospects, their motivation may diminish. Valence is another idea discussed by Victor Vroom, where valance is the value or desirability people place on the results of their activities (Mitchell & Knudsen, 1973). The concept of valence in cybersecurity involves an assessment of the perceived value of a career in cybersecurity and its benefits in the context of underprivileged populations. Financial stability, work security, and opportunities for professional growth and promotion may be among the benefits (Kuhl, 2021).

Process theory focuses on the cognitive processes and decision-making procedures people take while deciding on a professional route (Gandini, 2019). This theory can be useful in studying the decision-making processes of people from underprivileged communities who are considering jobs in cybersecurity (Milli et al., 2018). Process Theory provides a useful framework for understanding the decision-making processes of persons from underprivileged groups considering jobs in cybersecurity (Hagan et al., 2018) Process Theory can assist in highlighting the cognitive stages, motives, and barriers which influence their career decisions in this unique situation. According to Process Theory, the process of making career decisions is intentional and methodical (Milli et al., 2018). It starts with identifying prospective job alternatives, which may be impacted by variables such as field exposure, educational prospects, or personal preferences. Individuals analyze the numerous hurdles and facilitators they experience on their job path as they progress (Hagan et al., 2018). Financial restrictions, restricted access to educational resources, or fears about prejudice might all be barriers, while facilitators could include mentorship programs, scholarships, and the existence of a supportive community (Hagan et al., 2018). Potential cybersecurity professionals establish defined career objectives after recognizing the opportunities and assessing the difficulties (Corrandini, 2020). These goals involve identifying educational and training needs, as well as particular employment responsibilities they wish to pursue (Corrandini, 2020; Hagan et al., 2018). The last part of this decision-making process is weighing the advantages and disadvantages while taking into consideration personal circumstances, motives, and projected prospects in the cybersecurity industry (Corrandini, 2020). To utilize process theory successfully in the context of marginalized communities and cybersecurity, it is necessary to first understand the unique hurdles they confront. Financial restrictions, limited access to excellent education, prejudice and racism within the cybersecurity sector, and a lack of role models from comparable backgrounds are examples of these. (Cremer et al., 2022; Mishra et al., 2022) To overcome these challenges and assist marginalized community people in pursuing cybersecurity jobs, customized interventions and support systems must be implemented. Among the essential tools are scholarship programs, mentorship opportunities, educational outreach, and efforts encouraging diversity and inclusion in the sector (Mejias et al. 2018). Representational role models may be important sources of inspiration and encouragement for those experiencing comparable circumstances, providing direction and demonstrating achievement is possible (Mishra et al., 2022). Process Theory provides a systematic framework for understanding individuals' decision-making processes (Gandini, 2019). The use of process theory can help to influence the creation of more effective and focused measures to overcome the field's representation and participation gaps.

METHODOLOGY

The primary objective of this paper is to explore concepts of cybersecurity partnerships in underserved communities. To do so, a qualitative research exploratory approach is chosen as the methodology to provide data related to individuals' lived experiences. A complex problem exists in the lack of representation of cybersecurity partnerships aimed at underserved communities. The researcher will use a semi-structured constructivist focus group study. The researcher will conduct a survey study of nine individuals. The two questions from the problem statement will be asked to each participant along with three additional questions related to the study. Upon receiving all responses, the researcher will assess the themes and patterns to provide findings and results in the study.

The exploratory research methodology using focus groups is a research technique which exhibits a strong correlation to process theory, which views the world in terms of situations, events, people, and the processes that connect them (Mohr 1982; Maxwell, 1996). According to Maxwell (1996), the explanation of process theory primarily relies on how situations and events impact others. This approach is deeply rooted in comprehending the perspectives of underserved communities through their lived experiences (Lyon, 2020). The qualitative research method using focus groups is an effective way for researchers to explore a specific phenomenon deeply and determine the context, implementation, and outcomes of various decisions (Cronon, 2014; Lyon, 2020). The focus group essentially comprises five to twelve people who are interested in the topic and willing to participate constructively (Kruger, 1994; Robinson, 2002; Lazar et al., 2017). Homogenous groups of individuals with common backgrounds and experiences can promote discussion and provide viewpoints which represent a shared context (Lazar et al., 2017). By leveraging the focus group method, researchers can gather a range of opinions and insights which can be crucial for understanding complex issues.

The use of focus groups in exploratory research is closely aligned with process theory, which underscores the interconnectedness of situations, events, and people (Maxwell, 1996). Researchers gain valuable insights into the perspectives and experiences of underserved communities by comprehending how these factors impact one another. Focus groups allow for an in-depth examination of phenomena, taking into account context, implementation, and outcomes. To ensure productive discussions, scholars such as Lazar et al. (2017), Krueger (1994), and Robinson (2002) suggest smaller group sizes and selecting participants genuinely interested in making constructive contributions. Lazar et al. (2017) recommend homogeneous groups can facilitate discussion by providing shared context and experiences. Ultimately, these approaches promote inclusive dialogue and facilitate a comprehensive understanding of complex phenomena in research endeavors.

FINDINGS AND RESULTS

The findings and results from the focus group consist of qualitative exploratory research design responses. See Table 1. Survey Participants. Participants, Position Title, and Years of Service.

TABLE 1. Survey participants, position title, and years of service

PARTICIPANTS	POSITION TITLE	YEARS of SERVICE
Participant 1	Chief Operations Officer	15 Years
Participant 2	Project Director	2 Years
Participant 3	Chief of Critical and Emerging Technologies	20 Years
Participant 4	Computer Network Defense Analyst	5 Years
Participant 5	Forensic Analyst	14 Years
Participant 6	Computer Network Defense Analyst	15 Years
Participant 7	Cryptologic Intel Analyst	4 Years
Participant 8	Network Systems Engineer	6 Years
Participant 9	Computer Network Defense Analyst	15 Years

QUESTION 1:

(1) What cultural, educational, and economic factors influence the success or failure of cybersecurity partnerships in underserved communities? See Table 2. Success or Failure Influences of Cybersecurity Partnerships

TABLE 2. Success or failure influences of cybersecurity partnerships

Common Theme	Participant Similarities	Percentage of Concurrence with Data
Economic Barriers	Participant 1, 2, 4, 5, 8	The participants emphasize the lack of economic resources necessary for advanced education, training, or investment in cybersecurity infrastructure in underserved communities. Participants mention economic limitations hinder individuals' ability to access higher education and the resources needed to pursue careers in cybersecurity.
Educational Disparities	Participant 1, 2, 5, 7, 8	The participants stress how disparities in education, particularly in underserved communities, impact cybersecurity awareness, skills development, and access to opportunities within the industry. Participants highlight limited access to quality education prevents individuals from gaining the necessary knowledge and skills for cybersecurity careers.
Cultural Considerations	Participant 2-4, 9	Participants mention cultural factors playing a significant role in shaping perceptions and participation in cybersecurity partnerships. Building trust and relevance within the community is a highlighted theme. Participants also mention partnerships should involve community leaders and members in planning and execution to address the specific needs and challenges they face.
Visibility and Awareness	Participant 2, 4, 6, 7, 9	The lack of awareness of available cybersecurity partnerships due to limited visibility or funding constraints is a common theme. Participants mention increasing awareness and visibility of these opportunities is essential for fostering engagement and participation from community members.
Diversity and Representation	Participant 2, 4, 8	Prioritizing diversity and representation to ensure relevance and effectiveness within underserved communities is a theme found within responses. Participants state representation from individuals who share similar backgrounds can help foster trust and demonstrate the benefits of participation in cybersecurity partnerships.
Inclusive Planning and Execution	Participant 1, 9	Participants highlight successful partnerships require inclusive planning and execution, with input from the community to ensure initiatives meet their needs effectively. Participants mention community involvement is crucial for tailoring programs and resources to address specific challenges and barriers faced by underserved communities.

QUESTION 2:

(2) How would cybersecurity partnerships in underserved communities benefit organizations in cyber-intelligent markets? See Table 3. Benefits of Cybersecurity Partnerships

TABLE 3. Benefits of cybersecurity partnerships

Common Theme	Participant Similarities	Summary of Similarities
Diversity and Inclusion	Participant 1-9	All participants touch upon the importance of diversity and inclusion within cybersecurity partnerships in underserved communities. This includes the recognition of diverse backgrounds, experiences, and perspectives as valuable assets which contribute to innovation and problem-solving.
Access and Opportunity	Participant 1,2, 4,5, 7-9	Participants emphasize the importance of providing access and opportunities to underserved communities, particularly in terms of education, training, and employment within the cybersecurity sector. This includes addressing barriers such as unconscious biases and lack of resources.
Skill Development and Workforce Enhancement	Participant 2, 4-8	There is a consensus among participants on the potential for cybersecurity partnerships to enhance the skill development and workforce in underserved communities. Participants mention investing in education, training, and mentorship programs to cultivate a highly skilled workforce, which benefits both individuals and organizations.
Community Development and Socioeconomic Impact	Participant 2, 4, 5, 7, 8	Several participants highlight the broader impact of cybersecurity partnerships on community development and socioeconomic growth. Participants mention by providing resources and opportunities, these partnerships can empower individuals and communities to thrive economically and contribute positively to society.
Cybersecurity Industry Improvement	Participant 2-9	Participants acknowledge cybersecurity partnerships in underserved communities can help address existing challenges within the cybersecurity industry, such as the lack of diversity and talent shortages. By tapping into diverse talent pools and perspectives, organizations can enhance their effectiveness in addressing cybersecurity threats.
Innovation and Problem-Solving	Participant 1, 4, 6, 8	The diversity of backgrounds and perspectives brought by underserved communities is highlighted by participants and seen as essential for driving innovation and finding creative solutions to cybersecurity challenges. This diversity is viewed as a catalyst for generating new ideas and approaches within organizations.

THEMES AND PATTERNS

The participants' responses provide valuable information on the patterns and themes characterizing discussions surrounding the importance and value of cybersecurity partnerships in underserved communities (Atkins & Lawson, 2021; Payne et al., 2021). An important recurring theme which emerges from the responses is the importance of cybersecurity partnerships in underserved communities to promote diversity, equity, and inclusion within the cyber intelligence field (Atkins & Lawson, 2021). Another significant theme which arises is the potential for these partnerships to address the problem of diversity in the cybersecurity sector (Sultan,

2019; Cremer et al., 2022). Participants point out underserved communities offer a wealth of diverse backgrounds, experiences, and perspectives, which can foster innovation and creativity in organizations (Pusey, Gondree, & Peterson, 2016; Bicer, Lee, & Perihan, 2020; Payne et al., 2021). By tapping into this diverse pool of talent, organizations can benefit from a wider range of ideas and solutions, leading to increased innovation and competitiveness in the industry.

In addition, participants mention collaborations in cybersecurity are widely recognized as a pivotal means of addressing the systemic obstacles and subconscious prejudices which permeate the cyber intelligence domain (Sultan, 2019; Bicer, Lee, & Perihan, 2020; Cremer et al., 2022). Participants emphasize such partnerships offer a way for those who have been historically marginalized or underrepresented in the field to gain access and opportunities (Cremer et al., 2022; Renaud & Coles-Kemp, 2022). By promoting cooperation and sharing expertise in underserved communities, organizations can challenge prevailing norms and advance greater socioeconomic inclusivity, contributing to the creation of a more just workforce and industry landscape (Lyon, 2020; Mishra et al., 2022). Participants agree the advantages of cybersecurity collaborations go beyond organizational borders and have significant societal implications. Collaborators emphasize these partnerships can act as a driving force for community growth and empowerment (Payne et al., 2021; Jordan, 2022).

This is especially true for disadvantaged individuals who gain access to cybersecurity education, training, and career prospects (Pusey, Gondree, & Peterson, 2016; Payne et al., 2021). By investing in the aptitudes and abilities of individuals from underserved regions, organizations not only enhance their workforce but also contribute to the economic and social progress of these communities, resulting in a virtuous cycle of development and opportunity (Lyon, 2020; Bicer, Lee, & Perihan, 2020; Jordan, 2022). The establishment of cybersecurity partnerships is viewed by participants as a strategic solution to tackle workforce shortages and bolster organizational resilience (Finch et al., 2020; Atkins & Lawson, 2021). Participants have observed that by broadening their recruitment efforts to include underserved communities, businesses can tap into a diverse talent pool with distinct skills and perspectives which are advantageous in dealing with intricate cybersecurity issues. This diversification of the workforce not only fosters greater creativity and problem-solving capabilities but also fortifies overall cybersecurity resilience by integrating a wider array of insights and approaches to counter threats (Cremer et al., 2022; Mishra et al., 2022). Participants highlight cybersecurity partnerships have the power to bring about transformation, specifically in terms of creating a culture of inclusion and belonging within the industry (Atkins & Lawson, 2021; Payne et al., 2021). By proactively reaching out to underserved communities and offering career advancement opportunities in cybersecurity, organizations can foster an inclusive environment which recognizes the value of diversity and promotes equal opportunities for everyone (Sultan, 2019). Through the implementation of targeted education, training, and mentorship programs, these partnerships can empower individuals from different backgrounds to pursue fulfilling careers in cybersecurity, ultimately leading to a more dynamic and sustainable industry overall.

FUTURE RESEARCH ON THE SUBJECT

Future research on the utilization of what to expect as scholars, researchers, and practitioners in analyzing cybersecurity partnerships in underserved communities holds significant promise for advancing both theoretical understanding and practical applications in this critical area (Burrell, 2018; Chang et al., 2020; Atkins & Lawson, 2021). Expectancy Theory, which posits individuals motivated to act based on their expectations of achieving desired outcomes, provides a robust framework for examining the dynamics of partnerships in cybersecurity contexts, especially within underserved communities where unique challenges and opportunities exist (Pekrun, 2019; Atkins & Lawson, 2021; Kuhl, 2021; Payne et al., 2021).

One avenue for future research involves conducting comprehensive case studies across diverse underserved communities to explore how different factors such as trust, perceived capability, and resource availability influence the formation, success, and sustainability of cybersecurity partnerships (Chang et al., 2020; Atkins & Lawson, 2021). By examining these factors through the lens of Expectancy Theory, researchers can elucidate how stakeholders within these communities perceive the benefits of engaging in cybersecurity partnerships, what barriers they perceive, and how these perceptions influence their willingness to collaborate (Atkins & Lawson, 2021; Kuhl, 2021).

Additionally, future studies could focus on developing and validating measurement tools tailored to assessing expectancy-related factors in cybersecurity partnerships specifically within underserved communities (Atkins & Lawson, 2021; Jordan, 2022). The determinants could include scales to measure perceived partner competence, the clarity of partnership goals, and the alignment of partnership outcomes with community needs and expectations (Finch et al., 2020; Atkins & Lawson, 2021; Lyon, 2020). Such tools would not only aid in empirical research but also provide practical guidance for practitioners seeking to foster effective cybersecurity partnerships in diverse community settings (Pekrun, 2019; Atkins & Lawson, 2021; Renaud & Coles-Kemp, 2022).

Furthermore, longitudinal studies could track the evolution of cybersecurity partnerships over time within underserved communities, examining how initial expectations and motivations evolve in response to changing external threats, internal capacities, and community dynamics (Pekrun, 2019; Chang et al., 2020; Lyon, 2020). Such research would contribute valuable insights into the adaptive capabilities of cybersecurity partnerships and the resilience of underserved communities in the face of evolving cyber threats (Finch et al., 2020; Atkins & Lawson, 2021; Jordan, 2022). Overall, future research utilizing Expectancy Theory to analyze cybersecurity partnerships in underserved communities holds the potential to deepen our understanding of effective partnership dynamics, inform policy and practice recommendations, and ultimately enhance cybersecurity resilience and capacity building in vulnerable populations (Finch et al., 2020; Kuhl, 2021; Payne et al., 2021).

CONCLUSION

In analyzing Cybersecurity Partnerships in underserved communities through the lens of Expectancy Theory, we arrive at the conclusion that these partnerships can be significantly enhanced by aligning stakeholders' expectations with the anticipated outcomes of their collaborative efforts (Sultan, 2019; Finch et al., 2020; Atkins & Lawson, 2021; Kuhl, 2021). Expectancy Theory, which posits that individuals are motivated to act based on their expectations of desired rewards and the likelihood of achieving them, underscores the importance of clearly defined goals and perceived benefits in these partnerships (Jordan, 2022; Chang et al., 2020; Atkins & Lawson, 2021). For cybersecurity initiatives in underserved areas, it is crucial that all parties—whether they are community members, local organizations, or external partners—understand and believe in the tangible benefits of their involvement, such as improved security, skill development, and community resilience (Pusey, Gondree, & Peterson, 2016; Pekrun, 2019; Chang et al., 2020; Lyon, 2020). By setting realistic, achievable goals and ensuring that all stakeholders perceive a high probability of success and personal or communal gain, these partnerships can foster greater engagement and effectiveness (Payne et al., 2021; Jordan, 2022). Thus, the successful implementation of cybersecurity initiatives in these communities' hinges on managing expectations and demonstrating clear, mutually beneficial outcomes, ensuring that all involved are motivated to contribute to and sustain the effort (Renaud & Coles-Kemp, 2022).

Cybersecurity partnerships in underserved communities constitute a critical mechanism for addressing the workforce deficit, fostering diversity, and fortifying national cyber resilience (Finch et al., 2020; Lyon, 2020). The findings of this study underscore the imperative for strategic, interdisciplinary collaboration among industry leaders, policymakers, and community organizations to ensure the efficacy and sustainability of these initiatives (Burrell & Nobles, 2018; Rush & Landgraf, 2023). This section delineates actionable recommendations that practitioners and decision-makers can implement to enhance cybersecurity workforce development and promote inclusive participation within the field. To optimize the impact of cybersecurity partnerships, organizations must implement targeted recruitment and training initiatives that mitigate economic and educational disparities (Sultan, 2019). Establishing scholarship programs, mentorship frameworks, and structured workforce development pipelines will facilitate equitable access to cybersecurity career opportunities (Mejias et al., 2018). Concurrently, policymakers must advocate for increased financial allocations to educational institutions serving underrepresented demographics, ensuring these institutions are adequately resourced to deliver rigorous cybersecurity curricula and professional training (Morgan & Amerikaner, 2018; Nkrumah & Scott, 2022). A pivotal recommendation emerging from this research is the expansion of early cybersecurity education. Introducing students in underserved communities to cybersecurity principles at a formative stage cultivates sustained engagement and prepares them for future professional pathways (Bicer et al., 2020; Mejias et al., 2018). Collaborations with local educational institutions, community colleges, and Historically Black Colleges and Universities (HBCUs) should be leveraged to develop specialized coursework, internship opportunities, and apprenticeship programs (Cain, 2022). Furthermore, industry stakeholders must align academic curricula with evolving cybersecurity demands to ensure graduates possess industry-relevant competencies (Jordan, 2022; Payne et al., 2021). Ensuring the long-term viability of cybersecurity partnerships necessitates the adoption of inclusive hiring frameworks that dismantle barriers for underrepresented groups (Manuel & Karloff, 2020). Organizations must institutionalize bias-mitigating recruitment strategies—such as anonymized resume evaluations and diversified hiring panels—to enhance equitable talent acquisition (McGee, 2018). Additionally, implementing structured career advancement programs, executive leadership training, and mentorship networks will facilitate the retention and upward mobility of diverse professionals within cybersecurity organizations (Burrell, 2018; Jordan, 2022). These initiatives can help close gaps in leadership representation and provide a clearer pathway for professional growth, fostering a more inclusive industry. Community engagement represents a cornerstone of sustainable cybersecurity partnerships (Lazar et al., 2017). Organizations must engage directly with community stakeholders to ascertain localized challenges and co-develop tailored cybersecurity initiatives (Sultan, 2019). Establishing cybersecurity literacy campaigns, conducting public outreach workshops, and creating accessible training modules will enhance digital fluency and incentivize participation in cybersecurity career trajectories (Finch et al., 2020; Renaud & Coles-Kemp, 2022). Furthermore, financial assistance mechanisms—including grants, fellowships, and targeted scholarships—should be institutionalized to mitigate economic barriers and enhance workforce representation from historically marginalized communities (Holland, 2016; Vega, 2016).

Without financial support structures, many aspiring cybersecurity professionals from underserved backgrounds may struggle to enter and persist in the field. From a policy perspective, governmental agencies and industry leaders must coalesce to formulate standardized, equity-centered frameworks for cybersecurity partnerships (Atkins & Lawson, 2021; Santos et al., 2020). Establishing explicit diversity and inclusion benchmarks, monitoring progress through empirical metrics, and instituting accountability mechanisms will ensure that these initiatives yield substantive, long-term impact (Cremer et al., 2022; Mishra et al., 2022). Legislative advocacy should prioritize cybersecurity education within underserved populations, fostering systemic investment in talent development and workforce sustainability (National Initiative for Cybersecurity Careers and Studies, 2023). This commitment will contribute to closing the digital divide while simultaneously strengthening national security infrastructure.

The findings of this study affirm that cybersecurity partnerships in underserved communities serve as a catalyst for diversifying the workforce, bolstering national cyber defense, and enhancing economic mobility (Gonzalez & Kuenzi, 2014; Walton et al., 2021). By implementing these empirically grounded recommendations, organizations, policymakers, and community leaders can cultivate a more inclusive cybersecurity ecosystem, ensuring equitable opportunities for historically underrepresented groups. These strategic efforts will not only address the cybersecurity workforce gap but also drive systemic transformation, fostering an innovative, resilient, and adaptive cybersecurity infrastructure for the future (Pusey et al., 2016; Payne et al., 2021). The broader implications extend beyond workforce development, influencing policy, economic mobility, and digital equity in a rapidly evolving technological landscape.

REFERENCES

Alawida, M., Omolara, A. E., Abiodun, O. I., & Al-Rajab, M. (2022). A deeper look into cybersecurity issues in the wake of Covid-19: A survey. *Journal of King Saud University-Computer and Information Sciences*.

Atkins, S., & Lawson, C. (2021). Cooperation amidst competition: Cybersecurity partnership in the US financial services sector. *Journal of Cybersecurity*, *7*(1), tyab024. DOI: 10.1093/cybsec/tyab024

Baker, D., & Ellis, L. (2021). Future directions in digital information: scenarios and themes. In *Future Directions in Digital Information* (pp. 1–15). Chandos Publishing. DOI: 10.1016/B978-0-12-822144-0.00001-X

Bicer, A., Lee, Y., & Perihan, C. (2020). Inclusive STEM High School Factors Influencing Ethnic Minority Students' STEM Preparation. *Journal of Ethnic and Cultural Studies*, *7*(2), 147–172. https://www.jstor.org/stable/48710088. DOI: 10.29333/ejecs/384

Burrell, D. (2018). An Exploration of the Cybersecurity Workforce Shortage. *International Journal of Hyperconnectivity and the Internet of Things*, *2*(1), 29–41. DOI: 10.4018/IJHIoT.2018010103

Burrell, D. N., & Nobles, C. (2018). *Recommendations to Develop and Hire More Highly Qualified Women and Minorities Cybersecurity Professionals*. Academic Conferences International Limited.

Cain, C. C. (2022). A Shifting Research Agenda: Historically Black Colleges and Universities Must Prepare Students for Careers in Computing, Informatics, and Engineering. *Journal of Information Systems Education*, *33*(1), 41–50.

Carpenter, M. L. (2023). Retaining Racially Minoritized Students in Community College STEM Program. University of Southern California ProQuest Dissertations Publishing, 5-6.

Chang, B. L., Bakken, S., Brown, S. S., Houston, T. K., Kreps, G. L., Kukafka, R., Safran, C., & Stavri, P. Z. (2020). Bridging the digital divide: Reaching vulnerable populations. *Journal of the American Medical Informatics Association : JAMIA*, *11*(6), 448–457. DOI: 10.1197/jamia.M1535 PMID: 15299002

Cremer, F., Sheehan, B., Fortmann, M., Kia, A. N., Mullins, M., Murphy, F., & Materne, S. (2022). Cyber risk and cybersecurity: A systematic review of data availability. *The Geneva Papers on Risk and Insurance. Issues and Practice*, *47*(3), 698–736. DOI: 10.1057/s41288-022-00266-6 PMID: 35194352

Federal Grant: Cybersecurity Workforce Development and Training for Underserved Communities. (2023). US Fed News Service, Including US State News https://www.proquest.com/wire-feeds/federal-grant-cybersecurity-workforce-development/docview/2810047917/se-2

Finch, A., Burrell, D. N., Lu, S., Dawson, M., Springs, D., Bilberry, K., Anderson, D. P., & Modeste, R. (2020). Cybersecurity workforce development in minority, low income, and native American reservation communities. [IJSEUS]. *International Journal of Smart Education and Urban Society*, *11*(4), 35–52. DOI: 10.4018/IJSEUS.2020100103

Gandini, A. (2019). Labour process theory and the gig economy. *Human Relations*, *72*(6), 1039–1056. DOI: 10.1177/0018726718790002

Gonzalez, H. B., & Kuenzi, J. J. (2014). Science, technology, engineering, and mathematics (STEM) education. *PRiMER: Peer-Reviewed Reports in Medical Education Research.*

Hagan, J., McCarthy, B., Herda, D., & Cann Chandrasekher, A. (2018). Dual-process theory of racial isolation, legal cynicism, and reported crime. *Proceedings of the National Academy of Sciences of the United States of America*, *115*(28), 7190–7199. DOI: 10.1073/pnas.1722210115 PMID: 29987006

Hampton-Marcell, J., Bryson, T., Larson, J., Childers, T., Pasero, S., Watkins, C., Reed, T., Flucas-Payton, D., & Papka, M. E. (2023). Leveraging national laboratories to increase Black representation in STEM: Recommendations within the Department of Energy. *International Journal of STEM Education*, *10*(1), 4. DOI: 10.1186/s40594-022-00394-4

He, Y., Aliyu, A., Evans, M., & Luo, C. (2021). Health care cybersecurity challenges and solutions under the climate of COVID-19: Scoping review. *Journal of Medical Internet Research*, *23*(4), e21747. DOI: 10.2196/21747 PMID: 33764885

Holland, J. (2016). The Average Black Family Would Need 228 Years to Build the Wealth of a White Family Today. The Nation Journal. Retrieved from https://www.thenation.com/article/the-average-black-family-wouldneed-228-years-to-build-the-wealth-of-a-white-family-today

Jordan, C. A. (2022). Exploring the Cybersecurity Skills Gap: A Qualitative Study of Recruitment and Retention from a Human Resource Management Perspective (Order No. 29320493). Available from ProQuest Central; ProQuest Dissertations & Theses Global; ProQuest One Academic; Publicly Available Content Database. (2706752761). https://www.proquest.com/dissertations-theses/exploring-cybersecurity-skills-gap-qualitative/docview/2706752761/se-2

Khan, N. F., Ikram, N., & Saleem, S. (2023). Effects of socioeconomic and digital inequalities on cybersecurity in a developing country. *Security Journal*, •••, 1–31. PMID: 40478949

Kuhl, J. (2021). The expectancy-value approach within the theory of social motivation: Elaborations, extensions, critique. *Expectations and actions*, 125-160.

Lyon, V. (2020). Exploring Strategies for Recruiting and Retaining Diverse Cybersecurity Professionals (Order No. 27738274). Available from ProQuest Dissertations & Theses Global; ProQuest One Academic. (2378121182). https://www.proquest.com/dissertations-theses/exploring-strategies-recruiting-retaining-diverse/docview/2378121182/se-2

Manuel, B. A., & Karloff, D. B. (2020). Recruit and retain a diverse workforce. *Nature Reviews. Chemistry*, *4*(9), 435–437. DOI: 10.1038/s41570-020-0214-z PMID: 37127964

McGee, K. (2018). The influence of gender, and race/ethnicity on advancement in information technology (IT). *Information and Organization*, *28*(1), 1–36. DOI: 10.1016/j.infoandorg.2017.12.001

Mejias, M., Jean-Pierre, K., Anderson, K., Washington, G., Burge, L., & Washington, A. N. (2018). The Partnership for Early Engagement in Computer Science (PEECS) Program: Facilitating the Diversification of DC's Tech Workforce. In Proceedings of the International Conference on Frontiers in Education: Computer Science and Computer Engineering (FECS) (pp. 141-145). The Steering Committee of The World Congress in Computer Science, Computer Engineering and Applied Computing (WorldComp).

Milli, S., Lieder, F., & Griffiths, T. L. (2021). A rational reinterpretation of dual-process theories. *Cognition*, *217*, 104881. DOI: 10.1016/j.cognition.2021.104881 PMID: 34536658

Mishra, A., Alzoubi, Y. I., Anwar, M. J., & Gill, A. Q. (2022). Attributes impacting cybersecurity policy development: An evidence from seven nations. *Computers & Security*, *120*, 102820. DOI: 10.1016/j.cose.2022.102820

Mitchell, T. R., & Knudsen, B. W. (1973). Instrumentality theory predictions of students' attitudes towards business and their choice of business as an occupation. Academy of Management Journal (Pre-1986), 16(1), 41. https://www.proquest.com/scholarly-journals/instrumentality-theory-predictions-students/docview/229490746/se-2

Morgan, I., & Amerikaner, A. (2018). Funding Gaps 2018: An Analysis of School Funding Equity Across the U.S. Education Trust. Retrieved from https://edtrust.org/resource/funding-gaps-2018/

Morgan, S. (2016a, April, 7). African Americans Underrepresented In The Cybersecurity Field. Forbes. https://www.forbes.com/sites/stevemorgan/2016/04/07/african-americans-underrepresented-in-the-cybersecurity-field/?sh=58ea932115c9

Morgan, S. (2016b, March 28). Calling All Women: The Cybersecurity Field Needs You And There's A Million Jobs Waiting. Forbes. https://www.forbes.com/sites/stevemorgan/2016/03/28/calling-all-women-the-cybersecurity-field-. needs-you/#2470db2a381c

National Initiative for Cybersecurity Careers and Studies. (2023). Cybersecurity for underserved communities. https://niccs.cisa.gov/workforce-development/cybersecurity-underserved-communities

Nkrumah, T., & Scott, K. A. (2022). Mentoring in STEM higher education: A synthesis of the literature to (re)present the excluded women of color. *International Journal of STEM Education*, *9*(1), 50. Advance online publication. DOI: 10.1186/s40594-022-00367-7 PMID: 35919282

Payne, B. K., Mayes, L., Paredes, T., Smith, E., Wu, H., & Xin, C. (2021). Applying High Impact Practices in an Interdisciplinary Cybersecurity Program. *Journal of Cybersecurity Education, Research and Practice, 2020*(2).

Pekrun, R. (2019). Expectancy–value theory of anxiety: Overview and implications. *Anxiety*, •••, 23–42.

Pusey, P., Gondree, M., & Peterson, Z. (2016). The Outcomes of Cybersecurity Competitions and Implications for Underrepresented Populations. *IEEE Security and Privacy*, *14*(6), 90–95. DOI: 10.1109/MSP.2016.119

Renaud, K., & Coles-Kemp, L. (2022). Accessible and inclusive cyber security: A nuanced and complex challenge. *SN Computer Science*, *3*(5), 346. DOI: 10.1007/s42979-022-01239-1 PMID: 35755325

Rush, L. M., & Landgraf, K. B. (2023). High Impact Practices in Underserved Communities: Linking Open Educational Resources and Local Non-Profit in Business Communications Course Design. *Journal of Higher Education Theory and Practice*, *23*(8), 53–64. https://www.proquest.com/scholarly-journals/high-impact-practices-underserved-communities/docview/2821424061/se-2

Santos, D., Santos, D., Goel, S., Costanzo, J., Sagen, D., & Buddelmeyer, P. (2020). *A roadmap for successful regional alliances and multistakeholder partnerships to build the cybersecurity workforce*. US Department of Commerce, National Institute of Standards and Technology. DOI: 10.6028/NIST.IR.8287

Simms, A. (2023). Fiscal Fragility in Black Middle-Class Suburbia and Consequences for K–12 Schools and Other Public Services. *The Russell Sage Foundation Journal of the Social Sciences : RSF*, *9*(2), 204–225. DOI: 10.7758/RSF.2023.9.2.09

Steele, F. I. (1964). Work and Motivation by Victor H. Vroom. IMR; Industrial Management Review (Pre-1986), 6(1), 106. https://www.proquest.com/scholarly-journals/work-motivation-victor-h-vroom/docview/214194732/se-2

Sultan, A. H. M. A. D. (2019). Improving Cybersecurity Awareness in Underserved Populations. Center for Long Term Cybersecurity, UC Berkely. https://cltc. berkeley.edu/wpcontent/uploads/2019/04/CLTC_Underserved_Populations. Pdf.

Tariq, U., Ahmed, I., Bashir, A. K., & Shaukat, K. (2023). A Critical Cybersecurity Analysis and Future Research Directions for the Internet of Things: A Comprehensive Review. *Sensors (Basel)*, *23*(8), 4117. DOI: 10.3390/s23084117 PMID: 37112457

Vega, T. (2016). Blacks Will Take Hundreds of Years to Catch Up to White Wealth. https://money.cnn.com/2016/08/09/news/economy/blacks-white-wealth-gap/index.html

Vespa, J., Armstrong, D. M., & Medina, L. (2018). *Demographic turning points for the United States: Population projections for 2020 to 2060*. US Department of Commerce, Economics and Statistics Administration, US Census Bureau.

Walton, S., Wheeler, P. R., Zhang, Y., & Zhao, X. (2021). An integrative review and analysis of cybersecurity research: Current state and future directions. *Journal of Information Systems*, *35*(1), 155–186. DOI: 10.2308/ISYS-19-033

Chapter 8
Cloud-Driven Public Safety in Smart Cities:
Transforming Security and Overcoming Challenges

Saksham Sharma
School of Computer Engineering, Kalinga Institute of Industrial Technology (KIIT), Bhubaneswar-751024, Odisha, India

Sidhant Mishra
https://orcid.org/0009-0003-6920-5530
School of Computer Engineering, Kalinga Institute of Industrial Technology (KIIT), Bhubaneswar-751024, Odisha, India

Ravi Raj Shrivastava
https://orcid.org/0009-0004-3177-767X
School of Computer Engineering, Kalinga Institute of Industrial Technology (KIIT), Bhubaneswar-751024, Odisha, India

Kaustubh Srivastava
School of Computer Engineering, Kalinga Institute of Industrial Technology (KIIT), Bhubaneswar-751024, Odisha, India

Aashish Sahu
https://orcid.org/0009-0007-2585-5792
School of Computer Engineering, Kalinga Institute of Industrial Technology (KIIT), Bhubaneswar-751024, Odisha, India

Hitesh Mohapatra
https://orcid.org/0000-0001-8100-4860
School of Computer Engineering, Kalinga Institute of Industrial Technology (KIIT), Bhubaneswar-751024, Odisha, India

ABSTRACT

Cloud computing in smart cities has gradually transformed public security and emergency management. This report reviews the importance of cloud enabled safety systems with bonus details on IoT, big data, AI, and mobile technology. These benefits include; able to predict, and prevent crimes, quick and effective response to incidences, sharing of information, and citizens' participation in safety apps. However,

DOI: 10.4018/979-8-3373-0482-3.ch008

issues such as data privacy, artificial intelligence preconceptions, the digital divide, and cybersecurity issues are also explored. Both, Dubai and Singapore's cases are viable examples can be used here. The dependence on technology for smart cities; ethical innovation, and public involvement for safe, equal and resilient smart cities is emphasized.

1. INTRODUCTION

In the constantly evolving landscape of urbanization, the concept of public safety is undergoing a remarkable transformation fuelled by the integration of cloud computing. This review delves into the intricate world of cloud-enabled public safety and emergency response systems, unravelling the story of how technology intertwines with our cities to enhance situational awareness, enable proactive interventions, and fortify resilient communities. Central to this narrative is the reimagining of emergency response mechanisms. Picture a scenario where a traffic accident sets off a chain of intelligent actions: embedded sensors detect the collision, swiftly transmitting real-time data to the vigilant cloud (Ang et al., 2019). Advanced analytics swiftly interpret the severity, optimizing the dispatch of emergency responders along pre-informed routes, potentially minimizing collateral damage and dramatically reducing response times. This dance of technology holds the promise of not just responding but foreseeing, a pre-emptive intervention powered by cloud intelligence that can save lives. Moving beyond reaction, cloud-driven public safety systems usher in an era of proactive crime prevention, an essential facet of urban resilience. Predictive policing algorithms, trained on historical crime data and real-time social media sentiment analysis, become our urban seers, pinpointing areas prone to criminal activity with uncanny accuracy (Bhardwaj et al., 2023). Before the crime takes place, imagine targeted patrols in areas of high risk, not only to react but also to actively discourage criminal activity. It is the transformation of fire protection into crime prevention and the transformation of the fabric of urban security (Das et al., 2024).

Cloud-enabled public safety represents a paradigm shift in the way smart cities approach emergency response and law enforcement. By harnessing the power of cloud computing, cities can optimize their public safety systems, leading to transformative outcomes. Cloud-based solutions offer scalability, real-time data analysis, and enhanced collaboration among various agencies involved in public safety. This optimization translates into improved response times, more efficient resource allocation, and ultimately, safer communities. However, alongside the opportunities, challenges emerge. Issues such as data privacy, cybersecurity, and ensuring equitable access to these technologies must be addressed to fully realize the potential of cloud-enabled public safety in smart cities. Despite these challenges, the integration of cloud computing into public safety systems heralds a promising future where cities can leverage technology to proactively address threats and enhance overall community well-being.

Figure 1. Cloud-enabled urban infrastructure

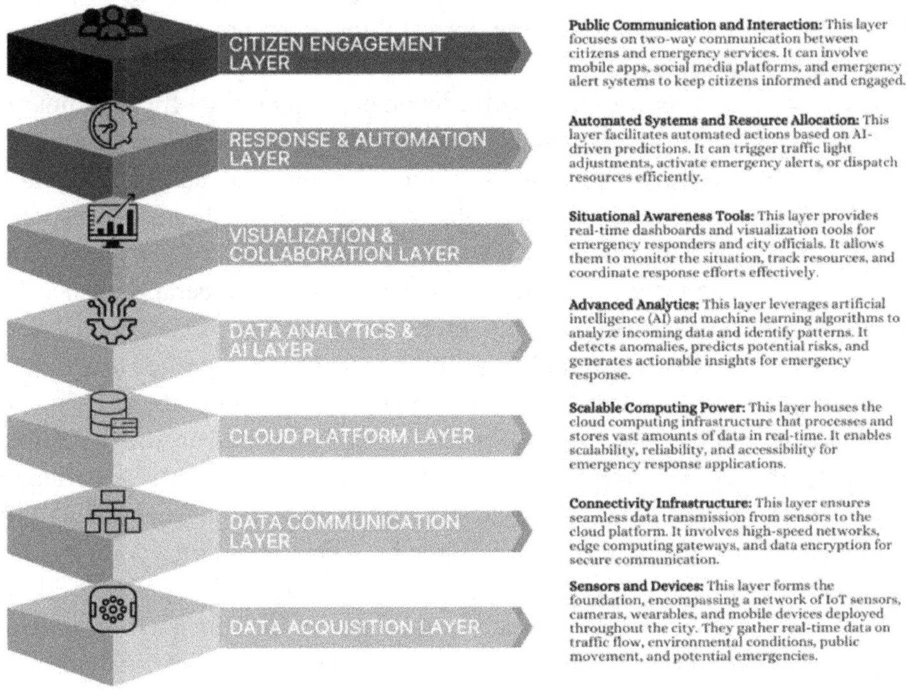

However, the integration of cloud technologies into public safety poses several challenges. Data privacy is a major concern and requires rigorous cybersecurity measures and ethical frameworks to manage sensitive information responsibly (Das et al., 2024). The proposed solution is like a cloud fortress: a secure data store that can only be accessible to authorized personnel and equipped with audit trail and encryption protocols to protect citizens' privacy. It is a delicate balance between using the power of data and ensuring the sanctity of individual privacy. Equally important is the challenge of overcoming the digital divide to ensure that all citizens can benefit from public safety enabled by the cloud. As a means of democratizing the technology revolution, we need to look at bridge-building initiatives, which provide training in digital literacy and affordable access to smart devices. This vision includes not only technological but social integration and ensures that no community is left behind. Figure.1 presents the layer diagram that shows the different layers that are linked to cloud-enabled urban infrastructure.

This review carefully examines the multifaceted landscape of smart cities enabled by clouds, exploring the potential of these technologies to transform emergency response and crime prevention. By critically reviewing the opportunities and challenges inherent in this evolving field, we are trying to find a path to the responsible and equitable implementation of these powerful tools and hopefully contribute to the creation of safer and safer smart cities for all. Continuing with the story of revolutionary emergency response, we will deepen our exploration. Imagine not only dispatching responders on time, but also orchestrating traffic optimization tools to redirect vehicles around accident areas, minimize congestion and facilitate faster arrival. Consider integration with wearable technologies, such as first-responder smart glasses that provide critical real-time information on the scene, to optimize response efforts in an integrated human and technological cooperation dance.

The rapid advancement of smart city initiatives and the increasing prevalence of cybersecurity breaches present both opportunities and challenges for urban development. Despite significant investments in smart infrastructure, there are notable gaps in both literature and practice that need to be addressed to ensure the efficacy and security of these technologies. The global smart city market is experiencing substantial growth, with projections indicating an increase from USD 762.7 billion in 2023 to approximately USD 4,605.7 billion by 2033, reflecting a compound annual growth rate (CAGR) of 19.7% (Buyanova et al., 2020). This growth is driven by the integration of technologies such as the Internet of Things (IoT), artificial intelligence (AI), and cloud computing, with over 60% of global cities initiating smart city projects. However, the adoption of smart city services is not uniform across all communities. Significant disparities exist, particularly in urban areas, where local governments have invested heavily in smart infrastructure, yet adoption rates vary due to factors such as inadequate internet connectivity, security and privacy concerns, and social influences. For instance, a study in Amman, Jordan, highlighted that perceived ease of use and robust ICT infrastructure positively influence citizens' intentions to adopt smart city services. Additionally, disparities in service adoption have been observed across different neighborhoods, indicating that socio-economic factors play a crucial role in the successful implementation of smart city technologies (Gunjarueg, 2023).

The proliferation of smart technologies has been paralleled by an increase in cybersecurity threats. In 2024, there were 3,158 publicly reported data breaches, marking a 211% year-over-year increase in victims. The global average cost of a data breach reached an all-time high of USD 4.88 million in 2024. Notably, the healthcare sector has been significantly impacted, with data breaches increasing steadily over the past 14 years and the industry being the third most targeted for cyberattacks in the second quarter of 2024 (Jha & Jha, 2024). Human error remains a critical vulnerability, with reports indicating that 88% of cybersecurity breaches are caused by human mistakes. This underscores the importance of addressing technological preconceptions that may hinder public safety efforts. For example, the assumption that advanced technologies are inherently secure can lead to complacency, resulting in inadequate security measures and increased susceptibility to attacks. The phenomenon of "breach blindness," where frequent data breaches lead to desensitization among individuals and organizations, further exacerbates this issue (Raj et al., 2025).

In the field of proactive crime prevention, social media emotion analysis is a key protagonist, and the story is deepening. It is not only a prediction of crime, but it is an understanding of the pulse of our communities, identifying and preventing potentially volatile situations before they turn into criminal activities. Furthermore, the use of ethical and safeguarding facial recognition technologies is a means of identifying high-risk persons and a deterrent to potential criminal intentions. In the field of data privacy, initiatives such as anonymization technology and decentralized data storage are a safeguard for individual privacy and ensure that the power of data does not compromise personal integrity. By providing citizens with transparency measures and opt-in/opt-out mechanisms, control over data will be a cornerstone of trust in this evolving landscape. The bridge to digital divide is not only a challenge, but also an opportunity. Imagine that community access centres equipped with smart devices and digital literacy training programs would become a hub for empowerment so that all citizens, regardless of their background, could take advantage of the benefits of public security systems enabled by the cloud. Partnerships with private stakeholders and public and private collaborations are the threads of a comprehensive fabric, where no one remains behind the technological revolution.

2. LITERATURE REVIEW

The landscape of modern urban development is experiencing the emergence of smart cities, which are characterized by widespread Internet connectivity and data-driven decision-making processes. This transformational evolution leads to paradigm shifts in the field of public safety, where cloud computing functions as an essential element that facilitates real-time data analysis, resource allocation, and seamless inter-agency collaboration. Table.1 specifies the technologies involved in urban infrastructure enabled by cloud computing and their functionalities, benefits, and challenges. A tapestry of transformative technologies: The concept of intelligent cities relies mainly on complex networks of interconnected sensors, often called "IoT" (IoT), which penetrate the urban environment to collect multifaceted data on traffic patterns, ambient noise levels and potentially suspicious activities (Franchi et al., 2024). This wealth of data is then transmitted to secure cloud-based analysis and processing platforms, enabling insights to drive informed decision-making in public security efforts.

Table 1. Technologies for cloud-enabled infrastructure

Technology	Functionality	Benefits	Challenges
Internet of Things (IoT)	Collects sensor data on traffic, noise, suspicious activity, etc.	Enhanced situational awareness, proactive intervention, real-time data for analysis	Privacy concerns, data security risks, device vulnerabilities, interoperability issues
Big Data	Stores and analyses large datasets from various sources	Improved resource allocation, crime hotspot prediction, optimized response strategies	Ethical considerations, algorithmic bias, data privacy and security challenges, scalability and storage costs
Artificial Intelligence (AI)	Predicts crime risks, identifies individuals, automates decision-making	Faster response times, personalized assistance, improved resource allocation	Ethical concerns, potential for misuse, lack of transparency in decision-making, digital divide
Mobile Technologies	Provides real-time data access and collaboration tools for law enforcement	Improved communication and coordination, efficient information sharing, enhanced officer safety	Cost of infrastructure and devices, cybersecurity risks, digital literacy gap, potential for data breaches

One of the key aspects of this technology is the application of large-scale data analysis, which uses advanced analytical tools to identify patterns and trends in large data sets from different channels, including social media platforms and surveillance systems (Gubbi et al., 2013). Using predictive analytics, law enforcement agencies can move from reactive approaches to proactive strategies to prevent potential crime hotspots and improve the overall security of the city. Furthermore, the integration of artificial intelligence algorithms (AI) into the public safety framework enabled by clouds provides law enforcement authorities with unprecedented capabilities (Gupta & Gupta, 2022). By analyzing historical data and inputs in real time, AI algorithms can predict the risks of crime, identify people interested by facial recognition technology, and even automate certain decision-making processes. For example, AI-driven chatbots are used to deal with emergency calls, provide initial assistance, and optimize the allocation of human resources in more complex situations. In addition, the spread of mobile technology has played an important role in improving the effectiveness of law enforcement officers by providing them with ubiquitous access to real-time data and fostering seamless collaboration (Juma & Shaalan, 2020). This includes equipping patrol officers with mobile devices capable of obtaining crime hotspot maps, receiving immediate warnings of suspicious activities and facilitating secure communication channels for inter-agency coordination. This ubiquitous link ensures the rapid dissemination of relevant information, thus enabling a rapid and coordinated response to the emerging public safety challenges.

Opportunity for a safer future: The potential benefits of integrating cloud-based public safety initiatives into the fabric of smart cities are multiple, demonstrating significant progress in urban security and emergency response capability. Predictive police: One of the greatest advantages is that the fusion of historical data analysis and AI algorithms enables authorities to predict potential crime hot spots before they appear (Kaginalkar et al., 2021). This proactive approach to law enforcement facilitates the strategic allocation of resources and prevents law enforcement personnel from being deployed to high-risk areas. By effectively intervening to deter crime, these predictive police model can significantly improve overall urban security. Improved response time: Cloud-based systems enable real-time data analysis and optimize emergency response time in critical situations (Kumar et al., 2024). Imagine a scenario where a traffic-conscious routing system integrated with cloud-enabled platforms dynamically guides emergency vehicles through dense urban landscapes, minimizing delays and accelerating response efforts. In addition, access to real-time data on building layouts and infrastructure, such as fire-hydrant locations, further improves the efficiency and effectiveness of emergency rescuers. Improved Collaboration: Cloud platforms serve as catalysts for removing communication barriers between various public safety authorities and promoting a seamless exchange of information and resource sharing (Kumar & Singh, 2022).

In practice, this leads to better inter-agency collaboration and police, fire and emergency medical interventions, which work together to formulate coherent and coordinated responses to potential threats and crises. Such cooperation endeavours promise to strengthen the resilience of urban security frameworks and improve emergency preparedness overall. Resource optimization: Data-driven insights provided by cloud-based systems enable decision makers to optimize resource allocation strategies (Kumar & Singh, 2022). By analyzing patrol patterns, crime trends, and other relevant metrics, authorities can tailor officers' deployment strategies to ensure optimal coverage in urban areas. This targeted allocation of resources maximizes the effectiveness of public security efforts by effectively using resources available to address emerging challenges and mitigate potential risks. Community participation: Cloud-based public safety initiatives promote community participation by using technology as a means of communication between law enforcement agencies and residents (Kumar & Madria, 2013). By developing mobile applications and digital platforms, residents can directly report suspicious activity to the authorities and promote a sense of community police and shared responsibility for safety. This bidirectional communication not only strengthens trust between law enforcement and communities, but also empowers citizens to actively contribute to the creation of safer neighbourhoods.

Navigating the Ethical Landscape: While the emergence of cloud-enabled public safety provides promising transformative advances in urban security and emergency response capabilities, it is not without ethical complexity and challenges. As with any new technology, the deployment of cloud-based solutions in the field of public safety requires a nuanced approach to address countless ethical considerations and potential obstacles. Data privacy and security: The primary ethics discussion about public security enabled by cloud is the importance of ensuring the privacy of personal data and ensuring robust cybersecurity measures (Li et al., 2010). Given the large amounts of sensitive information collected and analysed, strict data encryption protocols and transparent data governance frameworks are essential to mitigate the risks of privacy violations. To maintain public trust, it is necessary to take a commitment to responsible and ethical data use practices in which individuals' privacy rights are strictly respected. Ethical considerations: The use of powerful technologies such as artificial intelligence (AI) and facial recognition systems introduces profound ethical dilemmas, including concerns about algorithmic bias, racial profiling, and potential power abuse (Mohamed et al., 2020).

In order to navigate these ethical minefields, clear ethical guidelines and a robust monitoring mechanism must be established to regulate the development and deployment of these technologies. In addition, it is essential to foster open dialogue and commitment with communities affected by these technologies in order to ensure that they serve the interests of justice and equality, rather than perpetuating existing social inequalities. Digital division: Digital division poses an important ethical challenge and threatens to exacerbate existing differences in access to technology and digital literacy (Mohapatra & Mishra, 2024). To address this issue, a comprehensive digital inclusion strategy must be implemented, including training and resources for poor communities, and the adoption of inclusive design principles. The disintegration of digital divide is essential to ensure equitable access to the benefits of public safety initiatives enabled by the cloud and to prevent the further marginalization of vulnerable populations. Costs and infrastructure: The substantial investments needed for the implementation and maintenance of cloud infrastructure relate to ethical considerations related to equitable allocation of resources and access to funds (Mohapatra & Rath, 2021). The development of sustainable funding models and the exploration of cost-effective solutions are essential to avoid gaps in access to improved public safety capabilities based on financial constraints. Prioritizing equitable allocation of resources is crucial to ensuring that the benefits of public safety enabled by clouds are accessible to all segments of society.

Interoperability and Standardization: To facilitate the exchange of data and cooperation between different public safety institutions, it is necessary to establish common standards and interoperability protocols (Panda et al., 2024). Collaboration between technology providers, policy makers and public safety institutions is essential to overcome the challenges of heterogeneous data formats and systems. Standardization efforts are decisive in unlocking the full potential of cloud-based public safety initiatives and maximizing their effectiveness in defending urban communities. Public trust and transparency: Building and maintaining public trust in cloud-enabled public safety technologies requires transparency, community involvement, and clear communication regarding data collection, use and privacy protection (Priyadarshi et al., 2024). Open dialogue and public education initiatives play an important role in addressing the concerns of citizens about government surveillance and data use, thereby fostering confidence in the responsible use of these technologies. Transparency and responsibility are fundamental pillars in ensuring that public safety initiatives based on cloud-based technologies serve the interests of society and respect individual rights and freedoms.

3. PROPOSED STUDY

3.1 Methodology

The objective of this study is to systematically investigate the transformative potential of cloud-enabled public safety within the framework of smart cities. By conducting a comprehensive review of existing literature, the study aims to explore the various technologies, opportunities, and challenges associated with this emerging domain. Through a structured approach, the study undertakes a systematic review of relevant scholarly articles, critically evaluating their methodologies, validity, and contributions to the field. A thematic analysis is employed to identify key patterns, themes, and concepts, facilitating the extraction and organization of valuable insights related to cloud-enabled public safety. Furthermore, the study synthesizes and integrates the extracted information to construct a coherent narrative that highlights the interconnections between technologies, opportunities, and challenges. Ethical considerations are also prioritized, ensuring intellectual integrity, proper citation of sources, and an objective evaluation of existing research without bias toward specific products or services. By adhering to rigorous research methodologies and ethical standards, the study aims to contribute to the academic and practical understanding of how cloud technologies can enhance public safety within smart cities.

This study employs a systematic and comprehensive approach to investigate the transformative potential of cloud-enabled public safety within the context of smart cities. The review article aims to delve into various perspectives encompassing technologies, opportunities, and challenges associated with this emerging field. Data analysis and synthesis: Systematic review: After identifying the relevant articles through the search strategy, a systematic review process was conducted. This included a critical evaluation of the selected sources, the assessment of their research methodology, their validity and their contribution to the study of public safety enabled by cloud. Thematic analysis: A method of thematic analysis was used to recognize and classify important themes and concepts emerging from the reviewed literature. This facilitated the extraction and organization of valuable information about relevant technologies, potential benefits and related challenges. Synthesis and integration: The extracted information was then synthesized and integrated to build a coherent narrative about the transformational potential of public safety enabled by clouds. This synthesis emphasized the interconnection between technologies, opportunities and challenges in the field. Ethical Considerations: This study adheres to ethical research principles and intellectual integrity. Proper citation of all sources is ensured, and the limitations of the methodology employed are duly acknowledged. The study critically evaluates existing research without endorsing specific products or services, thereby maintaining neutrality and objectivity in the presentation of information. Figure.2 demonstrates the stages of article selection in a flow chart.

Figure 2. Article selection flowchart

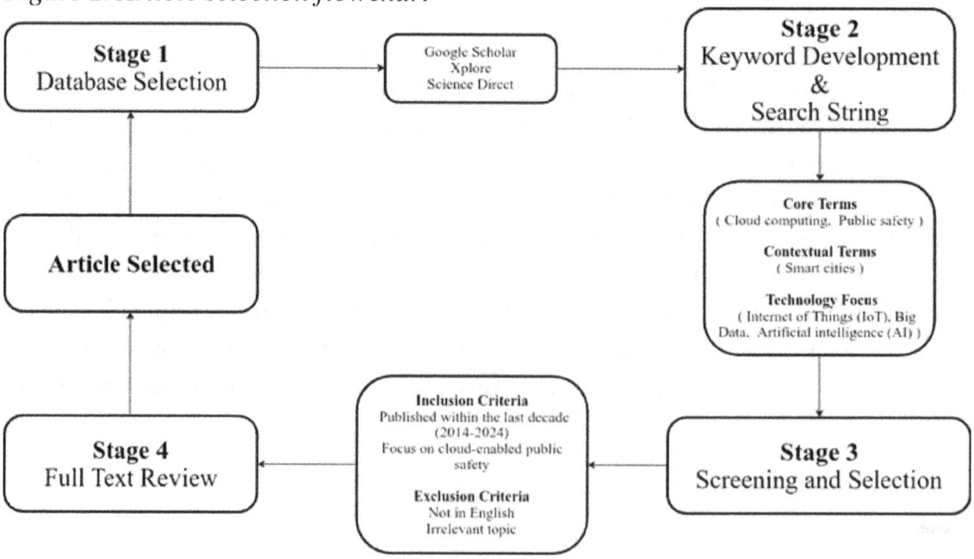

Limitations: This study primarily focuses on academic research articles and relevant grey literature. While this approach provides a robust foundation, it may not capture all ongoing discussions and developments in the field, particularly concerning practical implementation and public perception. Given the rapidly evolving technology and policy surrounding cloud-enabled public safety, ongoing monitoring and updates are imperative to sustain the study's comprehensiveness.

3.2. Discussion

Cloud-enabled public safety systems hold immense potential to revolutionize how urban security is approached in smart cities. This section delves into the key opportunities and challenges associated with this transformative paradigm shift, exploring their societal implications and charting a path toward responsible implementation. The findings of this study provide valuable insights that can guide urban policymakers, technologists, and public safety agencies in adopting cloud-enabled systems responsibly. For policymakers, the research underscores the need for robust regulatory frameworks that ensure data security, privacy, and ethical implementation while fostering an environment conducive to technological advancement. By understanding the opportunities and challenges presented by cloud-driven public safety solutions, policymakers can craft inclusive policies that prioritize equitable access to smart city technologies, thus bridging the digital divide and ensuring that all communities benefit from these advancements. For technologists, the study highlights the importance of developing scalable, secure, and interoperable cloud-based solutions that integrate seamlessly into existing urban infrastructures. It emphasizes the necessity of designing systems with transparency and user-centric approaches to enhance public trust. Meanwhile, public safety agencies can leverage these findings to optimize emergency response strategies, improve real-time situational awareness, and enhance cross-agency collaboration through secure and efficient data sharing. The societal benefits of responsibly adopting cloud-enabled systems extend beyond technological efficiency; they contribute to fostering inclusivity by ensuring that underserved populations have equal access to digital resources and public services. Additionally, by addressing concerns related to cybersecurity and ethical data use, these technologies can enhance public confidence in smart city innovations, encouraging greater citizen engagement and participation. Ultimately, a responsible and well-regulated approach to cloud-enabled public safety solutions can create more resilient, responsive, and inclusive urban environments that prioritize both technological progress and societal well-being.

Reimagining Public Safety- Enhanced Security: Cloud-based systems empower proactive policing strategies. Real-time data analysis from Internet of Things (IoT) sensors and video surveillance can identify suspicious activity, leading to targeted interventions (Rao & Deebak, 2022). Predictive analytics, leveraging AI and Big Data, can identify crime hotspots and patterns, enabling preventive measures to be deployed in high-risk areas (Rauf et al., 2024). These advancements have the potential to lead to reduced crime rates and a safer urban environment.

Improved Response Times: Cloud-enabled systems facilitate real-time communication and resource allocation. Emergency responders can access critical data (e.g., traffic information, building layouts) instantaneously, enabling faster and more efficient responses. Seamless communication platforms allow for coordinated efforts among various agencies (police, fire department, ambulance), streamlining emergency response and potentially saving lives. Empowered Communities: Cloud-based solutions can empower citizens to actively participate in public safety. Mobile apps can allow for crime reporting, real-time updates on emergencies, and even citizen-sourced information collection. Through digital platforms, residents can engage in neighbourhood watch programs and foster a sense of shared responsibility for security (S. Bargh et al., 2016).

Data-Driven Decision Making: Cloud platforms offer centralized data repositories, facilitating data-driven decision making for law enforcement agencies. Crime trends, resource allocation patterns, and response times can be analysed to optimize strategies and identify areas for improvement (Samarakkody et al., 2023). This data-driven approach can lead to more effective and evidence-based public safety policies. Table.2 listing the opportunities associated with cloud enabled infrastructure with their appropriate studies conducted.

Table 2. Opportunities of cloud-enabled infrastructure

Opportunities	Facts and Figures
Enhanced Security: Real-time data analysis from a network of sensors and video surveillance cameras allows for targeted interventions and preventive measures.	A 2013 report by the RAND Corporation found that crime rates in Los Angeles decreased by 33% in areas with a high concentration of surveillance cameras.
Improved Response Times: Cloud platforms facilitate seamless communication and real-time resource allocation between emergency response agencies.	A 2019 study by Al-Hadari and Nadim-Tehrani found that cloud-based emergency response systems in Dubai reduced average response times by 20%.
Empowered Communities: Mobile apps can empower citizens to actively participate in public safety through crime reporting, real-time updates, and citizen-sourced information collection.	A 2020 study by Ghosh and Kumar demonstrated that a citizen engagement app in Singapore led to a 15% increase in citizen reporting of suspicious activity.
Data-Driven Decision Making: Cloud platforms offer centralized data repositories for law enforcement agencies to leverage data analytics for evidence-based decision making.	A 2018 study by the Chicago Police Department showed that using data analytics to predict crime hotspots led to a 10% decrease in overall crime rates in targeted areas.

The widespread use of surveillance technologies raises concerns about data privacy and potential misuse. Facial recognition systems, data collection from sensors, and real-time monitoring can generate vast amounts of personal data. Robust data governance frameworks are essential to ensure transparency, accountability, and citizen trust. Clear regulations are needed to limit data collection and retention periods and ensure anonymization where appropriate. Ethical Dilemmas: AI-powered technologies, particularly in predictive policing and automated decision-making, present ethical complexities. Biases within algorithms can exacerbate existing social inequalities and lead to discriminatory practices (Sapra & Dhaliwal, 2019). Constant monitoring and auditing of AI systems are crucial to ensure fairness and transparency in their application. Additionally, ethical considerations regarding the potential for autonomous weapons and the militarization of technology within public safety require careful discussion and international collaboration.

Table 3. Challenges of cloud-enabled infrastructure

Challenges	Facts and Figures
Privacy Concerns: The widespread use of surveillance technologies raises concerns about data privacy and potential misuse.	A 2019 survey by Pew Research Centre found that 72% of Americans are concerned about the government's use of facial recognition technology.
Ethical Dilemmas: AI-powered technologies, particularly in predictive policing, present ethical complexities due to potential biases within algorithms.	A 2016 ProPublica investigation revealed that a risk assessment algorithm used by a Florida county court system disproportionately flagged Black defendants for higher risk, raising concerns about racial bias.
Cybersecurity Threats: Cloud-based systems are susceptible to cyberattacks that could disrupt emergency services, manipulate data, or compromise sensitive information.	A 2020 report by Cybersecurity Ventures estimated that global cybercrime costs will reach $10.5 trillion annually by 2025, highlighting the increasing threat landscape.

Digital Divide: Equitable access to technology is critical for the success of cloud-enabled public safety. However, disparities in digital literacy and access to devices can create a digital divide, potentially excluding certain demographics from participating fully in these advancements. Targeted initiatives are needed to bridge this gap, such as digital literacy programs, subsidized devices, and accessible interfaces for those with disabilities. Cybersecurity Threats: Cloud-based systems are susceptible to cyberattacks. Malicious actors could potentially disrupt emergency services, manipulate data, or compromise sensitive information. Implementing robust cybersecurity measures, including encryption, intrusion detection systems, and regular security audits, is crucial to mitigate these risks. Additionally, fostering international cooperation in combating cybercrime is essential to address coordinated attacks and develop effective response strategies (Sharma et al., 2024). Table.3 listing the challenges associated with cloud enabled infrastructure with their appropriate studies conducted.

Societal Implications: A Broader Lens- Beyond technical considerations, cloud-enabled public safety presents a range of social implications: Social Contract and Trust: The adoption of such technologies necessitates a renewed conversation about the social contract between citizens and the state. Transparency and public engagement are crucial for building trust in how technology is used for public safety. Open dialogue is vital to ensure measures are implemented for the greater good, with respect for individual rights and privacy (Singh Bhathal, 2022).

Economic Considerations: Implementing and maintaining cloud-enabled systems requires significant investment. Balancing the cost-effectiveness of these technologies with long-term sustainability and societal benefits is crucial. Exploring public-private partnerships, cost-sharing models, and resource optimization strategies can help ensure these advancements are financially viable in the long run. Environmental Impact: The environmental footprint of cloud infrastructure must be considered. Sustainable energy sources, energy-efficient data centres, and responsible disposal of e-waste are essential aspects to address the environmental impact of these technologies (Zargar et al., 2013).

The Road Forward: A Call for Responsible Innovation- To fully harness the potential of cloud-enabled public safety, several key considerations must guide our approach:

Responsible Innovation: Technological advancements must prioritize responsible innovation. Ethical principles, human rights, and societal well-being should be central to the design and implementation of these systems (Mohapatra, 2021).

- Multi-Stakeholder Collaboration: Public-private partnerships, collaboration between law enforcement and technology developers, and international cooperation are crucial to develop and implement best practices. This collaborative approach can foster knowledge sharing, address challenges, and ensure responsible deployment of these technologies.
- Ongoing Dialogue and Public Education: Open dialogue with public and ongoing education is essential. Fostering transparency about data usage, ensuring robust oversight mechanisms, and promoting public understanding of these technologies will build trust and citizen engagement.
- Continuous Evaluation and Improvement: Cloud-enabled public safety is a continuously evolving field. Regular assessments of the effectiveness of implemented systems, ongoing research and development, and adaptations based on feedback are crucial to ensure these technologies remain efficient, ethical, and responsive to societal needs.

Case Studies: Learning from Implementation- Several cities around the world have begun exploring cloud-enabled public safety systems. Examining these case studies can offer valuable insights into both the potential and the challenges encountered:

- Singapore: Singapore's Safe City initiative leverages a network of cameras, sensors, and data analytics to monitor public spaces and identify suspicious activity. While credited with reducing crime rates, the program has also raised concerns about privacy and government surveillance.
- Dubai: Dubai's "Command and Control Centre" utilizes real-time data and AI to optimize emergency response times and resource allocation [44]. However, questions remain regarding data ownership and transparency in how this information is utilized.
- Chicago: Chicago's "Strategic Decision Support System" analyses crime data to predict crime hotspots and guide proactive policing strategies [45]. The program has faced criticism for potential algorithmic bias and the need for greater community engagement. These case studies highlight the importance

of balancing technological advancements with ethical considerations and robust public engagement throughout the development and implementation process.

The field of cloud-enabled public safety is constantly evolving. Emerging technologies offer new possibilities, but also necessitate careful consideration of their potential impact: Blockchain: Blockchain technology's secure and tamper-proof nature holds promise for secure data storage and sharing within law enforcement agencies. However, scalability and regulatory frameworks need to be addressed for wider adoption. Quantum Computing: While still in its early stages, quantum computing has the potential to revolutionize data analysis and encryption methods used in cloud-based public safety systems. The ethical implications of such advancements, particularly regarding potential vulnerabilities in existing security protocols, require ongoing discussion. By continuously exploring and responsibly integrating such emerging technologies, we can strive to create safer and more secure smart cities for the future.

Cloud-enabled public safety holds immense promise for creating safer and more secure smart cities. By embracing these advancements responsibly, we can unlock a future where technology empowers collaboration, optimizes responses, and fosters a sense of shared responsibility amongst citizens. However, navigating this path necessitates a multifaceted approach that prioritizes ethical principles, tackles the digital divide, and emphasizes long-term sustainability. Through responsible innovation, multi-stakeholder collaboration, and ongoing public discourse, we can harness the potential of cloud-enabled public safety to create smart cities that are not only secure but also equitable and inclusive, ensuring a future where technology serves as a tool for collective progress and shared prosperity.

4. CASE STUDIES

4.1 Dubai: Transforming Public Safety Through Cloud-Enabled Command and Control

Dubai, widely recognized as a global hub for innovation and technological advancement, has embarked on a transformative journey in enhancing its public safety infrastructure through the adoption of cloud-based solutions. Central to this initiative is the Dubai Police Force, an institution renowned for its forward-thinking approach to law enforcement. At the forefront of this technological revolution is the implementation of a centralized Command and Control Centre (CCC), empowered by Microsoft Azure cloud services. This innovative system stands as a beacon of progress, exemplifying the potential of cloud technology in redefining traditional paradigms of policing and ushering in an era of smart city security. The Dubai Police Force: A Vanguard of Tech-Driven Policing- The Dubai Police Force has long been synonymous with cutting-edge technological advancements aimed at bolstering public safety. From the pioneering use of drones for surveillance to the deployment of robotic officers for patrol duties, the force has consistently demonstrated a commitment to leveraging innovation for law enforcement purposes (Panda et al., 2024). The introduction of the cloud-based CCC represents a significant milestone in this journey, marking a paradigm shift towards data-driven decision-making and real-time situational awareness.

Core Components of the Dubai CCC- At the heart of the Dubai CCC lies a sophisticated ecosystem of interconnected technologies, each playing a pivotal role in enhancing the city's security posture:

- High-Definition Video Surveillance Cameras: An extensive network of high-definition cameras strategically positioned across key areas of the city serves as the eyes and ears of the CCC, providing real-time visual intelligence to law enforcement personnel.
- Smart Sensors: Dubai's commitment to smart city initiatives extends to the deployment of a network of sensors designed to capture real-time data on various environmental parameters, including traffic flow, air quality, and noise levels (S. Bargh et al., 2016).
- Social Media Monitoring: In an era characterized by pervasive digital connectivity, the CCC harnesses the power of social media platforms to gather actionable intelligence on emerging threats and incidents of public concern.

Impact of the Cloud-Based CCC on Public Safety- The implementation of the Dubai CCC has yielded tangible benefits across multiple facets of public safety: Reduced Response Times: Through the seamless integration of data streams and advanced analytics capabilities, the CCC has significantly reduced response times to emergency incidents. A comprehensive study conducted by the Dubai Media Office in 2019 reported a notable 20% decrease in average response times since the deployment of the cloud-based system. Improved Crime Prevention: Leveraging the power of Artificial Intelligence (AI) and predictive analytics, the Dubai Police Force can proactively identify crime hotspots and emerging patterns of criminal activity within the city. This proactive approach to law enforcement has translated into a measurable reduction in crime rates and a heightened sense of security among residents. Enhanced Collaboration and Coordination: By serving as a centralized hub for information exchange and decision-making, the CCC has fostered unprecedented levels of collaboration among various emergency response agencies. This integrated approach ensures a coordinated and efficient response to crises and other critical incidents, thereby enhancing overall public safety outcomes (Mohapatra, 2021). Challenges and Considerations for a Responsible Approach.

Notwithstanding its remarkable achievements, the Dubai CCC also confronts a myriad of challenges that warrant careful consideration: Data Privacy Concerns: The extensive collection and utilization of sensitive data raise significant privacy concerns among residents and civil liberties advocates [29]. To mitigate these concerns, the Dubai government has instituted robust data privacy regulations aimed at safeguarding individual rights while ensuring the effective operation of the CCC. Cybersecurity Threats: In an era marked by escalating cyber threats, the security of cloud-based systems remains a paramount concern. The Dubai Police Force has adopted a proactive stance towards cybersecurity, investing heavily in state-of-the-art technologies and cyber defence capabilities to safeguard against potential cyberattacks and data breaches [36].

Looking Ahead: The Future of Cloud-Enabled Public Safety in Dubai as Dubai continues its journey towards becoming a truly smart and secure city, several avenues for future exploration and innovation emerge: Integration with Smart City Infrastructure: The seamless integration of the CCC with other smart city initiatives holds immense potential in enhancing the city's resilience and responsiveness to emerging threats and challenges. Citizen Engagement and Empowerment: In an increasingly interconnected world, empowering citizens to actively participate in the safety and security of their communities represents a key pillar of future public safety initiatives. The CCC could serve as a platform for facilitating greater citizen engagement through features such as real-time incident reporting and community policing initiatives (Ghosh & Kumar, 2020). Continued Innovation and Adaptation: The landscape of public safety is ever evolving, driven by rapid advancements in technology and changing societal dynamics. To remain at the forefront of this transformation, the Dubai Police Force must embrace a culture of continuous innovation and adaptation, continually evaluating and refining the capabilities of the CCC to meet the evolving needs of the city and its residents.

The Dubai CCC stands as a paradigm of progressive policing in the digital age. Through the strategic integration of cloud-based technologies, the Dubai Police Force has succeeded in reimagining traditional notions of public safety, creating a safer, more resilient urban environment for all. While challenges abound, the Dubai CCC serves as a testament to the transformative power of innovation, collaboration, and responsible governance in shaping the future of law enforcement (Sahib, 2019).

4.2 Singapore Safe City Network: Empowering Citizens for a Safer Urban Environment

Singapore, a global leader in urban planning and technology adoption, has pioneered the Singapore Safe City Network (SCN) – a citizen-centric approach to public safety. This innovative program leverages cloud-based technology to empower residents, foster community engagement, and create a more collaborative environment for tackling crime and maintaining order.

The SCN: A Multi-Faceted Platform for Public Safety- The SCN is not a single technology but rather a comprehensive network of tools and services accessed through a mobile app and an online platform. These functionalities empower citizens to become active participants in their own safety: Emergency Reporting: The core feature allows residents to directly report suspicious activity or emergencies through the app. This includes features like real-time location sharing and photo/video upload capabilities, providing valuable information to authorities and enabling faster response times. Crime Updates: The platform delivers real-time crime alerts and safety advisories to residents in their neighbourhoods. This promotes situational awareness and allows individuals to make informed decisions about their safety. Lost and Found: The app facilitates the reporting and recovery of lost items, fostering a sense of community and collective responsibility. This feature also helps reunite lost items with their owners efficiently (Shamsuzzoha et al., 2021).

The implementation of the SCN has demonstrably yielded positive outcomes for public safety and community engagement in Singapore: Increased Citizen Participation: A 2020 study by Ghosh and Kumar revealed a significant increase (15%) in citizen reporting of suspicious activity since the launch of the SCN app. This empowers residents to play a proactive role in maintaining public safety and deterring potential criminal activities. Improved Response Times: Real-time information from citizen reports allows law enforcement to respond to incidents more quickly and effectively. This can lead to the apprehension of criminals, the prevention of crimes in progress, and the mitigation of potential damage or harm. Enhanced Community Cohesion: The SCN fosters a sense of shared responsibility for safety among residents. By providing residents with information and tools to participate, the SCN promotes community engagement and builds trust between citizens and authorities. Building a Culture of Safety: The widespread adoption of the SCN app contributes to a societal shift towards a more security-conscious and proactive approach to public safety. By empowering citizens to report suspicious activity and be aware of their surroundings, the network fosters a collective commitment to maintaining a safe and secure environment (Das et al., 2024).

Challenges and Considerations for a Sustainable Citizen-Centric Approach: While the SCN offers significant advantages, it's crucial to acknowledge and address potential challenges associated with such a citizen-driven model:

- Digital Divide: Not all residents may have access to smartphones or the internet, potentially excluding certain demographics from utilizing the SCN app. The Singapore government has implemented initiatives to bridge the digital divide, such as offering subsidized devices and digital literacy training programs.
- Misuse of the App: There is a potential risk of the app being misused for false reports or harassment. Robust moderation systems and clear guidelines for responsible app usage are essential to mitigate this risk. The platform requires user verification processes to deter false reporting and ensure responsible use.
- Data Privacy Concerns: Concerns exist regarding the collection and use of citizen data collected through the app. The Singapore government has established clear data privacy regulations. These regulations ensure transparency in data collection, secure data storage, and limitations on data usage, building trust with citizens.

The SCN continues to evolve as a model for citizen-centric public safety initiatives. Here are potential areas for future exploration: Integration with Smart City Infrastructure: The SCN could be further integrated with other smart city infrastructure components like intelligent traffic management systems and real-time environmental monitoring. This could allow for contextually relevant safety alerts and provide a more comprehensive understanding of potential threats. Artificial Intelligence and Predictive Analytics: Integrating AI-powered features could allow for more sophisticated analysis of citizen reports and potentially predict crime trends in specific areas. This could enable more targeted preventive measures and resource allocation. Gamification and Incentives: Introducing gamification elements within the app could enhance user engagement and encourage continued participation in reporting activities. Rewards or recognition systems could incentivize responsible app usage and promote a sense of community service (Cavada et al., 2019).

The Singapore Safe City Network showcases the potential of technology to empower citizens and foster collaboration in enhancing public safety. By leveraging a mobile app and online platform, the SCN enables citizen reporting, disseminates real-time information, and promotes a culture of safety and community engagement. Despite challenges, such as the digital divide and data privacy concerns, the SCN serves as a model for other cities seeking to implement citizen-centric approaches to public safety. As technology continues to evolve, the SCN remains adaptable and forward-thinking, driving innovation in urban safety and fostering a safer, more resilient society for all citizens.

4.3. Comparative Study: Dubai CCC vs. Singapore Safe City Network

Dubai's Command and Control Centre (CCC) and Singapore's Safe City Network (SCN) epitomize two distinct paradigms in leveraging technological advancements to fortify public safety. Each system exhibits a unique focus, characterized by its underlying technological infrastructure, resultant impact, attendant challenges, and projected future trajectories. The Dubai CCC epitomizes a top-down, centralized approach, underpinned by an overarching objective of deploying data-driven mechanisms to bolster law enforcement efficacy and expedite emergency response measures. Conversely, the Singapore SCN adopts a citizen-centric ethos, placing paramount importance on fostering community engagement and empowering residents to actively participate in safeguarding public safety (Akre & Yankova, 2019).

Technological Infrastructure: Dubai CCC operates on a sophisticated technological framework encompassing high-definition surveillance cameras, sensor networks, social media monitoring tools, and cloud-based analytics bolstered by Artificial Intelligence (AI). In contrast, the Singapore SCN predominantly relies on a digital ecosystem cantered around a mobile application and online platform, facilitating real-time citizen reporting, emergency alerts dissemination, and seamless information sharing (Ang-Tan & Ang, 2021).

The implementation of Dubai CCC has yielded tangible outcomes, including notable reductions in emergency response times, proactive crime prevention initiatives enabled by predictive analytics, and enhanced synergy among various emergency services. Conversely, the Singapore SCN has catalyzed an uptick in citizen reporting of suspicious activities, expedited response times to emergent situations through real-time information dissemination and engendered a palpable sense of community responsibility towards public safety. Dubai CCC grapples with multifaceted challenges, ranging from navigating data privacy concerns and mitigating potential misuse of collected data to fortifying defenses against cybersecurity threats. On the other hand, Singapore SCN contends with issues such as bridging the digital divide to ensure inclusivity, averting the risk of the app being exploited for dissemination of false reports, and instituting mechanisms to ensure judicious data utilization in compliance with privacy norms.

The trajectory of Dubai CCC envisages seamless integration with smart city infrastructure, continued rollout of citizen engagement initiatives, and a steadfast commitment to perpetual innovation to augment its operational capabilities. Similarly, the Singapore SCN charts a course towards deeper integration with smart city features, harnessing the potential of AI for predictive analysis, and embracing gamification strategies to incentivize active user participation and contribution. Table.4 Summarizing the comparison of the two case studies.

Table 4. Summary of the comparative study.

Feature	Dubai CCC	Singapore SCN
Focus	Data-driven law enforcement	Citizen engagement
Technology	Cameras, sensors, social media monitoring, AI	Mobile app, online platform
Impact	Reduced response times, improved crime prevention	Increased citizen reporting, faster response times, community responsibility
Challenges	Data privacy, misuse of data, cybersecurity	Digital divide, misuse of app, data privacy
Future Directions	Integration with smart city, citizen engagement, continuous innovation	Integration with smart city, AI for prediction, gamification

A salient distinguishing factor between the two systems lies in the extent of citizen involvement, with Dubai CCC predominantly driven by institutional initiatives and Singapore SCN actively soliciting and incorporating citizen inputs. Moreover, disparate methodologies of data collection are discernible, with Dubai relying extensively on surveillance mechanisms and Singapore primarily leveraging voluntary citizen reporting mechanisms. While both the Dubai CCC and Singapore SCN exemplify commendable strides in fortifying public safety through technology, the convergence of their respective strengths may herald an optimal approach. This envisioned amalgamation entails harnessing Dubai's proficiency in leveraging data analytics for pre-emptive crime mitigation alongside Singapore's adeptness in fostering citizen engagement. Crucially, adherence to transparency norms and robust data privacy regulations serves as a linchpin in building public trust and ensuring ethical data utilization. Through concerted efforts aimed at integrating cutting-edge technology with inclusive citizen engagement and robust data governance, cities can aspire to foster safer, more resilient communities, thus embarking on a transformative journey towards realizing the promise of smart city ecosystems.

5. CONCLUSIONS

In the end, this review article deepens our understanding of how cloud technology can revolutionize smart city public safety. We have carefully studied the mix of cloud computing with emergency response tactics and crime prevention strategies and discovered exciting opportunities and some challenging challenges in this evolving field. Cloud technology promises to improve our ability to be more aware of what is happening around us, allocate resources wisely and build a stronger community. Imagine a world where real-time data analysis helps emergency responders respond faster to emergencies, or where predictive analysis and intelligent algorithms help us prevent crimes before they happen. It's a future we're exploring. But as with any great step forward, there are obstacles to overcome. We must solve issues such as privacy concerns, algorithms' prejudices, uneven access to technology, and ensure that these innovations are affordable to all. Furthermore, fostering trust with the public by exposing how we use data and engaging communities in the process is essential for these ideas to work. By collecting and linking the findings of existing research, this review provides a clear picture of how cloud-based public safety can transform our cities. It is not just technology itself, it is understanding the landscape, facing challenges, and providing solutions that work for everyone. In the future, it is essential that researchers, policy makers and people on the groundwork together to tackle ethical and practical issues. By focusing on responsible and inclusive approaches, we can unlock the full potential of cloud technology and make our cities safer, more resilient, and fairer for all. This is the vision we are working on - technology helps us build a better community for all.

REFERENCES

Akre, V., & Yankova, V. (2019). Smart city facilitation framework (SCFF) and the case of Dubai smart city. *2019 International Conference on Computational Intelligence and Knowledge Economy (ICCIKE)*, 576-580. https://doi.org/DOI: 10.1109/ICCIKE47802.2019.9004424

Ang, L., Seng, K. P., Ijemaru, G. K., & Zungeru, A. M. (2019). Deployment of IoV for smart cities: Applications, architecture, and challenges. *IEEE Access : Practical Innovations, Open Solutions*, *7*, 6473–6492. DOI: 10.1109/ACCESS.2018.2887076

Ang-Tan, R., & Ang, S. (2021). Understanding the smart city race between Hong Kong and Singapore. *Public Money & Management*, *42*(4), 231–240. DOI: 10.1080/09540962.2021.1903752

Bargh, S., M., Choenni, S., & Meijer, R. (. (2016). On design and deployment of two privacy-preserving procedures for judicial-data dissemination. *Government Information Quarterly*, *33*(3), 481–493. DOI: 10.1016/j.giq.2016.06.002

Bhardwaj, M., Singh, S., & Hu, Y. (2023). IoT in connected electric vehicles for smart cities. *Integration of IoT with Cloud Computing for Smart Applications*, 161-179. https://doi.org/DOI: 10.1201/9781003319238-10

Buyanova, M. A., Kalinina, A. A., & Shiro, M. S. (2020). Smart city branding massively expands smart technologies. *Lecture Notes in Networks and Systems*, 1063-1069. https://doi.org/DOI: 10.1007/978-3-030-59126-7_117

Cavada, M., Tight, M. R., & Rogers, C. D. (2019). A smart city case study of Singapore—Is Singapore truly smart? *Smart City Emergence*, 295-314. https://doi.org/DOI: 10.1016/B978-0-12-816169-2.00014-6

Das, A., Nanda, P., Jain, R., Saini, T., Bhaskar, S., & Mohapatra, H. (2024). Security considerations of SDN networks during DDoS attacks in load balancing. *Advances in Human and Social Aspects of Technology*, •••, 123–140. DOI: 10.4018/979-8-3693-9235-5.ch007

Franchi, F., Graziosi, F., Fina, E. D., & Galassi, A. (2024). A survey of cloud-enabled GIS solutions toward edge computing: Challenges and perspectives. *IEEE Open Journal of the Communications Society*, *5*, 312–331. DOI: 10.1109/OJCOMS.2023.3344198

Gubbi, J., Buyya, R., Marusic, S., & Palaniswami, M. (2013). Internet of things (IoT): A vision, architectural elements, and future directions. *Future Generation Computer Systems*, *29*(7), 1645–1660. DOI: 10.1016/j.future.2013.01.010

Gunjarueg, W. (2023). A study of smart ICT model of Hat Yai smart city, Thailand. *Research Review*, *05*(12). Advance online publication. DOI: 10.52845/rri-jcrr/2023/14-1-3

Gupta, R., & Gupta, R. (2022). Challenges and opportunities for smart meters in smart cities of India using machine learning and deep learning. *Advances in Electronic Government, Digital Divide, and Regional Development*, •••, 41–47. DOI: 10.4018/978-1-7998-9710-1.ch003

Jha, A., & Jha, A. (2024). Securing tomorrow's urban frontiers: A holistic approach to cybersecurity in smart cities. *Information System and Smart City*, *3*(1). Advance online publication. DOI: 10.59400/issc.v3i1.418

Juma, M., & Shaalan, K. (2020). Cyberphysical systems in the smart city: Challenges and future trends for strategic research. *Swarm Intelligence for Resource Management in Internet of Things*, 65-85. https://doi.org/DOI: 10.1016/B978-0-12-818287-1.00008-5

Kaginalkar, A., Kumar, S., Gargava, P., & Niyogi, D. (2021). Review of urban computing in air quality management as smart city service: An integrated IoT, AI, and cloud technology perspective. *Urban Climate*, *39*, 100972. DOI: 10.1016/j.uclim.2021.100972

Kumar, A., Bag, A., Anand, A., Saha, S., Mohapatra, H., & Kolhar, M. (2024). Examining healthcare services utilizing cloud technology in intelligent urban environments. *Advances in Healthcare Information Systems and Administration*, •••, 77–98. DOI: 10.4018/979-8-3693-7225-8.ch004

Kumar, A., Khan, S. B., Pandey, S. K., Shankar, A., Maple, C., Mashat, A., & Malibari, A. A. (2023). Development of a cloud-assisted classification technique for the preservation of secure data storage in smart cities. *Journal of Cloud Computing (Heidelberg, Germany)*, *12*(1), 92. Advance online publication. DOI: 10.1186/s13677-023-00469-9

Kumar, M., & Singh, A. (2022). Probabilistic data structures in smart city: Survey, applications, challenges, and research directions. *Journal of Ambient Intelligence and Smart Environments*, *14*(4), 229–284. DOI: 10.3233/AIS-220101

Kumar, V., & Madria, S. (2013). PIP: Privacy and integrity preserving data aggregation in wireless sensor networks. *2013 IEEE 32nd International Symposium on Reliable Distributed Systems*, 10-19. https://doi.org/DOI: 10.1109/SRDS.2013.10

Li, F., Luo, B., & Liu, P. (2010). Secure information aggregation for smart grids using homomorphic encryption. *2010 First IEEE International Conference on Smart Grid Communications*, 327-332. https://doi.org/DOI: 10.1109/SMARTGRID.2010.5622064

Mohamed, N., Al-Jaroodi, J., & Jawhar, I. (2020). Opportunities and challenges of data-driven cybersecurity for smart cities. *2020 IEEE Systems Security Symposium (SSS)*, 1-7. https://doi.org/DOI: 10.1109/SSS47320.2020.9174388

Mohapatra, H. (2021). Socio-technical challenges in the implementation of smart city. *2021 International Conference on Innovation and Intelligence for Informatics, Computing, and Technologies (3ICT)*, 57-62. https://doi.org/DOI: 10.1109/3ICT53449.2021.9581905

Mohapatra, H., & Mishra, S. R. (2024). Unlocking insights: Exploring data analytics and AI tool performance across industries. *Studies in Big Data*, 265-288. https://doi.org/DOI: 10.1007/978-981-97-0448-4_13

Mohapatra, H., & Rath, A. K. (2021). A fault tolerant routing scheme for advanced metering infrastructure: An approach towards smart grid. *Cluster Computing*, *24*(3), 2193–2211. DOI: 10.1007/s10586-021-03255-x

Panda, A. K., Lenka, A. A., Mohapatra, A., Rath, B. K., Parida, A. A., & Mohapatra, H. (2024). Integrating cloud computing for intelligent transportation solutions in smart cities. *Advances in Civil and Industrial Engineering*, •••, 121–142. DOI: 10.4018/979-8-3693-6695-0.ch005

Priyadarshi, S., Subudhi, S., Kumar, S., Bhardwaj, D., & Mohapatra, H. (2024). Analysis on enhancing urban mobility with IoT-integrated parking solutions. *Advances in Civil and Industrial Engineering*, •••, 143–172. DOI: 10.4018/979-8-3693-6695-0.ch006

Raj, S., Sheel, S., Singh, R., Ashar, S., & Mohapatra, H. (2025). Securing smart cities. *New Horizons in Leadership*, 487-512. https://doi.org/DOI: 10.4018/979-8-3693-6437-6.ch021

Rao, P. M., & Deebak, B. D. (2022). Security and privacy issues in smart cities/industries: Technologies, applications, and challenges. *Journal of Ambient Intelligence and Humanized Computing*, *14*(8), 10517–10553. DOI: 10.1007/s12652-022-03707-1

Rauf, A., Guru, A., & Mohapatra, H. (2024). Exploring the social model of smart home devices. *Advances in Human and Social Aspects of Technology*, •••, 233–256. DOI: 10.4018/979-8-3693-9235-5.ch012

Sahib, U. (2019). Smart Dubai: Sensing Dubai smart city for smart environment management. *Advances in 21st Century Human Settlements*, 437-489. https://doi.org/DOI: 10.1007/978-981-13-6822-6_12

Samarakkody, A., Amaratunga, D., & Haigh, R. (2023). Technological innovations for enhancing disaster resilience in smart cities: A comprehensive urban scholar's analysis. *Sustainability (Basel)*, *15*(15), 12036. DOI: 10.3390/su151512036

Sapra, R., & Dhaliwal, P. (2019). Blockchain for security issues of Internet of things (IoT). *Intelligent Systems Reference Library*, 599-626. https://doi.org/DOI: 10.1007/978-3-030-33596-0_24

Shamsuzzoha, A., Nieminen, J., Piya, S., & Rutledge, K. (2021). Smart city for sustainable environment: A comparison of participatory strategies from Helsinki, Singapore and London. *Cities (London, England)*, *114*, 103194. DOI: 10.1016/j.cities.2021.103194

Sharma, A., Anand, N., Mukherjee, S., Kumar, S., Kumar, S., & Mohapatra, H. (2024). Analyzing territorial variations in the implementation of IoT-based smart homes. *Advances in Electronic Government, Digital Divide, and Regional Development*, •••, 305–334. DOI: 10.4018/979-8-3693-6854-1.ch010

Singh Bhathal, G. (2022). Challenges and opportunities in mobile cloud computing for big data analytics. [IJSR]. *International Journal of Science and Research (Raipur, India)*, *11*(1), 1611–1615. DOI: 10.21275/ES24424211225

Zargar, S. T., Joshi, J., & Tipper, D. (2013). A survey of defense mechanisms against distributed denial of service (DDoS) flooding attacks. *IEEE Communications Surveys and Tutorials*, *15*(4), 2046–2069. DOI: 10.1109/SURV.2013.031413.00127

Chapter 9

Customer Satisfaction in Indigenous Telecommunication Companies in Nigeria: Role of Service Quality

Timilehin Olasoji Olubiyi
https://orcid.org/0000-0003-0690-7722
Babcock University, Ilishan-Remo, Nigeria

Adedayo Olufemi Ogunberu
Babcock University, Ilishan-Remo, Nigeria

Omolade Sunday Adeyemi
Oduduwa University, Ile-Ife, Nigeria

Adekunle Oluwole Binuyo
Babcock University, Ilishan-Remo, Nigeria

Balraj Verma
https://orcid.org/0000-0002-6542-3261
Chitkara University, Punjab, India

Bibin Xavier
https://orcid.org/0000-0001-6303-2067
Marian College, Kuttikkanam, India

ABSTRACT

Nigeria's telecommunication sector is strongly impacted by customer satisfaction and more so the sector is a competitive landscape where companies are vying to maintain their market share, ensure consumer satisfaction, and cultivate enduring service quality. Service quality is a major factor in determining customer satisfaction, especially regarding mobile service offerings, network reliability, data speed, and coverage. Therefore, this study examined the service quality and customer satisfaction of selected telecommunication firms in Nigeria. The study employed quantitative methods and survey research while the population for the study consisted of ninety-four service team members selected from three (3) telecommunication

DOI: 10.4018/979-8-3373-0482-3.ch009

firms with the largest number of subscribers in Nigeria. The study concluded that service quality affects customer satisfaction of selected telecommunication firms in Nigeria. It was recommended that firms should place more effort into improving the quality of products and services to improve customer satisfaction and help reduce customer attrition.

INTRODUCTION

Customer satisfaction in Nigeria's telecom sector is strongly impacted by service quality, which is still a crucial concern. Service quality is a major factor in determining customer loyalty, especially in relation to mobile services offering, network reliability, data speed, and coverage. Consumers want reliable service, yet many experience frequent interruptions, which makes them unhappy. Telecommunication firms need to enhance their service quality to aid customer satisfaction and be competitive. Low quality offerings erode consumer satisfaction among such firms as MTN, Airtel, and Glo (Ogunode & Oyebola, 2022). Furthermore, sustaining consumer satisfaction depends on the dependability of the product coming from executed services, although many Nigerian telecommunications firms have difficulty providing flawless services. Problems such as missed calls, sluggish internet connections, and coverage gaps irritate users. Despite the firms' efforts to increase its infrastructure, these problems still exist. Previous studies indicated that raising the service quality can greatly increase customer satisfaction since satisfied customers are more likely to stay loyal to a business, however, other studies were inconclusive on such (Mohammed et al., 2021). In addition, customers' growing demands for corporate accountability make the problem of dissatisfaction worse. This is known as "greenwashing," or making false environmental claims. While several Nigerian telecom companies tout their sustainability initiatives, these claims are undermined by poor product quality occasioned by the service quality at the beginning. Consumers place a high value on genuine and transparent product offerings, underscoring the necessity for the firms to match their marketing to the real quality produced and thus ensure customer satisfaction (Sharma, 2020). Therefore, Nigerian telecommunication firms need to make investments in reliable infrastructure, pay attention to service implementation and open communication to solve these problems. Raising the caliber of the product offering should increase customer satisfaction while lowering churn rates. A client-centric strategy is crucial, where the product's quality coming from executed service will match the expectations of the customer (Egena, 2018).

The researches of Moore, (2014); Awwal (2014); Pastuszak, Chadam, Phusavat and Polkowska (2013); Carl, (2016), Muhammad, Zohreh and Mojde (2013) among others studied. Awwal (2014); Carl, (2016); Moore, (2014); Muhammad,

Zohreh, and Mojde (2013); Pastuszak *et al.*, (2013) studied service quality, its dimensions and firm performance especially in the construction industry and were able to establish a relationship, however, scholarly reviews revealed that there are few studies on the relationship between service quality and customer satisfaction in the telecommunication industry as identified by Al-Dubai and Alaghbari (2018); Pastuszak *et al.,* (2013). Organisational performance in the Nigerian telecommunication industry has been impacted by reduction in customer satisfaction with many of the complaints on poor product and service quality (NCC, 2017), which was the end result of service execution. Service quality challenges in the industry included; improper target setting of products and services quality requirements and standards, inappropriate quality auditing and control on products and services and issues related to substandard equipment (Service Management Institute, 2014; Bunu, Muhammad & Adamu, 2019). Where these conditions were adhered to, products and services quality met with expectations but where this was not the case, unsatisfactory products and services such as drop calls, unsolicited messages, and loss of service were the result experienced. Further challenges also included drop in active voice and data subscriptions by subscribers (NCC, 2017). The documentation of these quality issues and how they impacted customer satisfaction in the industry have been limited to agencies with few researchers actually documenting them (Rolik, 2017).

LITERATURE REVIEW

Service Quality

Liberatore and Johnson (2013) defined service quality as the value placed on the product of a service from the perspective of the customer. This definition, however, was not expanded to consider other quality impacting measures such as cost and skills set of the service team, duration used on the service and so on. However, Goswami (2015) defined service quality as factors that affect service completion, impact budget and enable customer satisfaction. The purposes of service quality management implementation are to achieve the objectives of the service, prevent risks in the service delivery schedule and cause the least possible difficulty. Quality is considered an important outcome of a service since the performance measures of services are usually based on time, cost and quality, also known as the iron triangle (Orwig & Brennan, 2000). Quality has different attributes – both subjective and objective – some of which are difficult or impossible to quantify. Thus, a comprehensive approach to the assessment of service quality to include the traditional service success measures such as cost, schedule and safety, as well as measures such as customer satisfaction, leadership, employee involvement, teamwork, training and responsiveness is recommended. The characteristics of service quality management begins with quality planning, which involves identifying relevant quality standards needed by the service (Rose, 2005; Chang, Ishii, Lee & Tezuka, 2013). Identifying standards and requirements and determining how to satisfy them is one of the key activities during quality planning, and that is the foundation for quality being truly planned and built upon (Rose, 2005). Rose (2005) emphasised the importance of customer and requirement prioritization to be completed in early stage, even before service plan, so that the service starts in the right direction and customer quality considerations are known at an early stage. The quality planning stage helps to determine the expected quality standards of the service sponsors, determine relevant tools needed to achieve the set standard and also determine the tools needed, procedures to follow, the techniques and resources needed to achieve the quality expectations on the service.

As an advantage, service quality emphasizes the needs of the market, assures better quality performance in every sphere of activity, stresses on bringing attitudinal changes and improvements in the performance of employees by promoting proper work culture and effective team work, helps in checking non-productive activities and waste, Helpful in meeting the competition and helps in developing an adequate system of communication. Disadvantages of service quality include; Production Disruption: Implementing a quality management system in a company requires extensive training of employees and these requires them to take some time of their day to day work duties. While the improvements do reduce lead time, eliminate waste and improve productivity, the beginning stages of implementing a quality management in an organisation can reduce worker output; Employee Resistance: service quality requires change in mind-set, attitude and methods for performing their jobs. When management does not effectively communicate the team approach of service quality, workers may become fearful, which leads to employee resistance. When workers resist the programme, it can lower employee morale and productivity for the business.

Customer Satisfaction

Customer satisfaction is defined as the conclusion a customer takes on a particular product or service or its features such as cost and quality that satisfies expected fulfilment (Alanazi & Bach, 2016). Customer satisfaction is central to the performance, contributing to the success of any organisation and it is also important to the organisation for global competition and continued sustenance of the market share (Krajnakova, Navikaite & Navickas, 2015) and it is also considered as a crucial factor influencing customer loyalty (Gerpott, Rams & Schindler, 2001). Winning in today's marketplace entails the need to build customer relationship and not just building the products; building customer relationship means delivering superior value over competitors to the target customers (Krajnakova, Navikaite & Navickas, 2015). Whether an organisation provides quality services or not will depend on the customers' feedback on the satisfaction they get from consuming the products, since higher levels of quality lead to higher levels of customer satisfaction (Arokiasamy, 2013).

Customer satisfaction refers to a customer's evaluation of products and services after purchase as opposed to their expectation (Sayani, 2015). These definitions are in line with the cognitive based school of thought that, satisfaction with products and services is a product of pre-purchase expectations and disconfirmation. In other words, if the perceived performance of the product or service exceeds the expectations of the customer, then the result is positive disconfirmation and if the performance of the product is below expectations, it leads to negative disconfirmation. Positive disconfirmation allows for continuity and growth while negative disconfirmation results in discontinuity and negative word of mouth (Sayani, 2015). Kotler (2000) defined satisfaction as feelings of pleasure or disappointment resulting from comparing a product's perceived performance (or outcome) in relation to one's expectations.

According to Schiffman and Kanuk (2004), customer satisfaction is defined as the individual's perception of the performance of the products or services in relation to his or her expectations. Tsai, Tsai & Chang (2010) defined customer satisfaction as a judgment for the difference between the quality of the product or service and customer's own expectation. According to this argument, customers will be satisfied if the quality of the product or service above demands or expectation. On the other hand, if the quality of the product or service is below demands or expectation, customer will be dissatisfied.

Characteristics of customer satisfaction include; Product or Service quality where the associated attributes have the capacity to satisfy the needs and want of the customer. The quality of the product or service, where the quality is high, the customer can be over-satisfied and where the quality is low, the customer can be under-satisfied and can lead to rejection of the product or service and thus negatively impacting market share and organisational performance (Alanazi & Bach, 2016); pricing, which is crucial for dominance in the market. Pricing is usually influenced by service and product cost, anticipated volume and target market; Service quality where the response time and manner to calls and service requests from customers are important in mainly good perception of the product or service. Products and services with good support and after sales service responses tend to attract and sustain customers over time more than those products and services with poor service quality.

In the telecommunication industry, being a highly competitive and dynamic industry in Nigeria, customer satisfaction is largely dependent upon product and service quality offerings. Exceptional service or product quality is a significant source of distinctive competence in the market and often considered a key success factor in sustaining competitive advantage in the industry. Customer satisfaction create advantages such as buy-again opportunities. When customers are satisfied, they will continue to show loyalty through repeated purchases of service and product offering thus impacting sales and market share of the organisation. Customer satisfaction also helps to ensure that organisations are focused on improving service and product quality. This is quite important in telecommunication industry where competition is high and each organisation is constantly researching on improved services and products to gain competitive advantage. In an attempt to continually ensure customer satisfaction, organisations tend to maintain price reasonability and once the price is fairly stable, customers tend to be satisfied, so long as the quality of the service or product offering is not compromised (Rahman, 2014).

Service Quality and Customer Satisfaction

Moore (2014) studied the personality traits of successful service teams: Identifying service management team member personality characteristics. Using survey research design, data gathered from primary source was analysed using regression analysis. Similarly, Feng, Jingshan, Guoxian and Jorge (2013) investigated quality flow model in automotive paint shops. Secondary data were employed under the exploratory research design. Under the probability techniques simple random sampling technique was used by most researchers (Ogunberu, Akintelu & Olaposi, 2018; Moore, 2014; Beleiu, Crisan & Nistor, 2014; Dziekoski, 2017) for their studies to mention a few. Simple random sampling was advantageous to this study because it allows the sampling error to be calculated and reduces selection bias. A specific advantage is that it is the most straightforward method of probability sampling. A disadvantage of simple random sampling is that you may not select enough individuals with your characteristic of interest, especially if that characteristic is uncommon. A number of the researchers (El Sawalhi & Enshassi, 2013; Solis-Carcano, Corona-Suarez & Garcia-Ibarra, 2016) who employed simple random sampling also adopted stratified random sampling and some did not. Stratified sampling technique improves the accuracy and representativeness of the results by reducing sampling bias and helps to stratify the population, to ensure equal representation.

Arturo *et al.* (2015) studied the contextual and mediation analysis of total quality management (TQM) as a critical success factor in service excellence and found that designing a model that supports reliability and validity for implementing TQM as a success factor on services impacts the quality of service deliverables and leads to customer satisfaction. Maneesh, Khawaja, and Dianne (2014) studied the status of quality management practices in manufacturing SMEs and the finding revealed that the adoption of Six Sigma to quality management directly impacts customer satisfaction over time. The study explained that implementation of the process on service deliverables improves the quality, reduces errors and improves customer satisfaction. Sean and Gray (2013) studied inter-organisational quality management and found a positive relationship between quality and customer satisfaction. The study revealed that quality audit is important to the perception of consumer of products and services. Alanazi and Bach (2016) also studied the factors that affect and enhance Customer Satisfaction and found a positive relationship between quality and customer satisfaction. They found out that product quality, service quality, price quality affect customer satisfaction.

In addition, Christos, Evangelos, and Fotis (2010) while investigating total quality management practice among organisations revealed that the process of quality management and employee involvement influence service quality improvement and enhance customer satisfaction. Evangelos and Jiju (2015) reviewed the ISO 9001 quality management practices among organisations and found that continuous improvement process in quality measurement positively influences customer satisfaction and also prevents non-conformance, while Milunovic and Filipovic (2013) reviewed the methodology for quality management of services in manufacturing industries and found that customer satisfaction is influenced by the quality management in place in the organisation. The study also revealed that methodology for quality management can be specific to services. Suchanek, Richter and Kralova (2015) reviewed customer satisfaction, product quality and performance of companies and found that there is a positive correlation between customer satisfaction dimensions of customer need, satisfaction and repeat purchase. They were the major indicators influenced by service quality. The result showed that other customer satisfaction dimensions of recommendation, comparison and evaluation were not influenced by service and product quality. Similarly, the results of the study of Sugrova, Sedik, Kubelakova and Svetlikova (2017) on the impact of the product quality on consumer satisfaction and corporate brand, proved that there is a positive connection between service, product quality and customer satisfaction. The result further revealed that repeat purchase by customers is influenced by product quality. The result also showed that customers' behaviours, ages and tastes were also influencers to repeat purchase and satisfaction.

The study of Razak, Nirwanto and Triatmanto (2016) on the impact of product quality and price on customer satisfaction with the mediator of customer value, found that the functional value of a product to the customer is not optimal yet to be a major consideration for satisfaction but precisely the product quality conforming to set standards. The research further found that product quality dimensions of performance, features, reliability, conformity, durability, service capabilities, aesthetics and perceived quality, all have positive and significant effect on customer value and satisfaction. However, the result showed that a more affordable product price positively influences customer satisfaction. Olise and Ojiaku (2018), while studying the effect of product quality on customer satisfaction explained that the survival of a firm in a competitive environment depends on the quality of the products emanating from implemented services. The research explained further that customer satisfaction is dependent upon the ability of the firm to meet up with customer requirements and these must have been considered during the scope definition phase of the service. Based on the analysis, it was found that the quality of a product has a significant impact on the customers' satisfaction, and this in turn leads to high performance of the firms. Based on these, the researchers therefore recommended that apart from the product quality, there is a need for the customers to put into consideration other influencing factors that might affect customers" satisfaction, like customer services and price.

Hoe and Mansori (2018) studied the factors that can influence customer satisfaction and consequently customer loyalty. The study used Garvin's eight dimensions of product loyalty (performance, features, reliability, conformance, durability, serviceability, aesthetics and perceived quality) that affect customer satisfaction, which impacts loyalty. The result of the study indicated that durability, serviceability, aesthetics and perceived quality were significant and positively influences customer satisfaction with serviceability and perceived quality having the highest. The result also showed that performance, features and reliability had influence on customer satisfaction but this relationship was not significant. Similarly, Sitanggang, Sinulingga and Fachruddin (2019) while reviewing how product or service from a service meets its specification, explained that the consistency of the quality from such a product or service can contribute to the success of the firm reviewed through customer satisfaction, employee satisfaction and firm profitability. The research considered product quality dimensions of performance, features, reliability, conformance, durability, serviceability and perceived growth. The research found that there is a positive and significant effect between product quality dimensions of performance, reliability, serviceability and perceived growth with customer satisfaction while there is no significant effect of product quality dimensions of features and conformance on customer satisfaction.

Some authors also found positive relationships between service quality and customer satisfaction (Bogers, Chesbrough & Moedas, 2018; Wang, Zhang, Li, & Guo, 2018) while others have found negative correlation (Fageha & Aibinu, 2013). Having satisfied customers does not only hold the potential of increasing an organisation's customer base, but also increases the use of more volatile customer mix and increase the firm's reputation (Alabar, Egena & Gbande, 2017).

Hypothesis Development

Alabar et al., (2017); Rahman (2014), in an empirical study using questionnaire as research instrument found that there was positive relationship between service quality, service quality, product quality, product reliability and customer satisfaction. The positive finding also explained this relationship having direct impact on product innovativeness, customers demand, value added services and brand value of the organisations. Daria, Maurizio, Alessandro and Fabio (2012); Arturo, Araceli, Carolina and Lourdes (2015) investigated quality management and deduced that quality management especially Total Quality Management (TQM) process showed a high positive impact on internal process and production systems thus impacting operational performance of the organisation. The research of Alabar et al., (2017) in Nigeria, also determined that a relationship exists between service quality (SQ) or product delivery and customer satisfaction (CS), also between service quality reliability dimension and customer satisfaction, and finally, between customer satisfaction and switching intention among mobile phone users in Nigeria. The results have indicated that the two constructs (SQ and CS) were undeniably independent but were closely related and without a doubt, potential partners, implying that an increase in one was likely to cause a change in another. Ali and Abedalfattah (2013); Dara and Marc (2015), using quantitative method in their findings on the relationship between service quality and customer satisfaction showed that there was no relationship between service quality and customer satisfaction. Rather, the study established a relationship between quality management dimensions (leadership, strategic planning, customer focus, and employee relation), quality improvement plans of employees and organisational performance and not customer satisfaction. In light of the foregoing, this study hypothesised that:

H_{01}: Service quality does not have any significant effect on customer satisfaction of selected telecommunication firms in Nigeria.

Theoretical Foundation

The underpinning theory for this study on the interaction between service quality and customer satisfaction is the planning theory. The build-up for planning theory had commenced in the 1950s and the 1960s with several scholars postulating what really is planning and whether it can be introduced as a formal education for theorists and planners. However, planning theory was then propounded by Faludi (1973) as the application of scientific method, however crude, to policy making. It is a conscious effort made to increase the validity of policies in terms of the present and anticipated future of the environment. Validity is an attribute of the process by which decisions are made. It involves adviser, as the suppliers of scientific intelligence and decision makers. Advisers and decision makers interact thus forming a planning agency.

Supporting the theory, Koskela and Howell (2008) explained that it involves a process whereby methods and procedures are defined for setting goals, either for services or organisation, whereby these goals assist in the provision of options and providing directions towards achieving these objectives. It is a human action that translates know-how and planned objectives into meaning actions that help to achieve strategic view-points of the organisation. Similarly, The Service Management Institute (2017), supporting the theory, describes it from the view point of it broken down into different knowledge areas for service execution and these includes; scope planning, scope definition, activity definition, resource planning, activity sequencing, activity duration estimating, cost estimating, and schedule development, cost budgeting and service plan development. The output from these makes up an input to the executing processes.

The assumptions of the theory include the fact that it designs course of action for team members within a service, it provides opportunities for an evaluation of possible outcomes before implementation, it provides many options available for execution and team members can weigh these options and provide the pathway for the implementation of the chosen option. These assumptions form the foundation of the theory, which is similar to the planning processes utilised in service execution (Mulcahy, 2015).

Allmendinger (2002); Abukhater (2009) while critiquing the theory explained that planning is unique and its uniqueness stems partially from the inability to be defined in a single, narrow definition that fits it all. This is because planners are not a single entity that could fit into one category, nor can they fully agree on what planning really is. Rather, planners can vary across a continuum of interests, ranging from environmentalists and advocates, to even developers.

In explaining the relevance of planning to the study of service management, Szopik-Depczynska and Lanfranchi (2016); Service management institute (2017), explained that Planning is one of the elements of management, next to organising, motivating and control. It involves decision-making and action that will lead to the achievement of specific phenomena or objectives, the occurrence of which could not be spontaneous. Such objectives include staying ahead of competition, first-mover objectives and customer satisfaction initiatives.

Conceptual Framework

Figure 1. Authors conceptual model (2024)

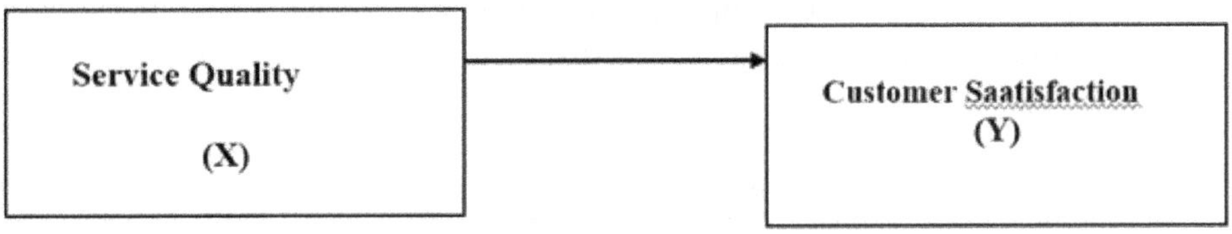

The above framework is further illustrated in the model equation below:

$Y_1 = \beta_0 + \beta_1 x_1 + e_i$ ---------------- equation 1

From equation (1), Y_1 is market share and x1 is service scope. β0 is the intercept, β1 is the Beta coefficient which captures all other variables that could explain market share outside the model.

Methodology

Quantitative methods and survey research designs were utilised to study the effect of service quality on customer satisfaction of selected telecommunication firms in Nigeria. The survey approach is employed to assess the opinions, attitudes, and feelings of various groups, allowing them to offer more dependable and honest input regarding the issue under inquiry. This study adopted the research methodology utilised by Adeyemi and Olubiyi, (2023), Arokodare, Falana, and Olubiyi, (2023), Olowoporoku, and Olubiyi,(2023), Olubiyi, (2023a), Olubiyi,(2023b), Olubiyi, (2022a), Olubiyi, Lawal, & Adeoye, (2022), Olubiyi, (2022b) and Olubiyi, (2022c) Olubiyi, Adeoye, Jubril, Adeyemi, and Eyanuku (2023) as well as Uwem, Oyedele, and Olubiyi, (2021) with cross-sectional have adopted this method in their respective studies and found it helpful. The study also used a proportionate sampling technique. The quantitative method was used in this study since it involved the utilisation and analysis of numerical data using specific statistical techniques to support or refute alternative knowledge claims as needed in this study. adapted structured questionnaire was used to gather primary data for the study. The primary population for this study consisted of three (3) selected telecommunication firms in Nigeria. These firms were chosen because they were the market leaders in the industry and had the largest number of subscribers in Nigeria (NCC subscriber data, 2022). The secondary population for the study included ninety-four (94) service employees in the Information System (IS) department of the selected telecommunication firms.

This population was less than two hundred (200) and thus the sample size used for this study was total enumeration as suggested by Ajay and Micah (2014). The sample size assisted in making inferences on the study population, reveal differences where necessary and help eliminate sampling error on the individuals in the population. Table 3.1 below presents the sample size distribution among the firms.

Table 1. Sample size distribution

S/N	Firm	No. of service employees in the IS department
1	MTN Nigeria	32
2	Airtel Nigeria	30
3	9 mobile	32
TOTAL		**94**

Source: Human Resource Department of Telecommunication Firms (2019)

Total enumeration was used to sample all the items in a universe leaving no element of chance to ensure that highest accuracy is obtained and it is used when the population is small. The respondents selected should be representative of the population concerned to give better responses representative enough for meaningful analysis and reporting (Kothari, 2004).

Data Analysis

Data analysis was performed by checking for consistency of filled questionnaire to ensure data cleansing, sorting and coding. Normality, Linearity, Homoscedasticity and Multicollinearity tests were performed on the data collected in line with the study objective. The objective of the study sought to evaluate the effect of service scope on market share of selected telecommunication firms in Nigeria. Study respondents were asked to indicate on a six-point Likert-type scale, their level of agreement on several statements describing service quality and its interaction with customer satisfaction. Using this scale, the study sought to know respondents' levels of agreement on various statements relating to service scope and market share of selected telecommunication firms.

Response Rate

The information system (IS) department personnel of the chosen telecommunication companies received ninety-four (94) copies of the research questionnaire. Seventy-four (74) questionnaires were correctly completed and given back to the researcher, yielding an equivalent response rate of 78.7%. This was a good representation and sufficient to draw conclusions from the study population. Table 4.1 present results of the response rate.

Table 2. Response rate

Responses	Frequency	Percent (%)
Completed usable copies of questionnaire	74	78.7%
Unusable, unreturned and disqualified questionnaires	20	21.3%
Total	94	100%

Source: Researcher's field survey (2019)

Demographics (n = 94)

This section discusses the independent variables first, then moves on to the dependent variables, providing an explanation of the descriptive statistical analysis of the respondents' opinions. For convenience of analysis, the responses were coded using numerical values on a six-point Likert-type scale. Five (5) for high (H), four (4) for moderately high (MH), three (3) for moderately low (ML), two (2) for low (L), and one (1) for very low (VL) were the values assigned. Descriptive statistics including percentages, means, and standard deviation were used to interpret the results.

The mean of the responses using a width of class interval were interpreted as follows: 5.50-6.00 implied very high degree, 4.50-5.49 implied high degree, 3.50-4.49 implied moderately high degree, 2.50-3.49 implied moderately low degree, 1.50-2.49 implied low degree and 0.50-1.49 implied very low degree. A standard deviation of more than one (1) indicated that the responses were widely distributed or no consensus, and less than 1 indicated consensus on responses obtained. The summarised responses as presented in the Tables below.

Table 3. Analysis of descriptive statistics of responses of respondents on service quality

Items	Very High	High	Moderately High	Moderately Low	Low	Very Low	Mean	Std. Dev.
Customer satisfaction	6.8%	83.8%	9.5%	0.0%	0.0%	0.0%	4.97	.405
Quality control	10.8%	50.0%	39.2%	0.0%	0.0%	0.0%	4.72	.652
Cost of Quality (cost of fixing issues) on the service	33.8%	50.0%	16.2%	0.0%	0.0%	0.0%	5.18	.690
Planning for quality on service	39.2%	50.0%	10.8%	0.0%	0.0%	0.0%	5.28	.652
Product acceptance	18.9%	41.9%	39.2%	0.0%	0.0%	0.0%	4.80	.740

Source: Field survey data (2024)

Table 2.1 presents respondents' responses to service quality. Table 2.1 shows that 6.8% of the respondents indicated that customer satisfaction is very high, 84.8% indicated high and 9.5% moderately high. On the average, the respondents indicated that customer satisfaction is high with a mean of 4.97 and standard deviation of 0.405. The results further show that 10.8% of the respondents responded very high to quality control, 50% indicated high and 39.2% moderately high. On the average, the respondents indicated that quality control is high with a mean of 4.72 and standard deviation of 0.652. The results reveal that 33.8% of the respondents indicated that cost of quality (cost of fixing issues) on the service is very high, 50% indicated high, 16.2% moderately high. On the average, the respondents indicated that cost of quality (cost of fixing issues) on the service is high with a mean of 5.18 and standard deviation of 0.690.

The results also indicated that 39.2% of the respondents responded very high to planning for quality on service, 50% indicated high, 10.8% moderately high. On the average, the respondents indicated that planning for quality on service is high with a mean of 5.28 and standard deviation of 0.652. Finally, the results in the Table shows that 18.9% of the respondents indicated that Product acceptance is very high, 41.9% indicated high, 39.2% indicated moderately high. On the average, the respondents indicated that product acceptance is high with a mean of 4.80 and standard deviation of 0.740.

The findings of the descriptive statistics of the variable, customer satisfaction are indicated on Table 2.2

Table 4. Analysis of descriptive statistics of responses of respondents on customer satisfaction

Items	Very High	High	Moderately High	Moderately Low	Low	Very Low	Mean	Std. Dev.
Customer acquisition	18.9%	67.6%	13.5%	0.0%	0.0%	0.0%	5.05	.571
Customer retention	13.5%	33.8%	51.4%	1.4%	0.0%	0.0%	4.59	.739
Customer feedback	24.3%	60.8%	13.5%	1.4%	0.0%	0.0%	5.08	.657
Customer attrition	45.9%	32.4%	21.6%	0.0%	0.0%	0.0%	5.24	.791
Customer complaints	17.6%	43.2%	37.8%	1.4%	0.0%	0.0%	4.77	.750

Source: Field survey data (2024)

Table 2.2 shows the perceptions of the participants on customer satisfaction. From the Table, about 18.9% of the respondents indicated that customer acquisition was very high, 67.6% indicated high and 13.5% moderately high. On the average, the respondents indicated that Customer acquisition was high with a mean of 5.05 and standard deviation of 0.571. The results towards customer retention indicated that 13.5% of the respondents responded very high, 33.8% indicated high, 51.4%

indicated moderately high and 1.4% indicated moderately low. On the average, the respondents indicated that customer retention was high with a mean of 5.08 and standard deviation of 0.657.

The results showed that 24.3% of the respondents indicated that customer feedback was very high, 60.8% indicated high, 13.5% moderately high and 1.4% indicated moderately low. On the average, the respondents indicated that customer feedback is high with a mean of 5.08 and standard deviation of 0.657. With regards to customer attrition, 45.9% of the respondents responded very high, 32.4% indicated high, 21.6% moderately high. On the average, the respondents indicated that customer attrition was high with a mean of 5.24 and a standard deviation of 0.791. Furthermore, 17.6% of the respondents that indicated that customer complaints were very high, 43.2% indicated high, 37.8% indicated moderately high. On the average, the respondents indicated that customer complaints were high with a mean of 4.77 and a standard deviation of 0.750.

Relating Tables 2.1 and 2.2 together, the descriptive statistics revealed that a larger percentage of the respondents rated most of the question items of service quality and customer satisfaction high and have similar pattern of increase with grand mean of 4.99 and 4.95, respectively. The findings revealed that planning for quality of service, cost of quality (cost of fixing issues) on the service and customer satisfaction are highly executed among telecommunication firms as most of the respondents' perceptions to these items tended towards "high" responses. In addition, the findings of the study revealed high customer attrition, customer feedback, and customer acquisition in the sequence. These findings, therefore, suggest that service quality may or may not affect customer satisfaction of selected telecommunication firms in Nigeria. This provided answer to the research question and enabled the researcher to achieve the objective of this study.

Test of Research Hypothesis

H_{01}: Service quality has no significant effect on customer satisfaction of selected telecommunication firms in Nigeria.

To test the hypothesis, linear regression analysis was used. Data for service quality and customer satisfaction were established by adding responses of all items for the variables. The resulting regression coefficients have been used to interpret the direction and magnitude of the relationship. The βeta coefficients showed the responsiveness of the dependent variable (customer satisfaction) as a result of unit change in the independent variable (service quality). The error term e_i captured the variations that cannot be explained by the model. The Regression results are presented in Table 2.3

Table 5. Results of regression of service quality on customer satisfaction

Variables	*B*	*Std. Error*	*t*	*p-value*	*R*	R^2
Constant	17.130	4.028	4.253	0.000	0.256	0.203
Service risk	0.515	0.064	8.059	0.000		

Source: Field survey results (2024)

Table 2.3 presents linear regression results on the effect of service quality on customer satisfaction of selected telecommunication firms in Nigeria. The result of the regression analysis revealed that service quality has a significant positive effect on the customer satisfaction of selected telecommunication firms in Nigeria ($\beta = 0.515$, $t = 8.059$, $p<0.05$). The value of t-statistics at 8.059 showed that the model parameter is statistically significant ($p<0.05$). Further, the result (Table 4.20) showed that there was a weak positive relationship between service quality and customer satisfaction of selected telecommunication firms ($R = 0.256$). This meant that an increase in service quality will lead to an increase in customer satisfaction of telecommunication firms.

From the results, R2 = 0.203, which indicated that about 20.3% changes in customer satisfaction of the selected telecommunication firms were explained by their service quality, while the remaining 79.7% changes in customer satisfaction of selected telecommunication firms in Nigeria were accounted for by other variables not captured in the model. This demand for an inquiry through research to find out the other variables that influence customer satisfaction of telecommunication firms in Nigeria. The simple regression model explaining the variation in customer satisfaction due to service quality is thus expressed as follows:

Customer Satisfaction = 17.130 + 0.515Service Quality .... Eq. 5

From the regression equation above, it was revealed that holding service quality constant at zero, customer satisfaction of selected telecommunication firms was at 17.130. The result showed that if there is an improvement in service quality by one unit in the measurement scale, customer satisfaction of the selected telecommunication firms is predicted to change, increase by 0.515 units. With the significant value in the model standing at 0.000, the level of significance is less than 0.05 ($p<0.05$). This meant that service quality significantly predicts customer satisfaction of telecommunication firms. Overall, the result shows that service quality has a weak positive effect on customer satisfaction of selected telecommunication firms in Nigeria. Therefore, the null hypothesis (H_{01}) that service quality does not have any significant effect on customer satisfaction of selected telecommunication firms in Nigeria is hereby rejected.

DISCUSSION AND CONCLUSION

The specific objective of this study sought to evaluate the effect of service quality on customer satisfaction of selected telecommunication firms in Nigeria. The result of the descriptive analysis for the objective shows that on the average majority of the respondents asserted customer satisfaction is high when service quality is high in the selected telecommunication firms in Nigeria, and there was convergence in the responses of the respondents around the mean. In this study, 83.3% of the respondent claimed that customer satisfaction in the selected telecommunication firms in Nigeria, while 50% of the respondents each affirmed high quality control and cost of quality (cost of fixing issues) on the service. The results also revealed that 67.6% of the respondents asserted Customer acquisition was high in selected telecommunication firms in Nigeria, however, findings unfolded that only 32.4% of respondents believed customer attrition was high in the selected telecommunication firms.

Besides, findings of the hypothesis (H_{01}) established a positive and statistically significant effect of service quality on the customer satisfaction in the selected telecommunication firms in Nigeria. Hence, the result of the descriptive statistics analysis for the objective and linear regression analysis testing of the hypothesis (H_{01}) affirmed that service quality has positive and significant effect on customer satisfaction in the selected telecommunication firms in Nigeria. The findings of this study were consistent with the research work of Arturo, Araceli, Carolina, and Lourde (2015) on contextual and mediation analysis of total quality management (TQM) as a critical success factor in service excellence found that designing a model that supports reliability and validity for implementing TQM as a success factor on services impacts the quality of service deliverables and lead to customer satisfaction. This position was corroborated with Maneesh, Khawaja, and Dianne (2014), who studied the status of quality management practices in manufacturing SMEs and the finding revealed that the adoption of Six Sigma to quality management directly impacts customer satisfaction over time. The study explained that implementation of the process on service deliverables improves the quality, reduces errors and improves customer satisfaction.

The work of Sean and Gray (2013), on inter-organisational quality management found a positive relationship between quality and customer satisfaction. The study revealed that quality audit is important to the perception of consumer of products and services. Alanazi and Bach (2016) found a positive relationship between quality and customer satisfaction. They found out that product quality, service quality, price quality affect customer satisfaction. Further, Christos, Evangelos, and Fotis (2010) found that the process of quality management and employee involvement influence service quality improvement and enhance customer satisfaction. Likewise, Evangelos and Jiju (2015) reviewed the ISO 9001 quality management practices among organisations and found that continuous improvement process in quality measurement positively influence customer satisfaction and prevent non-conformance, while Milunovic and Filipovic (2013) reviewed the methodology for quality management of services in manufacturing industries and found that customer satisfaction influenced by the quality management in place in the organisation. The study also revealed that the methodology for quality management can be specific to services.

Overall, current study has found out that service quality has a weak positive effect on customer satisfaction of selected telecommunication firms in Nigeria. Based on the findings of this study in collaboration with the findings from previous studies, the null hypotheses one ($H_0 1$), which states that service quality does not have any significant effect on customer satisfaction of selected telecommunication firms in Nigeria, is therefore rejected. The empirical study focused on investigating the relationship that exist between service quality and customer satisfaction of selected telecommunication firms in Nigeria and formulated a hypothesis that was analysed by simple linear regression. Result from the test of hypothesis showed that service quality has significant and positive effect on customer satisfaction. Therefore, the researcher concluded that service quality has a positive relationship with customer satisfaction and the more improved the quality of the products and services from the service, the more satisfied the customers.

Recommendation and Policy Implementation

The study further revealed that service quality and customer satisfaction have a positive relationship. This implies that the more improved the quality the more customer satisfaction experienced. There are high improvements in customer acquisition and retention while also, the customers provide many feedbacks and many complaints on the quality of products and services being rendered. It is, therefore, recommended that the firms should place more efforts in improving the quality of products and services in order to improve customer satisfaction and help reduce customer attrition.

Contribution to Knowledge and Suggestion for Further Studies

Conceptually, the study developed an improved perspective to customer satisfaction of telecommunication firms in Nigeria through the influence of service quality during service execution. The study explained the criticality of service quality to service execution and how it affects customer satisfaction of these firms. The study revealed that service quality targets customer satisfaction and are used on services to measure conform or non-conformance to quality standards. Conformance to quality standards aids customer satisfaction and buy-again opportunities and overall competitive advantage. The findings of this study indicated that there are other dimensions that influenced customer satisfaction apart from service quality, further research should be conducted to reveal these dimensions and how they influence customer satisfaction of telecommunication firms in Nigeria.

REFERENCES

Abukhater A. (2009). Rethinking planning theory and practice: A glimmer of light for prospects of integrated planning to combat complex urban realities. *Theoretical and empirical research in urban planning, 2*(11), 64 – 79.

Adeyemi, O. S., & Olubiyi, T. O.Adeyemi Omolade SundayOlubiyi Timilehin Olasoji. (2023). The Impact of Brand Awareness on Customer Loyalty in Selected Food and Beverage Businesses in Lagos State Nigeria. *Jurnal Multidisiplin Madani, 3*(3), 541–551. DOI: 10.55927/mudima.v3i3.3095

Adeyemi, T. (2009). Inferential statistics for social and behavioural research. *Research journal of mathematics and statistics 1*(2): 47-54.

Adeyemi, T. (2009). Inferential statistics for social and behavioural research. *Research journal of mathematics and statistics 1*(2): 47-54.

Adler, D. (2014). Scope change, flexibility and the management of services. *Review of integrative business and economics research, 4*(1), 469-483.

Aftab, H., Ismail, A., Ismaini, I.& Noor, Y. (2014). Time management practices in large construction services. *Colloquium on humanities, science and engineering, 5*(3), 61 - 65.

Ajay, S. & Micah, M. (2014). Sampling techniques & determination of sample size in applied statistics research: an overview. *International journal of economics, commerce and management, 2*(11), 1 – 22.

Ajay, S. & Micah, M. (2014). Sampling techniques & determination of sample size in applied statistics research: an overview. *International journal of economics, commerce and management, 2*(11), 1 – 22.

Akewushola, R., Olateju, O., Hammed, O., & Lawale, G. (2012). Effect of service management on service success. *Australian Journal of Business and Management Research, 2*(3), 1–11. DOI: 10.52283/NSWRCA.AJBMR.20120203A01

Alabar, T., Egena, E., & Gbande, I. (2017). Service quality and customer satisfaction in Nigerian mobile telephony. *British journal of marketing. Studies, 5*(3), 1–13.

Alanazi, A. & Bach, C. (2016). Factors that affect and enhance customer satisfaction. *Journal of research in business and management, 4*(9), 80 - 88.

Al_Dubai, M. & Alaghbari, M. (2018). Relationship between organisational factors towards service success. *Journal of internet banking and commerce, 23*(2), 20 - 32.

Ali, B. & Abedalfattah, Z. (2013). The effect of quality management practices on organisational performance in Jordan: An empirical study. *International journal of financial Research, 4*(1), 12 - 21.

Allmendinger, P. (2002). *Planning Theory*. Palgrave.

Arokiasamy, A. (2013). The impact of customer satisfaction on customer loyalty and intentions to switch in the banking sector in Malaysia. *The journal of commerce, 5*(1), 2220-6043.

Arokodare, M. A., Falana, R. B., & Olubiyi, T. O. (2023). Strategic agility, knowledge management and organisational performance in a post-pandemic era: A mediation analysis. *Journal of Family Business and Management Studies*, *27*, 83–108.

Arturo, C., Araceli, P., Carolina, R., & Lourdes, C. (2015). Contextual and mediation analysis between TQM critical factors and organisational results in the EFQM excellence model framework. *International Journal of Production Research, 25*(8), 923–934.

Assudani, R., & Kloppenborg, J. (2010). Managing stakeholders for service management success: An emergent model of stakeholders. *Journal of General Management, 36*(1), 67–80. DOI: 10.1177/030630701003500305

Awwal, M. (2014). Importance of strategic aspect in service management: A literature critique. *International journal of supply chain management, 3*(4), 96 - 99.

Beleiu, I., Crisan, E. & Nistor, R. (2014). Main factors influencing service success. *Interdisciplinary management research, 11*, 59-72.

Bogers, M., Chesbrough, H. & Moedas, C. (2018). Open innovation: Research, practices, and policies. *Sage journals, 60*(2), 1 - 10.

Brandon, D. (2006). *Service management for modern information system*. Idea group.

Bukit, I., Ismida, Y., Maulana, R.& Nasir, M. (2018). The influence of wage, age and experience to labor productivity in construction works in Kota Langsa, Aceh. *MATEC web of conferences, 147*(1), 10 - 14.

Bunu, S, Muhammad, M. & Adamu, H. (2019). Review and analysis on telecommunication networks infrastructure in the northwest province of Nigeria for optimisation: Problems and solutions. *International journal of computer science & engineering survey (IJCSES), 10*(1), 1 – 14.

Carl, O. (2016). Service management problems in small and medium enterprises in Nigeria. *Journal of entrepreneurship & organisation management, 5*(169), 1 - 3.

Chang, Y., Ishii, M., Lee, P.& Tezuka, K. (2013). A game theoretical analysis of port competition, transportation research part e: logistics and transportation review. *Elsevier, 49*(1), 92-106.

Christos, V., Evangelos, L., & Fotis, K. (2010). Investigating total quality management practice's inter-relationships in ISO 9001: 2000 certified organisations. *Total Quality Management & Business Excellence, 21*(5), 503–515. DOI: 10.1080/14783363.2010.481512

Cooper, L. & Nakanishi. (2014). *Market share analysis: Evaluating competitive marketing effectiveness*. Boston: Kluwer Academic Publishers.

Dara, S. & Marc, S. (2015). Quality management and innovation: New insights on a structural contingency framework. *International journal of quality innovation, 1*(2), 1 - 5.

Daria, B., Maurizio, F., Alessandro, P., & Fabio, S. (2012). Design of an integrated quality assurance strategy in production systems. *International Journal of Production Research, 50*(6), 1–20.

Dicksen, P. R. (1996). The static and dynamic mechanics of competitive theory. *Journal of Marketing, 60*, 102–106. DOI: 10.1177/002224299606000409

Dicksen, P. R. (1996). The static and dynamic mechanics of competitive theory. *Journal of Marketing, 60*, 102–106. DOI: 10.1177/002224299606000409

Donaldson, T., & Preston, L. (1995). The stakeholder theory of the corporation: Concepts, evidence, and implications. [El]. *Academy of Management Review, 20*(1), 501–522. DOI: 10.2307/258887

Dziekoski, K. (2017). Service managers' competencies model for construction industry in Poland. *Science direct, 182*, 174-181.

Egena, A. N. (2018). Service quality and customer satisfaction in Nigerian mobile telephony. *Journal of Business and Management, 7*(1), 112–130.

El Hajjar, S. (2018). Statistical analysis: internal-consistency reliability and construct validity. *International journal of quantitative and qualitative research methods, 6*(1), 27-38.

El Sawalhi, N. & Enshassi. (2013). Application of service time management tools and techniques to the construction industry in the Gaza strip. *The Australasian Journal of Construction Economics and Building, 5*(1), 1–8.

Evangelos, P., & Jiju, A. (2015). The effectiveness of the ISO 9001 quality management system and its influential critical factors in Greek manufacturing companies. *International Journal of Production Research, 53*(7), 2089–2099. DOI: 10.1080/00207543.2014.965353

Fageha, M., & Aibinu, A. (2013). Managing service scope definition to improve stakeholders' participation and enhance service outcome. *Procedia: Social and Behavioral Sciences, 74*(2), 154–164. DOI: 10.1016/j.sbspro.2013.03.038

Fageha, M., & Aibinu, A. (2013). Managing service scope definition to improve stakeholders' participation and enhance service outcome. *Procedia: Social and Behavioral Sciences, 74*(2), 154–164. DOI: 10.1016/j.sbspro.2013.03.038

Faludi, A. (1973). *A reader in planning theory* (1st ed.). Pergamon press.

Fashina, A., Abdilahi, S., Hassan, A., & Fakunle, F. (2020). The significant factors that influence the choice of service scope management practices in telecommunication companies in Somaliland. *PM World Journal., 9*(3), 1–12.

Fauziya, B., & Linge, K. (2019). Strategic Factors Influencing Market Share of Telecommunications in Kenya. *Journal of Marketing Communications, 2*(1), 80–91.

Feng, J., Jingshan, L., Guoxian, X., & Jorge, A. (2013). Quality flow model in automotive paint shops. *International Journal of Production Research, 48*(17), 5021–5030.

Fowler, J., & Floyd, J. (1995). *Improving survey questions: Design and evaluation*. Sage Publications.

Freeman, R. (1984). *Strategic management: A stakeholder approach*. Pitman/Ballinger.

Gerpott, T., Rams, W., & Schindler, A. (2001). Customer retention, loyalty and satisfaction in the German mobile cellular telecommunications market. *Telecommunications Policy, 25*(1), 249–269. DOI: 10.1016/S0308-5961(00)00097-5

Glasgow, P. (2005). *Fundamentals of survey research methodology*. Mitre.

Golini, R., Kalchschmidt, M., & Landoni, P. (2015). Adoption of service management practices: The impact on international development services of non-governmental organizations. *International Journal of Service Management., 11*(2), 21–35.

Goodpaster, K. (1991). Business ethics and stakeholder analysis. *Business Ethics Quarterly, 1*(1), 53–73.

Goswami, S. (2015). Role of quality management system in service completion. *Pipeline & gas journal, 242*(5), 101- 109.

Harrison, J., Freeman, R., & Abreu, M. (2015). Stakeholder theory as an ethical approach to effective management: Applying the theory to multiple contexts. *Revista Brasileira de Gestão de Negócios, 17*(55), 858–869. DOI: 10.7819/rbgn.v17i55.2647

Heravi, A., Coffey, V.& Trigunarsyah, B. (2015). Evaluating the level of stakeholder involvement during the service planning processes of building services. *International journal of service management, 33*(5), 1 - 9.

Hoe, L. & Mansori, S. (2018). The effects of product quality on customer satisfaction and loyalty: Evidence from Malaysian engineering industry. *International journal of industrial marketing, 3*(1), 20 -35.

Katuse, P., Ngari, J., & Owich, S. (2018). The strategy implementation and organization performance of companies at Nairobi securities exchange. *European Journal of Social Sciences, 5*(1), 37–48.

Koskela, L., & Howell, G. (2008). The underlying theory of service management is obsolete. *IEEE Engineering Management Review, 36*(2), 22–34. DOI: 10.1109/EMR.2008.4534317

Kothari, C. (2004). *Research methodology: methods and techniques* (2nd ed.). New age international publishers.

Krajnakova, E., Navikaite, A., & Navickas, V. (2015). Paradigm shift of small and medium-sized enterprises competitive advantage. *The Engineering Economist, 26*(3), 25–34.

Lancaster, G., & Massingham, L. (2013). *Essentials of marketing management* (2nd ed.). Routledge.

Liberatore, M. & Johnson, B. (2013). Improving service management decision making by modelling quality, time, and cost continuously. *Trans engineering management, 2*(9), 518–528.

Maneesh, K., Khawaja, K., & Dianne, W. (2014). Status of quality management practices in manufacturing SMEs: A comparative study between Australia and the UK. *International Journal of Production Research, 52*(21), 6482–6495. DOI: 10.1080/00207543.2014.948574

Manfio, N., & Lacerda, D. (2016). Definition of scope in new product development services for the food industry: A proposed method. *Gestão & Produção, 23*(1), 18–36. DOI: 10.1590/0104-530X1009-13

Milunovic, S., & Filipovic, J. (2013). Methodology for quality management of services in manufacturing industries. *Total Quality Management & Business Excellence, 24*(1-2), 91–107. DOI: 10.1080/14783363.2012.728851

Mohammed, A.. (2021). Product quality and customer satisfaction in the telecommunications sector. *JMR, Journal of Marketing Research, 12*(3), 223–235.

Moore, M. (2014). The personality traits of successful service teams: Identifying service management team member personality characteristics. *Journal of Health & Medical Informatics, 5*(3), 92–103.

Muhammad, N., Zohreh, P., & Mojde, S. (2013). Significance of scope in service success. *ScienceDirect, 9*(2), 722–729.

Muhammad, N., Zohreh, P., & Mojde, S. (2013). Significance of scope in service success. *ScienceDirect, 9*(2), 722–729.

Mulcahy, R. (2015). *PMP exam prep: Rita's course in a book for passing the PMP exam* (7th ed.). RMC publications.

Nibyiza, F., Shukla, J.& Ndabaga, E. (2015). Analysis of service scope change management as a tool for service success: Case study of Akazi Kanoze services. *European journal of business and social sciences, 4*(3), 29 – 41.

Nicholas, M., & Steyn, H. (2012). *Service management for engineering, business, and technology*. Routledge.

Nigerian Communications Commission (NCC) subscriber data (2017). Industry overview: Subscribers/Teledensity. Retrieved from https://www.ncc.gov.ng/stakeholder/statistics-reports/industry-overview

Nigerian Communications Commission (NCC) subscriber data (2018). Industry overview: Subscribers/Teledensity. Retrieved from https://www.ncc.gov.ng/stakeholder/statistics-reports/industry-overview

Ogunberu, A., Akintelu, S., & Olaposi, T. (2016). Factors affecting the choice of service scope management practices among telecommunication organizations. *Global journal of management and business research. Administrative Management, 16*(3), 13–19.

Ogunberu, A., Akintelu, S. & Olaposi, T. (2018). Application of service scope management practices on service success among telecommunication organizations in Nigeria. *International journal of development and sustainability, 7*(2), 518-532.

Ogunberu, A., Akintelu, S. & Olaposi, T. (2018). Application of service scope management practices on service success among telecommunication organizations in Nigeria. *International journal of development and sustainability, 7*(2), 518-532.

Ogunode, P. O., & Oyebola, S. A. (2022). Customer satisfaction and complaints management in Nigerian telecommunications. *British Journal of Management and Marketing Studies*, *5*(1), 18–35.

Olise, M. & Ojiaku, O. (2018), Effects of product quality on customer satisfaction: A review of manufacturing company's performance in Anambra state. *International journal of business & law research* *6*(1), 39-47.

Olowoporoku, A. A., & Olubiyi, T. O. (2023). Evaluating Service Quality and Business Outcomes Post-Pandemic: Perspective from Hotels in Emerging Market. *Sawala: Jurnal Administrasi Negara*, *11*(2), 182–201. DOI: 10.30656/sawala.v11i2.6975

Olubiyi, O. T., Lawal, A. T., & Adeoye, O. O. (2022). Succession planning and family business continuity: Perspectives from Lagos State, Nigeria. *Organization and Human Capital Development*, *1*(1), 40–52. DOI: 10.31098/orcadev.v1i1.865

Olubiyi, T. O. (2019). Knowledge management practices and family business profitability: Evidence from Lagos State, Nigeria. *Global Journal of Management and Business Research*, *19*(A11), 21–31. https://journalofbusiness.org/index.php/GJMBR/article/view/2872

Olubiyi, T. O. (2020). Knowledge management practices and family business profitability: Evidence from Lagos State, Nigeria [Nigerian Chapter]. *Arabian Journal of Business and Management Review*, *6*(1), 23–32.

Olubiyi, T. O. (2022a). Measuring technological capability and business performance post-COVID Era: Evidence from Small and Medium-Sized Enterprises (SMEs) in Nigeria. *Management & Marketing Journal*, *xx*(2), 234–248. DOI: 10.52846/MNMK.20.2.09

Olubiyi, T. O. (2022b). An investigation of sustainable innovative strategy and customer satisfaction in small and medium-sized enterprises (SMEs) in Nigeria. *Covenant Journal of Business and Social Sciences*, *13*(2), 1–24.

Olubiyi, T. O. (2023a). Unveiling the role of workplace environment in achieving the Sustainable Development Goal Eight (SDG8) and employee job satisfaction post-pandemic: Perspective from Africa. *Revista Management & Marketing Craiova*, *XXI*(2), 212–228. DOI: 10.52846/MNMK.21.2.02

Olubiyi T. O. (2023b). Leveraging competitive strategies on business outcomes post-covid-19 pandemic: Empirical investigation from Africa. *Journal of Management and Business: Research and Practice*, DOI: 10.54933/jmbrp-2023-15-2-1

Olubiyi, T. O. (2024). An investigation of the role of airline safety management and its impact on passenger satisfaction: a study of commercial airline businesses in Nigeria. Journal of the Management Sciences, 60(4). Retrieved from https://journals .unizik.edu.ng/jfms/article/view/3396 Nnamdi Azikiwe University, Awka, Nigeria

Olubiyi, T. O., Adeoye, O. O., Jubril, B., Adeyemi, O. S., & Eyanuku, J. P. (2023). Measuring Inequality in Sub-Saharan Africa Post-Pandemic: Correlation Results for Workplace Inequalities and Implication for Sustainable Development Goal ten. *International Journal of Professional Business Review*, *8*(4), e01405. DOI: 10.26668/ businessreview/2023.v8i4.1405

Olubiyi, T. O., & Akpa, V. A. (2023). Does innovative capability and artificial intelligence really matter for the profitability of consumer goods companies in developing economies? *SunText Review of Economics & Business*, *4*(3), 191–204.

Olubiyi, T. O., Jubril, B., Sojinu, O. S., & Ngari, R. (2022). Strengthening gender equality in small business and achieving sustainable development goals (SDGs), Comparative analysis of Kenya and Nigeria. *Sawala Jurnal Administrasi Negara*, *10*(2), 168–186. DOI: 10.30656/sawala.v10i2.5663

Omoyele, O. S., Olubiyi, T. O., Lanre-Babalola, F. O., Obadare, G. O., & Onikoyi, I. A. (2023). Business Model Innovation as a Catalyst for Sustainable Entrepreneurship: Empirical Findings from Small and Medium Enterprises in Nigeria. *Skyline Business Journal*, *19*(2), 55–64. DOI: 10.37383/SBJ190205

Orwig, R., & Brennan, L. (2000). An integrated view of service and quality management for service-based organizations. *International Journal of Quality & Reliability Management*, *17*(5), 351–363. DOI: 10.1108/02656710010298382

Orwig, R., & Brennan, L. (2000). An integrated view of service and quality management for service-based organizations. *International Journal of Quality & Reliability Management*, *17*(5), 351–363. DOI: 10.1108/02656710010298382

Osorio, P., Quelhas, O., Zotes, L., Shimoda, E., & Sergio, F. (2014). Critical success factors in service management: An exploratory study of an energy company in Brazil. *Global journal of management and business research. Administrative Management*, *14*(10), 39–50.

Pastuszak, Z., Chadam, J., Phusavat, K.& Polkowska, M. (2013). Strategic service management as component of innovative organisations. *Active citizenship by knowledge management and innovation, 8*(6), 11-31.

Rahman, H. (2014). Factors affecting customer satisfaction in mobile telecommunication industry in Bangladesh. *Business, management and education journal, 12*(1), 74–93.

Razak, I., Nirwanto, N. & Triatmanto, B. (2016). The impact of product quality and price on customer satisfaction with the mediator of customer value. *Journal of marketing and consumer research, 30(*1), 59 – 68.

Rolik, Y. (2017). Risk management in implementing wind energy services. *Procedia Engineering, 178*(19), 278–288. DOI: 10.1016/j.proeng.2017.01.115

Rose, K. (2005). *Service quality management: Why, what and how* (3rd ed.). USA: J. Ross publishing Inc.

Sarstedt, M., & Mooi, E. (2014). *A concise guide to market research*. Springer. DOI: 10.1007/978-3-642-53965-7

Sayani. (2015). Customer satisfaction and loyalty in the United Arab Emirates banking industry. *International journal of bank marketing, 33*(3), 351-375.

Schiffman, L., & Kanuk, L. (2004). *Consumer behaviour* (8th ed.). Prentice Hall.

Sean, M., & Gray, J. (2013). Inter-organisational quality management: The use of contractual incentives and monitoring mechanisms with outsourced manufacturing. *Production and Operations Management*, *22*(10), 1041–1056.

Sean, M., & Gray, J. (2013). Inter-organisational quality management: The use of contractual incentives and monitoring mechanisms with outsourced manufacturing. *Production and Operations Management*, *22*(10), 1041–1056.

Service Management Institute. (2017). *The PMBOK guide: A guide to the service management body of knowledge* (6th ed.). PMI Publications.

Sharma, A. (2020). Corporate accountability in telecommunications: Nigeria's case. *Journal of Corporate Responsibility*, *9*(2), 76–94.

Sitanggang, J., Sinulingga, S. & Fachruddin, K. (2019). Analysis of the effect of product quality on customer satisfaction and customer loyalty of Indihome ATPT Telkom regional 1 Sumatera, Medan, North Sumatra, Indonesia. *American international journal of business management (AIJBM), 2*(3), 26 – 37.

Solis-Carcano, G., Corona-Suarez, G.& Garcia-Ibarra, J. (2016). Time and cost control in construction services in southeast Mexico. *Journal of construction engineering, 18*(4), 411– 422.

Suchanek, P., Richter, J. & Kralova, M. (2015). Customer satisfaction, product quality and performance of companies. *Review of economic perspectives, 14*(4), 329 – 344.

Sugrova, M., Sedik, P., kubelakova A. & Svetlikova, V. (2017). The impact of the product quality on consumer satisfaction and corporate brand. *Economic Annals-XXI 165*(5-6), 133-137.

Suresh, B. (2005). *Scope creep management. The service perfect white paper collection*. USA: ResearchGate

Szopik-Depczynska, K. & Lanfranchi, G. (2016). The importance of planning in service management - Theoretical approach. *reports on economics and finance, 2*(1), 83 – 91.

Tsai, M., Tsai, C., & Chang, H. (2010). The effect of customer value, customer satisfaction, and switching costs on customer loyalty: An empirical study of hypermarkets in Taiwan. *Social behaviour and personality. International Journal (Toronto, Ont.), 38*(6), 729–740.

Vasista, T. (2017). Strategic cost management for construction service success: A systemic study. *Civil engineering and urban Planning. International Journal (Toronto, Ont.), 4*(1), 41–52.

Wael, H., & Zhiling, T. (2012). Service management literature: Gaps and opportunities. *E-Leader, 1*(1), 1–38.

Wang, C., Zhang, S., Li, X., & Guo, X. (2018). Understanding customers' compliance behaviour to frontline employees' fuzzy requests. *Journal of Services Marketing, 32*(2), 235–246. DOI: 10.1108/JSM-03-2016-0122

Yaghmale, F. (2003). Content validity and its estimation. *Journal of Medical Education, 3*(1), 25–27.

Chapter 10
Web Security Framework for Vulnerability Detection and Policy Enforcement

Akshita Sharma
https://orcid.org/0009-0003-7589-2517
Sharda School of Engineering and Technology, India

Astitva Bhardwaj
https://orcid.org/0009-0005-2256-9999
Sharda School of Engineering and Technology, India

Dharm Raj
https://orcid.org/0000-0001-8363-0515
Sharda School of Computing Science and Engineering, India

Amrit Kumar Agrawal
Sharda School of Computing Science and Engineering, India

Murari Kumar Singh
https://orcid.org/0000-0002-1251-6229
Sharda School of Computing Science and Engineering, India

Anil Kumar Sagar
Sharda School of Computing Science and Engineering, India

ABSTRACT

In an era, full of digital interactions and online connectivity, the importance of web security has become increasingly paramount. As our lives become more intertwined with the virtual realm, protecting sensitive data and countering cyber threats have gained unprecedented importance. Web security, comprising an extensive array of methods, tools, and tactics, can be used as the shield that can safeguard individuals and organizations against threats in the online domain. In this paper, we offer a concise yet comprehensive description of several attacks related to the web, the array of tools and techniques to tackle them, and the latest innovations in security

DOI: 10.4018/979-8-3373-0482-3.ch010

measures. The paper delves into detail about different kinds of attacks from cross-site scripting to SQL injections, and therefore, customized defenses are imperative. Further, the paper discusses several tools and techniques that can be used to keep web services secure. Finally, the paper provides a peep into the future with insight into recent advancements in security mechanisms.

1. INTRODUCTION

The Internet, a multidimensional, decentralized, and constantly growing system, is made up of different interconnected networks that communicate via Internet Protocol (IP) and packet switching (Park et al., 2005). Its vast and complicated nature makes complete evaluation difficult. As there is limited data available in real-world studies on cyber security, it is necessary to apply various measurement devices such as passive and active systems along with proper analysis methods that would help reveal the subject's position (Yu et al., 2008). The other side of this coin includes numerous aspects related to the internet, including users, protocols, platforms, app, technologies, devices, users and security threats. Measurement is rendered hard by these varied factors that shape the action for some systems among others. Moreover, given the transient and huge nature of the web, accurately predicting its behaviour in future is beyond possibility unless many trials and readings are done. This clearly demonstrates the significance of taking a multi-dimensional outlook on the issues related to the internet.

Given the growing use of web-based communications, web security is critical in the domain of cybersecurity (Attwood et al., 2020). Today, online data serves a variety of purposes, including interactions with web services acting as backend providers via custom applications and mobile apps. Social networks such as Facebook, Instagram, and TikTok, for example, provide both a web interface and mobile app services. As a result, protecting web applications and services is critical to avoiding misuse and potential risks (Tramontana et al., 2013). Because of the Internet's dynamic and opaque character, as well as its vital role in numerous services, continual monitoring, performance assessment, and network design are critical to ensuring dependability, security, and quality of service (Trestian et al., 2009).

Today, web application has become part and parcel of all business operations, providing communication, health, education, banking as well as IT services. The success of any business greatly depends on its security especially when it becomes very heterogeneous and complex. As a result, security testing emerges as a crucial task for web applications (Hasnain et al., 2020). Over time, a number of web vulnerabilities have been identified due to widespread usage of web-based applications.

As a result, attacks on web security are more frequent and may expose businesses to great risk (Desmet et al., 2008).

In the realm of web security, there exists a diverse array of cyberattacks that adversaries may exploit (Seo et al., 2004), such as data leakage (J et al., 2022), Cross-site Scripting(XSS) (Rodríguez et al., 2019), password guessing, application Denial of Service(DoS) (EtAl & E. C., 2016), cookie hijacking (Sivakorn et al., 2016),SQL injection attacks (Durai et al., 2020), and botnet-based attacks (Vignau et al., 2021). These weaknesses can provide unauthorized individuals with access to confidential data, such as credit card information, user profiles, and medical records. Moreover, these processes focus mainly on specific categories of weaknesses, especially those associated with the reallocation of memory, resulting in a system crash. However, these processes cannot completely resolve all security concerns (Satoh et al., 2010). This paper focuses on web attacks and emphasizes the necessity for strong security measures to protect against vulnerabilities present in web applications and secure web services

The continuous focus on user and entity privacy in the digital environment has encouraged the creation of countermeasures to prevent information breaches, which is both praiseworthy and important in the context of web security. These privacy safeguards, however, complicate the interpretation and collection of empirical cyber security data. As a result, web security is not always simple, and it frequently demands novel approaches to ensure accuracy and comprehensiveness (Fonseca et al., 2013, Kumar et al., 2021). In this sense, a systematic review of numerous types of web security attacks can tremendously aid researchers by providing insights into various points of view. Notably, our article is the first systematic review that focuses on extensively characterizing various kinds of attacks and the tools and techniques to prevent these attacks. The major contribution of this manuscript is as follows:

- A Description of web security that focused on various categories of the attacks specifically focusing on in detailed description of web-based attacks.
- An Overview of web systems, web applications, web application security, CIA triads, and category of attackers.
- A discussion about tools and techniques aimed at countering these web security threats. We offer a review of various data collection and analysis procedures used to tackle different categories of attacks.
- A review of the latest advancements in security measures within the realm of web security, outlining potential avenues for future research in this dynamic field.

Our systematic literature review encompasses a thorough examination of various papers. The structure of our paper is as follows: Section 2 comprises basic information about web, describing web applications, CIA triads, and categories of attackers, Section 3 is more analytical dealing with different kinds of attacks and Section 4 talks about measures and techniques for tackling the mentioned attacks while Section 5 discusses breakthroughs in security mechanisms aimed at combating the said attacks. Lastly, in Section 6 we sum up and conclude based on the observations made during the literature analysis.

Recent patterns show that there has been a definite escalation in web-related threats, which is closely attributed to a significant growing number of web-based applications accessing the major sectors of health care, finance, and governance. For example, from the Verizon 2023 Data Breach Investigations Report, web application vulnerabilities have taken part in more than over 40% of recognized breaches, thus signifying the urgent need for appropriate frameworks to detect and mitigate web vulnerabilities (Verizon, 2023). Even in the recent report by the European Union Agency for Cybersecurity (ENISA, 2024), it has been observed that sophisticated API-level attacks that attack cloud infrastructures have been greatly increasing, leading to a considerable number in financial and reputational damage to organizations that fall within this category. Thus, these statistics indicate a great need for systematic studies and proactive approaches toward web security frameworks, thus fuelling the current research toward conceiving the gap between vulnerability detection and policy enforcement practices.

1.1 Problem Statement

The persistence and escalation of internet-related cyber threats constitute a clear and empirically validated problem. Recent findings indicate that small-to- medium-sized enterprises (SMEs), in particular, are finding the going very tough against web threats because of limited resources and insufficient security-infrastructural investments. According to the Cisco Cybersecurity Report in 2024, around 65% of small and medium enterprises globally have suffered a serious cyber-attack in the previous year, among which web vulnerabilities are the highest exploited vector. Such vulnerabilities cause unauthorized access, leakage of data, and result into serious negative financial consequences. An IBM Security study (2024) also indicates that the average price for a data breach rose to USD 4.7 million per incident, thereby impacting the economy greatly. This evidence can be regarded as an empirically observably real problem, buttressing the claim that the very need-given this threat scenario-for a sound web security framework, which can be in position to conduct rapid vulnerability assessments and facilitate the enforcement of heavy-duty risk-alleviating security policies-is now of urgent priority.

1.2 Significance of the Study

Filling gaps in the detection of vulnerabilities and policy enforcement would play an essential role in significantly reducing cyber-attack exposure and possible damage due to such attacks. Current web security infrastructures, left unimproved or enhanced, will keep exposing significant areas such as health care, finance, e-commerce, and governmental institutions to high risk bounds that could lead to disastrous consequences like loss of finances, compromised privacy, and disruptions of indispensable services. For instance, modern attack trends on healthcare institutions have exposed the sensitive patient data and crippled efficiency and patient care delivery, proving need for advanced, robust security frameworks.

Theoretical perspectives and practical guidance come along with this study, empowering cybersecurity professionals, policy-makers, and organizational leaders with much needed substantial knowledge for building stronger defences against already sophisticated web-based threats. This study helps stakeholders understand the changing cyber threat landscape by identifying and classifying web vulnerabilities while studying the impact of currently existing security tools. More so, it offers a set of actionable and evidence-based recommendations which organizations can directly implement to improve their preparedness against and resilience towards threats manifesting through cyberspace (Fonseca et al., 2013, Kumar et al., 2021).

Moreover, the expected outputs of this study are very important as they provide empirical bases as well as clear pathways to build robust scalable security infrastructures for heterogeneous organizational environments, reaching from resource-scarce SMEs to any kind of organization. Also, most of the research findings will be worthwhile beyond short-term changes directed at improving cybersecurity. Effective means of detecting vulnerabilities and enforcing policies can translate into improved consumer confidence and regulatory compliance, as well as competitive advantage to the organizations demonstrating strong gains in cybersecurity maturity. It completes this research within the broader discourses on cybersecurity as it flags current inadequacies, puts forward practical solutions, and sets out future directions required for research and policy measures that are necessary to guarantee the safety of digital ecosystems in a connected world (Satoh et al., 2010).

2. OVERVIEW OF WEB

Due to the rapid expansion of the Internet, our daily lives have become closely intertwined with it. In order to harness the vast reservoir of data and information available on the Internet, the Web structure is constantly evolving and undergoing enhancements. There is a brief description of the web system in the subsections below.

2.1 Web System

Figure 1. The web platform

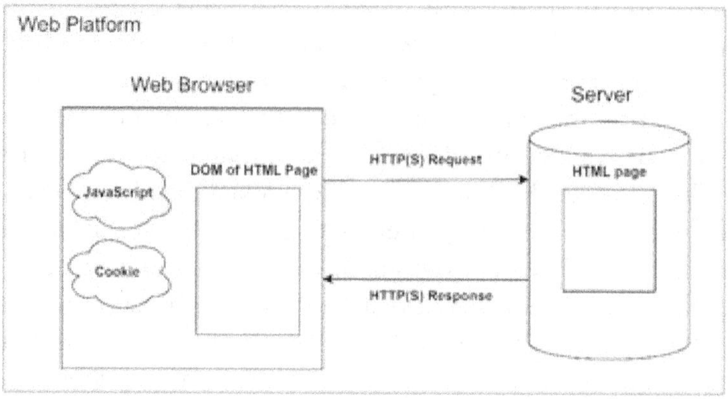

One of the main means to facilitate online services, from online banking to e-commerce is the Web system. It is a software system that facilitates various services through web pages which are comprised of HTML (Hyper Text Mark-up Language), CSS (Cascading Style Sheets), and JavaScript (Haley et al., 2008, Mai et al., 2018). It is comprised of various input interfaces (web pages fetched at the time of URL request). A huge set of data is handled by each interface which can be differentiated by the user roles. The web offers a uniform platform for resource sharing, publishing services, archiving and other global networking functions as the internet connects more things to the global network. Figure 1 depicts the working of web platform.

2.2 Web Application Security

A Web Application is a type of software that is often accessed using a web browser and frequently combines client-side and server-side scripts. It may be created using a variety of programming languages and operate on a variety of operating systems. Hypertext Transfer Protocol (HTTP) is used by web applications to communicate with web servers for all their functionality, and the results are commonly expressed in HTML. One of the important components of any web-related business is web application security. At various levels of complexity and scale, these web applications are vulnerable to attacks from multiple sources because of the nature of the internet. These days, the exchange of web data is required not only for browsing the web but also for using apps, and custom applications, to facilitate interaction with online services that function as providers for the backend. Since web applications are becoming more diverse and intricate, ensuring their security is vital for the success of businesses and organizations. As a result, security testing holds a significant position in the realm of web application security (Shar et al., 2014).

In order to foster application security, a well-known open and freely available community OWASP (Open Worldwide Application Security Project) is rummage-sale. It is in well collaboration with the Top 10 OWASP list, the development guide which describes how to create and develop a secure application for your project, code review guide which offers guidelines about how to verify the source code of your application to ensure its security, the testing guide offers guidelines about how to validate the security of working application (Eoin, 2013). In the interim, those who want to build a secure application can access all the documents, and tools freely provided by the OWASP.

2.3 CIA Triad

The CIA triad, which stands for Confidentiality, Integrity, and Availability, plays a fundamental role in information security and serves as a key principle. Network security is one of the crucial models governing information security policies within organizations. Figure 2 shows a diagram depicting the cia traids.

Figure 2. CIA triads

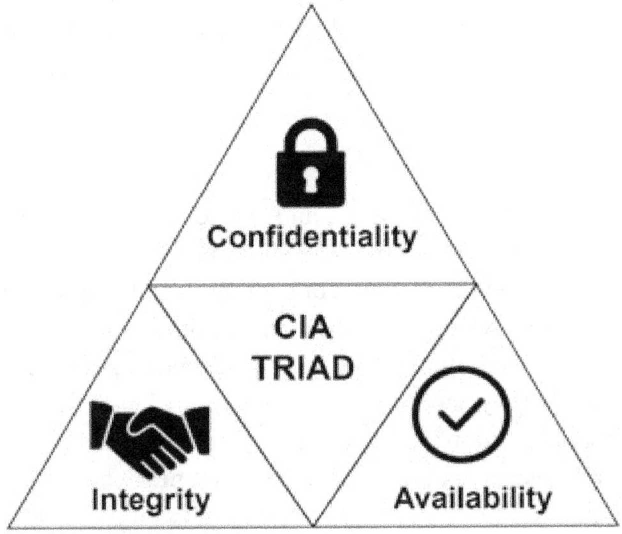

2.3.1 Confidentiality

Confidentiality involves restricting access to information to only those who have the proper authorization. This term encompasses the capability to ensure that sensitive or classified data can only be read by authorized individuals or systems, with unauthorized parties or systems being denied access to network data. To achieve this, a crucial approach is the use of a Virtual Private Network (VPN) tunnel for secure data transfer across the network. Additionally, encryption standards like Advanced Encryption Standard(AES) and Data Encryption Standard (DES) are employed to protect data. This ensures that even if an attacker gains access to the data, they would be unable to decipher it due to the strong encryption in place (Maene et al., 2018).

2.3.2 Integrity

Integrity of data transmission implies that the transmission remains undamaged, while the message or message content does not undergo any changes by someone else without his/her consent. This is the preservation of data integrity during the whole life cycle of information that keeps it authentic and internally and externally consistent. Encryption techniques can foster integrity and ensure that the data is accurate in order to maintain such integrity. Furthermore, the encryption system's process must be able either to stop any unauthorized alterations of data or to reveal such interventions. For instance, a slight alteration to somebody's medical notes or drug prescription may lead to severe consequences (Ge et al., 2021).

2.3.3 Availability

Availability ensures that information and services are readily accessible when necessary. This implies that network users should experience no issues accessing the network whenever they need This concept applies to both systems and data; they should be accessible when needed. To ensure the availability of networks and data, network and system administrators should regularly update their hardware and software. Additionally, they should have contingency plans and fail-over strategies in place for their organization's infrastructure. Such systems in disaster recovery management must however be based on such strategies which play a vital role at instances of infrastructural failure or immanent Distributed Denials of service (DDoS)disruptions that may endanger the company's valuable assets. With these strategies, they can smoothly transition to alternate infrastructure, thereby mitigating the impact of such failures or attacks (Hasan et al., 2023).

2.4 Category of Attackers

An attacker is someone who attempts to execute harmful activity to harm or disable systems. Web security primarily handles two types of attackers based on their target which are Web attacker and Network attacker which are described in the Table 1 and the subsections below.

Table 1. Various aspects of category of attacker

Attacker Type	Description	Attack Difficulty	Potential Consequences	Impact on HTTP Data	Server Control	Encryption Capabilities	Communication Capture
Web Attacker (Dai et al., 2020)	Controls at least one server, responds with malicious content.	Moderate	✓	✓	✓		
Network Attacker (Sourav et al., 2023)	Complex execution, total authority over HTTP-served web pages.	Challenging	✓	✓			✓

2.4.1 Web Attacker

A web attacker has authority over at least a single server, which replies to every HTTP(S) request it receives with malicious content of arbitrary nature, selected by the attacker. The capabilities of web attackers are expanded by network attackers, who possess the skill to identify and capture all communication transmitted between two endpoints within a network. All data transmitted via HTTP sent over the network is susceptible to corruption, forgery, and inspection by these attackers, but encryption is unbreakable to them (Dai et al., 2020).

2.4.2 Network Attacker

The network attackers are involved in sophisticated acts that involve sophisticated techniques used for breaching and compromising a network. However, what differentiates network attacks is their capability to cause massive harm and damage. In the successful implementation of a network attack, the attacker is provided with full privileges to access every page on the internet that are served using HTTP. This allows them to control, tamper with, hijack, as well as disable web services. Hence, despite substantial difficulties, network attackers constitute a severe possibility of wide-ranging service interruptions, data breaches, as well as substantial damage to an organization's esteem (Sourav et al., 2023).

3. SECURITY CHALLENGES AND ATTACKS IN WEBS

Balancing the concepts of sharing and openness always poses a challenge when considering security, trust, and privacy matters. These issues constitute the primary hurdles within the realm of the web. For better understanding let's explain it with an instance of something available on the web. In this context, the concern about privacy is related to the restriction of sharing this item exclusively with individuals having authorization to reach it. whereas the concern about security revolves around, determining who will be accessing the object and the actions he can perform with it. Lastly, the trust issue revolves around concerns related to the interaction of various entities on the web (HaddadPajouh et al., 2019). Various types of attacks are summarized in the Figure 3 and described in the subsections below.

Figure 3. Classification of various types of attacks

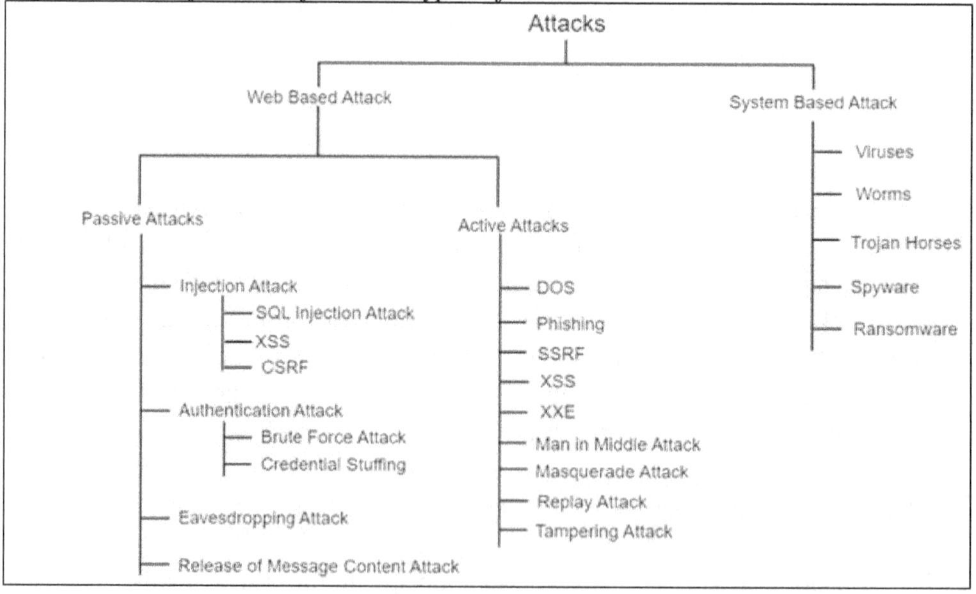

3.1 Web-Based Attacks

Exploitation of the vulnerabilities of websites, web applications, web servers, and related technologies through malicious activities is referred to as web-based attacks. The nature of these attacks is usually designed to compromise the integrity of online assets with associated repercussions like loss of data, breach of access, service interfering with normal operations, or whatsoever (Mitropoulos et al., 2017). Attackers utilize a range of methods to achieve their objectives, frequently focusing on vulnerabilities within the structure, configuration, or programming of web systems. It is important to have strong defensive measures, which include carrying out periodic security audits, updates, and installation of security tools within this constantly changing digital atmosphere (Bhushan et al., 2017). Several types of web-based attacks are described in the sub-sections below.

3.1.1 Active Attack

This attack mainly aims to harm the web system by modifying and altering the data. Table 2 categorizes various kinds of active attacks with their preventive measures. These attacks pose a threat to the system's integrity, reliability, and availability. hence these attacks result in alteration of the data and the system may get damaged. One positive aspect of this kind of attack is that it alerts the victim about the attack. Preventing these attacks is challenging because they exploit a wide range of software and physical vulnerabilities (Cai et al., 2019). Different active attacks are described in the subsection below.

Figure 4. Use case diagram for DoS attack

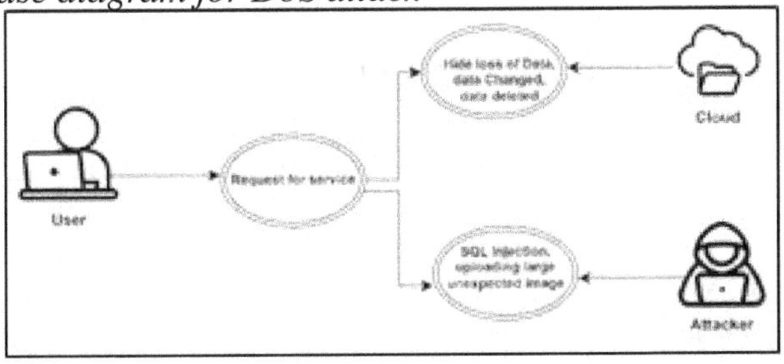

The use case diagram presented in the above Figure 4 illustrates a DoS attack scenario. In this scenario, an attacker leverages a cloud system to introduce vulnerabilities with the aim of obstructing legitimate users from accessing cloud services. Genuine users make service requests to the cloud, while the attacker engages in malicious actions like buffer overflows or SQL injections. Moreover, the perpetrator disturbs the system after sending malformed packets that make the volume of traffic in the communications channel of the cloud service provider increase greatly.

Figure 5. Sequence diagram for demonstrating DoS attack

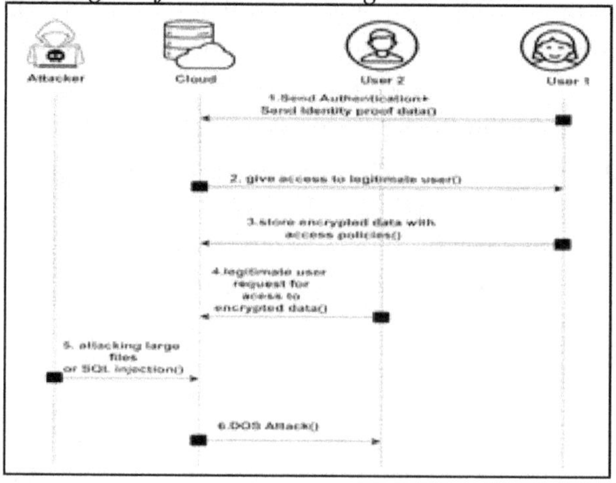

The Figure 5 depicts a DoS through a sequence diagram. In this sequence of events, a user submits their pertinent information to the webserver to establish their identity. Upon successful verification, the user is granted authorized access to encrypted data. Subsequently, an authorized and legitimate user initiates a request to access the data stored. However, the server is unable to provide the requested service to the user due to disruptive actions carried out by the attacker.

Figure 6. Use case diagram for phishing attack

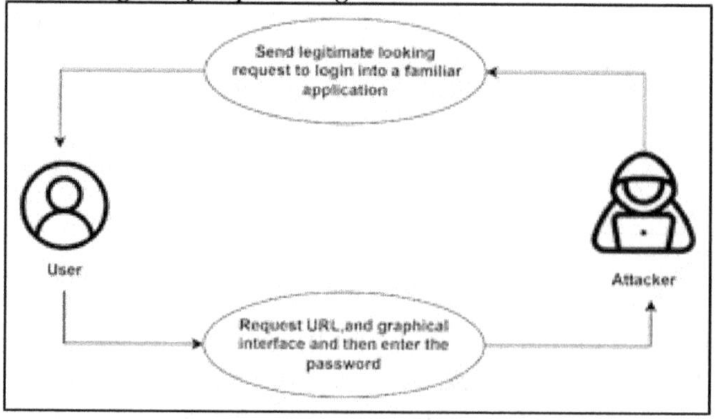

In Figure 6, there is a use case diagram illustrating a phishing attack scenario. In this figure, the attacker sends a website URL that appears to be legitimate to the user. The user, upon seeing the URL and graphical interface, believes it to be genuine. Subsequently, the user enters their username and password, which could be directly transmitted to the attacker's server and stored in their database. The Attacker will later use these stolen credentials to obtain the user's social security number, business-related information, and other private details.

Figure 7. Sequence diagram for demonstrating phishing attack

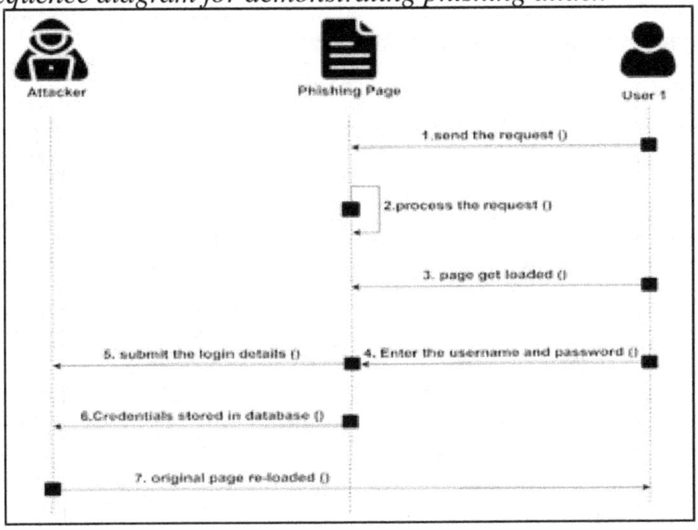

A sequence diagram that depicts the development of a phishing attack is shown in Figure 7. In this case, the user requests a webpage, but the attacker steps in by providing a URL to a fake webpage they have created. It is difficult for the user to tell the difference between this fake website and the real one since they are so similar to one another. At a critical point, the user recognizes the website via the URL the attacker gave. The user enters their credentials after mistaking it for the original. They are unaware that by doing this, the phisher's page may load without any problems. The attacker simultaneously gathers the user's private information by storing it in their database.

Figure 8. SSRF attack

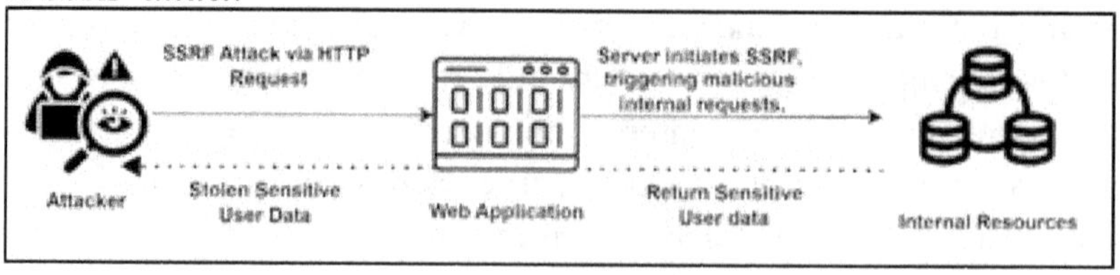

Table 2. Describing various types of active attack

Attack Type	Description	Methods	Impact	Prevention Measures
DOS (Mack et al., 2019)	Overloads networks to disrupt services	Flood attacks, Botnets	Loss of service, financial loss	DDoS protection, Network Monitoring
Phishing (Neupane et al., 2016, Das et al., 2019)	Deceptively steals personal info	Spoofed websites, Emails	Data breaches, Identity theft	User education, Email Filtering
SSRF (Kenyon et al., 2023, Al-Talak et al., 2021)	Forces servers to make unintended requests	Malicious payloads	Data exposure, Unauthorized access	Input validation, URL whitelisting
XSS (Van Der Loo & F., 2011)	Injects malicious scripts	Script injection	Data compromise, Privacy breaches	Input validation, Content Security Policy
XXE (Pourrahmani et al., 2023)	Exploits XML parser vulnerabilities	Malicious XML payloads	Unauthorized access, Data manipulation	Input validation, XML parser hardening
MitM (Sivasankari et al., 2022, Conti et al., 2016)	Intercepts and alters communications	Sniffing, manipulation	Data manipulation, Privacy breaches	Encryption, Certificate validation
Masquerade Attack (Kholidy et al., 2015)	Impersonates legitimate users	Stolen credentials, Bypassing auth	Unauthorized access, Privacy violation	Strong authentication, Access control
Replay Attack (Zaman et al., 2020)	Tampering with transmitted data	Capture and replay	Data integrity compromise, Confusion	Timestamps, Request validation
Tampering Attack (Liang et al., 2022)	Manipulates application data	Data modification, Logic flaws	Unauthorized changes, Data integrity	Code integrity checks, Input validation

3.1.2 Passive Attack

A passive attack is an attack where the data is not damaged or altered. It is referred to as the unauthorized eavesdropping on the activities on the web. The main focus of these attacks is to intercept the data without direct manipulation hence they preserve the data integrity and confidentiality. Table 3 describes the various types of passive attack with their preventive measures. These attacks are hard to detect as they do not include any kind of data alteration, due to which the victim is unaware of the attack (Ning et al., 2018). In the below subsections, various category of passive attacks is discussed.

Figure 9. Overview of SQL injection attack

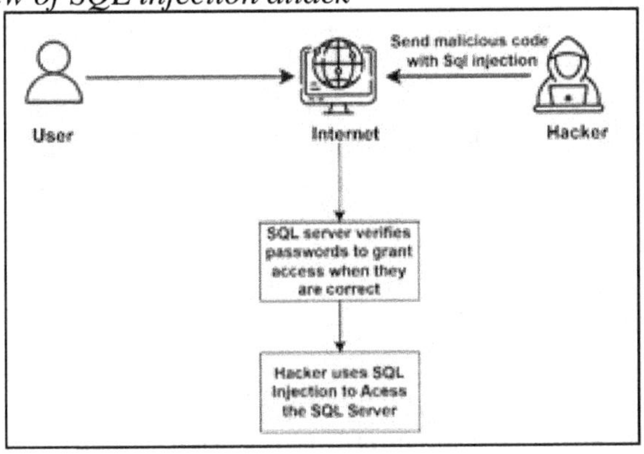

Table 3. Describing various types of passive attack

Attack Type	Description	Methods	Impact	Prevention Measures
Injection Attack (Guan et al., 2017)	Unauthorized data input	Malicious input	Data exposure, Unauthorized access	Input validation, Secure coding
SQL Injection (Mburano et al., 2018)	Exploits SQL vulnerabilities	Malicious SQL queries	Database compromise, Data breaches	Prepared statements, ORM, Input validation
XSS (Chaudhary et al., 2024)	Injects malicious scripts	Script injection	Data compromise, Privacy breaches	Input validation, Content Security Policy
CSRF (Alazmi et al., 2022)	Deceives users into taking unintended actions	Malicious requests	Unauthorized actions, Data manipulation	Anti-CSRF tokens, Session management

continued on following page

Table 3. Continued

Attack Type	Description	Methods	Impact	Prevention Measures
Authentication Attack (Cagalj et al., 2014)	Attempts to compromise authentication	Credential testing	Unauthorized access, Account compromise	Strong authentication, Multi-factor authentication
Brute Force Attack (Salamatian et al., 2020)	Repeated password guessing	Password guessing	Unauthorized access, Account compromise	Account lockout, Strong passwords
Credential Stuffing (Pal et al., 2019)	Reuses stolen passwords from breaches	Stolen credentials	Account compromise, Unauthorized access	Multi-factor authentication, Password policies
Eavesdropping (Ibrahim et al., 2015, Qin et al., 2019)	Unauthorized data interception	Sniffing, snooping	Data theft, Privacy breaches	Encryption, Secure network protocols
Release of Message Content (Arogundade & O., 2023)	Makes user information public	Data interception, keyloggers	Privacy breaches, Data theft	Encryption, Anti-malware software

3.2 System-Based Attacks

The attacks that aim mainly at the vulnerabilities of a computer system, targeting their confidentiality, integrity, or availability are referred to as system-based attacks also known as computer attacks or cyber-attacks. Table 4 discusses the various kinds of System based attacks with their preventive measures. Disrupting operations, stealing sensitive data, and unauthorized access are some of the main objectives of attackers. In order to defend the system against these attacks several security measures like firewalls, regular software patching, user education, etc. are required. The types of system attacks are discussed in the below sub-section are as follows:

Table 4. Describing various types of system based attacks

Attack Type	Description	Propagation Method	Object of Attack	Impact	Prevention Measures
Viruses (Abomhara et al., 2015)	Self-replicating code that infects files	File attachment, code integration	Computer files, programs	Data loss, System instability	Antivirus software, Regular updates
Worms (Sheikh & A., 2021)	Autonomous software propagating through networks	Email attachments, network	Networked systems, email servers	Network congestion, Denial of service	Network segmentation, Email Filtering
Trojan Horses (Sharma & S., 2018)	Disguised as legitimate files or programs	Concealed within software	User systems, data theft	Unauthorized access, Data compromise	Download from trusted sources, Scanning for malware
Spyware (Gagneja & K. K., 2017)	Collects user data and transmits to remote user	Program installation, downloads	User data, online habits	Privacy breaches, Data theft	Anti-spyware software, Secure downloads
Ransomware (Chesti et al., 2020)	Encrypts files and demands ransom for access	Malicious code execution	Computer files, user data	Data encryption, financial extortion	Regular backups, Security awareness training

4. WEB SECURITY TOOLS AND TECHNIQUES

In more recent years, illicit attempts at acquiring undue information from personal information have become quite rampant. Such measures often deal with stealing or blackmail in which case unsuspecting users are forced to "give up" some of their personal information or data (PS et al., 2018). It has highlighted how important cybersecurity is today, according to (Li et al., 2021). Some varied means of boosting cyber security. Anti-viruses, Firewalls, Authentication protocols, Encryption techniques, and Digital Signatures are examples of these which are described in Table 5. The following subsections provide a comprehensive discussion.

Table 5. Describing various types of security tools and techniques

Security Tool/ Technique	Description	Prevention	Detection	Authentication	Usage
Antivirus (Dhananjay et al., 2016)	Prevents and detects computer viruses	✓	✓		Malware protection
Firewalls (Kallepalli et al., 2021)	Controls network traffic to deter unauthorized access	✓			Network security
Authentication (Tabrizchi et al., 2020)	Verifies user identity using stored information	✓		✓	Identity validation
Encryption (Faheem et al., 2017)	Renders data unintelligible, requiring a decryption key	✓			Data security
Digital Signature (Kumar et al., 2014)	Provides authentication and data integrity verification	✓		✓	Data and user authentication

5. RECENT ADVANCEMENTS IN SECURITY MECHANISM

Recent academic endeavors in this area put more emphasis on turning toward newer techniques such as machine learning and deep learning towards addressing the difficult issues in web security. Cole et al. (2021) describe the DEFEAT strategy which uses deep learning to spot anomalies associated with cyber threats at earlier times for real-time detection systems. Such examples show the scope of real-time detection systems towards the development of prevention systems. In yet another instance, Robles-González et al. (2023) also went on to enhance the basic UDS model, that is, user-device-service, with advanced privacy add-ons, which serves to illuminate the emerging interdisciplinary approaches of his work at the confluence of cybersecurity and privacy-enhanced technologies. Definitely critical advancements were noted, but with appended needs for more comprehensive frameworks-scoping-and-scalable frameworks, primarily adaptable to SMEs and operating in stringently constrained resources.

Security mechanisms contains a range of techniques and technologies such as Authentication and Authorization, Data protection, Input Validation and security header, Monitoring and Incident Response, Access Control. Various recent advancements have been made by the researchers in these security mechanisms which are discussed in the subsections below.

5.1Authentication and Authorization

Authentication is considered a fundamental element of web security, providing a means to verify a user's identity based on the information stored within the system's security domain, as described in (Xue et al., 2022). Authorization refers to the actions that a user can take after being authenticated. It is used to decide which resources the end-user has access to and what activities they can conduct on those resources (Saxena et al., 2015). Below are some of the latest advancements in the realm of authentication and authorization

5.2 Data Protection

The process of securing sensitive information from destruction, corruption, or loss is known as Data protection.

It has become increasingly vital as the amount of data collected and stored has expanded at an unparalleled rate. Various recent advancements in this topic are discussed below:

5.3 Input Validation and Security Header

The enforcement implemented into software systems to ensure that only legitimate input is accepted in order to raise external consequences is known as input validation (Liu et al., 2008). Below, we have discussed several recent advancements in input validation and security header.

5.4 Monitoring and Incident Response

Most cyber security methods rely heavily on incident response and recovery. Incident response is a well-established concept for preparing for and responding to unexpected occurrences that negatively impact a business or organization (Smith et al., 2021). Below, we have mentioned various recent advancements in this security mechanism.

5.5 Access Control

An important tool for securing stored data is Access Control (AC). The primary goal of access control is to limit the extent to which subjects, such as individuals, devices, and processes, can access certain resources or objects (Ullah et al., 2023). (Sarfaraz et al., 2023) proposed AccessChain, an SCM access control framework based on an attribute-based access control (ABAC) paradigm that limits access to competing parties while allowing for network scalability. (Addobea et al., 2023) proposed an access control mechanism that incorporates numerous aspects of knowledge, competence, and possession to authenticate individuals to the blockchain. (Seo et al., 2023) proposed a new method that smoothly combines blockchain technology and substitution cipher techniques to heighten the security measures of the metaverse. (He et al., 2023) presented the use of smart contracts to study the method of fine-grained data access control, and to implement the attribute-based access control (ABAC) model. (Xi et al., 2023) proposed distributed access control policy and system based on blockchain. The focus is on enabling dynamic access policies for microservices collaboration. (Tegane et al., 2023) proposed An Attribute-Capability-Based Access Control (ACapBAC) solution for the Internet of Things. ACapBAC allows for fine-grained controlled delegation and flexible, dynamic access control. (Le et al., 2021) presented a semi-automated method for reverse-engineering AC policies from Web applications. (Park et al., 2021) presented the discussion about the fundamental characteristics and limits of existing access control methods, as well as the importance and need of activity management in smart collaborative ecosystems. (Bhatt et al., 2021) expanded on and extended a previously created access control model for AWS IoT known as the AWS-IoTAC model to provide a formal attribute-based access control (ABAC) model for AWS IoT. (Gan et al., 2020) proposed a solution that entails establishing the standard data format for an access control token, developing algorithms for equivalence, division, combination, and validation of these tokens, and diving into the system architecture for token-based access control.

Table 6. Security mechanisms techniques

Topic	Authors	Description
Authentication and Authorization	**(Robles-González et al., 2023)**	UDS framework with a privacy category, resulting in the UDSP framework for comprehensive evaluation.
	(Nguyen et al., 2023)	Method using RF fingerprint data to authenticate IoT nodes using deep learning.
	(Pant et al., 2022)	Dark web, data trading, and creating websites for secure user information.
	(Das et al., 2022)	Decentralized Open Web Cryptographic Standard (DOWCS) for safeguarding data in a decentralized manner.
	(Pohn et al., 2022)	Identity Management Service Model Framework (IMSMF) using ArchiMate for various protocols.
	(Cole et al., 2021)	DEFEAT strategy using deep learning for instant attack recognition.
	(Esposito et al., 2020)	blockchain technology for handling identity and authorization policies in distributed systems.
	(Iskhakov et al., 2021)	Technique for creating a profile of access subject authentication and developing adaptive verification algorithms.
	(Olanrewaju et al., 2021)	Frictionless user authentication system for web applications.
Data Protection	**(Ling et al., 2023)**	Studied the development of a web-based enterprise network system using Advanced Encryption Technology (AET).
	(Yao et al., 2023)	TLS encryption transmission mechanism for secure data transmission.
	(Perdices et al., 2022)	Identifying user online browsing based on IP addresses.
	(Olca et al., 2022)	Model for managing personal consent using semantic web technology for enhanced privacy.
	(Shandilya & S. K., 2022)	How NICS can improve web data and application security.
	(Zhang et al., 2022)	Prevalent issues in data protection on Internet enterprise platforms.
	(Jesus et al., 2022)	Literature review and analysis of Consent Receipts.
	(Duan et al., 2020)	ICSE (Interactive symmetric context encryption) using non-transparent data encryption.

continued on following page

Table 6. Continued

Topic	Authors	Description
Input Validation and security header	**(Fadlalla et al., 2023)**	Categorization for web application input validation vulnerabilities.
	(Chatzoglou et al., 2022)	Testbed to assess the efficacy of HTTP/3-related attacks on HTTP/3-capable servers.
	(García et al., 2023)	Browser Watcher for cross-browser website monitoring and browser console data collection.
	(Wu et al., 2023)	ZTWeb, a zero-trust-based defence model for website security.
	(Marashdih et al., 2023)	Static taint analysis in source code to track contaminated inputs.
	(Marashdih et al., 2022)	Machine learning method to identify input validation-related vulnerabilities from source code.
Monitoring and Incident Response	**(Maheswari et al., 2023)**	Intrusion detection system(IDS) for web and cloud computing environments.
	(Wang et al., 2023)	Application Monitoring (AM) technique for bug reproduction and data collection.
	(Bitzer et al., 2022)	Incident response management maturity model (IRM3) closely connected with practice needs.
	(Shaked et al., 2023)	Integrating operations models with incident response playbooks.
	(Palacios et al., 2022)	Heal the Breach (HTB) solution for mitigating BREACH attacks.
	(Catillo et al., 2021)	Analysed computer system logs with a focus on anomaly identification.
	(Staves et al., 2022)	Framework for enhanced response capabilities.
	(Fuentes-Garcia et al., 2021)	Taxonomy for features and modules of Network Security Monitoring (NSM) systems.
	(Kim et al., 2020)	Model for processing real-time, unencrypted HTTP data using CNN and LSTM.

continued on following page

Table 6. Continued

Topic	Authors	Description
Access Control	**(Ullah et al., 2023)**	AccessChain, an SCM access control framework based on attribute-based access control (ABAC).
	(Sarfaraz et al., 2023)	Access control mechanism based on knowledge, competence, and possession for blockchain authentication.
	(Addobea et al., 2023)	Blockchain and substitution cipher techniques for heightened metaverse security.
	(Seo et al., 2023)	Smart contracts to study fine-grained data access control using an attribute-based access control (ABAC) model.
	(Xi et al., 2023)	Distributed access control policies based on blockchain for micro services collaboration.
	(Tegane et al., 2023)	Attribute-Capability-Based Access Control (ACapBAC) solution for the Internet of Things. ACapBAC allows for fine-grained controlled delegation and flexible, dynamic access control.
	(Le et al., 2021)	Semi-automated method for reverse-engineering access control policies from web applications.
	(Park et al., 2021)	Characteristics of access control methods, the importance of activity management in collaborative ecosystems.
	(Bhatt et al., 2021)	AWS-IoTAC model for AWS IoT to provide formal attribute-based access control (ABAC).
	(Gan et al., 2020)	Standard data format for access control tokens and system architecture for token-based access control.

6. CONCLUSION

Internet is the base on which web-based communication and services create a multidimensional environment. The success of online communication, medical services, education, banking, and other computer-based activities depends highly on internet application security. Hence, it is necessary to protect these web-based applications and services from abuse and related risks. Accordingly, this paper examines the fundamental elements of web security. A general discussion about web security involves analysing the subject broadly and addressing issues like the internet, web applications, security of these web applications, possible ways through which the security of these web applications can be compromised, how these attacks can be mitigated, and new developments aimed at improving web security This paper discusses several types of attacks malicious actors can conduct on web security. This may involve web bugs, cross-site scripting, session fixation, data leakage, cookie hijacking, password guessing, application denial of service, botnet-based attacks, and SQL injection attacks. Such vulnerabilities can expose such data of individuals to outsiders leading to irreparable damage to people and organizations concerned. Lastly, the discussion will highlight the current advancement in security mechanisms with respect to web security. One must also observe network performance, restructure the network, and guarantee the security and reliability of service providers to safeguard the integrity and reliability of the web services. The Internet is a growing field and thus needs more advanced threat remedies while at the same time identifying vulnerabilities in the system. Various aspects of web security including an overview of web-related issues and the threats they pose, and how to tackle them are examined in this systematic review. The objective is to give institutions as well as researcher's ways and understanding towards safeguarding web apps against relentless and sophisticated web hazards.

These recommendations provide an outline of potential actions by organizational leaders, policymakers, and cybersecurity practitioners based on the insights and findings provided.

- Frameworks on Security Layers Implementation: Creating multi-tiered defence models integrating application level firewall-based and associated mechanisms along with robust authentication schemes as well as continuous vulnerability scanning tools.
- Prioritizing Detection in Real-time: Investing in machine learning-powered threat detection platforms, which enables immediate identification and response towards highly sophisticated web attacks.
- Periodic routine Security Audits: Everyone, design and carry out the assessment once per month which will penetrate, test and scan for vulnerabilities so that they can find and identify and resolve potential threats proactively.
- Add Training for Security: Include ongoing cybersecurity internal training software that emphasizes, above all, how to identify and mitigate in real time those attacks as common as XSS, phishing, social engineering, SQL injection, etc.
- Adopt the architectures of zero trust: Gradually align corporate security policies on a path toward zero trust: all users and devices that access sensitive resources have to be verified.
- Policy Enforcement Automation. Automated security policy enforcement tools would be used to enforce the rules accurately most of the time and reduce the chance of human error.
- Strengthen Regulatory Compliance. Ensure strong compliance with the relevant data protection laws like GDPR and HIPAA to directly lower the risks that have got to do with web vulnerabilities.

- Enhanced Incident Response Protocols: There must be established defined tested and documented incident response plans that would immediately respond to findings of cyber threats.
- Encourage Public-Private Collaboration: Creating partnerships with experts in the industry, cybersecurity companies, and national governments to share intelligence, improve threat awareness, and boost community resilience security.
- Regular Technology Update: Keep yourself up to date by timely software and patch management for all systems, while also promptly dealing with newly discovered vulnerabilities. The idea is to minimize the risk of their explication.

REFERENCES

Abomhara, M., & Kien, G. M. (2015). Cyber security and the Internet of Things: Vulnerabilities, threats, intruders and attacks. *Journal of Cyber Security and Mobility*, *4*(1), 65–88. DOI: 10.13052/jcsm2245-1439.414

Addobea, A. A., Li, Q., Obiri, I. A.Jr, & Hou, J. (2023). Secure multi-factor access control mechanism for pairing blockchains. *Journal of Information Security and Applications*, *74*, 103477. DOI: 10.1016/j.jisa.2023.103477

Al-Talak, K., & Abbass, O. (2021). Detecting Server-Side Request Forgery (SSRF) Attack by using Deep Learning Techniques. *International Journal of Advanced Computer Science and Applications*, *12*(12). Advance online publication. DOI: 10.14569/IJACSA.2021.0121230

Alazmi, S., & De Leon, D. C. (2022). A systematic literature review on the characteristics and effectiveness of web application vulnerability scanners. *IEEE Access : Practical Innovations, Open Solutions*, *10*, 33200–33219. DOI: 10.1109/ACCESS.2022.3161522

Arogundade, O. (2023). *Network Security Concepts, Dangers, and Defense Best Practical*. Computer Engineering and Intelligent Systems., DOI: 10.7176/CEIS/14-2-03

Attwood, S., Li, W., & Kharel, R. (2020). Evolutionary Algorithms in Web Security: Exploring untapped potential. 2022 13th International Symposium on Communication Systems, Networks and Digital Signal Processing (CSNDSP), 1–6. DOI: 10.1109/CSNDSP49049.2020.9249521

Bhatt, S., Pham, T. K., Gupta, M., Benson, J., Park, J., & Sandhu, R. (2021). Attribute-Based access control for AWS internet of things and secure industries of the future. *IEEE Access : Practical Innovations, Open Solutions*, *9*, 107200–107223. DOI: 10.1109/ACCESS.2021.3101218

Bhushan, B., & Sahoo, G. (2017). Recent advances in attacks, technical challenges, vulnerabilities and their countermeasures in wireless sensor networks. *Wireless Personal Communications*, *98*(2), 2037–2077. DOI: 10.1007/s11277-017-4962-0

Bitzer, M., Häckel, B., Leuthe, D., Ott, J., Stahl, B., & Strobel, J. (2022). Managing the Inevitable – a maturity model to establish incident response management capabilities. *Computers & Security*, *125*, 103050. DOI: 10.1016/j.cose.2022.103050

Cagalj, M., Perkovic, T., & Bugaric, M. (2014). Timing attacks on cognitive authentication schemes. *IEEE Transactions on Information Forensics and Security*, *10*(3), 584–596. DOI: 10.1109/TIFS.2014.2376177

Cai, N., & Hayashi, M. (2019). Secure network code for adaptive and active attacks with No-Randomness in intermediate nodes. *IEEE Transactions on Information Theory*, *66*(3), 1428–1448. DOI: 10.1109/TIT.2019.2957078

Catillo, M., Pecchia, A., & Villano, U. (2021). AutoLog: Anomaly detection by deep autoencoding of system logs. *Expert Systems with Applications*, *191*, 116263. DOI: 10.1016/j.eswa.2021.116263

Chakraborty, M., & Singh, M. (2020). Introduction to network Security Technologies. In Lecture notes in networks and systems (pp. 3–28). DOI: 10.1007/978-981-15-9317-8_1

Chatzoglou, E., Kouliaridis, V., Kambourakis, G., Karopoulos, G., & Gritzalis, S. (2022). A hands-on gaze on HTTP/3 security through the lens of HTTP/2 and a public dataset. *Computers & Security*, *125*, 103051. DOI: 10.1016/j.cose.2022.103051

Chaudhary, A., Krishna, K., Shadik, M., & Raj, D. (2023). A review on malicious link detection techniques. CRC Press eBooks, 768–777. DOI: 10.1201/9781003393580-114

Chaudhary, A., Krishna, K. C., Shadik, M., & Raj, D. (2024). Detection of phishing link using different machine learning techniques. In Lecture notes in networks and systems (pp. 63–77). DOI: 10.1007/978-981-99-9811-1_6

Chesti, I. A., Humayun, M., Sama, N. U., & Jhanjhi, N. (2020). Evolution, Mitigation, and Prevention of Ransomware. In 2020 2nd International Conference on Computer and Information Sciences (ICCIS) (pp. 1–6). DOI: 10.1109/ICCIS49240.2020.9257708

Cole, D., Newman, S., & Lin, D. (2021). A new facial authentication pitfall and remedy in web services. *IEEE Transactions on Dependable and Secure Computing*, *19*(4), 2635–2647. DOI: 10.1109/TDSC.2021.3067794

Conti, M., Dragoni, N., & Lesyk, V. (2016). A survey of Man in the middle attacks. *IEEE Communications Surveys and Tutorials*, *18*(3), 2027–2051. DOI: 10.1109/COMST.2016.2548426

Dai, P., Yu, W., Wang, H., Wen, G., & Lv, Y. (2020). Distributed reinforcement learning for Cyber-Physical system with multiple remote state estimation under DOS attacker. *IEEE Transactions on Network Science and Engineering*, *7*(4), 3212–3222. DOI: 10.1109/TNSE.2020.3018871

Das, A., Baki, S., Aassal, A. E., Verma, R., & Dunbar, A. (2019). SOK: A Comprehensive Reexamination of Phishing research from the security perspective. *IEEE Communications Surveys and Tutorials*, *22*(1), 671–708. DOI: 10.1109/COMST.2019.2957750

Das, D., Sethuraman, S. C., & Satapathy, S. C. (2022). A decentralized open web cryptographic standard. *Computers & Electrical Engineering*, *99*, 107751. DOI: 10.1016/j.compeleceng.2022.107751

Desmet, L., Verbaeten, P., Joosen, W., & Piessens, F. (2008). Provable Protection against Web Application Vulnerabilities Related to Session Data Dependencies. *IEEE Transactions on Software Engineering*, *34*(1), 50–64. DOI: 10.1109/TSE.2007.70742

Dhananjay, R. A., & Sheetal Kaushik. (2016). A comprehensive study of contemporary tools and techniques in the realm of cyber security. IITM Journal of Management and IT, 7(1), 109–110. https://www.IndianJournals.com

Duan, T., & Peng, Y. J. (2020). Interactive Symmetric Context Encryption in Framework of Asynchronous Data Exchange. In *2020 Chinese Control And Decision Conference (CCDC)*, Hefei, China, (Vol. 3, pp. 3665–3670). DOI: 10.1109/CCDC49329.2020.9164726

Durai, K. N., Subha, R., & Haldorai, A. (2020). A novel method to detect and prevent SQLIA using ontology to cloud web security. *Wireless Personal Communications*, *117*(4), 2995–3014. DOI: 10.1007/s11277-020-07243-z

Esposito, C., Ficco, M., & Gupta, B. B. (2020). Blockchain-based authentication and authorization for smart city applications. *Information Processing & Management*, *58*(2), 102468. DOI: 10.1016/j.ipm.2020.102468

EtAl, E. C. (. (2016). A network traffic representation model for detecting application layer attacks. *International Journal of Computing and Digital Systems*, *5*(1), 31–42. DOI: 10.12785/ijcds/050104

Fadlalla, F. F., & Elshoush, H. T. (2023). Input Validation Vulnerabilities in web Applications: Systematic review, Classification, and analysis of the current State-of-the-Art. *IEEE Access : Practical Innovations, Open Solutions*, *11*, 40128–40161. DOI: 10.1109/ACCESS.2023.3266385

Faheem, M., Jamel, S., Hassan, A. A. Z., Shafinaz, N., & Mat, M. (2017). A survey on the cryptographic encryption algorithms. *International Journal of Advanced Computer Science and Applications*, *8*(11). Advance online publication. DOI: 10.14569/IJACSA.2017.081141

Fonseca, J., Seixas, N., Vieira, M., & Madeira, H. (2013). Analysis of field data on web security vulnerabilities. *IEEE Transactions on Dependable and Secure Computing*, *11*(2), 89–100. DOI: 10.1109/TDSC.2013.37

Fuentes-Garcia, M., Camacho, J., & Macia-Fernandez, G. (2021). Present and future of network security Monitoring. *IEEE Access : Practical Innovations, Open Solutions*, *9*, 112744–112760. DOI: 10.1109/ACCESS.2021.3067106

Gagneja, K. K. (2017). Knowing the ransomware and building defense against it - specific to healthcare institutes. In *Third International Conference on Mobile and Secure Services (MobiSecServ)* (pp. 1–5). DOI: 10.1109/MOBISECSERV.2017.7886569

Gan, G., Chen, E., Zhou, Z., & Zhu, Y. (2020). Token-Based access control. *IEEE Access : Practical Innovations, Open Solutions*, *8*, 54189–54199. DOI: 10.1109/ACCESS.2020.2979746

García, B., Ricca, F., Del Alamo, J. M., & Leotta, M. (2023). Enhancing Web Applications Observability through Instrumented Automated Browsers. *Journal of Systems and Software*, *203*, 111723. DOI: 10.1016/j.jss.2023.111723

Ge, C., Susilo, W., Baek, J., Liu, Z., Xia, J., & Fang, L. (2021). Revocable Attribute-Based encryption with data integrity in clouds. *IEEE Transactions on Dependable and Secure Computing*, *19*(5), 2864–2872. DOI: 10.1109/TDSC.2021.3065999

Guan, Y., & Ge, X. (2017). Distributed attack detection and secure estimation of networked Cyber-Physical systems against false data injection attacks and jamming attacks. *IEEE Transactions on Signal and Information Processing Over Networks*, *4*(1), 48–59. DOI: 10.1109/TSIPN.2017.2749959

HaddadPajouh, H., Dehghantanha, A., Parizi, R. M., Aledhari, M., & Karimipour, H. (. (2019). A survey on internet of things security: Requirements, challenges, and solutions. *Internet of Things : Engineering Cyber Physical Human Systems*, *14*, 100129. DOI: 10.1016/j.iot.2019.100129

Haley, C., Laney, R., Moffett, J., & Nuseibeh, B. (2008). Security Requirements Engineering: A framework for representation and analysis. *IEEE Transactions on Software Engineering*, *34*(1), 133–153. DOI: 10.1109/TSE.2007.70754

Hasan, M. K., Habib, A. A., Islam, S., Safie, N., Abdullah, S. N. H. S., & Pandey, B. (2023). DDoS: Distributed denial of service attack in communication standard vulnerabilities in smart grid applications and cyber security with recent developments. *Energy Reports*, *9*, 1318–1326. DOI: 10.1016/j.egyr.2023.05.184

Hasnain, M., Pasha, M. F., & Ghani, I. (2020). Drupal core 8 caching mechanism for scalability improvement of web services. *Software Impacts*, *3*, 100014. DOI: 10.1016/j.simpa.2020.100014

He, G., Li, C., Shu, Y., & Luo, Y. (2023). Fine-grained access control policy in blockchain-enabled edge computing. *Journal of Network and Computer Applications*, *221*, 103706. DOI: 10.1016/j.jnca.2023.103706

Ibrahim, M., Elgamri, A., Babiker, S., & Mohamed, A. (2015). Internet of things based smart environmental monitoring using the Raspberry-Pi computer. In *Fifth International Conference on Digital Information Processing and Communications (ICDIPC)*, 2015. DOI: 10.1109/ICDIPC.2015.7323023

Iskhakov, A. Y., Iskhakova, A. O., & Meshcheryakov, R. V. (2021). Algorithm for building a cyberphysical system operator profile for adaptive authentication. *IFAC-PapersOnLine*, *54*(13), 493–498. DOI: 10.1016/j.ifacol.2021.10.497

Jesus, V., & Pandit, H. J. (2022). Consent receipts for a usable and auditable web of personal data. *IEEE Access : Practical Innovations, Open Solutions*, *10*, 28545–28563. DOI: 10.1109/ACCESS.2022.3157850

Kallepalli, K., & Chaudhry, U. B. (2021). Intelligent Security: Applying artificial intelligence to detect advanced cyber attacks. In Advanced sciences and technologies for security applications (pp. 287–320). DOI: 10.1007/978-3-030-87166-6_11

Kenyon, J., & Kenyon, J. (2023, September 14). Server-Side Request Forgery (SSRF) & the cloud resurgence. AppCheck | A Complete Enterprise Security Testing Solution -. https://appcheck-ng.com/server-side-request-forgery-ssrf/

Kholidy, H. K., Baiardi, F., & Hariri, S. (2015). DSGA: A data-driven semi-global alignment approach for detecting masquerade attacks. *IEEE Transactions on Dependable and Secure Computing*, *12*(2), 164–178. DOI: 10.1109/TDSC.2014.2327966

Kim, A., Park, M., & Lee, D. H. (2020). AI-IDS: Application of Deep Learning to Real-Time Web Intrusion Detection. *IEEE Access : Practical Innovations, Open Solutions*, *8*, 70245–70261. DOI: 10.1109/ACCESS.2020.2986882

Kumar, A., Bhushan, B., Malik, A., & Kumar, R. (2021). Protocols, solutions, and testbeds for Cyber-Attack Prevention in industrial SCADA systems. In Studies in big data (pp. 355–380). DOI: 10.1007/978-981-16-6210-2_17

Kumar, N., & Rao, K. (2014). Hash based approach for providing privacy and integrity in cloud data storage using digital signatures. *International Journal of Computer Science and Information Technologies*, *5*(6), 8074–8078.

Le, H. T., Shar, L. K., Bianculli, D., Briand, L. C., & Nguyen, C. D. (2021). Automated reverse engineering of role-based access control policies of web applications. *Journal of Systems and Software*, *184*, 111109. DOI: 10.1016/j.jss.2021.111109

Li, Y., & Liu, Q. (2021). A comprehensive review study of cyber-attacks and cyber security; Emerging trends and recent developments. *Energy Reports*, *7*, 8176–8186. DOI: 10.1016/j.egyr.2021.08.126

Liang, H., Zhu, L., Yu, F. R., & Wang, X. (2022). A Cross-Layer defense method for blockchain empowered CBTC systems against data tampering attacks. *IEEE Transactions on Intelligent Transportation Systems*, *24*(1), 501–515. DOI: 10.1109/TITS.2022.3211020

Ling, Y., Li, X., Bin, D., Yang, C., & Lu, J. (2023). Web Random Token Generation Technology Based on Asymmetric Encryption Technology. In 2023 IEEE 2nd International Conference on Electrical Engineering, Big Data and Algorithms (EEBDA), Changchun, China (pp. 804–808). DOI: 10.1109/EEBDA56825.2023.10090549

Liu, H., & Tan, H. B. K. (2008). Covering code behavior on input validation in functional testing. *Information and Software Technology*, *51*(2), 546–553. DOI: 10.1016/j.infsof.2008.07.001

Mack, J., Hu, Y., & Hoppa, M. A. (2019). A study of existing Cross-Site scripting detection and prevention techniques using XAMPP and VirtualBox. *Virginia Journal of Science*, *70*(3), 1. DOI: 10.25778/bx6k-2285

Maene, P., Gotzfried, J., Muller, T., De Clercq, R., Freiling, F., & Verbauwhede, I. (2018). Atlas: Application Confidentiality in Compromised embedded Systems. *IEEE Transactions on Dependable and Secure Computing*, *16*(3), 415–423. DOI: 10.1109/TDSC.2018.2858257

Maheswari, K., Siva, C., & Nalinipriya, G. (2023). Optimal cluster based feature selection for intrusion detection system in web and cloud computing environment using hybrid teacher learning optimization enables deep recurrent neural network. *Computer Communications*, *202*, 145–153. DOI: 10.1016/j.comcom.2023.02.003

Mai, P. X., Goknil, A., Shar, L. K., Pastore, F., Briand, L. C., & Shaame, S. (2018). Modeling Security and Privacy Requirements: A Use Case-Driven Approach. *Information and Software Technology*, *100*, 165–182. DOI: 10.1016/j.infsof.2018.04.007

Marashdih, A. W., Zaaba, Z. F., & Suwais, K. (2022). Predicting input validation vulnerabilities based on minimal SSA features and machine learning. *Journal of King Saud University. Computer and Information Sciences*, *34*(10), 9311–9331. DOI: 10.1016/j.jksuci.2022.09.010

Marashdih, A. W., Zaaba, Z. F., & Suwais, K. (2023). An enhanced static taint analysis approach to detect input validation vulnerability. *Journal of King Saud University. Computer and Information Sciences, 35*(2), 682–701. DOI: 10.1016/j.jksuci.2023.01.009

Mburano, B., & Si, W. (2018). Evaluation of web vulnerability scanners based on OWASP Benchmark. In *26th Int. Conf. Syst. Eng. (ICSEng)* (pp. 1–6). DOI: 10.1109/ICSENG.2018.8638176

Mitropoulos, D., Louridas, P., Polychronakis, M., & Keromytis, A. D. (2017). Defending against web application attacks: Approaches, challenges and implications. *IEEE Transactions on Dependable and Secure Computing, 16*(2), 188–203. DOI: 10.1109/TDSC.2017.2665620

Neupane, A., Saxena, N., Maximo, J. O., & Kana, R. (2016). Neural Markers of Cybersecurity: An FMRI study of Phishing and Malware warnings. *IEEE Transactions on Information Forensics and Security, 11*(9), 1970–1983. DOI: 10.1109/TIFS.2016.2566265

Nguyen, D. D. N., Sood, K., Xiang, Y., Gao, L., Chi, L., & Yu, S. (2023). Toward IoT node authentication mechanism in next generation networks. *IEEE Internet of Things Journal, 10*(15), 13333–13341. DOI: 10.1109/JIOT.2023.3262822

Ning, J., Xu, J., Liang, K., Zhang, F., & Chang, E. (2018). Passive attacks against searchable encryption. *IEEE Transactions on Information Forensics and Security, 14*(3), 789–802. DOI: 10.1109/TIFS.2018.2866321

Olanrewaju, R. F., Khan, B. U. I., Morshidi, M. A., Anwar, F., & Kiah, L. B. M. (2021). A frictionless and secure user authentication in Web-Based premium applications. *IEEE Access : Practical Innovations, Open Solutions, 9*, 129240–129255. DOI: 10.1109/ACCESS.2021.3110310

Olca, E., & Can, O. (2022a). DICON: A Domain-Independent Consent Management for Personal Data Protection. *IEEE Access : Practical Innovations, Open Solutions, 10*, 95479–95497. DOI: 10.1109/ACCESS.2022.3204970

Olca, E., & Can, O. (2022b). DICON: A Domain-Independent Consent Management for Personal Data Protection. *IEEE Access : Practical Innovations, Open Solutions, 10*, 95479–95497. DOI: 10.1109/ACCESS.2022.3204970

Pal, B., Daniel, T., Chatterjee, R., & Ristenpart, T. (2019). Beyond credential stuffing: password similarity models using neural networks. *2022 IEEE Symposium on Security and Privacy (SP)*, 417–434. DOI: 10.1109/SP.2019.00056

Palacios, R., Fernandez-Portillo, A. F., Sanchez-Ubeda, E. F., & Garcia-De-Zuniga, P. (2022). HTB: A very effective method to protect web servers against BREACH attack to HTTPS. *IEEE Access : Practical Innovations, Open Solutions, 10*, 40381–40390. DOI: 10.1109/ACCESS.2022.3166175

Pant, P., Rajawat, A. S., Goyal, S., Bedi, P., Verma, C., Raboaca, M. S., & Enescu, F. M. (2022). Authentication and authorization in modern web apps for data security using NoDEJs and role of dark web. *Procedia Computer Science, 215*, 781–790. DOI: 10.1016/j.procs.2022.12.080

Park, J., Sandhu, R., Gupta, M., & Bhatt, S. (2021). Activity control design principles: Next generation access control for smart and collaborative systems. *IEEE Access : Practical Innovations, Open Solutions, 9*, 151004–151022. DOI: 10.1109/ACCESS.2021.3126201

Park, K. S., Shin, H. D., Park, B. L., Cheong, H. S., Choa, Y. M., Lee, H. K., Lee, J., Lee, J., Kim, H. T., Han, B. G., Kim, J. W., Koh, I., Kim, Y. J., Kimm, K., & Oh, B. (2005). Genetic polymorphisms in the transforming growth factor beta-induced gene associated with BMI. *Human Mutation, 25*(3), 322. DOI: 10.1002/humu.9315 PMID: 15712349

Perdices, D., De Vergara, J. E. L., González, I., & De Pedro, L. (2022). Web browsing privacy in the deep learning era: Beyond VPNs and encryption. *Computer Networks, 220*, 109471. DOI: 10.1016/j.comnet.2022.109471

Pohn, D., & Hommel, W. (2022). Reference Service Model Framework for Identity Management. *IEEE Access : Practical Innovations, Open Solutions, 10*, 120984–121009. DOI: 10.1109/ACCESS.2022.3219044

Pourrahmani, H., Yavarinasab, A., Monazzah, A. M. H., & Van Herle, J. (2023). A review of the security vulnerabilities and countermeasures in the Internet of Things solutions: A bright future for the Blockchain. *Internet of Things : Engineering Cyber Physical Human Systems, 23*, 100888. DOI: 10.1016/j.iot.2023.100888

Qin, W., Chen, S., & Peng, M. (2019). Recent advances in Industrial Internet: Insights and challenges. *Digital Communications and Networks, 6*(1), 1–13. DOI: 10.1016/j.dcan.2019.07.001

Robles-González, A., Arias-Cabarcos, P., & Parra-Arnau, J. (2023). Privacy-centered authentication: A new framework and analysis. *Computers & Security, 132*, 103353. DOI: 10.1016/j.cose.2023.103353

Rodríguez, G. E., Torres, J. G., Flores, P., & Benavides, D. E. (2019). Cross-site scripting (XSS) attacks and mitigation: A survey. *Computer Networks, 166*, 106960. DOI: 10.1016/j.comnet.2019.106960

Salamatian, S., Huleihel, W., Beirami, A., Cohen, A., & Medard, M. (2020). Centralized vs Decentralized Targeted Brute-Force Attacks: Guessing With Side-Information. *IEEE Transactions on Information Forensics and Security, 15*, 3749–3759. DOI: 10.1109/TIFS.2020.2998949

Sarfaraz, A., Chakrabortty, R. K., & Essam, D. L. (2023). AccessChain: An access control framework to protect data access in blockchain enabled supply chain. *Future Generation Computer Systems, 148*, 380–394. DOI: 10.1016/j.future.2023.06.009

Satoh, F., & Tokuda, T. (2010). Security Policy composition for composite web services. *IEEE Transactions on Services Computing, 4*(4), 314–327. DOI: 10.1109/TSC.2010.40

Saxena, N., Choi, B. J., & Lu, R. (2015). Authentication and Authorization Scheme for various user roles and devices in smart Grid. *IEEE Transactions on Information Forensics and Security, 11*(5), 907–921. DOI: 10.1109/TIFS.2015.2512525

Seo, J., & Park, S. (2023). SBAC: Substitution cipher access control based on blockchain for protecting personal data in metaverse. *Future Generation Computer Systems, 151*, 85–97. DOI: 10.1016/j.future.2023.09.022

Seo, N. J., Kim, N. H., Cho, N. S., & Cha, N. S. (2004). Web server attack categorization based on root causes and their locations. In Information Technology: Coding and Computing, 2004. Proceedings. ITCC 2004. International Conference onVolume: 1 (pp. 90-96 Vol.1). DOI: 10.1109/ITCC.2004.1286431

Shaked, A., Cherdantseva, Y., Burnap, P., & Maynard, P. (2023). Operations-informed incident response playbooks. *Computers & Security, 134*, 103454. DOI: 10.1016/j.cose.2023.103454

Shandilya, S. K. (2022). Paradigm shift in adaptive cyber defense for securing the web data: The future ahead. *Journal of Web Engineering*. Advance online publication. DOI: 10.13052/jwe1540-9589.21416

Shar, L. K., Briand, L. C., & Tan, H. B. K. (2014). Web application vulnerability prediction using hybrid program analysis and machine learning. *IEEE Transactions on Dependable and Secure Computing, 12*(6), 688–707. DOI: 10.1109/TDSC.2014.2373377

Sharma, S. (2018). Design and implementation of malware detection Scheme. *International Journal of Computer Network and Information Security, 10*(8), 58–66. DOI: 10.5815/ijcnis.2018.08.07

Sheikh, A. (2021). Certified Ethical Hacker (CEH) Preparation guide. In Apress eBooks. DOI: 10.1007/978-1-4842-7258-9

Sivakorn, S., Polakis, I., & Keromytis, A. D. (2016). The cracked cookie jar: HTTP cookie hijacking and the exposure of private information. *2022 IEEE Symposium on Security and Privacy (SP)*. DOI: 10.1109/SP.2016.49

Sivasankari, N., & Kamalakkannan, S. (2022). Detection and prevention of man-in-the-middle attack in iot network using regression modeling. *Advances in Engineering Software, 169*, 103126. DOI: 10.1016/j.advengsoft.2022.103126

Smith, R., Janicke, H., He, Y., Ferra, F., & Albakri, A. (2021). The Agile Incident Response for Industrial Control Systems (AIR4ICS) framework. *Computers & Security, 109*, 102398. DOI: 10.1016/j.cose.2021.102398

Sourav, S., & Chen, B. (2023). Exposing hidden attackers in industrial control systems using Micro-Distortions. *IEEE Transactions on Smart Grid, 15*(2), 2089–2101. DOI: 10.1109/TSG.2023.3300710

Staves, A., Anderson, T., Balderstone, H., Green, B., Gouglidis, A., & Hutchison, D. (2022). A Cyber Incident response and recovery framework to support operators of industrial control systems. *International Journal of Critical Infrastructure Protection, 37*, 100505. DOI: 10.1016/j.ijcip.2021.100505

Tabrizchi, H., & Rafsanjani, M. K. (2020). A survey on security challenges in cloud computing: Issues, threats, and solutions. *The Journal of Supercomputing, 76*(12), 9493–9532. DOI: 10.1007/s11227-020-03213-1

Tegane, S., Semchedine, F., & Boudries, A. (2023). An extended Attribute-based access control with controlled delegation in IoT. *Journal of Information Security and Applications, 76*, 103473. DOI: 10.1016/j.jisa.2023.103473

The Open Web Application Security Project. (n.d.). Testing guide. In The Open Web Application Security Project (pp. 1–207) [Book]. https://owasp.org/www-project-web-security-testing-guide/assets/archive/OWASP_Testing_Guide_v4.pdf

Tramontana, P., Amalfitano, D., & Fasolino, A. R. (2013, September 1). Reverse engineering techniques: From web applications to rich Internet applications. In 2013 15th IEEE International Symposium on Web Systems Evolution (WSE), Eindhoven, Netherlands. DOI: 10.1109/WSE.2013.6642421

Trestian, I., Ranjan, S., Kuzmanovic, A., & Nucci, A. (2009). Googling the Internet: Profiling internet endpoints via the world wide web. *IEEE/ACM Transactions on Networking*, *18*(2), 666–679. DOI: 10.1109/TNET.2009.2031175

Ullah, S. S., Oleshchuk, V., & Pussewalage, H. S. G. (2023). A survey on blockchain envisioned attribute based access control for internet of things: Overview, comparative analysis, and open research challenges. *Computer Networks*, *235*, 109994. DOI: 10.1016/j.comnet.2023.109994

Van Der Loo, F. (2011). Comparison of penetration testing tools for web applications [Thesis]. https://www.cs.ru.nl/masters-theses/2011/F_vd_Loo___Comparison_of _penetration_testing_tools_for_web_applications.pdf

Vignau, B., Khoury, R., Hallé, S., & Hamou-Lladj, A. (2021). The Botnet Simulator: A simulation tool for understanding the interaction between botnets. *Software Impacts*, *10*, 100173. DOI: 10.1016/j.simpa.2021.100173

Voronkov, A., Martucci, L. A., & Lindskog, S. (2020). Measuring the usability of firewall rule sets. *IEEE Access : Practical Innovations, Open Solutions*, *8*, 27106–27121. DOI: 10.1109/ACCESS.2020.2971093

Wang, D., Galster, M., & Morales-Trujillo, M. (2023). Application Monitoring for bug reproduction in web-based applications. *Journal of Systems and Software*, *207*, 111834. DOI: 10.1016/j.jss.2023.111834

Wu, A., Feng, Z., Li, X., & Xiao, J. (2023). ZTWeb: Cross site scripting detection based on zero trust. *Computers & Security*, *134*, 103434. DOI: 10.1016/j.cose.2023.103434

Xi, N., Liu, J., Li, Y., & Qin, B. (2023). Decentralized access control for secure microservices cooperation with blockchain. *ISA Transactions*, *141*, 44–51. DOI: 10.1016/j.isatra.2023.07.018 PMID: 37541856

Xue, K., Luo, X., Ma, Y., Li, J., Liu, J., & Wei, D. S. L. (2022). A distributed authentication scheme based on smart contract for roaming service in mobile vehicular networks. *IEEE Transactions on Vehicular Technology*, *71*(5), 5284–5297. DOI: 10.1109/TVT.2022.3148303

Yao, W., & Song, T. (2023). A covert TLS encryption transmission method based on network covert channel. *2022 IEEE Symposium on Computers and Communications (ISCC)*, 1344–1347. DOI: 10.1109/ISCC58397.2023.10217970

Yu, N. W., Wang, N. X., Fu, N. X., Xuan, N. D., & Zhao, N. W. (2008). An invisible localization attack to internet threat monitors. *IEEE Transactions on Parallel and Distributed Systems*, *20*(11), 1611–1625. DOI: 10.1109/TPDS.2008.255

Zaman, A., Safarinejadian, B., & Birk, W. (2020). Security analysis and fault detection against stealthy replay attacks. *International Journal of Control, 95*(6), 1562–1575. DOI: 10.1080/00207179.2020.1862917

Zhang, J., Yang, A., & Shuaishuai, F. (2022). Data protection of internet enterprise platforms in the era of big data. *Journal of Web Engineering*. Advance online publication. DOI: 10.13052/jwe1540-9589.21314

Compilation of References

Abomhara, M., & Kien, G. M. (2015). Cyber security and the Internet of Things: Vulnerabilities, threats, intruders and attacks. *Journal of Cyber Security and Mobility*, *4*(1), 65–88. DOI: 10.13052/jcsm2245-1439.414

Abukhater A. (2009). Rethinking planning theory and practice: A glimmer of light for prospects of integrated planning to combat complex urban realities. *Theoretical and empirical research in urban planning,* 2(11), 64 – 79.

Achdiat, I., Mulyani, S., Azis, Y., & Sukmadilaga, C. (2023). Roles of organizational learning culture in promoting innovation. *The Learning Organization*, *30*(1), 76–92. DOI: 10.1108/TLO-01-2021-0013

Addobea, A. A., Li, Q., Obiri, I. A.Jr, & Hou, J. (2023). Secure multi-factor access control mechanism for pairing blockchains. *Journal of Information Security and Applications*, *74*, 103477. DOI: 10.1016/j.jisa.2023.103477

Adeyemi, T. (2009). Inferential statistics for social and behavioural research. *Research journal of mathematics and statistics 1*(2): 47-54.

Adeyemi, O. S., & Olubiyi, T. O.Adeyemi Omolade SundayOlubiyi Timilehin Olasoji. (2023). The Impact of Brand Awareness on Customer Loyalty in Selected Food and Beverage Businesses in Lagos State Nigeria. *Jurnal Multidisiplin Madani*, *3*(3), 541–551. DOI: 10.55927/mudima.v3i3.3095

Adler, D. (2014). Scope change, flexibility and the management of services. *Review of integrative business and economics research,* 4(1), 469-483.

Admass, W. S., Munaye, Y. Y., & Diro, A. A. (2024). Cyber security: State of the art, challenges and future directions. *Cyber Security and Application Journal*, *2*, 1–10. DOI: 10.1016/j.csa.2023.100031

Aftab, H., Ismail, A., Ismaini, I.& Noor, Y. (2014). Time management practices in large construction services. *Colloquium on humanities, science and engineering, 5*(3), 61 - 65.

AGC. (2020a) Construction is an essential industry. News release https://www.agc.org/news/2020/03/21/construction-essential-industry#:~:text=Partnered%20with%20the%20buildings%20trades,COVID%2D19%2Drelated%20shutdowns

Agnihotri, A. (2016). Extending boundaries of blue ocean strategy. *Journal of Strategic Marketing, 24*(6), 519–528. DOI: 10.1080/0965254X.2015.1069882

Agroia, H., Reno, R., Spezeski, J., Mousli, L., Sarabia, R., & Starzyk, E. (2024). A Case Study to Investigate Factors Influencing the Santa Clara County Getting to Zero Initiative's Collective Impact Model. *Journal of Social, Behavioral and Health Sciences, 18*(1), 45–55. DOI: 10.5590/JSBHS.2024.18.1.04

Ahmad, S., & Liu, Y. (2024). Microaggressions at work: Psychological costs and organizational remedies. *Journal of Occupational Health Psychology, 29*(1), 12–26.

Ahmed, I. Z., Abid, G., Arshad, M., Ashfaq, F., Athar, M. A., & Hassan, Q. (2021). Impact of authoritative and laissez-Faire leadership on thriving at work: The moderating role of conscientiousness. *European Journal Investigation in Health. European Journal of Investigation in Health, Psychology and Education, 11*(3), 667–685. DOI: 10.3390/ejihpe11030048

AIHR. (n.d.). How to impact the company's culture with organizational citizenship behavior. Retrieved from https://www.aihr.com/

Ajay, S. & Micah, M. (2014). Sampling techniques & determination of sample size in applied statistics research: an overview. *International journal of economics, commerce and management, 2*(11), 1 – 22.

Ajzen, I. (1991). The theory of planned behavior. *Organizational Behavior and Human Decision Processes, 50*(2), 179–211. DOI: 10.1016/0749-5978(91)90020-T

Ajzen, I., & Fishbein, M. (1980). *Understanding attitudes and predicting social behavior*. Prentice-Hall.

Akewushola, R., Olateju, O., Hammed, O., & Lawale, G. (2012). Effect of service management on service success. *Australian Journal of Business and Management Research, 2*(3), 1–11. DOI: 10.52283/NSWRCA.AJBMR.20120203A01

Akpa, V. O., Asikhia, O. U., & Nneji, N. E. (2021). Organizational culture and organizational performance: A review of literature. *International Journal of Advances in Engineering and Management, 3*(1), 361–372.

Akre, V., & Yankova, V. (2019). Smart city facilitation framework (SCFF) and the case of Dubai smart city. *2019 International Conference on Computational Intelligence and Knowledge Economy (ICCIKE)*, 576-580. https://doi.org/DOI: 10.1109/ICCIKE47802.2019.9004424

Al Amri, T., & Marey, P. M. (2021). Project delays and cost overruns between the public and private sectors in Oman. *Journal of Public Affairs (14723891), 21*(3), 1–10. https://doi-org.captechu.idm.oclc.org/10.1002/pa.2262

Al Amri, T., & Marey-Pérez, M. (2020). Impact of Covid-19 on Oman's Construction Industry. *Technium Soc Sci J, 9*, 661–670. DOI: 10.47577/tssj.v9i1.1021

Al_Dubai, M. & Alaghbari, M. (2018). Relationship between organisational factors towards service success. *Journal of internet banking and commerce, 23*(2), 20 - 32.

Alabar, T., Egena, E., & Gbande, I. (2017). Service quality and customer satisfaction in Nigerian mobile telephony. *British journal of marketing. Studies, 5*(3), 1–13.

Alanazi, A. & Bach, C. (2016). Factors that affect and enhance customer satisfaction. *Journal of research in business and management, 4*(9), 80 - 88.

Alawida, M., Omolara, A. E., Abiodun, O. I., & Al-Rajab, M. (2022). A deeper look into cybersecurity issues in the wake of Covid-19: A survey. *Journal of King Saud University-Computer and Information Sciences*.

Alazmi, S., & De Leon, D. C. (2022). A systematic literature review on the characteristics and effectiveness of web application vulnerability scanners. *IEEE Access : Practical Innovations, Open Solutions, 10*, 33200–33219. DOI: 10.1109/ACCESS.2022.3161522

Alhazmi, A. A., & Kaufmann, A. (2022). Phenomenological Qualitative Methods Applied to the Analysis of Cross-Cultural Experience in Novel Educational Social Contexts. *Frontiers in Psychology, 13*(1), 785134. Advance online publication. DOI: 10.3389/fpsyg.2022.785134 PMID: 35548502

Ali, B. & Abedalfattah, Z. (2013). The effect of quality management practices on organisational performance in Jordan: An empirical study. *International journal of financial Research, 4*(1), 12 - 21.

Al-Janabi, A. S. H., Mhaibes, H. A., & Hussein, S. A. (2022). The role of learning organizations in crisis management strategy: A case study. *Corporate & Business Strategy Review, 3*(1), 8–21. DOI: 10.22495/cbsrv4i1art1

Allan-Blitz, L.-T., Turner, I., Hertlein, F., & Klausner, J. D. (2020). High Frequency and Prevalence of Community-Based Asymptomatic SARS-CoV-2 Infection. *medRxiv* 2020 DOI: 10.1101/2020.12.09.20246249

Allmendinger, P. (2002). *Planning Theory*. Palgrave.

Almeida, F., & Ferreira, J. J. M. (2022). Agile leadership and capability building in dynamic environments: A model for effective decision-making. *Journal of Strategy and Management*, *15*(2), 198–213.

Al-Mekhlafi, A. B. A. (2024). The importance of effective human resources management in creating a more secure work environment by improving safety culture. *International Journal of Intellectual Human Resource Management*, *5*(01), 14–23.

Almohtaseb, A., Aljohani, K., & Gabel, A. (2021). Transformational leadership and organizational resilience: Evidence from the mental health sector. *Journal of Leadership & Organizational Studies*, *28*(1), 45–58. DOI: 10.1177/15480518211007217

Almohtaseb, N., Moyo, L., Santoso, N. R., & Pratama, B. P. (2021). Transformational leadership during the COVID-19 pandemic: Strengthening employee engagement through internal communication. *The Journal of Communication Inquiry*, *47*(2), 67–82. DOI: 10.1177/01968599221095182

Alsharef, A., Banerjee, S., Uddin, S. M. J., Albert, A., & Jaselskis, E. (2021). Early Impacts of the COVID-19 Pandemic on the United States Construction Industry. *International Journal of Environmental Research and Public Health*, *18*(4), 1559. MDPI AG. Retrieved from DOI: 10.3390/ijerph18041559

Al-Talak, K., & Abbass, O. (2021). Detecting Server-Side Request Forgery (SSRF) Attack by using Deep Learning Techniques. *International Journal of Advanced Computer Science and Applications*, *12*(12). Advance online publication. DOI: 10.14569/IJACSA.2021.0121230

Altunoğlu, A. E., Kocakula, Ö., & Özer, A. (2022). *Demographic differences matter on job outcomes: Psychological contract's mediating role*. Journal Business, Management and Economics Engineering., DOI: 10.3846/bmee.2022.14895

Anand, A., Muskat, B., Creed, A., Zutshi, A., & Csepregi, A. (2021). Knowledge sharing, knowledge transfer and SMEs: Evolution, antecedents, outcomes and directions. *Personnel Review*, *50*(9), 1873–1893. DOI: 10.1108/PR-05-2020-0372

Anderson, H. J. (2017). Organizational-Citizen Behavior. In Zeigler-Hill, V., & Shackelford, T. (Eds.), *Encyclopedia of Personality and Individual Differences*. Springer. DOI: 10.1007/978-3-319-28099-8_788-1

Andrea, S. B., Eisenberg-Guyot, J., Blaikie, K. J., Owens, S., Oddo, V. M., Peckham, T., Minh, A., & Hajat, A. (2022). Inequitable Burden of the COVID-19 Pandemic Among Marginalized Older Workers in the United States: An Intersectional Approach. *The Journals of Gerontology. Series B, Psychological Sciences and Social Sciences*, *77*(10), 1928–1937. https://doi-org.captechu.idm.oclc.org/10.1093/geronb/gbac095. DOI: 10.1093/geronb/gbac095 PMID: 35863041

Ang, L., Seng, K. P., Ijemaru, G. K., & Zungeru, A. M. (2019). Deployment of IoV for smart cities: Applications, architecture, and challenges. *IEEE Access : Practical Innovations, Open Solutions*, *7*, 6473–6492. DOI: 10.1109/ACCESS.2018.2887076

Ang-Tan, R., & Ang, S. (2021). Understanding the smart city race between Hong Kong and Singapore. *Public Money & Management*, *42*(4), 231–240. DOI: 10.1080/09540962.2021.1903752

Arditi, David, Nayak, Shruti, Damci, Atilla. (2017). Effect of organizational culture on delay in construction. *International Journal of Project Management*, (Vol. 35, Issue 2, P. 136-147). https://doi.org/.DOI: 10.1016/j.ijproman.2016.10.018

Arı, K., Coplugil, K. B., Gönültas, I., & Artan, D. (2022). A Survey on the Effects of the Covid-19 Pandemic at Construction Sites. *IOP Conference Series. Earth and Environmental Science*, *1101*(3), 032011. DOI: 10.1088/1755-1315/1101/3/032011

Arksey, H., & O'Malley, L. (2005). Scoping studies: Towards a methodological framework. *International Journal of Social Research Methodology*, *8*(1), 19–32. DOI: 10.1080/1364557032000119616

Arogundade, O. (2023). *Network Security Concepts, Dangers, and Defense Best Practical*. Computer Engineering and Intelligent Systems., DOI: 10.7176/CEIS/14-2-03

Arokiasamy, A. (2013). The impact of customer satisfaction on customer loyalty and intentions to switch in the banking sector in Malaysia. *The journal of commerce*, *5*(1), 2220-6043.

Arokodare, M. A., Falana, R. B., & Olubiyi, T. O. (2023). Strategic agility, knowledge management and organisational performance in a post-pandemic era: A mediation analysis. *Journal of Family Business and Management Studies*, *27*, 83–108.

Arturo, C., Araceli, P., Carolina, R., & Lourdes, C. (2015). Contextual and mediation analysis between TQM critical factors and organisational results in the EFQM excellence model framework. *International Journal of Production Research*, *25*(8), 923–934.

Associated General Contractors of America (AGC) Diversity & Inclusion Council. AGC of America., The Business Case for Diversity & Inclusion in the Construction Industry 5 (2018). https://www.agc.org/sites/default/files/Files/Advocacy/AGC%20 Report%20on%20Biz%20Case%20for%20D%26I%20FINAL.pdf

Assudani, R., & Kloppenborg, J. (2010). Managing stakeholders for service management success: An emergent model of stakeholders. *Journal of General Management*, *36*(1), 67–80. DOI: 10.1177/030630701003500305

Atkins, S., & Lawson, C. (2021). Cooperation amidst competition: Cybersecurity partnership in the US financial services sector. *Journal of Cybersecurity*, *7*(1), tyab024. DOI: 10.1093/cybsec/tyab024

Attwood, S., Li, W., & Kharel, R. (2020). Evolutionary Algorithms in Web Security: Exploring untapped potential. 2022 13th International Symposium on Communication Systems, Networks and Digital Signal Processing (CSNDSP), 1–6. DOI: 10.1109/CSNDSP49049.2020.9249521

Awwal, M. (2014). Importance of strategic aspect in service management: A literature critique. *International journal of supply chain management, 3*(4), 96 - 99.

Ayat, M., & Kang, C. W. (2021). Effects of the COVID-19 pandemic on the construction sector: A systemized review. *Engineering, Construction, and Architectural Management.*

Ayob, A. L., & Nor, N. M. (2019). *Predictors of employee engagement in Malaysia, and the moderating effects of job demands and total reward.* Asian Academy of Management Journal., DOI: 10.21315/aamj2019.24.s2.3

Ayodeji-Ogundiran, A. I., Burrell, D. N., & Lewis, E. J. (2021). Strategic Adaptive Leadership and Emerging Approaches to Online Marketing of a US Small Business Real Estate Firm in Response to COVID-19. [IJOM]. *International Journal of Online Marketing*, *11*(3), 1–14. DOI: 10.4018/IJOM.2021070101

Baczyńska, A., He, H., He, T., Li, X., & Xinyi He, X. (2024). Servant leadership and employees' work safety behavior: The moderating role of corporate social responsibility to employees. *International Journal of Organizational Leadership*, *13*(4), 778–801.

Bag, S., Pretorius, J. H. C., Gupta, S., & Dwivedi, Y. K. (2021). Role of institutional pressures and resources in the adoption of big data analytics: A resource-based view perspective. *Production Planning and Control*, *32*(12), 1041–1056.

Bailey, Z. D., Krieger, N., Agénor, M., Graves, J., Linos, N., & Bassett, M. T. (2017). Structural racism and health inequities in the USA: Evidence and interventions. *Lancet, 389*(10077), 1453–1463. DOI: 10.1016/S0140-6736(17)30569-X PMID: 28402827

Bajo, B. M. (1990). From transactional to transformational leadership: Learning to share the vision. *Organizational Dynamics, 18*(3), 19–31. DOI: 10.1016/0090-2616(90)90061-S

Baker, D., & Ellis, L. (2021). Future directions in digital information: scenarios and themes. In *Future Directions in Digital Information* (pp. 1–15). Chandos Publishing. DOI: 10.1016/B978-0-12-822144-0.00001-X

Baker, M. G., Peckham, T. K., & Seixas, N. S. (2020). Estimating the burden of United States workers exposed to infection or disease: A key factor in containing risk of COVID-19 infection. *PLoS One, 15*(4), 1–8. https://doi-org.captechu.idm.oclc.org/10.1371/journal.pone.0232452. DOI: 10.1371/journal.pone.0232452 PMID: 32343747

Baral, A., Liang, Y., Li, M., Gonzalez, M., Shahandashti, M., & Ashuri, B. (2022). Impact of COVID-19 on the Diversity of the Construction Workforce. *Natural Hazards Review, 23*(3), 04022015. DOI: 10.1061/(ASCE)NH.1527-6996.0000560

Baral, S., Rao, A., Rwema, J. O. T., Lyons, C., Cevik, M., Kågesten, A. E., Diouf, D., Sohn, A. H., Phaswana-Mafuya, R. N., Kamarulzaman, A., Millett, G., Marcus, J. L., & Mishra, S. (2022). Competing health risks associated with the COVID-19 pandemic and early response: A scoping review. *PLoS One, 17*(8), 1–21. https://doi-org.captechu.idm.oclc.org/10.1371/journal.pone.0273389. DOI: 10.1371/journal.pone.0273389 PMID: 36037216

Bargh, S., M., Choenni, S., & Meijer, R. (. (2016). On design and deployment of two privacy-preserving procedures for judicial-data dissemination. *Government Information Quarterly, 33*(3), 481–493. DOI: 10.1016/j.giq.2016.06.002

Barling, J., Loughlin, C., & Kelloway, E. K. (2002). Development and test of a model linking safety-specific transformational leadership and occupational safety. *The Journal of Applied Psychology, 87*(3), 488–496. DOI: 10.1037/0021-9010.87.3.488 PMID: 12090606

Barnard, C. I. (1938). *The functions of the Executive*. Harvard University.

Basford, T. E., & Chen, J. (2023). Inclusive climates and workplace discrimination: A review and future directions. *The Academy of Management Annals, 17*(1), 134–167. DOI: 10.5465/annals.2021.0111

Bass, B. M., & Avolio, B. J. (1994). Transformational leadership and organizational culture. *International Journal of Public Administration, 17*(3–4), 541–554. DOI: 10.1080/01900699408524907

Basu, E., Pradhan, R. K., & Tewari, H. R. (2021). Impact of Organizational Citizenship Behavior at Work UPINCASE 2020 *Journal of Physics: Lecture Series* 1823 (2021) 012005 IOP Publishing DOI: 10.1088/1742-6596/1823/1/012005

Bateman, T. S., & Organo, D. W. (1983). Job satisfaction and the good soldier: The relationship between the employee's affection and "citizenship.". *Journal of the Academy of Management, 26*(4), 587–595. DOI: 10.2307/255908

Battisti, E., Alfiero, S., & Leonidou, E. (2022). Remote working and digital transformation during the COVID-19 pandemic: Economic-financial impacts and psychological drivers for employees. *Journal of Business Research, 150*, 38–50. DOI: 10.1016/j.jbusres.2022.06.010 PMID: 35706830

Beleiu, I., Crisan, E. & Nistor, R. (2014). Main factors influencing service success. *Interdisciplinary management research, 11*, 59-72.

Bell, A., & Adams, S. (2022). Challenges and opportunities in virtual mental health care: A case study of telehealth implementation. *Journal of Mental Health Technology, 38*(2), 113–126. DOI: 10.1080/15332985.2022.2035093

Bertrand, M., & Mullainathan, S. (2004). Are Emily and Greg more employable than Lakisha and Jamal? A field experiment on labor market discrimination. *The American Economic Review, 94*(4), 991–1013. DOI: 10.1257/0002828042002561

Best, A. L., Fletcher, F. E., Kadono, M., & Warren, R. C. (2021). Institutional distrust among African Americans and building trustworthiness in the COVID-19 response: implications for ethical public health practice. *Journal of health care for the poor and*

Bezrukova, K., Jehn, K. A., & Spell, C. S. (2016). Reviewing diversity training: Where we have been and where we should go. *Academy of Management Learning & Education, 11*(2), 207–227. DOI: 10.5465/amle.2008.0090

Bhardwaj, M., Singh, S., & Hu, Y. (2023). IoT in connected electric vehicles for smart cities. *Integration of IoT with Cloud Computing for Smart Applications*, 161-179. https://doi.org/DOI: 10.1201/9781003319238-10

Bhattacharyya, A., & Hastak, M. (2023). Impact Analysis of Covid-19 Pandemic on Construction Employment in the United States. In *Canadian Society of Civil Engineering Annual Conference* (pp. 411-420). Springer, Singapore. DOI: 10.1007/978-981-19-0968-9_33

Bhatt, S., Pham, T. K., Gupta, M., Benson, J., Park, J., & Sandhu, R. (2021). Attribute-Based access control for AWS internet of things and secure industries of the future. *IEEE Access : Practical Innovations, Open Solutions*, *9*, 107200–107223. DOI: 10.1109/ACCESS.2021.3101218

Bhushan, B., & Sahoo, G. (2017). Recent advances in attacks, technical challenges, vulnerabilities and their countermeasures in wireless sensor networks. *Wireless Personal Communications*, *98*(2), 2037–2077. DOI: 10.1007/s11277-017-4962-0

Bibbins-Domingo, K. (2020). This time must be different: Disparities during the COVID-19 pandemic. *Annals of Internal Medicine*, *173*(3), 233–234. DOI: 10.7326/M20-2247 PMID: 32343767

Bicer, A., Lee, Y., & Perihan, C. (2020). Inclusive STEM High School Factors Influencing Ethnic Minority Students' STEM Preparation. *Journal of Ethnic and Cultural Studies*, *7*(2), 147–172. https://www.jstor.org/stable/48710088. DOI: 10.29333/ejecs/384

Bitzer, M., Häckel, B., Leuthe, D., Ott, J., Stahl, B., & Strobel, J. (2022). Managing the Inevitable – a maturity model to establish incident response management capabilities. *Computers & Security*, *125*, 103050. DOI: 10.1016/j.cose.2022.103050

Blackwell, A. (2017). The Curb-Cut Effect. Laws and programs designed to benefit vulnerable groups, such as the disabled or people of color, often end up benefiting all of society. Stanford Social Innovation Review. https://ssir.org/chapters/entry/the _ curb_cut_effect

Blau, P. (1964). *Exchange and power in social life*. Wiley.

Blog, N. I. O. S. H. "COVID-19 Poses Big Challenges for Small Construction Firms," at: https://blogs.cdc.gov/niosh-science-blog/2021/03/09/construction_covid/

Bloomberg, D. L & Volpe. M. (2016). Completing your Qualitative Dissertation: A road map from beginning to end. 3rd edition, Sage Publications, Thousand Oaks, California.

Boatswain, M. (2016). Increasing Jobsite ess for Women in Construction. *Construction Executive:*http://constructionexec.com/chapter/increasing-jobsite-safety-for-women-in-construction

Bogers, M., Chesbrough, H. & Moedas, C. (2018). Open innovation: Research, practices, and policies. *Sage journals, 60*(2), 1 - 10.

Bogers, M., Sims, J., & West, J. (2019). What is an ecosystem? Incorporating 25 years of ecosystem research. *Proceedings - Academy of Management, 2019*(1), 11080. DOI: 10.5465/AMBPP.2019.11080abstract

Boliño, M. C. (1999). Citizenship and print management: Good soldiers or good actors? *Academy of Management Review, 24*(1), 82–98. DOI: 10.2307/259038

Bolino, M. C., Hsing, H.-H., Harvey, J., & LePine, A. (2015). "Well, I'm tired of trying." Organizational citizenship behavior. *The Journal of Applied Psychology, 100*(1), 56–74. DOI: 10.1037/a0037583 PMID: 25111252

Bolino, M. C., Klotz, A. C., Turnley, W. H., & Harvey, J. (2013). Exploring the dark side of organizational citizenship behavior. *Journal of Organizational Behavior, 34*(4), 542–559. DOI: 10.1002/job.1847

Bonilla-Silva, E. (2001). *White Supremacy and Racism in the Post-Civil Rights Era*. Lynne Reinner Publishers, Inc. DOI: 10.1515/9781685850272

Bonilla-Silva, E. (2019). *Racism without racists: Color-blind racism and the persistence of racial inequality in America*. Rowman & Littlefield.

Bou Hatoum, M., Faisal, A., Nassereddine, H., & Sarvari, H. (2021). Analysis of COVID-19 concerns raised by the construction workforce and development of mitigation practices. *Frontiers in Built Environment, 7*, 66. DOI: 10.3389/fbuil.2021.688495

Brandon, D. (2006). *Service management for modern information system*. Idea group.

Bridges, J. (2023, October 31). How to make a change management plan (templates included). *ProjectManager*. https://www.projectmanager.com/training/how-to-make-a-change-management-plan

Brief, A. P., & Motowidlo, S. J. (1986). Prosocial organizational behaviors. *Journal of the Academy of Management, 11*, 710–725.

Brooksbank, R. (1994). The anatomy of marketing positioning strategy. *Marketing Intelligence & Planning, 12*(4), 10–14. DOI: 10.1108/02634509410060695

Brown, S., Brooks, R. D., & Dong, X. S. (2020). Coronavirus and health disparities in construction.

Brown, S., Brooks, R. D., & Dong, X. S. (2020). Impact of COVID-19 on construction workers and businesses.

Brown, S., Brooks, R. D., Harris, W., & Dong, X. S. (2021). Construction employment, businesses, and COVID-19 vaccinations during the pandemic.

Brown, T. L. (2021). Workplace conflict resolution and the role of organizational policies. *Journal of Organizational Development, 35*(2), 45–58.

Bryman, A. (2016). *Social research methods* (5th ed.). Oxford University Press.

Bui, D. P., McCaffrey, K., Friedrichs, M., LaCross, N., Lewis, N. M., Sage, K., Barbeau, B., Vilven, D., Rose, C., & Braby, S. **(2020).** Racial and ethnic disparities among COVID-19 cases in workplace outbreaks by industry sector—Utah, March 6–June 5, 2020. *Morbid. Mortal. Week. Rep, 69*, 1133–1138.

Bukit, I., Ismida, Y., Maulana, R.& Nasir, M. (2018). The influence of wage, age and experience to labor productivity in construction works in Kota Langsa, Aceh. *MATEC web of conferences, 147*(1), 10 - 14.

Bunu, S, Muhammad, M. & Adamu, H. (2019). Review and analysis on telecommunication networks infrastructure in the northwest province of Nigeria for optimisation: Problems and solutions. *International journal of computer science & engineering survey (IJCSES), 10*(1), 1 – 14.

Burke, W. W. (2008). *Organizational change: Theory and practice* (2nd ed.). Sage.

Burrell, D. (2018). An Exploration of the Cybersecurity Workforce Shortage. *International Journal of Hyperconnectivity and the Internet of Things, 2*(1), 29–41. DOI: 10.4018/IJHIoT.2018010103

Burrell, D. N., Lewis, E. J., & Richardson, K. (2023). Adaptive Marketing, Management Strategy, and Technology Innovation in Beverage and Hospitality Markets. [IJIDE]. *International Journal of Innovation in the Digital Economy, 14*(1), 1–10. DOI: 10.4018/IJIDE.324096

Burrell, D. N., & Nobles, C. (2018). *Recommendations to Develop and Hire More Highly Qualified Women and Minorities Cybersecurity Professionals*. Academic Conferences International Limited.

Buyanova, M. A., Kalinina, A. A., & Shiro, M. S. (2020). Smart city branding massively expands smart technologies. *Lecture Notes in Networks and Systems*, 1063-1069. https://doi.org/DOI: 10.1007/978-3-030-59126-7_117

Cagalj, M., Perkovic, T., & Bugaric, M. (2014). Timing attacks on cognitive authentication schemes. *IEEE Transactions on Information Forensics and Security, 10*(3), 584–596. DOI: 10.1109/TIFS.2014.2376177

Cai, N., & Hayashi, M. (2019). Secure network code for adaptive and active attacks with No-Randomness in intermediate nodes. *IEEE Transactions on Information Theory, 66*(3), 1428–1448. DOI: 10.1109/TIT.2019.2957078

Cain, C. C. (2022). A Shifting Research Agenda: Historically Black Colleges and Universities Must Prepare Students for Careers in Computing, Informatics, and Engineering. *Journal of Information Systems Education*, *33*(1), 41–50.

Cairns, G., & Wright, G. (2018). Scenario thinking and practice: A review and call for future research. *Journal of Business Research*, *91*, 548–556.

Cakir, M. S., Wardman, J. K., & Trautrims, A. (2023). Ethical leadership supports safety voice by increasing risk perception and reducing ethical ambiguity: Evidence from the COVID-19 pandemic. *Risk Analysis*, *43*(9), 1902–1916. DOI: 10.1111/risa.14053 PMID: 36261397

Callaghan, W. M. (2012). Overview of maternal mortality in the United States. *Seminars in Perinatology*, *36*(1), 2–6. DOI: 10.1053/j.semperi.2011.09.002 PMID: 22280858

Cameron, K. S., & Quinn, R. E. (2011). Diagnosing and Changing Organizational Culture Based on the Competing Values Framework (3rd ed.). San Francisco Jossey-Bass. - References - Scientific Research Publishing. (n.d.). Www.scirp.org. https://www.scirp.org/reference/referencespapers?referenceid=1871430

Cameron, E., & Green, M. (2020). *Making sense of change management: A complete guide to the models, tools, and techniques of organizational change* (6th ed.). Kogan Page.

Caracuzzo, E., Caputo, A., Callea, A., Cortese, C., & Urbini, F. (2024). Playful work design in fostering organizational citizenship behaviors and performance: Two studies on the mediating role of work engagement. *Management Research Review*, *47*(9), 1422–1440. Advance online publication. DOI: 10.1108/MRR-05-2023-0354

Care Without Coverage.; 2002. doi: https://doi.org/DOI: 10.17226/10367

Carl, O. (2016). Service management problems in small and medium enterprises in Nigeria. *Journal of entrepreneurship & organisation management, 5*(169), 1 - 3.

Carpenter, M. L. (2023). Retaining Racially Minoritized Students in Community College STEM Program. University of Southern California ProQuest Dissertations Publishing, 5-6.

Carter, R. T., Lau, M. Y., Johnson, V., & Kirkinis, K. (2017). Racial discrimination and health outcomes among racial/ethnic minorities: A meta-analytic review. *Journal of Multicultural Counseling and Development*, *45*(4), 232–259. DOI: 10.1002/jmcd.12076

Casillas, E., Jr., Wu, G., Iantorno, S., & Ning, W. V. Joon Choi, Chan, P., & Lee, M. M. (2021). COVID-19: Highlighting Health Disparities in the Los Angeles Latinx Community. *Clinical Medicine & Research, 19*(4), 161–168. https://doi-org.captechu.idm.oclc.org/10.3121/cmr.2021.1654

Castilla, E. J., & Benard, S. (2010). The paradox of meritocracy in organizations. *Administrative Science Quarterly, 55*(4), 543–676. DOI: 10.2189/asqu.2010.55.4.543

Catillo, M., Pecchia, A., & Villano, U. (2021). AutoLog: Anomaly detection by deep autoencoding of system logs. *Expert Systems with Applications, 191*, 116263. DOI: 10.1016/j.eswa.2021.116263

Causation and Injustice. Locating the injustice of racial and ethnic health disparities. (2022). *Bioethics, 36*(3), 260–266. https://doi-org.captechu.idm.oclc.org/10.1111/bioe.12994

Cavada, M., Tight, M. R., & Rogers, C. D. (2019). A smart city case study of Singapore—Is Singapore truly smart? *Smart City Emergence*, 295-314. https://doi.org/DOI: 10.1016/B978-0-12-816169-2.00014-6

Cavico, F. J., Muffler, S., & Mujtaba, B. G. (2012). Appearance discrimination in employment: Legal and ethical implications of "lookism" and "look phobia." *ResearchGate*. https://www.researchgate.net/publication/263365558

Center for Disease Control and Prevention. (2022, August 3). *Interpretation of Forecasts of New and Total Deaths*. Updated 2022, Aug. 3, from COVID-19 Forecasts: Deaths | CDC)

Centers for Disease Control and Prevention. (2023). Health workers face a mental health crisis. *Centers for Disease Control and Prevention*. https://www.cdc.gov/vitalsigns/health-worker-mental-health/index.html

Centers for Disease Control and Prevention. Flu Disparities Among Racial and Ethnic Minority Groups.

Cerruti, C., Tavoletti, E., & Grieco, C. (2019). Management consulting: A review of fifty years of scholarly research. *Management Research Review, 42*(8), 902–925. DOI: 10.1108/MRR-03-2018-0100

Chakma, S. (2020). Racism in India: The need for criminalization of racism and racial crimes. *National Campaign Against Torture*. http://www.uncat.org/press-release/racism-in-india-the-need-for-criminalization-of-racism-and-racial-crimes/

Chakraborty, M., & Singh, M. (2020). Introduction to network Security Technologies. In Lecture notes in networks and systems (pp. 3–28). DOI: 10.1007/978-981-15-9317-8_1

Chang, Y., Ishii, M., Lee, P.& Tezuka, K. (2013). A game theoretical analysis of port competition, transportation research part e: logistics and transportation review. *Elsevier, 49*(1), 92-106.

Chang, B. L., Bakken, S., Brown, S. S., Houston, T. K., Kreps, G. L., Kukafka, R., Safran, C., & Stavri, P. Z. (2020). Bridging the digital divide: Reaching vulnerable populations. *Journal of the American Medical Informatics Association : JAMIA, 11*(6), 448–457. DOI: 10.1197/jamia.M1535 PMID: 15299002

Chatzoglou, E., Kouliaridis, V., Kambourakis, G., Karopoulos, G., & Gritzalis, S. (2022). A hands-on gaze on HTTP/3 security through the lens of HTTP/2 and a public dataset. *Computers & Security, 125*, 103051. DOI: 10.1016/j.cose.2022.103051

Chaudhary, A., Krishna, K. C., Shadik, M., & Raj, D. (2024). Detection of phishing link using different machine learning techniques. In Lecture notes in networks and systems (pp. 63–77). DOI: 10.1007/978-981-99-9811-1_6

Chaudhary, A., Krishna, K., Shadik, M., & Raj, D. (2023). A review on malicious link detection techniques. CRC Press eBooks, 768–777. DOI: 10.1201/9781003393580-114

Chen, Q., & Mills, T. Dynamic Interplay between Safety Culture and Workplace Diversity. Retrieved from http://www.irbnet. de/daten/iconda/CIB20338.pdf

Chesti, I. A., Humayun, M., Sama, N. U., & Jhanjhi, N. (2020). Evolution, Mitigation, and Prevention of Ransomware. In 2020 2nd International Conference on Computer and Information Sciences (ICCIS) (pp. 1–6). DOI: 10.1109/ICCIS49240.2020.9257708

Cheung-Judge, M.-Y., & Holbeche, L. (2015). *Organization development: A practitioner's guide for OD and HR*. Kogan Page.

Chiaburu, D. S., Oh, I.-S., Berry, C. M., Li, N., & Gardner, R. G. (2011). The Five-Factor Model of Personality Traits and Organizational Citizenship Behaviors: A goal J.L. Pletzer *Personality and Individual Differences* 173 (2021) 110550

Chiaburu, D. S., & Baker, D. F. (2006). Extra-role behavior as a response to perceived organizational support: The role of social exchange relationships. *Journal of Managerial Psychology, 21*(5), 471–488.

Chien-Ho, K., & Abdulmajeed, H. A. (2022). Improving Construction Safety: Lessons Learned from COVID-19 in the United States. *Sustainability (Basel), 14*(12), 7137. DOI: 10.3390/su14127137

Choi, B., & Lee, S. H. (2022). The psychological mechanism of construction workers' safety participation: The social identity theory perspective. *Journal of Safety Research, 82*, 194–206. DOI: 10.1016/j.jsr.2022.05.011 PMID: 36031247

Choi, E. (2022). A paradigm shift in beauty education in response to the digital transformation era-based on analysis of trends in the cosmetics and beauty industry. *Journal of the Korean Society of Cosmetology, 28*(4), 675–688. DOI: 10.52660/JKSC.2022.28.4.675

Choi, J. O., Shrestha, P. P., Lim, J., & Shrestha, B. K. (2018, March). An investigation of construction workforce inequalities and biases in the architecture, engineering, and construction (AEC) industry. In *Construction Research Congress 2018: Sustainable Design and Construction and Education*. DOI: 10.1061/9780784481301.007

Chong, J. X. Y., & Gagné, M. (2019). Self-Determination Theory for Work Motivation. *Management*. Advance online publication. DOI: 10.1093/obo/9780199846740-0182

Choudhury, S., & Kumar, S. (2021). Understanding identity, conflict, and trauma through literary texts of selected women writers of North-East India. *ResearchGate*. https://www.researchgate.net/publication/355768748

Choudhury, P., Foroughi, C., & Larson, B. Z. (2020). Work-from-anywhere: The productivity effects of geographic flexibility. *Strategic Management Journal, 42*(4), 655–683. DOI: 10.1002/smj.3251

Christian, M. S., Bradley, J. C., Wallace, J. C., & Burke, M. J. (2009). Workplace safety: A meta-analysis of the roles of person and situation factors. *The Journal of Applied Psychology, 94*(5), 1103–1127. DOI: 10.1037/a0016172 PMID: 19702360

Christos, V., Evangelos, L., & Fotis, K. (2010). Investigating total quality management practice's inter-relationships in ISO 9001: 2000 certified organisations. *Total Quality Management & Business Excellence, 21*(5), 503–515. DOI: 10.1080/14783363.2010.481512

Christy, V., Manoharan, J., & Yokesh, M. (2019). Psychological well-being as a mediator between psychological contract breach and organisational citizenship behaviour. *Medico-Legal Update, 19*(1), 118. Advance online publication. DOI: 10.5958/0974-1283.2019.00024.0

Chughtai, M. S., Khalid, Y., Mushtaque, I., Yusrini, L., & Akhtar, N. (2022). A test of job demands and resources theory for leaders and subordinates change-related behaviors: A perspective from emerging economy. Journal of Innovative Research in Management Sciences. DOI: 10.62270/jirms.vi.34

Cialdini, R. B., & Kenrick, D. T. (1976). Altruism as Hedonism: A Social Development Perspective on the Relationship Between Negative Mood and Help. *Journal of Personality and Social Psychology*, *40*(5), 1039–1046. DOI: 10.1037/0022-3514.34.5.907

Ciekanowski, Z. S., Żurawski, S., Wysokińska, A., & Kacprzak, A. (2025). The Role of a leader in shaping the safety culture of an organization. *European Research Studies*, *28*(1), 589–598. DOI: 10.35808/ersj/3923

Clampitt, P. G., DeKoch, R. J., & Cashman, T. (2000). A strategy for communicating about uncertainty. *The Academy of Management Perspectives*, *14*(4), 41–57. DOI: 10.5465/ame.2000.3979815

Clarke, S. (2013). Safety leadership: A meta-analytic review of transformational and transactional leadership styles as antecedents of safety behaviours. *Journal of Occupational and Organizational Psychology*, *86*(1), 22–49. DOI: 10.1111/j.2044-8325.2012.02064.x

Clark, R., & Estes, F. (2008). *Turning research into results: A guide to selecting the right performance solutions*. Information Age Publications.

Cohen, S. (1980). Side effects of stress on human performance and social behavior: A review of research and theory. *Psychol. Bowl.Isaiah*, *88*, 82–108. PMID: 7403392

Cole, D., Newman, S., & Lin, D. (2021). A new facial authentication pitfall and remedy in web services. *IEEE Transactions on Dependable and Secure Computing*, *19*(4), 2635–2647. DOI: 10.1109/TDSC.2021.3067794

Collazo, J. (2020, August 3). The Importance Of Communication When There Is Change In A Company. *Forbes*. Retrieved December 5, 2022, from https://www.forbes.com/sites/forbesbusinesscouncil/2020/08/03/the-importance-of-communication-when-there-is-change-in-a-company/?sh=4335d5f3739e

Colquitt, J. A. (2001). On the dimensionality of organizational justice: A construct validation of a measure. *The Journal of Applied Psychology*, *86*(3), 386–400. DOI: 10.1037/0021-9010.86.3.386 PMID: 11419799

Compilation from U.S. Census Bureau Current Population Survey (CPD) Questionnaire. Available at: https://www.census.gov/programs-surveys/cps/technical-documentation/questionnaires.html

Conti, M., Dragoni, N., & Lesyk, V. (2016). A survey of Man in the middle attacks. *IEEE Communications Surveys and Tutorials, 18*(3), 2027–2051. DOI: 10.1109/COMST.2016.2548426

Cooper, L. & Nakanishi. (2014). *Market share analysis: Evaluating competitive marketing effectiveness*. Boston: Kluwer Academic Publishers.

Cooper, M. D. (2000). Towards a model of safety culture. *Safety Science Journal, 36*, 111–136. DOI: 10.1016/S0925-7535(00)00035-7

Copulsky, J. R., & Wolf, M. J. (1990). Relationship marketing: Positioning for the future. *The Journal of Business Strategy, 11*(4), 16–20. DOI: 10.1108/eb060069 PMID: 10106864

Cortina, L. M., & Magley, V. J. (2009). Patterns and profiles of response to incivility in the workplace. *Journal of Occupational Health Psychology, 14*(3), 272–288. DOI: 10.1037/a0014934 PMID: 19586222

Coyle-Shapiro, J. A. M., & Kessler, I. (2000). *Mutuality, Stability and Psychological Breach of the Contract: A Longitudinal Study*. Paper presented at the Academy of Management, Toronto, August.

Coyle-Shapiro, J. A. M., Morrow, P. C., & Kessler, I. (2006). Serving Two Organizations: Exploring the Employment Relationship of Hired Employees. *Human Resource Management, 45*(4), 561–583. DOI: 10.1002/hrm.20132

Cremer, F., Sheehan, B., Fortmann, M., Kia, A. N., Mullins, M., Murphy, F., & Materne, S. (2022). Cyber risk and cybersecurity: A systematic review of data availability. *The Geneva Papers on Risk and Insurance. Issues and Practice, 47*(3), 698–736. DOI: 10.1057/s41288-022-00266-6 PMID: 35194352

Crenshaw, K. (1989). Demarginalizing the intersection of race and sex: A black feminist critique of antidiscrimination doctrine, feminist theory, and antiracist politics. *University of Chicago Legal Forum, 1989*(1), 139–167.

Creswell, J. W., & Plano Clark, V. L. (2011). *Designing and Conducting Mixed Methods Research* (2nd ed.). Sage Publications.

Creswell, J. W., & Poth, C. N. (2018). *Qualitative inquiry and research design: Choosing among five approaches* (4th ed.). Sage Publications.

Currie, L, Iannone, A; Mandato, C. (2021). *The Construction Lawyer; Chicago Vol. 41*(1), (Winter 2021), p. 23-33.

Daft, R. L. (2010). *Management* (9th ed.). South-Western. Cengage Learning

Dai, P., Yu, W., Wang, H., Wen, G., & Lv, Y. (2020). Distributed reinforcement learning for Cyber-Physical system with multiple remote state estimation under DOS attacker. *IEEE Transactions on Network Science and Engineering*, *7*(4), 3212–3222. DOI: 10.1109/TNSE.2020.3018871

Dalal, R. S., Lam, H., Weiss, M., Welch, E. R., & Hulin, C. (2009). Intrafaceted approach to work behavior and performance: Concurrent and lagging associations between citizenship and counter-productivity, and dynamic relationships with affect and overall work performance. *Academy of Management Journal*, *52*(5), 1051–1066. DOI: 10.5465/amj.2009.44636148

Dangelico, R. M., Pujari, D., & Pontrandolfo, P. (2017). Green product innovation in manufacturing firms: A sustainability-oriented dynamic capability perspective. *Business Strategy and the Environment*, *26*(4), 490–506. DOI: 10.1002/bse.1932

Dara, S. & Marc, S. (2015). Quality management and innovation: New insights on a structural contingency framework. *International journal of quality innovation, 1*(2), 1 - 5.

Daria, B., Maurizio, F., Alessandro, P., & Fabio, S. (2012). Design of an integrated quality assurance strategy in production systems. *International Journal of Production Research*, *50*(6), 1–20.

Das, A., Baki, S., Aassal, A. E., Verma, R., & Dunbar, A. (2019). SOK: A Comprehensive Reexamination of Phishing research from the security perspective. *IEEE Communications Surveys and Tutorials*, *22*(1), 671–708. DOI: 10.1109/COMST.2019.2957750

Das, A., Nanda, P., Jain, R., Saini, T., Bhaskar, S., & Mohapatra, H. (2024). Security considerations of SDN networks during DDoS attacks in load balancing. *Advances in Human and Social Aspects of Technology*, •••, 123–140. DOI: 10.4018/979-8-3693-9235-5.ch007

Das, D., Sethuraman, S. C., & Satapathy, S. C. (2022). A decentralized open web cryptographic standard. *Computers & Electrical Engineering*, *99*, 107751. DOI: 10.1016/j.compeleceng.2022.107751

Davis, R. J. (2018). The long-term effects of racial discrimination on career trajectories. *Human Resources Quarterly*, *29*(4), 123–140. DOI: 10.1002/hrq.2018.29.4.123

Davis, R., McCallum, S., & Jenkins, M. (2023). Collaborative care models in mental health: Challenges and opportunities in integrated service delivery. *Community Mental Health Journal*, *59*(1), 75–89. DOI: 10.1007/s10597-023-01089-0

Day, M., Magnan, G. M., Hughes, J., & Webb, M. (2008). Strategic supplier relationship management. *Supply Chain Management Review*, *12*(4), 40–48.

Dekker, S. (2012). *Just culture: Balancing safety and accountability*. CRC Press.

Del Campo, R. (2007). Psychological Breach of Contract: A Perspective on Individual Difference, *International Journal of Management*. Thursday, March 1, 2007. 11 of the Constitution.

DeMaria, J. (2017, April 12). Organizational Safety Culture. Institute for Safety and Health Management. Retrieved from https://ishm.org/organizational-safety-culture/

Denison, D. R., & Mishra, A. K. (1995). Toward a Theory of Organizational Culture and Effectiveness. *Organization Science*, *6*(2), 204–223. https://www.jstor.org/stable/2635122. DOI: 10.1287/orsc.6.2.204

Desmet, L., Verbaeten, P., Joosen, W., & Piessens, F. (2008). Provable Protection against Web Application Vulnerabilities Related to Session Data Dependencies. *IEEE Transactions on Software Engineering*, *34*(1), 50–64. DOI: 10.1109/TSE.2007.70742

DeWalt, K. M., & DeWalt, B. R. (2011). *Participant observation: A guide for fieldworkers* (2nd ed.). Rowman & Littlefield.

Dhananjay, R. A., & Sheetal Kaushik. (2016). A comprehensive study of contemporary tools and techniques in the realm of cyber security. IITM Journal of Management and IT, 7(1), 109–110. https://www.IndianJournals.com

Dhillon, R., Agarwal, B., & Rajput, N. (2022). *Experiential marketing strategies used by luxury cosmetics companies*. Innov. Mark. DOI: 10.21511/im.18(1).2022.05

Dicksen, P. R. (1996). The static and dynamic mechanics of competitive theory. *Journal of Marketing*, *60*, 102–106. DOI: 10.1177/002224299606000409

Dlamini, J. (2020). *Safari nation: A social history of the Kruger National Park*. Ohio University Press. DOI: 10.2307/j.ctv21zp25d

Dobbin, F., & Kalev, A. (2021). Why diversity programs fail. *Harvard Business Review*, *94*(7/8), 52–60. https://hbr.org/2016/07/why-diversity-programs-fail

Dolgui, A., Ivanov, D., & Sokolov, B. (2020). Reconfigurable supply chain: The X-network. *International Journal of Production Research*, *58*(13), 4138–4163. DOI: 10.1080/00207543.2020.1774679

Donaldson, T., & Preston, L. (1995). The stakeholder theory of the corporation: Concepts, evidence, and implications. [El]. *Academy of Management Review*, *20*(1), 501–522. DOI: 10.2307/258887

Dong, X. S., Wang, X., Katz, R., Trahan Cain, C., Rinehart, R. (2018). Fatal injuries among small construction establishments. Available at: publications_ Quarter3-QDR-2018_0.pdf (cpwr.com)

Doubraski, B. (2016, December 13). Increasing Jobsite Safety for Women in Construction. Construction Executive. Retrieved from http://constructionexec.com/chapter/increasingjobsite-safety-for-women-in-construction

Dovidio, J. F., & Gaertner, S. L. (2010). Intergroup bias. In Fiske, S. T., Gilbert, D. T., & Lindzey, G. (Eds.), *Handbook of social psychology* (2nd ed., pp. 1084–1121). John Wiley & Sons. DOI: 10.1002/9780470561119.socpsy002029

Duan, T., & Peng, Y. J. (2020). Interactive Symmetric Context Encryption in Framework of Asynchronous Data Exchange. In *2020 Chinese Control And Decision Conference (CCDC)*, Hefei, China, (Vol. 3, pp. 3665–3670). DOI: 10.1109/CCDC49329.2020.9164726

Dubey, R., Gunasekaran, A., Childe, S. J., Papadopoulos, T., & Hazen, B. T. (2021). Big data analytics capability in supply chain agility: The moderating effect of organizational flexibility. *Management Decision*, *59*(1), 179–196.

Durai, K. N., Subha, R., & Haldorai, A. (2020). A novel method to detect and prevent SQLIA using ontology to cloud web security. *Wireless Personal Communications*, *117*(4), 2995–3014. DOI: 10.1007/s11277-020-07243-z

Dwivedi, Y. K., Ismagilova, E., Carlson, J., Filieri, R., Jacobson, J., Kumar, V., & Wang, Y. (2021). Social media marketing and consumer engagement: A review and future research agenda. *Journal of Business Research*, *137*, 275–285.

Dziekoski, K. (2017). Service managers' competencies model for construction industry in Poland. *Science direct, 182*, 174-181.

Easo, K., Balaji, M. S., & Anbazhagan, B. (2020). Organizational Citizenship Behavior, Its Background, and Outcomes: An Empirical Analysis, *Shanlax. International Journal of Management (Kolkata)*, *7*(3), 74–77. DOI: 10.34293/management.v7i3.1610

Edmons, A. E. (2012). The link between job satisfaction and company value, with implications for corporate social responsibility. *Acts*, *26*(4), 1–19.

Egena, A. N. (2018). Service quality and customer satisfaction in Nigerian mobile telephony. *Journal of Business and Management*, *7*(1), 112–130.

El Hajjar, S. (2018). Statistical analysis: internal-consistency reliability and construct validity. *International journal of quantitative and qualitative research methods, 6*(1), 27-38.

El Sawalhi, N. & Enshassi. (2013). Application of service time management tools and techniques to the construction industry in the Gaza strip. *The Australasian Journal of Construction Economics and Building*, *5*(1), 1–8.

Elizalde, R. R. (2022). COVID-19 in the Construction Sector. *Encyclopedia*, *2*(2), 717–728. DOI: 10.3390/encyclopedia2020050

Ely, R. J., & Thomas, D. A. (2020). Cultural diversity at work: The effects of diversity perspectives on work group processes and outcomes. *Administrative Science Quarterly*, *46*(2), 229–273. DOI: 10.2307/2667087

Engelen, A., Brettel, M., & Wiest, G. (2012). Cross-functional integration and new product performance, the impact of national and corporate culture. *Journal of International Management*, *18*(1), 52–65. DOI: 10.1016/j.intman.2011.07.001

Esposito, C., Ficco, M., & Gupta, B. B. (2020). Blockchain-based authentication and authorization for smart city applications. *Information Processing & Management*, *58*(2), 102468. DOI: 10.1016/j.ipm.2020.102468

EtAl, E. C. (. (2016). A network traffic representation model for detecting application layer attacks. *International Journal of Computing and Digital Systems*, *5*(1), 31–42. DOI: 10.12785/ijcds/050104

Evangelos, P., & Jiju, A. (2015). The effectiveness of the ISO 9001 quality management system and its influential critical factors in Greek manufacturing companies. *International Journal of Production Research*, *53*(7), 2089–2099. DOI: 10.1080/00207543.2014.965353

Fadlalla, F. F., & Elshoush, H. T. (2023). Input Validation Vulnerabilities in web Applications: Systematic review, Classification, and analysis of the current State-of-the-Art. *IEEE Access : Practical Innovations, Open Solutions*, *11*, 40128–40161. DOI: 10.1109/ACCESS.2023.3266385

Fageha, M., & Aibinu, A. (2013). Managing service scope definition to improve stakeholders' participation and enhance service outcome. *Procedia: Social and Behavioral Sciences*, *74*(2), 154–164. DOI: 10.1016/j.sbspro.2013.03.038

Faheem, M., Jamel, S., Hassan, A. A. Z., Shafinaz, N., & Mat, M. (2017). A survey on the cryptographic encryption algorithms. *International Journal of Advanced Computer Science and Applications*, *8*(11). Advance online publication. DOI: 10.14569/IJACSA.2017.081141

Faludi, A. (1973). *A reader in planning theory* (1st ed.). Pergamon press.

Farh, J. L., Zhong, C. B., & Organ, D. W. (2002). *An inductive analysis of the construct domain of organizational citizenship behavior.In the People's Republic of China. A. S. Tsui, C.M. Lau (Eds.), The Management of Enterprises in the People's Republic of China* (445-470), Kluwer Academic Press, Boston, MA. DOI: 10.1007/978-1-4615-1095-6_18

Farh, J. L., Earley, P. C., & Lin, S. C. (1997). Impetus for Action: Acultural Analysis of Justice and the Behavior of Organizational Citizenship in Chinese Society. *Quarterly Journal of Administrative Sciences*, *42*(3), 421–444. DOI: 10.2307/2393733

Farh, J. L., Zhong, C. B., & Organ, D. W. (2004). Behavior of organizational citizenship in the People's Republic of China. *Organization Science*, *15*(2), 241–253. DOI: 10.1287/orsc.1030.0051

Fashina, A., Abdilahi, S., Hassan, A., & Fakunle, F. (2020). The significant factors that influence the choice of service scope management practices in telecommunication companies in Somaliland. *PM World Journal.*, *9*(3), 1–12.

Fauziya, B., & Linge, K. (2019). Strategic Factors Influencing Market Share of Telecommunications in Kenya. *Journal of Marketing Communications*, *2*(1), 80–91.

Federal Grant: Cybersecurity Workforce Development and Training for Underserved Communities. (2023). US Fed News Service, Including US State News https://www.proquest.com/wire-feeds/federal-grant-cybersecurity-workforce-development/docview/2810047917/se-2

Fein, E., Yildiz, H., & Romi, A. (2023). Organizational Citizenship Behavior and Self-Defeating Work Behavior: A Comprehensive Framework for Understanding Employee Behaviors. *Frontiers in Psychology*, •••, 14.

Fellows, R., & Liu, A. (2022). *Research methods for construction* (5th ed.). John Wiley & Sons Ltd.

Feng, J., Jingshan, L., Guoxian, X., & Jorge, A. (2013). Quality flow model in automotive paint shops. *International Journal of Production Research*, *48*(17), 5021–5030.

Ferdinand, K. C., & Nasser, S. A. (2015). Racial/ethnic disparities in prevalence and care of patients with type 2 diabetes mellitus. *Current Medical Research and Opinion*, *31*(5), 913–923. DOI: 10.1185/03007995.2015.1029894 PMID: 25772230

Finch, A., Burrell, D. N., Lu, S., Dawson, M., Springs, D., Bilberry, K., Anderson, D. P., & Modeste, R. (2020). Cybersecurity workforce development in minority, low income, and native American reservation communities. [IJSEUS]. *International Journal of Smart Education and Urban Society*, *11*(4), 35–52. DOI: 10.4018/IJSEUS.2020100103

Fiscella, K., & Sanders, M. R. (2016). Racial and ethnic disparities in the quality of health care. *Annual Review of Public Health*, *37*(1), 375–394. DOI: 10.1146/annurev-publhealth-032315-021439 PMID: 26789384

Fischer, R. J., Halibozek, E. P., & Walters, D. C. (2018). Contingency Planning Emergency Response and Safety. *International Security*, *2019*, 249–268. DOI: 10.1016/B978-0-12-805310-2.00011-1

Fishbein, M. (1979). A theory of reasoned action: Some applications and implications. *Nebraska Symposium on Motivation*, *27*, 65–116. PMID: 7242751

Fitzpatrick, P. J. (2023). Improving health literacy using the power of digital communications to achieve better health outcomes for patients and practitioners. *Frontiers in Digital Health*, *17*(5), 1–13. DOI: 10.3389/fdgth.2023.1264780 PMID: 38046643

Fonseca, J., Seixas, N., Vieira, M., & Madeira, H. (2013). Analysis of field data on web security vulnerabilities. *IEEE Transactions on Dependable and Secure Computing*, *11*(2), 89–100. DOI: 10.1109/TDSC.2013.37

Ford, M. T., Matthews, R. A., Wooldridge, J. D., Mishra, V., Kakar, U., & Strahan, S. R. (2021). How do occupational stressor-strain effects vary with time? A review and meta-analysis of the relevance of time lags in longitudinal studies. *Work and Stress*, *35*(2), 104–130. DOI: 10.1080/02678373.2020.1837731

Fowler, J., & Floyd, J. (1995). *Improving survey questions: Design and evaluation*. Sage Publications.

Franchi, F., Graziosi, F., Fina, E. D., & Galassi, A. (2024). A survey of cloud-enabled GIS solutions toward edge computing: Challenges and perspectives. *IEEE Open Journal of the Communications Society*, *5*, 312–331. DOI: 10.1109/OJCOMS.2023.3344198

Freeman, R. (1984). *Strategic management: A stakeholder approach*. Pitman/Ballinger.

Fuentes-Garcia, M., Camacho, J., & Macia-Fernandez, G. (2021). Present and future of network security Monitoring. *IEEE Access : Practical Innovations, Open Solutions*, *9*, 112744–112760. DOI: 10.1109/ACCESS.2021.3067106

Gagneja, K. K. (2017). Knowing the ransomware and building defense against it - specific to healthcare institutes. In *Third International Conference on Mobile and Secure Services (MobiSecServ)* (pp. 1–5). DOI: 10.1109/MOBISECSERV.2017.7886569

Gakovic, A., & Tetrick, L. E. (2003). Perceived organizational support and employment status: A comparison of the employment relationship of part-time and full-time employees attending the college class. *Journal of Organizational Behavior*, *24*, 649–666. DOI: 10.1002/job.206

Gamil, Y., & Alhagar, A. (2020). The impact of the pandemic crisis on the survival of the construction industry: A case of COVID-19. *Mediterranean Journal of Social Sciences*, *11*(4), 122. DOI: 10.36941/mjss-2020-0047

Gandini, A. (2019). Labour process theory and the gig economy. *Human Relations*, *72*(6), 1039–1056. DOI: 10.1177/0018726718790002

Gan, G., Chen, E., Zhou, Z., & Zhu, Y. (2020). Token-Based access control. *IEEE Access : Practical Innovations, Open Solutions*, *8*, 54189–54199. DOI: 10.1109/ACCESS.2020.2979746

García, B., Ricca, F., Del Alamo, J. M., & Leotta, M. (2023). Enhancing Web Applications Observability through Instrumented Automated Browsers. *Journal of Systems and Software*, *203*, 111723. DOI: 10.1016/j.jss.2023.111723

Garcia, M. A., Homan, P. A., García, C., & Brown, T. H. (2021). The Color of COVID-19: Structural Racism and the Disproportionate Impact of the Pandemic on Older Black and Latinx Adults. *The Journals of Gerontology. Series B, Psychological Sciences and Social Sciences*, *76*(3), e75–e80. https://doi-org.captechu.idm.oclc.org/10.1093/geronb/gbaa114. DOI: 10.1093/geronb/gbaa114 PMID: 32756973

Garcia, M. A., Thierry, A. D., & Pendergrast, C. B. (2022). Devastating Economic Impact of COVID-19 on Older Black and Latinx Adults: Implications for Health and Well-Being. *The Journals of Gerontology. Series B, Psychological Sciences and Social Sciences*, *77*(8), 1501–1507. https://doi-org.captechu.idm.oclc.org/10.1093/geronb/gbab218. DOI: 10.1093/geronb/gbab218 PMID: 34850887

Garcia, M., Taylor, R., & Chen, L. (2020). Breaking barriers: Addressing racial discrimination in modern organizations. *Diversity and Inclusion Review*, *12*(3), 98–112.

Ge, C., Susilo, W., Baek, J., Liu, Z., Xia, J., & Fang, L. (2021). Revocable Attribute-Based encryption with data integrity in clouds. *IEEE Transactions on Dependable and Secure Computing*, *19*(5), 2864–2872. DOI: 10.1109/TDSC.2021.3065999

Gerpott, T., Rams, W., & Schindler, A. (2001). Customer retention, loyalty and satisfaction in the German mobile cellular telecommunications market. *Telecommunications Policy*, *25*(1), 249–269. DOI: 10.1016/S0308-5961(00)00097-5

Ghadge, A., Dani, S., Ojha, R., & Caldwell, N. (2017). Using risk sharing contracts for supply chain risk mitigation: A buyer-supplier power and dependence perspective. *Computers & Industrial Engineering*, *103*, 262–270. DOI: 10.1016/j.cie.2016.11.034

Gil, R. M., Marcelin, J. R., Zuniga-Blanco, B., Marquez, C., Mathew, T., Piggott, D. A., & Macias Gil, R. (2020). COVID-19 Pandemic: Disparate Health Impact on the Hispanic/Latinx Population in the United States. *The Journal of Infectious Diseases*, *222*(10), 1592–1595. https://doi-org.captechu.idm.oclc.org/10.1093/infdis/jiaa474. DOI: 10.1093/infdis/jiaa474 PMID: 32729903

Glasgow, P. (2005). *Fundamentals of survey research methodology*. Mitre.

Golini, R., Kalchschmidt, M., & Landoni, P. (2015). Adoption of service management practices: The impact on international development services of non-governmental organizations. *International Journal of Service Management.*, *11*(2), 21–35.

Gonzalez, H. B., & Kuenzi, J. J. (2014). Science, technology, engineering, and mathematics (STEM) education. *PRiMER: Peer-Reviewed Reports in Medical Education Research.*

Gonzalez, R., & Harper, L. (2025). Inclusive leadership and organizational belonging: A pathway to dismantling systemic discrimination. *The Academy of Management Perspectives.*

Goodpaster, K. (1991). Business ethics and stakeholder analysis. *Business Ethics Quarterly*, *1*(1), 53–73.

Göritz, A. S. (2010). Organizational citizen behavior and job satisfaction. *Journal of Managerial Psychology*, *25*(8), 758–775.

Goswami, S. (2015). Role of quality management system in service completion. *Pipeline & gas journal, 242*(5), 101- 109.

Goyal, R. (2020). Racial discrimination: An undiagnosed sickness in India. *Law School Policy Review & Kautilya Society*. https://lawschoolpolicyreview.com/2020/05/26/racial-discrimination-an-undiagnosed-sickness-in-india/56

Graham, J. W. (1989). *Organizational Citizenship Behavior: Redefinition, Operationalization, and Validation of Constructs*. Unpublished working paper, Loyola University Chicago, Chicago, IL, 68.

Graham, J. W. (1991). An essay on the behavior of organizational citizenship. *Use Reply Rights J, 4*(3), 249–270. DOI: 10.1007/BF01385031

Grant, A. M., & Mayer, D. M. (2009). Good soldiers and good actors: Prosocial and impression management motives as interactive predictors of affiliated citizenship behaviors. *The Journal of Applied Psychology, 94*(4), 900–912. DOI: 10.1037/a0013770 PMID: 19594233

Grant, A. M., & Mayer, D. M. (2009). Good Soldiers: The Impact of Leadership on Employee Citizen Behavior. *The Leadership Quarterly, 20*(1), 56–71.

Gravlee, C. C. (2020). Systemic racism, chronic health inequities, and COVID-19: A syndemic in the making? *American Journal of Human Biology, 32*(5), e23482. DOI: 10.1002/ajhb.23482 PMID: 32754945

Greenberg, J. (1987). A taxonomy of organizational justice theories. *Academy of Management Review, 12*(1), 9–22. DOI: 10.2307/257990

Greene, J., Hamilton, S., & Parker, R. (2023). Financial instability in mental health organizations during the COVID-19 pandemic. *Journal of Health Economics, 49*(1), 47–56. DOI: 10.1016/j.jhec.2023.01.005

Grewal, D., Roggeveen, A. L., & Nordfält, J. (2020). The future of retailing. *Journal of Retailing, 96*(1), 86–95.

Griffin, M. A., & Neal, A. (2000). Perceptions of safety at work: A framework for linking safety climate to safety performance, knowledge, and motivation. *Journal of Occupational Health Psychology, 5*(3), 347–358. DOI: 10.1037/1076-8998.5.3.347 PMID: 10912498

Guan, Y., & Ge, X. (2017). Distributed attack detection and secure estimation of networked Cyber-Physical systems against false data injection attacks and jamming attacks. *IEEE Transactions on Signal and Information Processing Over Networks, 4*(1), 48–59. DOI: 10.1109/TSIPN.2017.2749959

Gubbi, J., Buyya, R., Marusic, S., & Palaniswami, M. (2013). Internet of things (IoT): A vision, architectural elements, and future directions. *Future Generation Computer Systems, 29*(7), 1645–1660. DOI: 10.1016/j.future.2013.01.010

Gunjarueg, W. (2023). A study of smart ICT model of Hat Yai smart city, Thailand. *Research Review, 05*(12). Advance online publication. DOI: 10.52845/rrijcrr/2023/14-1-3

Guo, K. L. (2009). Effective communication in health care: Strategies to improve outcomes. *The Health Care Manager, 28*(3), 222–229. DOI: 10.1097/HCM.0b013e3181b3e2b2

Guo, K. L., & Sanchez, Y. (2009). Workplace communication. *Organization Development Journal, 27*(4), 9–22.

Gupta, R., & Gupta, R. (2022). Challenges and opportunities for smart meters in smart cities of India using machine learning and deep learning. *Advances in Electronic Government, Digital Divide, and Regional Development*, •••, 41–47. DOI: 10.4018/978-1-7998-9710-1.ch003

Gürel, E., & Tat, M. (2017). SWOT analysis: A theoretical review. *Journal of International Social Research, 10*(51), 994–1006. DOI: 10.17719/jisr.2017.1832

Haas, E. J., Demich, B., & McGuire, J. (2020). Learning from Workers' Near-miss Reports to Improve Organizational Management. *Mining, Metallurgy & Exploration, 37*(3), 873–885. DOI: 10.1007/s42461-020-00206-9 PMID: 32875278

HaddadPajouh, H., Dehghantanha, A., Parizi, R. M., Aledhari, M., & Karimipour, H. (. (2019). A survey on internet of things security: Requirements, challenges, and solutions. *Internet of Things : Engineering Cyber Physical Human Systems, 14*, 100129. DOI: 10.1016/j.iot.2019.100129

Hadley, P. (2025). Leadership's impact on employees' perception of their safety culture in a public transportation organization (Doctoral dissertation, University of Massachusetts Global).

Hagan, J., McCarthy, B., Herda, D., & Cann Chandrasekher, A. (2018). Dual-process theory of racial isolation, legal cynicism, and reported crime. *Proceedings of the National Academy of Sciences of the United States of America, 115*(28), 7190–7199. DOI: 10.1073/pnas.1722210115 PMID: 29987006

Hakanen, J. J., Bakker, A. B., & Jokisaari, M. (2011). A 35-year follow-up study on burnout among Finnish employees. *Journal of Occupational Health Psychology, 16*(3), 345–360. DOI: 10.1037/a0022903 PMID: 21728440

Haley, C., Laney, R., Moffett, J., & Nuseibeh, B. (2008). Security Requirements Engineering: A framework for representation and analysis. *IEEE Transactions on Software Engineering, 34*(1), 133–153. DOI: 10.1109/TSE.2007.70754

Hampton-Marcell, J., Bryson, T., Larson, J., Childers, T., Pasero, S., Watkins, C., Reed, T., Flucas-Payton, D., & Papka, M. E. (2023). Leveraging national laboratories to increase Black representation in STEM: Recommendations within the Department of Energy. *International Journal of STEM Education, 10*(1), 4. DOI: 10.1186/s40594-022-00394-4

Harkness, A., Gattamorta, K. A., Estrada, Y., Jimenez, D., Kanamori, M., Prado, G., & Behar-Zusman, V. (2020). Latinx Health Disparities Research During COVID-19: Challenges and Innovations. *Annals of Behavioral Medicine*, *54*(8), 544–547. https://doi-org.captechu.idm.oclc.org/10.1093/abm/kaaa054. DOI: 10.1093/abm/kaaa054 PMID: 32716033

Harrison, J., Freeman, R., & Abreu, M. (2015). Stakeholder theory as an ethical approach to effective management: Applying the theory to multiple contexts. *Revista Brasileira de Gestão de Negócios*, *17*(55), 858–869. DOI: 10.7819/rbgn.v17i55.2647

Harrison, T., McLeod, J., & Watkins, P. (2022). Barriers to telehealth adoption in mental health care: A review of COVID-19 impacts. *Telemedicine Journal and e-Health*, *28*(9), 1156–1163. DOI: 10.1089/tmj.2022.0128

Hasan, M. K., Habib, A. A., Islam, S., Safie, N., Abdullah, S. N. H. S., & Pandey, B. (2023). DDoS: Distributed denial of service attack in communication standard vulnerabilities in smart grid applications and cyber security with recent developments. *Energy Reports*, *9*, 1318–1326. DOI: 10.1016/j.egyr.2023.05.184

Haslam, S. A. (2004). *Psychology in organizations: The social identity approach* (2nd ed.). Sage.

Hasnain, M., Pasha, M. F., & Ghani, I. (2020). Drupal core 8 caching mechanism for scalability improvement of web services. *Software Impacts*, *3*, 100014. DOI: 10.1016/j.simpa.2020.100014

Hatch, J., & Zweig, J. (2001). *Strategic flexibility: The key to growth*. Ivey Business Journal.Judge, W., & Douglas, T. (2009). Organizational change capacity: The systematic development of a scale. *Journal of Organizational Change Management*, *22*(6), 635–649. DOI: 10.1108/09534810910997041

He, Q., Rowangould, D., Karner, A., Palm, M., & LaRue, S. (2022). COVID-19 pandemic impacts on essential transit riders: Findings from a U.S. Survey. *Transportation Research: Part D, 105*, N.PAG. https://doi-org.captechu.idm.oclc.org/10.1016/j.trd.2022.103217

He, G., Li, C., Shu, Y., & Luo, Y. (2023). Fine-grained access control policy in blockchain-enabled edge computing. *Journal of Network and Computer Applications*, *221*, 103706. DOI: 10.1016/j.jnca.2023.103706

Helfrich, C., Hwang, T., & Fisher, D. (2022). Crisis preparedness in mental health organizations: A framework for resilience. *Journal of Organizational Psychology*, *35*(2), 112–124. DOI: 10.1016/j.jop.2022.02.004

Heravi, A., Coffey, V.& Trigunarsyah, B. (2015). Evaluating the level of stakeholder involvement during the service planning processes of building services. *International journal of service management, 33*(5), 1 - 9.

Herhausen, D., Binder, J., Schoegel, M., & Herrmann, A. (2022). Integrating bricks with clicks: Retailer-level and channel-level outcomes of online–offline channel integration. *Journal of Retailing*, *98*(1), 80–94.

Herscovitch, L., & Meyer, J. P. (2002). Commitment to organizational change: Extension of a three-component model. *The Journal of Applied Psychology*, *87*(3), 474–487. DOI: 10.1037/0021-9010.87.3.474 PMID: 12090605

He, Y., Aliyu, A., Evans, M., & Luo, C. (2021). Health care cybersecurity challenges and solutions under the climate of COVID-19: Scoping review. *Journal of Medical Internet Research*, *23*(4), e21747. DOI: 10.2196/21747 PMID: 33764885

Hirsh, E., & Lyons, C. J. (2010). Perceiving discrimination on the job: Legal consciousness, workplace context, and the construction of race discrimination. *Law & Society Review*, *44*(2), 269–298. DOI: 10.1111/j.1540-5893.2010.00403.x

Hoe, L. & Mansori, S. (2018). The effects of product quality on customer satisfaction and loyalty: Evidence from Malaysian engineering industry. *International journal of industrial marketing, 3*(1), 20 -35.

Hofmann, D. A., & Mark, B. (2006). An investigation of the relationship between safety climate and medication errors as well as other nurses and patient outcomes. *Personnel Psychology*, *59*(4), 847–869. DOI: 10.1111/j.1744-6570.2006.00056.x

Hofstede, G. (1980). *Consequences of culture: International differences in work-related values*. Sage Publications.

Hogg, M. A., & Terry, D. J. (2000). Social identity and self-categorization processes in organizational contexts. *Academy of Management Review*, *25*(1), 121–140. DOI: 10.2307/259266

Holder, M., Jones, J., & Masterson, T. (2021). The Early Impact of Covid-19 on Job Losses among Black Women in the United States. *Feminist Economics*, *27*(1/2), 103–116. https://doi-org.captechu.idm.oclc.org/10.1080/13545701.2020.1849766. DOI: 10.1080/13545701.2020.1849766

Holland, J. (2016). The Average Black Family Would Need 228 Years to Build the Wealth of a White Family Today. The Nation Journal. Retrieved from https://www.thenation.com/article/the-average-black-family-wouldneed-228-years-to-build-the-wealth-of-a-white-family-today

Holland, S., Mason, J., & Brice, M. (2020) Trump declares coronavirus national emergency, says he will most likely be tested. Reuters. https://www.reuters.com/chapter/us-health-coronavirus-usa-emergency/trump-declares-coronavirus-national-emergency-says-he-will-most-likely-be-tested-idUSKBN2102G3. Accessed 12 Feb 2021\

Homans, G. C. (1961). *Social behavior: its elementary forms*. Harcourt, Brace, and the World.

Huang, Y.-H., Ho, M., Smith, G. S., & Chen, P. Y. (2006). Safety climate and self-reported injury: Assessing the mediating role of employee safety control. *Accident; Analysis and Prevention*, *38*(3), 425–433. DOI: 10.1016/j.aap.2005.07.002 PMID: 16442068

Husted, B. W., & Folger, R. (2004). Equity and transaction costs: The contribution of organizational justice theory to an integrative model of economic organization. *Organization Science*, *15*(6), 719–729. DOI: 10.1287/orsc.1040.0088

Ibrahim, M., Elgamri, A., Babiker, S., & Mohamed, A. (2015). Internet of things based smart environmental monitoring using the Raspberry-Pi computer. In *Fifth International Conference on Digital Information Processing and Communications (ICDIPC)*, 2015. DOI: 10.1109/ICDIPC.2015.7323023

Ijomah, T., Eyo-Udo, N., & Anjorin, K. (2024). The role of big data analytics in customer relationship management: Strategies for improving customer engagement and retention. *World Journal of Advanced Science and Technology*, 6.

Iskhakov, A. Y., Iskhakova, A. O., & Meshcheryakov, R. V. (2021). Algorithm for building a cyberphysical system operator profile for adaptive authentication. *IFAC-PapersOnLine*, *54*(13), 493–498. DOI: 10.1016/j.ifacol.2021.10.497

Ivankova, N. V., Creswell, J. W., & Stick, S. L. (2006). Using mixed-methods sequential explanatory design: From theory to practice. *Field Methods*, *18*(1), 3–20. DOI: 10.1177/1525822X05282260

Ivanov, D., & Dolgui, A. (2021). A digital supply chain twin for managing the disruption risks and resilience in the era of Industry 4.0. *Production Planning and Control, 32*(9), 775–788. DOI: 10.1080/09537287.2020.1768450

Iyer, P., Davari, A., Zolfagharian, M., & Paswan, A. (2019). Market orientation, positioning strategy, and brand performance. *Industrial Marketing Management, 81*, 16–29. DOI: 10.1016/j.indmarman.2018.11.004

James, M. (2014). *Positioning theory and strategic communication: A new approach to public relations research and practice*. Routledge. DOI: 10.4324/9781315886084

Jenkins, K. (2023). *The COVID-19 Implications on the United States Failing Infrastructure and Its Affect on Future Generations* (Order No. 30987911). Available from ProQuest One Academic. (2915913865). https://www.proquest.com/dissertations-theses/covid-19-implications-on-united-states-failing/docview/2915913865/se-2

Jeon, J., Padhye, S., Bhattacharyya, A., Cai, H., & Hastak, M. (2022). Impact of COVID-19 on the US Construction Industry as Revealed in the Purdue Index for Construction. *Journal of Management Engineering, 38*(1), 1–13. https://doi-org.captechu.idm.oclc.org/10.1061/(ASCE)ME.1943-5479.0000995. DOI: 10.1061/(ASCE)ME.1943-5479.0000995

Jesus, V., & Pandit, H. J. (2022). Consent receipts for a usable and auditable web of personal data. *IEEE Access : Practical Innovations, Open Solutions, 10*, 28545–28563. DOI: 10.1109/ACCESS.2022.3157850

Jha, A., & Jha, A. (2024). Securing tomorrow's urban frontiers: A holistic approach to cybersecurity in smart cities. *Information System and Smart City, 3*(1). Advance online publication. DOI: 10.59400/issc.v3i1.418

Johnson-Agbakwu, C. E., Ali, N. S., Oxford, C. M., Wingo, S., Manin, E., & Coonrod, D. V. (2022). Racism, COVID-19, and Health Inequity in the USA: A Call to Action. *Journal of Racial and Ethnic Health Disparities, 9*(1), 52–58. DOI: 10.1007/s40615-020-00928-y PMID: 33197038

Johnson, P., & Lee, S. (2019). The psychological impact of workplace discrimination on employee well-being. *The Journal of Applied Psychology, 74*(6), 551–565. DOI: 10.1037/apl0000381

Jordan, C. A. (2022). Exploring the Cybersecurity Skills Gap: A Qualitative Study of Recruitment and Retention from a Human Resource Management Perspective (Order No. 29320493). Available from ProQuest Central; ProQuest Dissertations & Theses Global; ProQuest One Academic; Publicly Available Content Database. (2706752761). https://www.proquest.com/dissertations-theses/exploring-cybersecurity-skills-gap-qualitative/docview/2706752761/se-2

Juaneda-Ayensa, E., Mosquera, A., & Sierra Murillo, Y. (2020). Omnichannel customer behavior: Key drivers of technology acceptance and use and their effects on purchase intention. *Frontiers in Psychology*, *11*, 890. PMID: 27516749

Judge, D. A., & Burrell, D. N. (2021). Exploring the Nature of Business Strategy Change for Mental Health Practices in the Age of COVID-19. [IJBSA]. *International Journal of Business Strategy and Automation*, *2*(4), 1–11. DOI: 10.4018/IJBSA.20211001.oa1

Juma, M., & Shaalan, K. (2020). Cyberphysical systems in the smart city: Challenges and future trends for strategic research. *Swarm Intelligence for Resource Management in Internet of Things*, 65-85. https://doi.org/DOI: 10.1016/B978-0-12-818287-1.00008-5

Kaginalkar, A., Kumar, S., Gargava, P., & Niyogi, D. (2021). Review of urban computing in air quality management as smart city service: An integrated IoT, AI, and cloud technology perspective. *Urban Climate*, *39*, 100972. DOI: 10.1016/j.uclim.2021.100972

Kalahasthi, P., & Usha, N. (2024). Redefining the future of work: A mediation model enabling workplace transformation for medium-sized IT product companies of South India. IIM Kozhikode Society & Management Review. DOI: 10.1177/22779752241259508

Kallepalli, K., & Chaudhry, U. B. (2021). Intelligent Security: Applying artificial intelligence to detect advanced cyber attacks. In Advanced sciences and technologies for security applications (pp. 287–320). DOI: 10.1007/978-3-030-87166-6_11

Kaluarachchi, Y., Nartallo, P., & Emuze, F. (2022). How can the construction industry improve their workers' health and well-being in a post-COVID-19 era. *IOP Conference Series. Earth and Environmental Science*, *1101*(3), 032013. DOI: 10.1088/1755-1315/1101/3/032013

Kane, G. C., Nanda, R., Phillips, A. N., & Copulsky, J. R. (2021). *The transformation myth: Leading your organization through uncertain times*. MIT Press. DOI: 10.7551/mitpress/13965.001.0001

Kao, K., Hsu, H.-H., Thomas, C. L., Cheng, Y.-C., Lin, M., & Li, H.-F. (2021). Motivating employees to speak up: Linking job autonomy, P-O fit, and employee voice behaviors through work engagement. *Current Psychology (New Brunswick, N.J.)*. Advance online publication. DOI: 10.1007/s12144-020-01222-0

Kara, D., Uysal, M., Sirgy, M. J., & Lee, G. (2021). The moderating role of team adaptive capacity in the relationship between inclusive leadership and strategic goal attainment. *Journal of Business Research*, *134*, 731–740.

Katuse, P., Ngari, J., & Owich, S. (2018). The strategy implementation and organization performance of companies at Nairobi securities exchange. *European Journal of Social Sciences*, *5*(1), 37–48.

Katz, D., & Kahn, R. L. (1966). *The Social Psychology of Organizations*. Wiley.

Kaur, G., Sharma, R. R. K., & Verma, P. (December 8, 2016). Aligning Culture Typologies to Innovative Employee Benefits: Using Cameron and Quinn's Competing Value Framework. University of Sri Jayewardenepura, Sri Lanka, 13th International Conference on Business Management (ICBM).DOI: 10.2139/ssrn.2910213

Kelloway, E. K., & Barling, J. (2010). Leadership development as an intervention in occupational health psychology. *Work and Stress*, *24*(3), 260–279. DOI: 10.1080/02678373.2010.518441

Kenyon, J., & Kenyon, J. (2023, September 14). Server-Side Request Forgery (SSRF) & the cloud resurgence. AppCheck | A Complete Enterprise Security Testing Solution -. https://appcheck-ng.com/server-side-request-forgery-ssrf/

Kestenbaum, R. (2018, September 9). The Biggest Trends in the Beauty Industry. *Forbes*. Retrieved December 5, 2022, from https://www.forbes.com/sites/richardkestenbaum/2018/09/09/beauty-industry-biggest-trends-skin-care-loreal-shiseido-lauder/?sh=27a588f76982

Khan, N. F., Ikram, N., & Saleem, S. (2023). Effects of socioeconomic and digital inequalities on cybersecurity in a developing country. *Security Journal*, •••, 1–31. PMID: 40478949

Kholidy, H. K., Baiardi, F., & Hariri, S. (2015). DSGA: A data-driven semi-global alignment approach for detecting masquerade attacks. *IEEE Transactions on Dependable and Secure Computing*, *12*(2), 164–178. DOI: 10.1109/TDSC.2014.2327966

Kim, A. J., & Sullivan, P. (2019). Emotional branding speaks to consumers' hearts: The case of fashion brands with DTC strategies. *Fashion and Textiles*, *6*(1), 1–16. DOI: 10.1186/s40691-018-0164-y

Kim, A., Park, M., & Lee, D. H. (2020). AI-IDS: Application of Deep Learning to Real-Time Web Intrusion Detection. *IEEE Access : Practical Innovations, Open Solutions*, *8*, 70245–70261. DOI: 10.1109/ACCESS.2020.2986882

Kissi, E., Asare, O. A., & Agyekum, K. (2019).. . *Determining the Effects of the Interaction Between Organizational Citizenship Behavior, Work Overload, and Employee Performance in Ghana's Construction Industry*, *68*(7), 1235–1249. DOI: 10.1108/IJPPM07-2018-0262

Kline, N., Webb, N. J., Thompson, E. L., Griner, S. B., & Schrimshaw, E. W. (2022). Latinx COVID-19 Disparities and Work As a Social Determinant of Health: A Research and Policy Agenda. *Population Health Management*, *25*(2), 284–287. https://doi-org.captechu.idm.oclc.org/10.1089/pop.2021.0368. DOI: 10.1089/pop.2021.0368 PMID: 35442792

Kniffin, K. M., Narayanan, J., Anseel, F., Antonakis, J., Ashford, S. P., Bakker, A. B., Bamberger, P., Bapuji, H., Bhave, D. P., Choi, V. K., Creary, S. J., Demerouti, E., Flynn, F. J., Gelfand, M. J., Greer, L. L., Johns, G., Kesebir, S., Klein, P. G., Lee, S. Y., & Vugt, M. (2021). COVID-19 and the workplace: Implications, issues, and insights for future research and action. *The American Psychologist*, *76*(1), 63–77. DOI: 10.1037/amp0000716 PMID: 32772537

Konovsky, M. A., & Organ, D. W. (1996). Dispositional and contextual determinants of organizational citizenship behavior. *Journal of Organizational Behavior*, *17*(3), 253–266. DOI: 10.1002/(SICI)1099-1379(199605)17:3<253::AID-JOB747>3.0.CO;2-Q

Kopf, D., & Detrixhe, J. A coronavirus-led recession could hit jobs for young people and minorities hardest https://qz.com/1822762/coronavirus-led-recession-in-us-could-hit-people-of-color-hardest/

Korkmaz, M., & Korkmaz, A. (2011). The moderating role of organizational culture in the relationship between organizational citizenship behaviors (OCB) and perceptions of justice. *Emerald insight*. https://doi.org/DOI: 10.1108/01409171111178836

Koskela, L., & Howell, G. (2008). The underlying theory of service management is obsolete. *IEEE Engineering Management Review*, *36*(2), 22–34. DOI: 10.1109/EMR.2008.4534317

Kothari, C. (2004). *Research methodology: methods and techniques* (2nd ed.). New age international publishers.

Kotler, P. (1993). The major tasks of marketing management. *Marketing Management*, *2*(3), 52.

Kotter, J. P. (1996). *Leading change*. Harvard Business Review Press.

Koys, D. J. (2001). The effects of employee satisfaction, organizational citizenship behavior, and turnover on organizational effectiveness: a longitudinal unit-level study. *Pers. psychol.,* 54(1): 101-114 (14 pages).

Kozlenkova, I. V., Samaha, S. A., & Palmatier, R. W. (2014). Resource-based theory in marketing. *Journal of the Academy of Marketing Science*, *42*(1), 1–21. DOI: 10.1007/s11747-013-0336-7

Kraemer, B., & Swanson, E. B. (2021). Communication technologies and remote work: Implications for managing employee safety and engagement. *Journal of Organizational Computing and Electronic Commerce*, *31*(2), 129–147. DOI: 10.1080/10919392.2021.1907167

Krajnakova, E., Navikaite, A., & Navickas, V. (2015). Paradigm shift of small and medium-sized enterprises competitive advantage. *The Engineering Economist*, *26*(3), 25–34.

Kraus, S., Durst, S., Ferreira, J. J., Veiga, P., Kailer, N., & Weinmann, A. (2022). Digital transformation in business and management research: An overview of the current status quo. *International Journal of Information Management*, *63*, 102466. DOI: 10.1016/j.ijinfomgt.2021.102466

Krebs, D. J. (1970). Altruism: An Examination of the Concept and a Review of the Literature. *Psychological Bulletin*, *73*(4), 258–302. DOI: 10.1037/h0028987

Krishnan, L., Ogunwole, S. M., & Cooper, L. A. (2020). Historical insights on coronavirus disease 2019 (COVID-19), the 1918 influenza pandemic, and racial disparities: Illuminating a path forward. *Annals of Internal Medicine*, *173*(6), 474–481. DOI: 10.7326/M20-2223 PMID: 32501754

Kuhl, J. (2021). The expectancy-value approach within the theory of social motivation: Elaborations, extensions, critique. *Expectations and actions*, 125-160.

Kumar, A., Bhushan, B., Malik, A., & Kumar, R. (2021). Protocols, solutions, and testbeds for Cyber-Attack Prevention in industrial SCADA systems. In Studies in big data (pp. 355–380). DOI: 10.1007/978-981-16-6210-2_17

Kumar, V., & Madria, S. (2013). PIP: Privacy and integrity preserving data aggregation in wireless sensor networks. *2013 IEEE 32nd International Symposium on Reliable Distributed Systems*, 10-19. https://doi.org/DOI: 10.1109/SRDS.2013.10

Kumar, A., Bag, A., Anand, A., Saha, S., Mohapatra, H., & Kolhar, M. (2024). Examining healthcare services utilizing cloud technology in intelligent urban environments. *Advances in Healthcare Information Systems and Administration*, •••, 77–98. DOI: 10.4018/979-8-3693-7225-8.ch004

Kumar, A., Khan, S. B., Pandey, S. K., Shankar, A., Maple, C., Mashat, A., & Malibari, A. A. (2023). Development of a cloud-assisted classification technique for the preservation of secure data storage in smart cities. *Journal of Cloud Computing (Heidelberg, Germany)*, *12*(1), 92. Advance online publication. DOI: 10.1186/s13677-023-00469-9

Kumar, M., & Singh, A. (2022). Probabilistic data structures in smart city: Survey, applications, challenges, and research directions. *Journal of Ambient Intelligence and Smart Environments*, *14*(4), 229–284. DOI: 10.3233/AIS-220101

Kumar, N., & Rao, K. (2014). Hash based approach for providing privacy and integrity in cloud data storage using digital signatures. *International Journal of Computer Science and Information Technologies*, *5*(6), 8074–8078.

Lamm, E., Tosti-Kharas, J., & King, C. E. (2015). Enhancing employee sustainability: Perceived organizational support for the environment. *Journal of Business Ethics*, *128*(1), 207–220. DOI: 10.1007/s10551-014-2093-z

Lancaster, G., & Massingham, L. (2013). *Essentials of marketing management* (2nd ed.). Routledge.

Langton, N., Robbins, S. P., Judge, T. A., Yap, R., & Perry, E. (2023). *Organizational behaviour: Concepts, controversies, applications* (9th Canadian ed.). Pearson Canada.

Lapshun, A. L., & Fusch, G. E. (2023). Times of Uncertainties Require Embracing Leadership and Feedback. *The Qualitative Report*, *28*(3), 828–847. DOI: 10.46743/2160-3715/2023.5609

Lau, K. H. V., Anand, P., Ramirez, A., & Phicil, S. (2022). Disparities in Telehealth use During the COVID-19 Pandemic. *Journal of Immigrant and Minority Health*, *24*(6), 1–4. https://doi-org.captechu.idm.oclc.org/10.1007/s10903-022-01381-1. DOI: 10.1007/s10903-022-01381-1 PMID: 35976473

Laurencin, C. T., & McClinton, A. (2020). The COVID-19 pandemic: A call to action to identify and address racial and ethnic disparities. *Journal of Racial and Ethnic Health Disparities*, *7*(3), 398–402. DOI: 10.1007/s40615-020-00756-0 PMID: 32306369

Lawrence, K., Anderson, A., Susi, G., Sutton, S., Kubisch, A., & Codrington, R. (2009). A Practical Guide for Designing Strategies to Close Chronic Racial Outcome Gaps. https://www.aspeninstitute.org/wp-content/uploads/files/content/images/Roundtable%20on%20Community%20Change%20RETOC.pdf

Lawther, S., Hastings, G. B., & Lowry, R. (1997). De-marketing: Putting Kotler and Levy's ideas into practice. *Journal of Marketing Management, 13*(4), 315–325. DOI: 10.1080/0267257X.1997.9964475

Leavy, B. (2018). Value innovation and how to successfully incubate "blue ocean" initiatives. *Strategy and Leadership, 46*(3), 10–20. DOI: 10.1108/SL-02-2018-0020

Lee, J. (2020). The role of organizational citizenship behavior in improving employee performance: a meta-analysis approach.

Lee, H. A. (2018). Affirmative action in Malaysia: Education and employment outcomes since the 1990s. *Journal of Contemporary Asia, 48*(2), 262–284.

Lee, J. S., Kim, J. K., & Kim, S. K. (2019). The impact of organizational communication and employee safety participation and safety compliance on frequency of industrial accidents. *The Journal of the Korea Contents Association, 19*(12), 558–564.

Lee, S., & Kamradt, R. (2022). Integrating mental health into primary care: A review of models and outcomes. *Journal of Health Integration, 29*(6), 218–231. DOI: 10.1016/j.jhii.2023.02.015

Le, H. T., Shar, L. K., Bianculli, D., Briand, L. C., & Nguyen, C. D. (2021). Automated reverse engineering of role-based access control policies of web applications. *Journal of Systems and Software, 184*, 111109. DOI: 10.1016/j.jss.2021.111109

Lemon, K. N., & Verhoef, P. C. (2016). Understanding customer experience throughout the customer journey. *Journal of Marketing, 80*(6), 69–96. DOI: 10.1509/jm.15.0420

Leonardi, P. M. (2021). COVID-19 and the new technologies of organizing: Digital exhaust, digital footprints, and artificial intelligence in the wake of remote work. *Journal of Management Studies, 58*(1), 249–253. DOI: 10.1111/joms.12648

Lê-Scherban, F., Headen, I., Klem, A. M., Traister, K., Gilliam, E., Beverly, M., Jannetti, M., Ferroni, J., & Carroll-Scott, A. (2023). Research and Evaluation in a Child-Focused Place-Based Initiative: West Philly Promise Neighborhood. *International Journal of Environmental Research and Public Health, 20*(9), 5716. DOI: 10.3390/ijerph20095716 PMID: 37174234

Liang, H., Zhu, L., Yu, F. R., & Wang, X. (2022). A Cross-Layer defense method for blockchain empowered CBTC systems against data tampering attacks. *IEEE Transactions on Intelligent Transportation Systems*, *24*(1), 501–515. DOI: 10.1109/TITS.2022.3211020

Liang, Y., Baral, A., Shahandashti, M., & Ashuri, B. (2022). Availability Heuristic in Construction Workforce Decision-Making amid COVID-19 Pandemic: Empirical Evidence and Mitigation Strategy. *Journal of Management Engineering*, *38*(5), 1–9. https://doi-org.captechu.idm.oclc.org/10.1061/(ASCE)ME.1943-5479.0001077. DOI: 10.1061/(ASCE)ME.1943-5479.0001077

Lian, H., Li, J., Du, C., Wu, W., Xia, Y., & Lee, C. (2022). Disaster or opportunity? How COVID-19-associated changes in environmental uncertainty and job insecurity relate to organizational identification and performance. *The Journal of Applied Psychology*, *107*(5), 693–706. Advance online publication. DOI: 10.1037/apl0001011 PMID: 35254851

Liberatore, M. & Johnson, B. (2013). Improving service management decision making by modelling quality, time, and cost continuously. *Trans engineering management, 2*(9), 518–528.

Li, F., Luo, B., & Liu, P. (2010). Secure information aggregation for smart grids using homomorphic encryption. *2010 First IEEE International Conference on Smart Grid Communications*, 327-332. https://doi.org/DOI: 10.1109/SMARTGRID.2010.5622064

Ling, Y., Li, X., Bin, D., Yang, C., & Lu, J. (2023). Web Random Token Generation Technology Based on Asymmetric Encryption Technology. In 2023 IEEE 2nd International Conference on Electrical Engineering, Big Data and Algorithms (EEBDA), Changchun, China (pp. 804–808). DOI: 10.1109/EEBDA56825.2023.10090549

Lingard, H., Zhang, R. P., Räisänen, C., Goh, Y. M., Bowen, P., & Bhandari, S. (2021). Special issue: what have we learnt from the COVID-19 global pandemic: improving the construction industry's abilities to foresee, respond to and recover from future endemic catastrophes. *Construction Management and Economics*, *39*(2), 192–197. DOI: 10.1080/01446193.2020.1869480

Liu, H., & Tan, H. B. K. (2008). Covering code behavior on input validation in functional testing. *Information and Software Technology*, *51*(2), 546–553. DOI: 10.1016/j.infsof.2008.07.001

Li, Y., & Liu, Q. (2021). A comprehensive review study of cyber-attacks and cyber security; Emerging trends and recent developments. *Energy Reports*, *7*, 8176–8186. DOI: 10.1016/j.egyr.2021.08.126

Locker, K. O., & Findlay, J. (2011). *Business communication: Building critical skills* (5th Canadian ed.). McGraw-Hill Ryerson.

Lo, H., Chen, W., & Zhang, L. (2023). Adapting to change: Mental health organizations and the shift to telehealth. *Mental Health Research Review, 12*(4), 223–235. DOI: 10.1016/j.mhrv.2023.04.003

Löwstedt, M., & Räisänen, C. (2014). Social identity in construction: Enactments and outcomes. *Construction Management and Economics, 32*(11), 1093–1105. DOI: 10.1080/01446193.2014.956132

Lukas, B. A., Hult, G. T. M., & Ferrell, O. C. (1996). A theoretical perspective of the antecedents and consequences of organizational learning in marketing channels. *Journal of Business Research, 36*(3), 233–244. DOI: 10.1016/0148-2963(95)00154-9

Lyon, V. (2020). Exploring Strategies for Recruiting and Retaining Diverse Cybersecurity Professionals (Order No. 27738274). Available from ProQuest Dissertations & Theses Global; ProQuest One Academic. (2378121182). https://www.proquest.com/dissertations-theses/exploring-strategies-recruiting-retaining-diverse/docview/2378121182/se-2

Macias Gil, R., Touzard-Romo, F., Sanchez, M. C., Pandita, A., Kalligeros, M., Mylona, E. K., Shehadeh, F., Mylonakis, E., & Gil, R. M. (2021). Characteristics and outcomes of Hispanic/Latinx patients with coronavirus disease 19 (COVID-19) requiring hospitalization in Rhode Island: A retrospective cohort study. *Annals of Epidemiology, 58*, 64–68. https://doi-org.captechu.idm.oclc.org/10.1016/j.annepidem.2021.03.003. DOI: 10.1016/j.annepidem.2021.03.003 PMID: 33737227

Mack, J., Hu, Y., & Hoppa, M. A. (2019). A study of existing Cross-Site scripting detection and prevention techniques using XAMPP and VirtualBox. *Virginia Journal of Science, 70*(3), 1. DOI: 10.25778/bx6k-2285

Maene, P., Gotzfried, J., Muller, T., De Clercq, R., Freiling, F., & Verbauwhede, I. (2018). Atlas: Application Confidentiality in Compromised embedded Systems. *IEEE Transactions on Dependable and Secure Computing, 16*(3), 415–423. DOI: 10.1109/TDSC.2018.2858257

Maheswari, K., Siva, C., & Nalinipriya, G. (2023). Optimal cluster based feature selection for intrusion detection system in web and cloud computing environment using hybrid teacher learning optimization enables deep recurrent neural network. *Computer Communications, 202*, 145–153. DOI: 10.1016/j.comcom.2023.02.003

Mahmoud, A., Berman, A., Reisel, W., Fuxman, L., & Hack-Polay, D. (2023). Examining generational differences as a moderator of extreme-context perception and its impact on work alienation organizational outcomes: Implications for the workplace and remote work transformation. *Scandinavian Journal of Psychology*. Advance online publication. DOI: 10.1111/sjop.12955 PMID: 37596807

Mahmoud, A., Hack-Polay, D., Reisel, W., Fuxman, L., Grigoriou, N., Mohr, I., & Aizouk, R. (2021). Who's more vulnerable? A generational investigation of COVID-19 perceptions' effect on Organisational citizenship Behaviours in the MENA region: Job insecurity, burnout and job satisfaction as mediators. *BMC Public Health*, *21*(1), 1951. Advance online publication. DOI: 10.1186/s12889-021-11976-2 PMID: 34706702

Mai, P. X., Goknil, A., Shar, L. K., Pastore, F., Briand, L. C., & Shaame, S. (2018). Modeling Security and Privacy Requirements: A Use Case-Driven Approach. *Information and Software Technology*, *100*, 165–182. DOI: 10.1016/j.infsof.2018.04.007

Malila, C., Daya, P., & Bick, G. (2023). *The future of work: A hybrid work model in a public sector organisation*. The Case Writing Centre, University of Cape Town, Graduate School of Business., DOI: 10.1108/CASEUCT-2023-000001

Mamon, P. (2020). Organizational Culture. https://www.researchgate.net/publication/341266529_Organizational_Culture

Maneesh, K., Khawaja, K., & Dianne, W. (2014). Status of quality management practices in manufacturing SMEs: A comparative study between Australia and the UK. *International Journal of Production Research*, *52*(21), 6482–6495. DOI: 10.1080/00207543.2014.948574

Manfio, N., & Lacerda, D. (2016). Definition of scope in new product development services for the food industry: A proposed method. *Gestão & Produção*, *23*(1), 18–36. DOI: 10.1590/0104-530X1009-13

Mannheim, J., Konda, S., & Logan, L. K. (2022). Racial, ethnic and socioeconomic disparities in SARS-CoV-2 infection amongst children. *Paediatric and Perinatal Epidemiology*, *36*(3), 337–346. https://doi-org.captechu.idm.oclc.org/10.1111/ppe.12865. DOI: 10.1111/ppe.12865 PMID: 35076946

Manuel, B. A., & Karloff, D. B. (2020). Recruit and retain a diverse workforce. *Nature Reviews. Chemistry*, *4*(9), 435–437. DOI: 10.1038/s41570-020-0214-z PMID: 37127964

Marashdih, A. W., Zaaba, Z. F., & Suwais, K. (2022). Predicting input validation vulnerabilities based on minimal SSA features and machine learning. *Journal of King Saud University. Computer and Information Sciences, 34*(10), 9311–9331. DOI: 10.1016/j.jksuci.2022.09.010

Marashdih, A. W., Zaaba, Z. F., & Suwais, K. (2023). An enhanced static taint analysis approach to detect input validation vulnerability. *Journal of King Saud University. Computer and Information Sciences, 35*(2), 682–701. DOI: 10.1016/j.jksuci.2023.01.009

Marić, M., Hernaus, T., Vujčić, M., & Černe, M. (2019). Job characteristics and organizational citizenship behavior: A multisource study on the role of work engagement. Drustvena istrazivanja. DOI: 10.5559/di.28.1.02

Marshall, J., Roache, D., & Marshall, R. (2020). Crisis leadership: A critical examination of Educational leadership in higher education in the midst of the COVID-19 Pandemic *International Studies in Educational Administration (Commonwealth Council for Educational Administration & Management)*, 48(3), 1-30.

Martin, J. A. (2021). Adaptive leadership in practice: Driving innovation through continuous learning. *Leadership and Organization Development Journal, 42*(3), 423–437.

Marx, D. (2001). Just culture: Balancing safety and accountability. *Human Factors Journal, 43*(2), 168–178.

Marzouk, M. M., El Kherbawy, A. A., & Khalifa, M. (2013). Factors influencing subcontractors selection in construction projects. *Housing and Building Research Center Journal, 9*(2), 150–158. DOI: 10.1016/j.hbrcj.2013.05.001

Massey, D. S., & Denton, N. A. (1993). *American apartheid: Segregation and the making of the underclass*. Harvard University Press.

Masters, G. A., Asipenko, E., Bergman, A. L., Person, S. D., Brenckle, L., Moore Simas, T. A., Ko, J. Y., Robbins, C. L., & Byatt, N. (2021). Impact of the COVID-19 pandemic on mental health, access to care, and health disparities in the perinatal period. *Journal of Psychiatric Research, 137*, 126–130. https://doi-org.captechu.idm.oclc.org/10.1016/j.jpsychires.2021.02.056. DOI: 10.1016/j.jpsychires.2021.02.056 PMID: 33677216

Masterson, S. S. (2011). A trickle-down model of organizational justice: Relating employee and customer perceptions and reactions to equity. *The Journal of Applied Psychology, 86*(4), 594–604. DOI: 10.1037/0021-9010.86.4.594 PMID: 11519644

Maynes, T. D., & Podsakoff, P. M. (2014). An examination of the nature, background, and consequences of an expanded set of employee voice behaviors. *The Journal of Applied Psychology*, *99*(1), 87–112. DOI: 10.1037/a0034284 PMID: 24041119

Mayo, M. (2022). Untreated mental illness and its impact on public health: A review of economic, emotional, and societal costs. *Journal of Health Policy*, *15*(2), 78–83.

Mays, V. M., Cochran, S. D., & Barnes, N. W. (2007). Race, race-based discrimination, and health outcomes among African Americans. *Annual Review of Psychology*, *58*(1), 201–225. DOI: 10.1146/annurev.psych.57.102904.190212 PMID: 16953796

Mays, V. M., Coleman, L. M., & Jackson, J. S. (2007). Perceived race-based discrimination, employment status, and job stress in a national sample of Black women: Implications for health outcomes. *Journal of Occupational Health Psychology*, *12*(3), 301–318. DOI: 10.1037/1076-8998.12.3.301 PMID: 17638495

Mazanec, J. A., Wöber, K., & Zins, A. H. (2020). Tourism destination competitiveness: From definition to explanation? A methodologically sophisticated approach. *Journal of Travel Research*, *59*(3), 459–478.

Mburano, B., & Si, W. (2018). Evaluation of web vulnerability scanners based on OWASP Benchmark. In *26th Int. Conf. Syst. Eng. (ICSEng)* (pp. 1–6). DOI: 10.1109/ICSENG.2018.8638176

McCoy, H. (2020). Black lives matter, and yes, you are racist: The parallelism of the twentieth and twenty-first centuries. *Child & Adolescent Social Work Journal*, *37*(5), 463–475. DOI: 10.1007/s10560-020-00690-4 PMID: 32836724

McGee, K. (2018). The influence of gender, and race/ethnicity on advancement in information technology (IT). *Information and Organization*, *28*(1), 1–36. DOI: 10.1016/j.infoandorg.2017.12.001

McShane, S. L., Tasa, K., & Steen, S. (2021). *Canadian organizational behaviour* (11th ed.). McGraw-Hill Education.

Meier, L. L., Semmer, N. K., Elfering, A., & Jacobshagen, N. (2008). The double meaning of control: Three-way interactions between internal resources, job control, and stressors at work. *Journal of Occupational Health Psychology*, *13*(3), 244–258. DOI: 10.1037/1076-8998.13.3.244 PMID: 18572995

Mejias, M., Jean-Pierre, K., Anderson, K., Washington, G., Burge, L., & Washington, A. N. (2018). The Partnership for Early Engagement in Computer Science (PEECS) Program: Facilitating the Diversification of DC's Tech Workforce. In Proceedings of the International Conference on Frontiers in Education: Computer Science and Computer Engineering (FECS) (pp. 141-145). The Steering Committee of The World Congress in Computer Science, Computer Engineering and Applied Computing (WorldComp).

Meliala, Y. H. (2023). The Influence of Organizational Culture and Transformational Leadership on Organizational Citizenship Behavior (OCB) Mediated Organizational Commitment and Job Satisfaction: Acces la Success. *Calitatea*, *24*(195), 235–246. DOI: 10.47750/QAS/24.195.28

Mena, J. A., & Chabowski, B. R. (2015). The role of organizational learning in stakeholder marketing. *Journal of the Academy of Marketing Science*, *43*(4), 429–452. DOI: 10.1007/s11747-015-0442-9

Men, L. R. (2014). Internal communication in organizations: An essential guide. *Journal of Communication Management (London)*, *18*(3), 268–280. DOI: 10.1108/JCOM-02-2014-0011

Men, L. R., & Yue, C. A. (2019). Creating a positive emotional culture: Effect of internal communication and leadership style. *Public Relations Review*, *45*(3), 101764. DOI: 10.1016/j.pubrev.2019.03.001

Meza, E., Giglio, L., Franco, A. O., Rodriguez, E., Stock, L., Balmes, J., Torres, J. M., & Fernandez, A. (2022, August 9). Worker Perspectives on COVID-19 Risks: A Qualitative Study of Latino Construction Workers in Oakland, California. *International Journal of Environmental Research and Public Health*, *19*(16), 9822. DOI: 10.3390/ijerph19169822 PMID: 36011454

Mezentseva, A., Gracia, F. J., Silla, I., & Martínez-Córcoles, M. (2023). The role of empowering leadership, safety culture and safety climate in the prediction of mindful organizing in an air traffic management company. *Safety Science*, *168*, 1–27. DOI: 10.1016/j.ssci.2023.106321

Michels, D., & Murphy, K. (2021). How good is your company at Change? *Harvard Business Review*.

Michigan Department of Health and Human Services. Coronavirus Outbreak Reporting. Available online: https://www.michigan.gov/coronavirus/0,9753,7-406-98163_98173_102057---,00.html (accessed on 15 October 2020).

Milaković, M., Koren, H., Bradvica-Kelava, K., Bubaš, M., Nakić, J., Jeličić, P., Bucić, L., Bekavac, B., Čvrljak, J., & Capak, M. (2023). Telework-related risk factors for musculoskeletal disorders. *Frontiers in Public Health*, *3*(11), 1–6. DOI: 10.3389/fpubh.2023.1155745 PMID: 37465175

Miller, A., & Johnson, M. (2022). Organizational change and crisis management: A review of frameworks in the healthcare sector. *Journal of Healthcare Management*, *67*(3), 197–210. DOI: 10.1097/00115514-202207000-00006

Millett, G. A., Jones, A. T., Benkeser, D., Baral, S., Mercer, L., Beyrer, C., Honermann, B., Lankiewicz, E., Mena, L., Crowley, J. S., Sherwood, J., & Sullivan, P. S. (2020). Assessing differential impacts of COVID-19 on black communities. *Annals of Epidemiology*, *47*, 37–44. DOI: 10.1016/j.annepidem.2020.05.003 PMID: 32419766

Milli, S., Lieder, F., & Griffiths, T. L. (2021). A rational reinterpretation of dual-process theories. *Cognition*, *217*, 104881. DOI: 10.1016/j.cognition.2021.104881 PMID: 34536658

Milunovic, S., & Filipovic, J. (2013). Methodology for quality management of services in manufacturing industries. *Total Quality Management & Business Excellence*, *24*(1-2), 91–107. DOI: 10.1080/14783363.2012.728851

Mishra, A., Alzoubi, Y. I., Anwar, M. J., & Gill, A. Q. (2022). Attributes impacting cybersecurity policy development: An evidence from seven nations. *Computers & Security*, *120*, 102820. DOI: 10.1016/j.cose.2022.102820

Mitchell, T. R., & Knudsen, B. W. (1973). Instrumentality theory predictions of students' attitudes towards business and their choice of business as an occupation. Academy of Management Journal (Pre-1986), 16(1), 41. https://www.proquest.com/scholarly-journals/instrumentality-theory-predictions-students/docview/229490746/se-2

Mitropoulos, D., Louridas, P., Polychronakis, M., & Keromytis, A. D. (2017). Defending against web application attacks: Approaches, challenges and implications. *IEEE Transactions on Dependable and Secure Computing*, *16*(2), 188–203. DOI: 10.1109/TDSC.2017.2665620

Mohamed, L. (2024). The Role of Leadership and Effective Communication in Crisis Management. https://hdl.handle.net/2437/373711

Mohamed, N., Al-Jaroodi, J., & Jawhar, I. (2020). Opportunities and challenges of data-driven cybersecurity for smart cities. *2020 IEEE Systems Security Symposium (SSS)*, 1-7. https://doi.org/DOI: 10.1109/SSS47320.2020.9174388

Mohammed, A.. (2021). Product quality and customer satisfaction in the telecommunications sector. *JMR, Journal of Marketing Research*, *12*(3), 223–235.

Mohapatra, H., & Mishra, S. R. (2024). Unlocking insights: Exploring data analytics and AI tool performance across industries. *Studies in Big Data*, 265-288. https://doi.org/DOI: 10.1007/978-981-97-0448-4_13

Mohapatra, H. (2021). Socio-technical challenges in the implementation of smart city. *2021 International Conference on Innovation and Intelligence for Informatics, Computing, and Technologies (3ICT)*, 57-62. https://doi.org/DOI: 10.1109/3ICT53449.2021.9581905

Mohapatra, H., & Rath, A. K. (2021). A fault tolerant routing scheme for advanced metering infrastructure: An approach towards smart grid. *Cluster Computing*, *24*(3), 2193–2211. DOI: 10.1007/s10586-021-03255-x

Molnar, M. M., Schwarz, U., Hellgren, J., Hasson, H., & Tafvelin, S. (2022). Leading for safety: A question of leadership focus. *Safety and Health at Work*, *10*(2), 180–187. DOI: 10.1016/j.shaw.2018.12.001 PMID: 35664905

Moore, M. (2014). The personality traits of successful service teams: Identifying service management team member personality characteristics. *Journal of Health & Medical Informatics*, *5*(3), 92–103.

Moorman, R. H. (1991). Relationship Between Organizational Justice and Organizational Citizenship Behaviors: Do Perceptions of Equity Influence Employee Citizenship? *The Journal of Applied Psychology*, *76*(6), 845–855. DOI: 10.1037/0021-9010.76.6.845

Morgan, I., & Amerikaner, A. (2018). Funding Gaps 2018: An Analysis of School Funding Equity Across the U.S. Education Trust. Retrieved from https://edtrust.org/resource/funding-gaps-2018/

Morgan, S. (2016a, April, 7). African Americans Underrepresented In The Cybersecurity Field. Forbes. https://www.forbes.com/sites/stevemorgan/2016/04/07/african-americans-underrepresented-in-the-cybersecurity-field/?sh=58ea932115c9

Morgan, S. (2016b, March 28). Calling All Women: The Cybersecurity Field Needs You And There's A Million Jobs Waiting. Forbes. https://www.forbes.com/sites/stevemorgan/2016/03/28/calling-all-women-the-cybersecurity-field-. needs-you/#2470db2a381c

Morrison, E. W. (1994). Role Definitions and Organizational Citizenship Behavior: The Importance of the Employee Perspective. *Academy of Management Journal*, *37*(6), 1543–1567. DOI: 10.2307/256798

Moyo, M. (2019). Leadership and innovation in times of crisis: The role of transformational leadership in the health sector. *International Journal of Healthcare Management, 23*(4), 305–318. DOI: 10.1080/123456789

Muhammad, N., Zohreh, P., & Mojde, S. (2013). Significance of scope in service success. *ScienceDirect, 9*(2), 722–729.

Mulcahy, R. (2015). *PMP exam prep: Rita's course in a book for passing the PMP exam* (7th ed.). RMC publications.

Mullen, J., & Kelloway, E. K. (2009). Safety leadership: A longitudinal study of the effects of transformational leadership on safety outcomes. *Journal of Occupational and Organizational Psychology, 82*(2), 253–272. DOI: 10.1348/096317908X325313

Mumby, D. K., & Kuhn, T. R. (2019). Leadership, communication, and organizational culture: Using sensemaking to make sense of sensemaking. *Management Communication Quarterly, 33*(1), 5–13. DOI: 10.1177/0893318918809184

Nahrgang, J. D., Morgeson, F. P., & Hofmann, D. A. (2011). Safety at work: A meta-analytic investigation of the link between job demands, job resources, burnout, engagement, and safety outcomes. *The Journal of Applied Psychology, 96*(1), 71–94. DOI: 10.1037/a0021484 PMID: 21171732

Naji, G., Isha ASN, Mohyaldinn, M, E., Leka, S., Saleem, M, S., Rahman, S., Alzoraiki, M. (2021). Impact of safety culture on safety performance: Mediating role of psychosocial hazard: An integrated modelling approach. *International Journal of Environment Res.* 13, 18(16):8568. .DOI: 10.3390/ijerph18168568

Nath, P., Nachiappan, S., & Ramanathan, R. (2010). The impact of marketing capability, operations capability, and diversification strategy on performance: A resource-based view. *Industrial Marketing Management, 39*(2), 317–329. DOI: 10.1016/j.indmarman.2008.09.001

National Center for Health Statistics. (2019). *Health.* United States Spotlight Racial and Ethnic Disparities in Heart Disease.

National Initiative for Cybersecurity Careers and Studies. (2023). Cybersecurity for underserved communities. https://niccs.cisa.gov/workforce-development/cybersecurity-underserved-communities

NCBI. (2021). Impact of prosocial motivation on organizational citizenship. Obtained dehttps://www.ncbi.nlm.nih.gov/

Neal, A., & Griffin, M. A. (2006). A study of the lagged relationships among safety climate, safety motivation, safety behavior, and accidents at the individual and group levels. *The Journal of Applied Psychology, 91*(4), 946–953. DOI: 10.1037/0021-9010.91.4.946 PMID: 16834517

Netemeyer, R. G., & Bearden, W. O. (1992). A comparative analysis of two models of behavioral intention. Journal of the Academy of Marketing Science, *20*(1), 49–59. https://doi-org/DOI: 10.1007/BF02723475

Neupane, A., Saxena, N., Maximo, J. O., & Kana, R. (2016). Neural Markers of Cybersecurity: An FMRI study of Phishing and Malware warnings. *IEEE Transactions on Information Forensics and Security, 11*(9), 1970–1983. DOI: 10.1109/TIFS.2016.2566265

Nguyen, D. D. N., Sood, K., Xiang, Y., Gao, L., Chi, L., & Yu, S. (2023). Toward IoT node authentication mechanism in next generation networks. *IEEE Internet of Things Journal, 10*(15), 13333–13341. DOI: 10.1109/JIOT.2023.3262822

Nguyen, H. T. (2020). Dismantling systemic barriers in the workplace: A guide to equitable practices. *Equality Studies Journal, 8*(1), 32–48.

Nguyen, M. H., Tu, H. H., & Pham, L. T. (2020). The role of psychological safety in fostering team agility and organizational resilience. *Journal of Organizational Effectiveness: People and Performance, 7*(3), 289–308.

Nibyiza, F., Shukla, J.& Ndabaga, E. (2015). Analysis of service scope change management as a tool for service success: Case study of Akazi Kanoze services. *European journal of business and social sciences, 4*(3), 29 – 41.

Nicholas, M., & Steyn, H. (2012). *Service management for engineering, business, and technology*. Routledge.

Niedzwiecki, M. J., Hsia, R. Y., & Shen, Y. C. (2018). Not all insurance is equal: Differential treatment and health outcomes by insurance coverage among nonelderly adult patients with heart attack. *Journal of the American Heart Association, 7*(11), e008152. Advance online publication. DOI: 10.1161/JAHA.117.008152 PMID: 29871858

Nieves, J., & Diaz-Meneses, G. (2020). Organizational learning capability and innovation: The moderating role of environmental scanning. *European Journal of Innovation Management, 23*(3), 478–501.

Nigerian Communications Commission (NCC) subscriber data (2017). Industry overview: Subscribers/Teledensity. Retrieved from https://www.ncc.gov.ng/stakeholder/statistics-reports/industry-overview

Nigerian Communications Commission (NCC) subscriber data (2018). Industry overview: Subscribers/Teledensity. Retrieved from https://www.ncc.gov.ng/stakeholder/statistics-reports/industry-overview

NikkhahManesh. S., Choi, J., & Shrestha, P. (2020, March). Critical literature review on the diversity and inclusion of women and ethnic minorities in construction and civil engineering industry and education. In *Construction Research Congress* 2020.

Ning, J., Xu, J., Liang, K., Zhang, F., & Chang, E. (2018). Passive attacks against searchable encryption. *IEEE Transactions on Information Forensics and Security, 14*(3), 789–802. DOI: 10.1109/TIFS.2018.2866321

NIOSH Absenteeism in the Workplace at. https://www.cdc.gov/niosh/topics/absences/default.html Compilation from U.S. Census Bureau Current Population Survey (CPS) Questionnaire. Available at: https://www.census.gov/programs-surveys/cps/technical-documentation/questionnaires.html

Nkomo, S. M. (2020). Gender and ethnic discrimination in African workplaces. *Equality, Diversity and Inclusion, 39*(2), 123–136.

Nkrumah, T., & Scott, K. A. (2022). Mentoring in STEM higher education: A synthesis of the literature to (re)present the excluded women of color. *International Journal of STEM Education, 9*(1), 50. Advance online publication. DOI: 10.1186/s40594-022-00367-7 PMID: 35919282

Noe, R. A., Hollenbeck, J. R., Gerhart, B., & Wright, P. M. (2022). *Human Resource Management: Gaining a Competitive Advantage* (12th ed.). McGraw-Hill Education.

Noh, E.-M., & Lee, K.-H. (2022). *The empirical research on professional isolation during remote work in context of COVID-19 and organizational citizenship behavior*. Korean Journal of Industrial and Organizational Psychology., DOI: 10.24230/kjiop.v35i3.513-558

Nwaogu, J. M., Chan, A. P. C., & Tetteh, M. O. (2022). Staff resilience and coping behavior as protective factors for mental health among construction tradesmen. *Journal of Engineering, Design and Technology, 20*(3), 671–695. DOI: 10.1108/JEDT-11-2020-0464

Odonkor, C. A., Sholas, M. G., Verduzco-Gutierrez, M., Zafonte, R. D., & Silver, J. K. (2020). African American Patient Disparities in COVID-19 Outcomes: A Call to Action for Physiatrists to Provide Rehabilitation Care to Black Survivors. *American Journal of Physical Medicine & Rehabilitation, 99*(11), 986–987. https://doi-org.captechu.idm.oclc.org/10.1097/PHM.0000000000001568. DOI: 10.1097/PHM.0000000000001568 PMID: 32804715

Ogunberu, A., Akintelu, S. & Olaposi, T. (2018). Application of service scope management practices on service success among telecommunication organizations in Nigeria. *International journal of development and sustainability, 7*(2), 518-532.

Ogunberu, A., Akintelu, S., & Olaposi, T. (2016). Factors affecting the choice of service scope management practices among telecommunication organizations. *Global journal of management and business research. Administrative Management, 16*(3), 13–19.

Ogunode, P. O., & Oyebola, S. A. (2022). Customer satisfaction and complaints management in Nigerian telecommunications. *British Journal of Management and Marketing Studies*, *5*(1), 18–35.

Oikarinen, T., Hyypia, M., & Pihkala, T. (2007). *Effects of human resource management practices on the OCB of employees within networks.* Paper prepared for the 19th Conference of the Nordic Academy of Management in Bergen, Norway.

Okonkwo, R. N., & Adetunji, A. (2021). Tribal affiliations and hiring practices in Nigeria. *African Journal of Business Ethics*, *15*(1), 89–102.

Olanrewaju, R. F., Khan, B. U. I., Morshidi, M. A., Anwar, F., & Kiah, L. B. M. (2021). A frictionless and secure user authentication in Web-Based premium applications. *IEEE Access : Practical Innovations, Open Solutions*, *9*, 129240–129255. DOI: 10.1109/ACCESS.2021.3110310

Olatoye, O. (2022). *Social and Psychological Impact of Covid-19 Pandemic on Construction Projects* (Order No. 29994627). Available from ProQuest One Academic. (2770728354). https://www.proquest.com/dissertations-theses/social-psychological-impact-covid-19-pandemic-on/docview/2770728354/se-2

Olca, E., & Can, O. (2022a). DICON: A Domain-Independent Consent Management for Personal Data Protection. *IEEE Access : Practical Innovations, Open Solutions*, *10*, 95479–95497. DOI: 10.1109/ACCESS.2022.3204970

Oleksa-Marewska, K., & Tokar, J. (2022). Facing the post-pandemic challenges: The role of leadership effectiveness in shaping the affective well-being of healthcare providers working in a hybrid work mode. *International Journal of Environmental Research and Public Health*, *19*(21), 14388. Advance online publication. DOI: 10.3390/ijerph192114388 PMID: 36361264

Olise, M. & Ojiaku, O. (2018), Effects of product quality on customer satisfaction: A review of manufacturing company's performance in Anambra state. *International journal of business & law research* *6*(1), 39-47.

Oliver, M., & Shapiro, T. (1997). *Black Wealth/White Wealth: A New Perspective on Racial Inequality*. Routledge.

Olowoporoku, A. A., & Olubiyi, T. O. (2023). Evaluating Service Quality and Business Outcomes Post-Pandemic: Perspective from Hotels in Emerging Market. *Sawala: Jurnal Administrasi Negara, 11*(2), 182–201. DOI: 10.30656/sawala.v11i2.6975

Olubiyi T. O. (2023b). Leveraging competitive strategies on business outcomes post-covid-19 pandemic: Empirical investigation from Africa. *Journal of Management and Business: Research and Practice*, DOI: 10.54933/jmbrp-2023-15-2-1

Olubiyi, T. O. (2024). An investigation of the role of airline safety management and its impact on passenger satisfaction: a study of commercial airline businesses in Nigeria. Journal of the Management Sciences, 60(4). Retrieved from https://journals.unizik.edu.ng/jfms/article/view/3396 Nnamdi Azikiwe University, Awka, Nigeria

Olubiyi, O. T., Lawal, A. T., & Adeoye, O. O. (2022). Succession planning and family business continuity: Perspectives from Lagos State, Nigeria. *Organization and Human Capital Development, 1*(1), 40–52. DOI: 10.31098/orcadev.v1i1.865

Olubiyi, T. O. (2019). Knowledge management practices and family business profitability: Evidence from Lagos State, Nigeria. *Global Journal of Management and Business Research, 19*(A11), 21–31. https://journalofbusiness.org/index.php/GJMBR/article/view/2872

Olubiyi, T. O. (2020). Knowledge management practices and family business profitability: Evidence from Lagos State, Nigeria [Nigerian Chapter]. *Arabian Journal of Business and Management Review*, *6*(1), 23–32.

Olubiyi, T. O. (2022a). Measuring technological capability and business performance post-COVID Era: Evidence from Small and Medium-Sized Enterprises (SMEs) in Nigeria. *Management & Marketing Journal, xx*(2), 234–248. DOI: 10.52846/MNMK.20.2.09

Olubiyi, T. O. (2022b). An investigation of sustainable innovative strategy and customer satisfaction in small and medium-sized enterprises (SMEs) in Nigeria. *Covenant Journal of Business and Social Sciences, 13*(2), 1–24.

Olubiyi, T. O. (2023a). Unveiling the role of workplace environment in achieving the Sustainable Development Goal Eight (SDG8) and employee job satisfaction post-pandemic: Perspective from Africa. *Revista Management & Marketing Craiova, XXI*(2), 212–228. DOI: 10.52846/MNMK.21.2.02

Olubiyi, T. O., Adeoye, O. O., Jubril, B., Adeyemi, O. S., & Eyanuku, J. P. (2023). Measuring Inequality in Sub-Saharan Africa Post-Pandemic: Correlation Results for Workplace Inequalities and Implication for Sustainable Development Goal ten. *International Journal of Professional Business Review*, *8*(4), e01405. DOI: 10.26668/businessreview/2023.v8i4.1405

Olubiyi, T. O., & Akpa, V. A. (2023). Does innovative capability and artificial intelligence really matter for the profitability of consumer goods companies in developing economies? *SunText Review of Economics & Business*, *4*(3), 191–204.

Olubiyi, T. O., Jubril, B., Sojinu, O. S., & Ngari, R. (2022). Strengthening gender equality in small business and achieving sustainable development goals (SDGs), Comparative analysis of Kenya and Nigeria. *Sawala Jurnal Administrasi Negara*, *10*(2), 168–186. DOI: 10.30656/sawala.v10i2.5663

Olugbemiga, E. O., Jang, Y., Song, K., & Ahn, J. (2023). Impact of COVID-19 on Social and Psychological Well-Being of Workers in Construction Projects: Comparative Analysis of Managers and Laborers. *Buildings (Basel, Switzerland)*, *13*(8), 1902. DOI: 10.3390/buildings13081902

Omidi, L., Karimi, H., Pilbeam, C., Mousavi, S., & Moradi, G. (2023). Exploring the relationships among safety leadership, safety climate, psychological contract of safety, risk perception, safety compliance, and safety outcomes. *Frontiers in Public Health*, *11*, 1–7. DOI: 10.3389/fpubh.2023.1235214 PMID: 37937077

Omi, M., & Winant, H. (1994). *Racial Formation in the United States from the 1960s to the 1990s* (2nd ed.). Routledge.

Omoyele, O. S., Olubiyi, T. O., Lanre-Babalola, F. O., Obadare, G. O., & Onikoyi, I. A. (2023). Business Model Innovation as a Catalyst for Sustainable Entrepreneurship: Empirical Findings from Small and Medium Enterprises in Nigeria. *Skyline Business Journal*, *19*(2), 55–64. DOI: 10.37383/SBJ190205

Ong, P., & Valenzuela, A. (1996). The Labor Market: Immigrant Effects and Racial Disparities. In Waldinger, R., & Bozorgmehr, M. (Eds.), *Ethnic Los Angeles* (pp. 165–191). Russell Sage Foundation.

Organ, D. W. (2015). Behavior of Organizational Citizenship, Second Edition, vol. 17, no. 1938. Elsevier, 2015. DOI: 10.1016/B978-0-08-097086-8.22031-X

Organ, D. W. (2017). Behavior of Organizational Citizenship: Recent Trends and Developments, *Annu. Rev. Organ. Psychol. Organ. Behave,* no. November 2017, pp. 1-12, 2018, doi: DOI: 10.1146/annurev-orgpsych-032117-104536

Organ, D. W. (1977). A re-evaluation and reinterpretation of the satisfaction-causes-performance hypothesis. *Academy of Management Review, 2*(1), 46–53. DOI: 10.2307/257604

Organ, D. W. (1988). *Organizational Citizenship Behavior: The Good Soldier Syndrome*. Lexington Books.

Organ, D. W., & Konovsky, M. (1989). Cognitive versus affective determinants of organizational citizenship behavior. *The Journal of Applied Psychology, 74*(1), 157–164. DOI: 10.1037/0021-9010.74.1.157

Organ, D. W., Podsakoff, P. M., & MacKenzie, S. B. (2006). *Behavior of organizational citizenship: its nature, antecedents and consequences*. Sage Publications. DOI: 10.4135/9781452231082

Organ, D. W., & Ryan, K. (1995). A meta-analytic review of attitudinal and dispositional predictors of organizational citizenship behavior. *Personnel Psychology, 48*(4), 775–802. DOI: 10.1111/j.1744-6570.1995.tb01781.x

Orwig, R., & Brennan, L. (2000). An integrated view of service and quality management for service-based organizations. *International Journal of Quality & Reliability Management, 17*(5), 351–363. DOI: 10.1108/02656710010298382

Osorio, P., Quelhas, O., Zotes, L., Shimoda, E., & Sergio, F. (2014). Critical success factors in service management: An exploratory study of an energy company in Brazil. *Global journal of management and business research. Administrative Management, 14*(10), 39–50.

Pager, D., & Shepherd, H. (2008). The sociology of discrimination: Racial discrimination in employment, housing, credit, and consumer markets. *Annual Review of Sociology, 34*(1), 181–209. DOI: 10.1146/annurev.soc.33.040406.131740 PMID: 20689680

Palacios, R., Fernandez-Portillo, A. F., Sanchez-Ubeda, E. F., & Garcia-De-Zuniga, P. (2022). HTB: A very effective method to protect web servers against BREACH attack to HTTPS. *IEEE Access : Practical Innovations, Open Solutions, 10*, 40381–40390. DOI: 10.1109/ACCESS.2022.3166175

Pal, B., Daniel, T., Chatterjee, R., & Ristenpart, T. (2019). Beyond credential stuffing: password similarity models using neural networks. *2022 IEEE Symposium on Security and Privacy (SP)*, 417–434. DOI: 10.1109/SP.2019.00056

Pamidimukkala, A., & Kermanshachi, S. (2021). Impact of COVID-19 on field and office workforce in the construction industry, Project Leadership, and Society. Volume 2, 100018, ISSN 2666-7215, https://doi.org/DOI: 10.1016/j.plas.2021.100018

Panda, A. K., Lenka, A. A., Mohapatra, A., Rath, B. K., Parida, A. A., & Mohapatra, H. (2024). Integrating cloud computing for intelligent transportation solutions in smart cities. *Advances in Civil and Industrial Engineering*, ●●●, 121–142. DOI: 10.4018/979-8-3693-6695-0.ch005

Pantano, E., Pizzi, G., Scarpi, D., & Dennis, C. (2020). Competing during a pandemic? Retailers' ups and downs during the COVID-19 outbreak. *Journal of Business Research, 116*, 209–213. DOI: 10.1016/j.jbusres.2020.05.036 PMID: 32501307

Pant, P., Rajawat, A. S., Goyal, S., Bedi, P., Verma, C., Raboaca, M. S., & Enescu, F. M. (2022). Authentication and authorization in modern web apps for data security using NoDEJs and role of dark web. *Procedia Computer Science, 215*, 781–790. DOI: 10.1016/j.procs.2022.12.080

Park, J., Sandhu, R., Gupta, M., & Bhatt, S. (2021). Activity control design principles: Next generation access control for smart and collaborative systems. *IEEE Access : Practical Innovations, Open Solutions, 9*, 151004–151022. DOI: 10.1109/ACCESS.2021.3126201

Park, K. S., Shin, H. D., Park, B. L., Cheong, H. S., Choa, Y. M., Lee, H. K., Lee, J., Lee, J., Kim, H. T., Han, B. G., Kim, J. W., Koh, I., Kim, Y. J., Kimm, K., & Oh, B. (2005). Genetic polymorphisms in the transforming growth factor beta-induced gene associated with BMI. *Human Mutation, 25*(3), 322. DOI: 10.1002/humu.9315 PMID: 15712349

Parku, K. E., Obuobisa-Darko, T., & Asiedu, E. (2023). *Psychological contract fulfilment: A suitable umpire between transformational leadership and employee engagement in the Ghanaian public sector*. International Journal of Applied Research in Business and Management., DOI: 10.51137/ijarbm.2023.4.1.5

Pasco, R. F., Fox, S. J., Johnston, S. C., Pignone, M., & Meyers, L. A. (2020). Estimated association of construction work with risks of COVID-19 infection and hospitalization in Texas. [Google Scholar] [CrossRef] [PubMed]. *JAMA Network Open, 3*(10), e2026373. DOI: 10.1001/jamanetworkopen.2020.26373 PMID: 33119111

Pastuszak, Z., Chadam, J., Phusavat, K.& Polkowska, M. (2013). Strategic service management as component of innovative organisations. *Active citizenship by knowledge management and innovation, 8*(6), 11-31.

Patel, V., Thornicroft, G., & Walker, R. (2021). Mental health disparities: Reducing the gap in access and outcomes for underserved populations. *American Journal of Public Health, 111*(2), 154–161. DOI: 10.2105/AJPH.2021.306512

Payne, B. K., Mayes, L., Paredes, T., Smith, E., Wu, H., & Xin, C. (2021). Applying High Impact Practices in an Interdisciplinary Cybersecurity Program. *Journal of Cybersecurity Education, Research and Practice, 2020*(2).

Payne, M., Roache, D., Subero, J., & Zhang, G. P. (2024). How safety leadership styles impact safety performance: A case study. *Journal of Safety Research, 93*, 214–228. DOI: 10.1016/j.jsr.2025.02.006 PMID: 40483057

Pekrun, R. (2019). Expectancy–value theory of anxiety: Overview and implications. *Anxiety*, •••, 23–42.

Perdices, D., De Vergara, J. E. L., González, I., & De Pedro, L. (2022). Web browsing privacy in the deep learning era: Beyond VPNs and encryption. *Computer Networks, 220*, 109471. DOI: 10.1016/j.comnet.2022.109471

Phadermrod, B., Crowder, R. M., & Wills, G. B. (2019). Importance-performance analysis based SWOT analysis. *International Journal of Information Management, 44*, 194–203. DOI: 10.1016/j.ijinfomgt.2016.03.009

Piotrowicz, W., & Cuthbertson, R. (2019). Exploring omnichannel retailing: Common expectations and diverse realities. *Journal of Retailing and Consumer Services, 50*, 1–7.

Pipeline & Gas Journal. Phillips 66: Red Oak, Liberty, ACE Pipelines Deferred by Cost Cuts. Available online: https://pgjonline.com/news/2020/03-march/phillips-66-red-oak-liberty-ace-pipelines-deferred-by-cost-cuts (accessed on 26 October 2020).

Podsakoff, P.M., & Mackenzie, S.B. (1994). Behavior of organizational citizenship and effectiveness of the sales unit. Journal of Market Research, 31, 351-363. 28.

Podsakoff, N. P., Whiting, S. W., Podsakoff, P. M., & Blume, B. D. (2009). Individual and organizational-level consequences of organizational citizenship behaviors: A meta-analysis. *The Journal of Applied Psychology, 94*(1), 122–141. DOI: 10.1037/a0013079 PMID: 19186900

Podsakoff, N. P., Whiting, S. W., Podsakoff, P. M., & Mishra, P. M. (2011). Effects of organizational citizenship behaviors on selection decisions in job interviews. *The Journal of Applied Psychology, 96*(2), 310–326. DOI: 10.1037/a0020948 PMID: 20919791

Podsakoff, P. M., MacKenzie, S. B., Paine, J. B., & Bachrach, D. G. (2000). Organizational Citizenship Behaviors: A Critical Review of the Theoretical and Empirical Literature and Suggestions for Future Research. *Journal of Management, 26*(3), 513–563. DOI: 10.1177/014920630002600307

Pohn, D., & Hommel, W. (2022). Reference Service Model Framework for Identity Management. *IEEE Access : Practical Innovations, Open Solutions, 10*, 120984–121009. DOI: 10.1109/ACCESS.2022.3219044

Pournader, M., Kach, A., & Talluri, S. (2020). A review of the existing and emerging topics in the supply chain risk management literature. *Decision Sciences, 51*(4), 867–919. DOI: 10.1111/deci.12470 PMID: 34234385

Pourrahmani, H., Yavarinasab, A., Monazzah, A. M. H., & Van Herle, J. (2023). A review of the security vulnerabilities and countermeasures in the Internet of Things solutions: A bright future for the Blockchain. *Internet of Things : Engineering Cyber Physical Human Systems, 23*, 100888. DOI: 10.1016/j.iot.2023.100888

Priyadarshi, S., Subudhi, S., Kumar, S., Bhardwaj, D., & Mohapatra, H. (2024). Analysis on enhancing urban mobility with IoT-integrated parking solutions. *Advances in Civil and Industrial Engineering*, •••, 143–172. DOI: 10.4018/979-8-3693-6695-0.ch006

Priya, V. (n.d.). *Why is citizen behavior so important for organizations?* LinkedIn. Retrieved from LinkedIn.

Priyono, A., & Hidayat, A. (2022). Dynamic capabilities for open innovation: A typology of pathways toward aligning resources, strategies and capabilities. *Journal of Open Innovation, 8*(4), 206. DOI: 10.3390/joitmc8040206

Pusey, P., Gondree, M., & Peterson, Z. (2016). The Outcomes of Cybersecurity Competitions and Implications for Underrepresented Populations. *IEEE Security and Privacy, 14*(6), 90–95. DOI: 10.1109/MSP.2016.119

Qin, W., Chen, S., & Peng, M. (2019). Recent advances in Industrial Internet: Insights and challenges. *Digital Communications and Networks, 6*(1), 1–13. DOI: 10.1016/j.dcan.2019.07.001

Quansah, P. E., Zhu, Y., & Guo, M. (2023). Assessing the effects of safety leadership, employee engagement, and psychological safety on safety performance. *Journal of Safety Research, 86*, 226–244. Advance online publication. DOI: 10.1016/j.jsr.2023.07.002 PMID: 37718051

Rahman, H. (2014). Factors affecting customer satisfaction in mobile telecommunication industry in Bangladesh. *Business, management and education journal, 12*(1), 74–93.

Rahman, M., Hamid, S., & Zafar, T. (2020). Migrant worker exploitation in the gig economy of Southeast Asia. *Asian Journal of Social Science, 48*(3), 345–362.

Raj, S., Sheel, S., Singh, R., Ashar, S., & Mohapatra, H. (2025). Securing smart cities. *New Horizons in Leadership*, 487-512. https://doi.org/DOI: 10.4018/979-8-3693-6437-6.ch021

Rao, P. M., & Deebak, B. D. (2022). Security and privacy issues in smart cities/industries: Technologies, applications, and challenges. *Journal of Ambient Intelligence and Humanized Computing*, *14*(8), 10517–10553. DOI: 10.1007/s12652-022-03707-1

Raoufi, M., & Fayek, A. R. (2021). Identifying actions to control and mitigate the effects of the COVID-19 pandemic on construction organizations: Preliminary findings. *Public Works Management & Policy*, *26*(1), 47–55. DOI: 10.1177/1087724X20969164

Rapp, A. A., Bachrach, D. G., & Rapp, T. L. (2013). The influence of time management skill on the curvilinear relationship between organizational citizenship behavior and task performance. *The Journal of Applied Psychology*, *98*(4), 668–677. DOI: 10.1037/a0031733 PMID: 23379912

Rauf, A., Guru, A., & Mohapatra, H. (2024). Exploring the social model of smart home devices. *Advances in Human and Social Aspects of Technology*, •••, 233–256. DOI: 10.4018/979-8-3693-9235-5.ch012

Razak, I., Nirwanto, N. & Triatmanto, B. (2016). The impact of product quality and price on customer satisfaction with the mediator of customer value. *Journal of marketing and consumer research, 30(*1), 59 – 68.

Renaud, K., & Coles-Kemp, L. (2022). Accessible and inclusive cyber security: A nuanced and complex challenge. *SN Computer Science*, *3*(5), 346. DOI: 10.1007/s42979-022-01239-1 PMID: 35755325

Roache, D. (2023). Transformational leadership style: Management and communication taxonomies for organizational effectiveness. In Roache, D. (Ed.), *Transformational leadership styles, management strategies, and communication for global leaders* (pp. 1–27). IGI Global Publisher. DOI: 10.4018/978-1-6684-8822-5.ch001

Roache, D. (2024). Ethical values and organizational optimization: morality and social responsibility of leaders. In Roache, D. (Ed.), *Ethical quandaries in business practices: Exploring morality and social responsibility* (pp. 1–26). IGI Global Publisher. DOI: 10.4018/979-8-3693-3948-0.ch001

Roberts, L. M., & Nour, S. E. (2023). Rethinking organizational diversity initiatives: The central role of psychological safety. *Organizational Behavior and Human Decision Processes*, *174*, 104216. DOI: 10.1016/j.obhdp.2023.104216

Robinson, S.L., & Rousseau, D.M. (1994). Violating the psychological contract: it is not the exception but the norm. *Journal of Organizational Behavior*, 15, 245-259. Article 29.

Robinson, C. (2024). *How to impact the company's culture with organizational citizenship behavior. Forbes*. Retrieved from Forbes.

Robinson, S. L., & Morrison, E. W. (1995). Psychological Contracts and OCB: The Effect of Unfulfilled Obligations on Civic Virtue Behavior. *Journal of Organizational Behavior, 16*(3), 289–298. DOI: 10.1002/job.4030160309

Robles-González, A., Arias-Cabarcos, P., & Parra-Arnau, J. (2023). Privacy-centered authentication: A new framework and analysis. *Computers & Security, 132*, 103353. DOI: 10.1016/j.cose.2023.103353

Rockstuhl, T., Dulebohn, J. H., Ang, S., & Shore, L. M. (2012). Leader-Member Exchange (LMX) and Culture: A Meta-Analysis of LMX Correlates in 23 Countries. *The Journal of Applied Psychology, 97*(6), 1097–1130. DOI: 10.1037/a0029978 PMID: 22985117

Rodríguez, G. E., Torres, J. G., Flores, P., & Benavides, D. E. (2019). Cross-site scripting (XSS) attacks and mitigation: A survey. *Computer Networks, 166*, 106960. DOI: 10.1016/j.comnet.2019.106960

Roethlisberger, F. J., & Dickson, W. J. (1939). *Management and the worker*. Harvard University Press.

Roggeveen, A. L., & Sethuraman, R. (2020). How the COVID-19 pandemic may change the world of retailing. *Journal of Retailing, 96*(2), 169–171. DOI: 10.1016/j.jretai.2020.04.002

Rolik, Y. (2017). Risk management in implementing wind energy services. *Procedia Engineering, 178*(19), 278–288. DOI: 10.1016/j.proeng.2017.01.115

Romi, A., Yildiz, H., & Somech, A. (2019). Job satisfaction as a predictor of organizational citizenship behavior: evidence from multiple industries.

Rose, K. (2005). *Service quality management: Why, what and how* (3rd ed.). USA: J. Ross publishing Inc.

Rousseau, D. M. (1995). *Psychological Contracts in Organizations: Understanding Written and Unwritten Agreements*. SAGE. DOI: 10.4135/9781452231594

Rueda, R. (2011). *The 3 dimensions of improving student performance: finding the right solutions to the right problems*. Teachers College, Columbia University.

Rush, L. M., & Landgraf, K. B. (2023). High Impact Practices in Underserved Communities: Linking Open Educational Resources and Local Non-Profit in Business Communications Course Design. *Journal of Higher Education Theory and Practice*, *23*(8), 53–64. https://www.proquest.com/scholarly-journals/high-impact-practices-underserved-communities/docview/2821424061/se-2

S&P Global. Pennsylvania's Orders to Stem Coronavirus Outbreak Pause Several Gas Pipeline Projects. Available online: https://www.spglobal.com/platts/en/market-insights/latest-news/natural-gas/032520-pennsylvanias-orders-to-stem-coronavirus-outbreak-pause-several-gas-pipeline-projects

Sabatello, M., Jackson Scroggins, M., Goto, G., Santiago, A., McCormick, A., Morris, K. J., Daulton, C. R., Easter, C. L., & Darien, G. (2021). Structural Racism in the COVID-19 Pandemic: Moving Forward. *The American Journal of Bioethics*, *21*(3), 56–74. https://doi-org.captechu.idm.oclc.org/10.1080/15265161.2020.1851808. DOI: 10.1080/15265161.2020.1851808 PMID: 33345745

Sahib, U. (2019). Smart Dubai: Sensing Dubai smart city for smart environment management. *Advances in 21st Century Human Settlements*, 437-489. https://doi.org/DOI: 10.1007/978-981-13-6822-6_12

Salamatian, S., Huleihel, W., Beirami, A., Cohen, A., & Medard, M. (2020). Centralized vs Decentralized Targeted Brute-Force Attacks: Guessing With Side-Information. *IEEE Transactions on Information Forensics and Security*, *15*, 3749–3759. DOI: 10.1109/TIFS.2020.2998949

Samarakkody, A., Amaratunga, D., & Haigh, R. (2023). Technological innovations for enhancing disaster resilience in smart cities: A comprehensive urban scholar's analysis. *Sustainability (Basel)*, *15*(15), 12036. DOI: 10.3390/su151512036

Santos, D., Santos, D., Goel, S., Costanzo, J., Sagen, D., & Buddelmeyer, P. (2020). *A roadmap for successful regional alliances and multistakeholder partnerships to build the cybersecurity workforce*. US Department of Commerce, National Institute of Standards and Technology. DOI: 10.6028/NIST.IR.8287

Sapra, R., & Dhaliwal, P. (2019). Blockchain for security issues of Internet of things (IoT). *Intelligent Systems Reference Library*, 599-626. https://doi.org/DOI: 10.1007/978-3-030-33596-0_24

Sarfaraz, A., Chakrabortty, R. K., & Essam, D. L. (2023). AccessChain: An access control framework to protect data access in blockchain enabled supply chain. *Future Generation Computer Systems*, *148*, 380–394. DOI: 10.1016/j.future.2023.06.009

Sarstedt, M., & Mooi, E. (2014). *A concise guide to market research*. Springer. DOI: 10.1007/978-3-642-53965-7

Satoh, F., & Tokuda, T. (2010). Security Policy composition for composite web services. *IEEE Transactions on Services Computing*, *4*(4), 314–327. DOI: 10.1109/TSC.2010.40

Saxena, N., Choi, B. J., & Lu, R. (2015). Authentication and Authorization Scheme for various user roles and devices in smart Grid. *IEEE Transactions on Information Forensics and Security*, *11*(5), 907–921. DOI: 10.1109/TIFS.2015.2512525

Sayani. (2015). Customer satisfaction and loyalty in the United Arab Emirates banking industry. *International journal of bank marketing, 33*(3), 351-375.

Schiffman, L., & Kanuk, L. (2004). *Consumer behaviour* (8th ed.). Prentice Hall.

Schumm, L. P., Giurcanu, M. C., Locey, K. J., Ortega, J. C., Zhang, Z., & Grossman, R. L. (2022). Racial and ethnic disparities in the observed COVID-19 case fatality rate among the U.S. population. *Annals of Epidemiology*, *74*, 118–124. https://doi-org.captechu.idm.oclc.org/10.1016/j.annepidem.2022.07.010. DOI: 10.1016/j.annepidem.2022.07.010 PMID: 35940395

Sean, M., & Gray, J. (2013). Inter-organisational quality management: The use of contractual incentives and monitoring mechanisms with outsourced manufacturing. *Production and Operations Management*, *22*(10), 1041–1056.

Seo, N. J., Kim, N. H., Cho, N. S., & Cha, N. S. (2004). Web server attack categorization based on root causes and their locations. In Information Technology: Coding and Computing, 2004. Proceedings. ITCC 2004. International Conference onVolume: 1 (pp. 90-96 Vol.1). DOI: 10.1109/ITCC.2004.1286431

Seo, J., & Park, S. (2023). SBAC: Substitution cipher access control based on blockchain for protecting personal data in metaverse. *Future Generation Computer Systems*, *151*, 85–97. DOI: 10.1016/j.future.2023.09.022

Serrano, F., Blutinger, E. J., Vargas-Torres, C., Bilal, S., Counts, C., Straight, M., & Lin, M. P. (2022). Racial and Ethnic Disparities in Hospitalization and Clinical Outcomes Among Patients with COVID-19. *Western Journal of Emergency Medicine: Integrating Emergency Care with Population Health, 23*(5), 601–612. https://doi-org.captechu.idm.oclc.org/10.5811/westjem.2022.3.53065

Service Management Institute. (2017). *The PMBOK guide: A guide to the service management body of knowledge* (6th ed.). PMI Publications.

Sethi, D., & Seth, M. (2009). Interpersonal communication: Lifeblood of an organization. *The IUP Journal of Soft Skills*, *III*(3&4), 32–40. https://www.researchgate.net/profile/Deepa_Sethi/publication/228271402_Interpersonal_Communication_Lifeblood_of_an_Organization/links/55af387808ae98e661a6fd03/Interpersonal-Communication-Lifeblood-of-an-Organization.pdf

Sfantou, D. F., Laliotis, A., Patelarou, A. E., Sifaki-Pistolla, D., Matalliotakis, M., & Patelarou, E. (2017). Importance of leadership style towards quality of care measures in healthcare settings: A systematic review. *Healthcare (Basel)*, *5*(4), 73. DOI: 10.3390/healthcare5040073 PMID: 29036901

Shah, S.Z., *et al.* (2022). Leadership styles and their impact on organizational citizenship behaviors: a review study.

Shaked, A., Cherdantseva, Y., Burnap, P., & Maynard, P. (2023). Operations-informed incident response playbooks. *Computers & Security*, *134*, 103454. DOI: 10.1016/j.cose.2023.103454

Shams, R., Vrontis, D., Belyaeva, Z., Ferraris, A., & Czinkota, M. R. (2021). Strategic agility in international business: A conceptual framework for "agile" multinationals. *Journal of International Management*, *27*(1), 100737. DOI: 10.1016/j.intman.2020.100737

Shamsuzzoha, A., Nieminen, J., Piya, S., & Rutledge, K. (2021). Smart city for sustainable environment: A comparison of participatory strategies from Helsinki, Singapore and London. *Cities (London, England)*, *114*, 103194. DOI: 10.1016/j.cities.2021.103194

Shandilya, S. K. (2022). Paradigm shift in adaptive cyber defense for securing the web data: The future ahead. *Journal of Web Engineering*. Advance online publication. DOI: 10.13052/jwe1540-9589.21416

Shar, L. K., Briand, L. C., & Tan, H. B. K. (2014). Web application vulnerability prediction using hybrid program analysis and machine learning. *IEEE Transactions on Dependable and Secure Computing*, *12*(6), 688–707. DOI: 10.1109/TDSC.2014.2373377

Sharma, A. (2020). Corporate accountability in telecommunications: Nigeria's case. *Journal of Corporate Responsibility*, *9*(2), 76–94.

Sharma, A., Anand, N., Mukherjee, S., Kumar, S., Kumar, S., & Mohapatra, H. (2024). Analyzing territorial variations in the implementation of IoT-based smart homes. *Advances in Electronic Government, Digital Divide, and Regional Development*, •••, 305–334. DOI: 10.4018/979-8-3693-6854-1.ch010

Sharma, S. (2018). Design and implementation of malware detection Scheme. *International Journal of Computer Network and Information Security*, *10*(8), 58–66. DOI: 10.5815/ijcnis.2018.08.07

Sheikh, A. (2021). Certified Ethical Hacker (CEH) Preparation guide. In Apress eBooks. DOI: 10.1007/978-1-4842-7258-9

Shields, S. A. (2008). Gender: An intersectionality perspective. *Sex Roles*, *59*(5-6), 301–311. DOI: 10.1007/s11199-008-9501-8

Simms, A. (2023). Fiscal Fragility in Black Middle-Class Suburbia and Consequences for K–12 Schools and Other Public Services. *The Russell Sage Foundation Journal of the Social Sciences : RSF*, *9*(2), 204–225. DOI: 10.7758/RSF.2023.9.2.09

Simon, S. M., & Varghese, K. (2018, July). Assessment of organizational culture in construction–A case study approach. In *26th Annual Conference of the International Group to Lean Construction (IGLC).* Chennai, India (p.348-357) DOI: 10.24928/2018/0396

Simon, T., Goldberg, A., & Bruria Adini, B. (2015). Socializing in emergencies—A review of the use of social media in emergency situations. *International Journal of Information Management*, *35*(5), 609–619. DOI: 10.1016/j.ijinfomgt.2015.07.001

Singh Bhathal, G. (2022). Challenges and opportunities in mobile cloud computing for big data analytics. [IJSR]. *International Journal of Science and Research (Raipur, India)*, *11*(1), 1611–1615. DOI: 10.21275/ES24424211225

Singh, P., & Loncar, N. (2010). Pay Satisfaction, Job Satisfaction, and Turnover Intent. Relations Industrielles. *Industrial Relations*, *65*(3), 470–490. https://www.jstor.org/stable/23078304. DOI: 10.7202/044892ar

Sirmon, D. G., Hitt, M. A., Ireland, R. D., & Gilbert, B. A. (2011). Resource orchestration to create competitive advantage: Breadth, depth, and life cycle effects. *Journal of Management*, *37*(5), 1390–1412. DOI: 10.1177/0149206310385695

Sitanggang, J., Sinulingga, S. & Fachruddin, K. (2019). Analysis of the effect of product quality on customer satisfaction and customer loyalty of Indihome ATPT Telkom regional 1 Sumatera, Medan, North Sumatra, Indonesia. *American international journal of business management (AIJBM)*, *2*(3), 26 – 37.

Sivakorn, S., Polakis, I., & Keromytis, A. D. (2016). The cracked cookie jar: HTTP cookie hijacking and the exposure of private information. *2022 IEEE Symposium on Security and Privacy (SP)*. DOI: 10.1109/SP.2016.49

Sivasankari, N., & Kamalakkannan, S. (2022). Detection and prevention of man-in-the-middle attack in iot network using regression modeling. *Advances in Engineering Software, 169*, 103126. DOI: 10.1016/j.advengsoft.2022.103126

Smela, B., Toumi, M., Świerk, K., Francois, C., Biernikiewicz, M., Clay, E., & Boyer, L. (2023). Rapid literature review: Definition and methodology. *Journal of Market Access & Health Policy, 11*(1), 2241234. DOI: 10.1080/20016689.2023.2241234 PMID: 37533549

Smith, C. A., Organ, D. W., & Near, J. P. (1983). Behavior of organizational citizenship: Its nature and background. *The Journal of Applied Psychology, 68*(4), 653. DOI: 10.1037/0021-9010.68.4.653

Smith, K., Daniels, L., & Roberts, M. (2023). The rise of telehealth during the COVID-19 pandemic: Mental health perspectives. *Journal of Telemedicine and Telecare, 29*(3), 168–175. DOI: 10.1177/1357633X20982595

Smith, R., Janicke, H., He, Y., Ferra, F., & Albakri, A. (2021). The Agile Incident Response for Industrial Control Systems (AIR4ICS) framework. *Computers & Security, 109*, 102398. DOI: 10.1016/j.cose.2021.102398

Snodgrass, S. J., Weerasekara, I., Edwards, S., Heneghan, N. R., Puentedura, E. J., & James, C. (2022). Relationships between the physical work environment, postures and musculoskeletal pain during COVID-19: A survey of frequent computer users. *Journal of Occupational and Environmental Medicine, 64*(11), e782–e791. DOI: 10.1097/JOM.0000000000002698 PMID: 36075375

Solis-Carcano, G., Corona-Suarez, G.& Garcia-Ibarra, J. (2016). Time and cost control in construction services in southeast Mexico. *Journal of construction engineering, 18*(4), 411– 422.

Somech, A., & Ohayon, L. (2019). The role of organizational culture in fostering organizational citizenship behavior among employees.

Somech, A., & Drach-Zahavy, A. (2004). Exploring organizational citizenship behavior from an interpersonal perspective: The role of team member behavior in promoting citizenship behavior. *The Journal of Applied Psychology, 89*(5), 893–901.

Somech, A., & Drach-Zahavy, A. (2004b). Organizational Citizenship Behaviors: Definitions and Dimensions. *Journal of Managerial Psychology, 19*(6), 609–622. DOI: 10.1108/02683940410558073

Song, L., Wang, Y., Chen, B., Tan, Y., Zhang, W., & Wang, Y. (2020). The association between health insurance and all-cause, cardiovascular disease, cancer, and cause-specific mortality: A prospective cohort study. *International Journal of Environmental Research and Public Health, 17*(5), 1525. DOI: 10.3390/ijerph17051525 PMID: 32120888

Sott, M. K., & Bender, M. S. (2025). The Role of Adaptive Leadership in Times of Crisis: A Systematic Review and Conceptual Framework. *Merits, 5*(1), 2. DOI: 10.3390/merits5010002

Sourav, S., & Chen, B. (2023). Exposing hidden attackers in industrial control systems using Micro-Distortions. *IEEE Transactions on Smart Grid, 15*(2), 2089–2101. DOI: 10.1109/TSG.2023.3300710

Spradley, J. P. (1980). *Participant observation*. Holt, Rinehart and Winston.

Srinivasan, R., & Swink, M. (2018). An investigation of visibility and flexibility as complements to supply chain analytics: An organizational information processing theory perspective. *Production and Operations Management, 30*(6), 1770–1791. DOI: 10.1111/poms.12746

Standard Social Innovation Review Collective Impact https://ssir.org/chapters/entry/collective_impact# 124. Tai, D. B. G., Shah, A., Doubeni, C. A., Sia, I. G., & Wieland, M. L. (2021). The Disproportionate Impact of COVID-19 on Racial and Ethnic Minorities in the United States. *Clinical Infectious Diseases, 72*(4), 703–706. https://doi-org.captechu.idm.oclc.org/10.1093/cid/ciaa815\

Staves, A., Anderson, T., Balderstone, H., Green, B., Gouglidis, A., & Hutchison, D. (2022). A Cyber Incident response and recovery framework to support operators of industrial control systems. *International Journal of Critical Infrastructure Protection, 37*, 100505. DOI: 10.1016/j.ijcip.2021.100505

Steele, F. I. (1964). Work and Motivation by Victor H. Vroom. IMR; Industrial Management Review (Pre-1986), 6(1), 106. https://www.proquest.com/scholarly-journals/work-motivation-victor-h-vroom/docview/214194732/se-2

Suchanek, P., Richter, J. & Kralova, M. (2015). Customer satisfaction, product quality and performance of companies. *Review of economic perspectives, 14*(4), 329 – 344.

Sugrova, M., Sedik, P., kubelakova A. & Svetlikova, V. (2017). The impact of the product quality on consumer satisfaction and corporate brand. *Economic Annals-XXI 165*(5-6), 133-137.

Sultan, A. H. M. A. D. (2019). Improving Cybersecurity Awareness in Underserved Populations. Center for Long Term Cybersecurity, UC Berkely. https://cltc. berkeley. edu/wpcontent/uploads/2019/04/CLTC_Underserved_Populations. Pdf.

Suresh, B. (2005). *Scope creep management. The service perfect white paper collection.* USA: ResearchGate

Suwannarat, P., & Wijaya, A. (2022). Regional identity and employment discrimination in Thailand and Indonesia. *Southeast Asian Journal of Social Science, 10*(4), 210–225.

Syed-Yahya, S. N., Idris, M. A., & Noblet, A. J. (2022). The relationship between safety climate and safety performance: A review. *Journal of Safety Research, 83*, 105–118. DOI: 10.1016/j.jsr.2022.08.008 PMID: 36481002

Szalaty, P. M., & Derda, I. (2020). "Revolutionizing Beauty Industry": Co-Creation and Customer Engagement for Brand Image Development. Case Study Research of a Crowdsource-Driven Cosmetics Company Volition Beauty. *International Journal of Marketing, Communication and New Media, 8*(14).

Szopik-Depczynska, K. & Lanfranchi, G. (2016). The importance of planning in service management - Theoretical approach. *reports on economics and finance, 2*(1), 83 – 91.

Tabrizchi, H., & Rafsanjani, M. K. (2020). A survey on security challenges in cloud computing: Issues, threats, and solutions. *The Journal of Supercomputing, 76*(12), 9493–9532. DOI: 10.1007/s11227-020-03213-1

Tajfel, H., & Turner, J. C. (1986). The social identity theory of intergroup behavior. In Worchel, S., & Austin, W. G. (Eds.), *Psychology of intergroup relations* (pp. 7–24). Nelson-Hall.

Tamers, S. L., Streit, J., Pana-Cryan, R., Ray, T., Syron, L., Flynn, M. A., Castillo, D., Roth, G., Geraci, C., Guerin, R., Schulte, P., Henn, S., Chang, C. C., Felknor, S., & Howard, J. (2020). Envisioning the future of work to safeguard the safety, health, and well-being of the workforce: A perspective from the CDC's National Institute for Occupational Safety and Health. *American Journal of Industrial Medicine, 63*(12), 1065–1084. DOI: 10.1002/ajim.23183 PMID: 32926431

Tariq, U., Ahmed, I., Bashir, A. K., & Shaukat, K. (2023). A Critical Cybersecurity Analysis and Future Research Directions for the Internet of Things: A Comprehensive Review. *Sensors (Basel), 23*(8), 4117. DOI: 10.3390/s23084117 PMID: 37112457

Taylor, J., & Adams, P. (2022). Creating inclusive workplaces: Policies for safety and security. *Management Studies Quarterly*, *67*(1), 15–30. DOI: 10.1177/01708406221094017

Teece, D. J., Peteraf, M., & Leih, S. (2016). Dynamic capabilities and organizational agility: Risk, uncertainty, and strategy in the innovation economy. *California Management Review*, *62*(4), 5–35. DOI: 10.1525/cmr.2016.58.4.5

Tegane, S., Semchedine, F., & Boudries, A. (2023). An extended Attribute-based access control with controlled delegation in IoT. *Journal of Information Security and Applications*, *76*, 103473. DOI: 10.1016/j.jisa.2023.103473

The Associated General Contractors of America. (2018, August 29). *Eighty Percent of Contractors Report Difficulty Finding Qualified Craft Workers to Hire as the Association Calls for Measures to Rebuild the Workforce.* https://www.agc.org/news/2018/08/29/ eighty-percent-contractors-report-difficulty finding-qualified-craft-workers-hire

The Associated General Contractors of America. Myers-Lawson School of Construction—Virginia Tech. (2017). *Preventing Fatalities in the Construction Industry.* https://www.agc.org/ sites/ default/files/Files/Safety%20%26%20 Health/AGC-VT%20Fatality%20Report%20%5BFinal %5D_0.pdf

The Open Web Application Security Project. (n.d.). Testing guide. In The Open Web Application Security Project (pp. 1–207) [Book]. https://owasp.org/www-project-web-security-testing-guide/assets/archive/OWASP_Testing_Guide_v4.pdf

Tjemkes, B., Vos, P., & Burgers, K. (2023). *Strategic alliance management.* Routledge. DOI: 10.4324/9781003222187

Toseef, M., Kiran, A., Zhuo, S., Jahangir, M., Riaz, S., Wei, Z., Ghauri, T. A., Ullah, I., & Ahmad, S. B. (2022). Inspirational leadership and innovative communication in sustainable organizations: A mediating role of mutual trust. *Frontiers in Psychology*, *13*, 1–13. DOI: 10.3389/fpsyg.2022.846128 PMID: 36003091

Tramontana, P., Amalfitano, D., & Fasolino, A. R. (2013, September 1). Reverse engineering techniques: From web applications to rich Internet applications. In 2013 15th IEEE International Symposium on Web Systems Evolution (WSE), Eindhoven, Netherlands. DOI: 10.1109/WSE.2013.6642421

Trestian, I., Ranjan, S., Kuzmanovic, A., & Nucci, A. (2009). Googling the Internet: Profiling internet endpoints via the world wide web. *IEEE/ACM Transactions on Networking*, *18*(2), 666–679. DOI: 10.1109/TNET.2009.2031175

Trougakos, J. P., Beal, D. J., Cheng, B. H., Hideg, I., & Zweig, D. (2015). Too Exhausted to Help: A Resource Depletion Perspective on Everyday Interpersonal Citizenship Behaviors. *The Journal of Applied Psychology*, *100*(1), 227–236. DOI: 10.1037/a0038082 PMID: 25314365

Tsai, M., Tsai, C., & Chang, H. (2010). The effect of customer value, customer satisfaction, and switching costs on customer loyalty: An empirical study of hypermarkets in Taiwan. *Social behaviour and personality. International Journal (Toronto, Ont.)*, *38*(6), 729–740.

Tsai, Y. (2011). Relationship between organizational culture, leadership behavior and job satisfaction. *BMC Health Services Research*, *11*(98), 1–9. DOI: 10.1186/1472-6963-11-98 PMID: 21569537

Tsung-Lin, W., & Liu, H. (2023). Causal Model Analysis of the Effect of Policy Formalism, COVID-19 Fear, Social Support and Work Stress on Construction Workers' Anxiety during the Epidemic. *Buildings (Basel, Switzerland)*, *13*(1), 10. DOI: 10.3390/buildings13010010

Turnley, W. H., & Feldman, D. C. (2000). Re-examining the effects of psychological violations of contract: Unmet expectations and job dissatisfaction as mediators. *Journal of Organizational Behavior*, *21*(1), 25–42. DOI: 10.1002/(SICI)1099-1379(200002)21:1<25::AID-JOB2>3.0.CO;2-Z

U.S. Bureau of Labor Statistics (BLS). Current Employment Statistics—National. Available online: https://www.bls.gov/ces/ (accessed on 10 November 2020).

U.S. Bureau of Labor Statistics. (2022, April). *Spotlight on statistics: The Construction Industry: Characteristics of the Employed*, 2003–20. from https://www.bls.gov/spotlight/2022/the-construction-industry-labor-force-2003-to-2020/home.htm

U.S. Bureau of Labor Statistics. (2022, January 20). *Labor force statistics from the current population survey*. From https://www.bls.gov/cps/cpsaat18.htm

Uddin, M. A., Mahmood, M., & Fan, L. (2019). Why Individual Employee Engagement Matters for Team Performance?: Mediating Effects of Employee Engagement and Organizational Citizenship Behavior. *Team Performance Management*, *25*(1–2), 47–68. DOI: 10.1108/TPM-12-2017-0078

Ullah, S. S., Oleshchuk, V., & Pussewalage, H. S. G. (2023). A survey on blockchain envisioned attribute based access control for internet of things: Overview, comparative analysis, and open research challenges. *Computer Networks*, *235*, 109994. DOI: 10.1016/j.comnet.2023.109994

Uru, F. O., Gozukara, E., & Tezcan, L. (2022). The moderating roles of remote, hybrid, and onsite working on the relationship between work engagement and organizational identification during the COVID-19 pandemic. *Sustainability (Basel), 14*(24), 16828. Advance online publication. DOI: 10.3390/su142416828

Vable, A. M., Cohen, A. K., Leonard, S. A., Glymour, M. M., Duarte, C. D. P., & Yen, I. H. (2018). Do the health benefits of education vary by sociodemographic subgroup? Differential returns to education and implications for health inequities. *Annals of Epidemiology, 28*(11), 759–766.e5. Advance online publication. DOI: 10.1016/j.annepidem.2018.08.014 PMID: 30309690

Van Der Loo, F. (2011). Comparison of penetration testing tools for web applications [Thesis]. https://www.cs.ru.nl/masters-theses/2011/F_vd_Loo___Comparison_of_penetration_testing_tools_for_web_applications.pdf

Varadarajan, R. (2020). Customer information resources advantage, marketing strategy, and business performance: A market resources-based view. *Industrial Marketing Management, 89*, 89–97. DOI: 10.1016/j.indmarman.2020.03.003

Vargas, N., & Stainback, K. (2016). *Documenting contested racial identities among self-identified Latinos, Asians, Blacks, and Whites*. American Behavioral Scientist., DOI: 10.1177/0002764215613396

Varvasovszky, Z., & Brugha, R. (2000). A stakeholder analysis. *Health Policy and Planning, 15*(3), 338–345. DOI: 10.1093/heapol/15.3.338 PMID: 11012410

Vasista, T. (2017). Strategic cost management for construction service success: A systemic study. *Civil engineering and urban Planning. International Journal (Toronto, Ont.), 4*(1), 41–52.

Vega, T. (2016). Blacks Will Take Hundreds of Years to Catch Up to White Wealth. https://money.cnn.com/2016/08/09/news/economy/blacks-white-wealth-gap/index.html

Verhoef, P. C., Broekhuizen, T., Bart, Y., Bhattacharya, A., Dong, J. Q., Fabian, N., & Haenlein, M. (2021). Digital transformation: A multidisciplinary reflection and research agenda. *Journal of Business Research, 122*, 889–901. DOI: 10.1016/j.jbusres.2019.09.022

Vespa, J., Armstrong, D. M., & Medina, L. (2018). *Demographic turning points for the United States: Population projections for 2020 to 2060*. US Department of Commerce, Economics and Statistics Administration, US Census Bureau.

Vidman, Å., & Strömberg, A. (2020). Leadership for a healthy work environment - a question about who, what and how. *Leadership in Health Services*, *34*(1), 1–15. DOI: 10.1108/LHS-06-2020-0041 PMID: 33818972

Vignau, B., Khoury, R., Hallé, S., & Hamou-Lladj, A. (2021). The Botnet Simulator: A simulation tool for understanding the interaction between botnets. *Software Impacts*, *10*, 100173. DOI: 10.1016/j.simpa.2021.100173

Voronkov, A., Martucci, L. A., & Lindskog, S. (2020). Measuring the usability of firewall rule sets. *IEEE Access : Practical Innovations, Open Solutions*, *8*, 27106–27121. DOI: 10.1109/ACCESS.2020.2971093

Wael, H., & Zhiling, T. (2012). Service management literature: Gaps and opportunities. *E-Leader*, *1*(1), 1–38.

Wakeel, F., & Njoku, A. (2021, February). Application of the weathering framework: Intersection of racism, stigma, and COVID-19 as a stressful life event among African Americans. [). MDPI.]. *Health Care*, *9*(2), 145. PMID: 33540498

Walton, S., Wheeler, P. R., Zhang, Y., & Zhao, X. (2021). An integrative review and analysis of cybersecurity research: Current state and future directions. *Journal of Information Systems*, *35*(1), 155–186. DOI: 10.2308/ISYS-19-033

Walz, S. M., & Niehoff, B. P. (2000). Organizational citizenship behaviors: Their relationship with organizational effectiveness. *Journal of Hospitality & Tourism Research (Washington, D.C.)*, *24*(3), 301–319. DOI: 10.1177/109634800002400301

Wang, B., Liu, Y., Qian, J., & Parker, S. K. (2021). Achieving effective remote working during the COVID-19 pandemic: A work design perspective. *Applied Psychology*, *70*(1), 16–59. DOI: 10.1111/apps.12290 PMID: 33230359

Wang, C., Zhang, S., Li, X., & Guo, X. (2018). Understanding customers' compliance behaviour to frontline employees' fuzzy requests. *Journal of Services Marketing*, *32*(2), 235–246. DOI: 10.1108/JSM-03-2016-0122

Wang, D., Galster, M., & Morales-Trujillo, M. (2023). Application Monitoring for bug reproduction in web-based applications. *Journal of Systems and Software*, *207*, 111834. DOI: 10.1016/j.jss.2023.111834

Wang, Z., Chen, X., & Jiang, Y. (2022). Telehealth expansion during the COVID-19 pandemic: Impacts on mental health care. *Journal of Health Technology & Policy*, *28*(6), 120–133. DOI: 10.1080/00138020.2022.2035208

Warren, M. A., & Warren, M. T. (2023). The EThIC Model of Virtue-Based Allyship Development: A New Approach to Equity and Inclusion in Organizations: JBE. *Journal of Business Ethics, 182*(3), 783–803. DOI: 10.1007/s10551-021-05002-z PMID: 34840369

Washington State Department of Health. Statewide COVID-19 Outbreak Report. Available online: https://www.doh.wa.gov/Portals/1/Documents/1600/coronavirus/data-tables/StatewideCOVID-19OutbreakReport.pdf

Weitzman, B. C., PhD., Abrams, C., M.A., Starr, B., M.P.H., Hasan, I., M.P.A., Shire, A., Elbel, B., & Berry, C. (2023). Exploring Flexibility in Philanthropic Funding for Place-Based Efforts to Improve Community Health: Reflections on a New York State Multisite Initiative. *The Foundation Review, 15*(2), 66-81,88. https://doi.org/ DOI: 10.9707/1944-5660.1656

Werr, A., & Stjernberg, T. (2003). Exploring management consulting firms as knowledge systems. *Organization Studies, 24*(6), 881–908. DOI: 10.1177/0170840603024006004

White, S. (2021, March 4). L'Oreal Responds to push for natural ingredients in make-up. *Reuters*. Retrieved November 18, 2022, from https://www.reuters.com/business/environment/loreal-responds-push-natural-ingredients-make-up-2021-03-04/

Wiewiora, A., Trigunarsyah, B., Murphy, G., Coffey, V. (2013). Organizational culture and willingness to share knowledge: A competing values perspective in the Australian context, International Journal of Project Management, (Vol. 31, Issue 8, P. 1163-1174). https://doi.org/.DOI: 10.1016/j.ijproman.2012.12.014

Williams, D. P., Jones, N. M., & Holman, E. A. (2022). Racial and ethnic differences in perseverative cognition at the onset of the COVID-19 pandemic. *Social Science & Medicine, 306*, N.PAG. https://doi-org.captechu.idm.oclc.org/10.1016/j.socscimed.2022.115105

Williams, D. R., & Mohammed, S. A. (2013). Racism and health II: A needed research agenda for effective interventions. *The American Behavioral Scientist, 57*(8), 1200–1226. DOI: 10.1177/0002764213487341 PMID: 24347667

Williams, L. J., & Anderson, S. E. (1991). Job satisfaction and organizational commitment as predictors of organizational citizenship and role behaviors. *Journal of Management, 17*(3), 601–617. DOI: 10.1177/014920639101700305

Williams, L. R. (2021). Job satisfaction and turnover intentions in discriminatory environments. *Employee Relations Journal, 39*(2), 78–95.

Williamson, O. E. (1975). *Markets and hierarchies*. Prensa Libre.

Williamson, O. E. (1993). Calculation, confidence and economic organization. *J. Derecho Econ., 36*, 453–486.

Williamson, T. (2005). Work-based learning: A leadership development example from an action research study of shared governance implementation. *Journal of Nursing Management, 13*(6), 490–499. DOI: 10.1111/j.1365-2934.2005.00576.x PMID: 16238690

Wingo, S. N. (2019). Black Uteri Matter. *Obstetrics and Gynecology, 133*(1), 4–5. DOI: 10.1097/AOG.0000000000003035 PMID: 30531579

Wirtz, B. W., Pistoia, A., Ullrich, S., & Göttel, V. (2023). Dynamic capabilities and strategic agility: Developing strategic responsiveness through adaptive leadership. *Journal of Business Research, 161*, 113897.

World Health Organization (WHO). (2020). *Mental health and COVID-19: Early evidence of the pandemic's impact*. Retrieved from https://www.who.int/news-room/feature-stories/detail/mental-health-and-covid-19

Wörtler, B., Van Yperen, N. V., & Barelds, D. (2020). Do individual differences in need strength moderate the relations between basic psychological need satisfaction and organizational citizenship behavior? *Motivation and Emotion, 44*(3), 315–328. DOI: 10.1007/s11031-019-09775-9

Wright, G., & Goodwin, P. (2009). Decision making and planning under low levels of predictability: Enhancing the scenario method. *International Journal of Forecasting, 25*(4), 813–825. DOI: 10.1016/j.ijforecast.2009.05.019

Wu, A., Feng, Z., Li, X., & Xiao, J. (2023). ZTWeb: Cross site scripting detection based on zero trust. *Computers & Security, 134*, 103434. DOI: 10.1016/j.cose.2023.103434

Wu, T.-C., Wang, F.-C., & Li, C.-C. (2008). An empirical study of end-user computing and work performance: A safety perspective. *Safety Science, 46*(9), 1381–1396. DOI: 10.1016/j.ssci.2007.09.001

Xi, N., Liu, J., Li, Y., & Qin, B. (2023). Decentralized access control for secure microservices cooperation with blockchain. *ISA Transactions, 141*, 44–51. DOI: 10.1016/j.isatra.2023.07.018 PMID: 37541856

Xue, K., Luo, X., Ma, Y., Li, J., Liu, J., & Wei, D. S. L. (2022). A distributed authentication scheme based on smart contract for roaming service in mobile vehicular networks. *IEEE Transactions on Vehicular Technology, 71*(5), 5284–5297. DOI: 10.1109/TVT.2022.3148303

Xu, M., Zhang, Y., Sun, H., Tang, Y., & Li, J. (2024). How digital transformation enhances corporate innovation performance: The mediating roles of big data capabilities and organizational agility. *Heliyon*, *10*(14), e34905. DOI: 10.1016/j.heliyon.2024.e34905 PMID: 39149071

Yaghmale, F. (2003). Content validity and its estimation. *Journal of Medical Education*, *3*(1), 25–27.

Yao, W., & Song, T. (2023). A covert TLS encryption transmission method based on network covert channel. *2022 IEEE Symposium on Computers and Communications (ISCC)*, 1344–1347. DOI: 10.1109/ISCC58397.2023.10217970

Yates, C., & Thomas, P. (2021). Mental health care during COVID-19: A review of global practices. *International Journal of Mental Health Care*, *30*(2), 78–88. DOI: 10.1111/inm.12356

Yildiz, H., *et al.* (2023). Understanding Mandatory Citizenship Behaviors in Organizations: Implications for Management Practices.

Yilmaz, G. (2014). Let's Peel the Onion Together: An Application of Schein's Model of Organizational Culture. *Communication Teacher*, *28*(4), 224–228. DOI: 10.1080/17404622.2014.939674

Yücel, S. (2021). Transformational leadership in healthcare: An analysis of its impact on employee satisfaction and organizational performance. *Health Care Management Review*, *44*(2), 105–117. DOI: 10.1097/HMR.0000000000000304

Yu, N. W., Wang, N. X., Fu, N. X., Xuan, N. D., & Zhao, N. W. (2008). An invisible localization attack to internet threat monitors. *IEEE Transactions on Parallel and Distributed Systems*, *20*(11), 1611–1625. DOI: 10.1109/TPDS.2008.255

Yusoff, W. F. W. (2021). Racial bias in Malaysian recruitment: A field experiment. *International Journal of Manpower*, *42*(3), 456–472.

Zaman, A., Safarinejadian, B., & Birk, W. (2020). Security analysis and fault detection against stealthy replay attacks. *International Journal of Control*, *95*(6), 1562–1575. DOI: 10.1080/00207179.2020.1862917

Zargar, S. T., Joshi, J., & Tipper, D. (2013). A survey of defense mechanisms against distributed denial of service (DDoS) flooding attacks. *IEEE Communications Surveys and Tutorials*, *15*(4), 2046–2069. DOI: 10.1109/SURV.2013.031413.00127

Zhang, H., Lu, Y., Gupta, S., & Zhao, L. (2022). What motivates customers to continue using mobile apps? The role of personalized marketing. *Journal of Interactive Marketing*, *58*, 28–42.

Zhang, J., Yang, A., & Shuaishuai, F. (2022). Data protection of internet enterprise platforms in the era of big data. *Journal of Web Engineering*. Advance online publication. DOI: 10.13052/jwe1540-9589.21314

Zhao, F., Meng, T., Wang, W., Alam, F., & Zhang, B. (2023). Digital Transformation and Firm Performance: Benefit From Letting Users Participate. *Journal of Global Information Management*, *31*(1), 1–23. DOI: 10.4018/JGIM.322104

Zhao, N., Hong, J., & Lau, K. (2023). Impact of supply chain digitalization on supply chain resilience and performance: A multi-mediation model. *International Journal of Production Economics*, *259*, 108817. DOI: 10.1016/j.ijpe.2023.108817 PMID: 36852136

Zheng, P., Zhan, X., & Liu, W. (2021). Mental health during the COVID-19 pandemic: A review of global trends. *Psychiatry Research*, *54*(1), 78–85.

Zhou, X., Nguyen-Feng, V. N., Wamser-Nanney, R., & Lotzin, A. (2022). Racism, Posttraumatic Stress Symptoms, and Racial Disparity in the U.S. COVID-19 Syndemic. *Behavioral Medicine (Washington, D.C.)*, *48*(2), 85–94. https://doi-org.captechu.idm.oclc.org/10.1080/08964289.2021.2006131. DOI: 10.1080/08964289.2021.2006131 PMID: 35318897

Zohar, D. (2002). The effects of leadership dimensions, safety climate, and assigned priorities on minor injuries in work groups. *Journal of Organizational Behavior*, *23*(1), 75–92. DOI: 10.1002/job.130

Zohar, D., & Luria, G. (2003). The use of supervisory practices as leverage to improve safety behavior: A cross-level intervention model. *Journal of Safety Research*, *34*(5), 567–577. DOI: 10.1016/j.jsr.2003.05.006 PMID: 14733991

Zsidisin, G. A., & Henke, J. W. (2019). Strategic supplier relationship management and risk mitigation. *Journal of Business Logistics*, *40*(2), 94–109.

About the Contributors

Kim L. Brown-Jackson holds a Ph.D.-Cybersecurity Leadership, Doctorate of Business Admin (DBA)-Quality Systems Mgmt. (business process improvement) conc. Health Systems, a Master's-Biomedical Sciences in Pathology & Molecular Oncology with additional Ph.D. course work, an Associates-Biotechnology and Forensic Science, an executive professional MBA certificate, and Bachelors in Biological Sciences with a cluster minor in Business Administration. She is certified in numerous professional areas. Dr. Brown-Jackson has 30 years of experience as a practitioner, academician, quality healthcare leader and performance and learning strategist guiding business process improvement through biomedical services, public health, pandemics, advanced drug development, telemedicine/ telehealth initiatives, and leadership development. Specializes in regulatory compliant industries (pharmaceutical-drugs, therapeutics, biologics, medical devices, financial). She has taught at the collegiate, government, and corporate levels. She has contributed to over 16 book chapters and 30+ peer-reviewed journals, and delivered numerous presentations at conferences and on panels.

Darrell Norman Burrell is a faculty member at Marymount University. He is a post-doctoral researcher at the University of Maryland- Baltimore School of Pharmacy. He is a visiting researcher at the Pellegrino Center at the Georgetown School of Medicine. He is visiting scholar at the Samuel DeWitt Proctor Institute for Leadership, Equity, and Justice at Rutgers University. Dr. Burrell has 3 doctorate degrees and five graduate degrees. He has over 200 peer reviewed publications. He has over 20 years of management, teaching, and training experience in academia, government, and private industry. Dr. Burrell can be reached at dnburrell@captechu .edu

Lauren Catherine Conley is a doctoral candidate in the Doctor of Business Administration (DBA) program at Marymount University, specializing in Business Intelligence. She holds dual master's degrees in both international business and international marketing from Hult International Business School, where she graduated with honors and Dean's List distinction. Her professional background spans over seven years of experience in strategic marketing, digital communications, and data-driven campaign management. She currently serves as Marketing Manager for North America at ChemPoint, where she leads integrated marketing strategies in the plastics and elastomers sector. Her research interests include consumer behavior, green marketing, generational sustainability attitudes, and applied data analytics in strategic decision-making. Lauren brings a practitioner-scholar perspective to her academic work, drawing on both corporate and consultancy experience across sectors. She is committed to producing applied research that bridges the gap between business theory and real-world marketing practices that advance sustainable consumer engagement.

Marlena Daryousef holds an MBA and Doctor of Management degree from Colorado Technical University with over ten years of business development and business consulting across multiple business verticals. Marlena has a proven track record of helping both startups and established businesses improve their business optimization, stakeholder engagement, quality and risk management processes, and problem-solving. It is important to be apart of social change while assisting businesses to defend their unique place in their industry.

Brian Douglas began his academic journey at North Carolina A&T State University, one of the nation's most innovative universities, where he earned a BS in Business with a concentration in Marketing. He later received an MBA in Human Resource Management from Webster University. His interest in workplace behavior led him to pursue a Ph.D. in Business Psychology at The Chicago School in Los Angeles, a school known for excellence in psychology. Dr. Douglas's research focused on understanding how technological advancements affect employee engagement. Currently, Dr. Douglas serves as a full professor at Clinton College, a historic and intimate HBCU in South Carolina. In addition to his teaching responsibilities, he advises students, recruits adjunct faculty, and supports accreditation efforts through curriculum and assessment development. His expertise in business and psychology allows him to inspire and prepare students to become effective leaders in today's dynamic workplace.

Terrence Duncan holds a Doctor of Business Administration degree from Walden University (2016), and a MBA-Healthcare Services Concentration from Park University (2006). He has over fifteen years industry experience in healthcare ranging from enterprise risk management, claims administration, and patient safety. Dr. Duncan currently serves on two non-profit boards and works extensively with the regional chamber of commerce on subject areas including healthcare, economic development, diversity, and leadership. Dr. Duncan has self-published two books on leadership and personal motivation.

Thomas Cephus Gibbs III is a Capitol Technology Alumnus. He obtained his Construction Science Ph.D. at Capitol Technology University. He is also a Lincoln Vibrant Communities fellow at Claremont Lincoln University. He graduated from the University of the Pacific McGeorge School of Law and obtained his master's in public administration. He has an African American Studies research certification from The Bunche Center at the University of California Los Angeles UCLA. He is a graduate of the Small Business Academy from the University of Southern California (USC). He is a graduate of the Sacramento Planning Academy. An Alumnus of the Sacramento Transportation Planning Academy. He is an AmeriCorps Alumni, serving three terms. He served one term as an AmeriCorps Volunteer for Hands on Atlanta. He also served two terms as an AmeriCorps Vista for the Sacramento Promise Zone. Mr. Gibbs is also a Morehouse College alumnus who graduated with a B.A. in African American Studies. While at Morehouse, he Completed his senior practicum and thesis on the prison industrial complex while teaching a cultural diversity class on Hip Hop at the Atlanta Federal Penitentiary. Mr. Gibbs is an active member of the National Bison Association and a devoted husband and loving father. Additionally, He is a Bison Conservationist. He is the Founder and the Director of Development for glimmering Rainbow Bison Ranch Company. In his current role with Glimmering Rainbow Bison Ranch, Mr. Gibbs focuses his energy, expertise, and efforts on using what the ranch has to accommodate the needs of local communities. He is a serial entrepreneur, Real Estate Developer, and Former Co-owner of the Fresh Lines Barber Shop franchise. Before pivoting into the agricultural industry, Mr. Gibbs, as a small business owner, used economic development strategies in the Sacramento Promise Zone to accelerate job growth and later became a national Opportunity Fund Manager. Mr. Gibbs has an extensive background in government initiatives. He employs his skill sets to create and build effective partnerships with local government entities, small businesses, community and faith-based organizations, future ranchers, and bison enthusiasts.

Eugene J. Lewis is a Professor specializing in Information Systems and Cyber Security. He has taught courses across various disciplines, including Marketing, Management, Logistics, and Information Systems, and has made significant contributions as a researcher in business and technical core competencies. Currently, he works with the Aviation and Missile Command (AMCOM) within the Aviation & Defense Industry, focusing on the Cargo CH-47 Helicopters Foreign Military Sales (FMS) Program Office for the U.S. Army. Previously, Dr. Lewis served as an Assistant Professor of Marketing at Oakwood University, where he held both full-time and part-time teaching roles in Marketing, Leadership, and Computer Information Systems. He has also taught courses at Lindsey Wilson University and Edward Waters University (EWU), covering topics such as global marketing, marketing management, organizational dynamics, project management, database management, logistics, and supply chain strategies. A practitioner in his field, Dr. Lewis's education and extensive experience exemplify the integration of marketing, management, and technology. As an International Program Manager (IPM), he regularly delivers briefings to dignitaries and foreign leaders worldwide, focusing on logistics and supply chain management. Much of his career has been dedicated to introducing innovative ideas that help consumers understand the value of emotional intelligence (EQ) and business intelligence (BI) through technological integration. Beyond his professional pursuits, Dr. Lewis is passionate about giving back to the community. He dedicates much of his free time to mentoring youth in underserved areas, instructing in the art of boxing. With over 13 years of experience as a boxing coach and instructor, he is a registered coach with the United States Boxing Association for the Southeastern Region. Originally from Seattle, Washington, where his family remains, Dr. Lewis enjoys traveling, writing poetry, playing guitar, and engaging with inspiring individuals.

Quatavia McLester is a PhD candidate in the Healthcare Technology program at Capitol Technology University. She holds a Master of Science in Industrial/Organizational Psychology from Austin Peay State University. She holds a Bachelor of Science in Psychology and a minor in Applied Statistics and Data Analysis from Kennesaw State University. She is currently serving as a Board Certified Behavior Analyst for a mental healthcare service provider. Her research interests include processes and outcomes of organizational development and change at the individual, group, and systems levels within the healthcare field, the effects of destructive leadership within organizations, and the use of healthcare technology in the mental healthcare space.

Hitesh Mohapatra received the B.E. degree in Information Technology from Biju Patnaik University of Technology (BPUT), Odisha in 2006, and the MTech. Degree in CSE from Odisha University of Technology and Research (OUTR) University, Odisha in 2009. He received his Ph.D. in Computer Science & Engineering in 2021 from Veer Surendra Sai University of Technology (VSSUT), Burla, India. He has contributed 30 SCI and Scopus indexed research papers, 21 international/national conferences and books on Software Engineering and C Programming respectively. He has 15 years of teaching experience both in industry and academia. He has served the research community with various capacities like session chair, technical chair, keynote speaker etc. His research interests include wireless sensor network, smart city, smart grid and smart water. Currently he is working as Associate Professor at School of Computer Engineering, KIIT DU, Bhubaneswar, and Odisha.

Maria R. Mondala-Duncan serves as the Senior Management Analyst for the City of Simi Valley. Dr. Mondala-Duncan is a generalist and a business professional with over 18 years of combined management experience, 13 of which have been in the public sector. Her broad range of experience entail the areas of labor negotiations, monitoring revenue and expenditures, review/analyze legislation for impact on the agency, building relationships with elected officials, and developing new ideas, in addition to operations and administration, organizational leadership/human resources, budgets, contracts, procurement, project management, accounting and finance, and law. Dr. Mondala-Duncan holds a BA in Sociology, an MBA with two concentrations in Organizational Leadership and Project Management, and Doctoral of Business Administration in Business Intelligence. She has published several journal articles, a member of The Honor Society of Phi Kappa Phi and National Society of Leadership and Success, and a 2024 Honored Listee in the Marquis Who's Who.

Roger Muntu is a distinguished media professional, educator, and multilingual communicator with over 25 years of experience in broadcasting, education, and digital media production. Roger has demonstrated a passion for media, language, and education, consistently contributing to global broadcasting and local educational initiatives. His career spans various roles, from television and radio hosting to production management, which has shaped his expertise in cross-cultural communication, Leadership, and project management. Roger is pursuing a Doctorate in Business Administration (DBA) in Business Intelligence at Marymount University, where he continues to refine his leadership skills and deepen his knowledge of business analytics and strategy. This academic pursuit complements his robust professional experience in media and education as he strives to integrate his vast knowledge of international communication with data-driven decision-making. Roger holds a Master of Business Administration (MBA) in Leadership, a with a Minor in Business Management from Marymount University, and an associate degree in Information

Timi Olubiyi is an Entrepreneurship and Small Business Management expert with a Ph.D in Business Administration. A Babcock University Business School Affiliated Scholar and senior government official. He is a prolific investment coach, business engineer, Chartered Member of the Chartered Institute for Securities & Investment (CISI), and a financial literacy specialist.

William Quisenberry resides in Lexington, KY, and has a diverse background that includes studying and practicing within the field of business administration, coordinating implementation projects for Fortune 500 clients, managing and overseeing vendors/suppliers, operations management, project management, marketing, research analysis, consulting, and teaching at the collegiate level. Dr. Quisenberry has collaborated and worked on projects with a variety of major organizations in the marketplace that include: Lexmark International, Halliburton, Branch Banking and Trust, The U.S. Department of Veterans Affairs, Wal-Mart, The U.S. Army Corps of Engineers, Accenture, IBM, Best Buy, Lockheed Martin, John Hancock Financial, and the World Trade Center Association. Dr. Quisenberry holds a Bachelor of Business Administration (BBA) degree in Finance, a BBA in Marketing, as well as a Master of Business Administration degree from Sullivan University's Graduate School of Business, and a Post-Graduate Certification in Forensic Accounting from Davenport University. He also possesses a Doctor of Business Administration (DBA) degree with a specialization in Leadership from Walden University.

Jimmy Thankachan is an Associate Professor at CHRIST (Deemed to be University) Bangalore, India. She completed her M. Com in Human Resource Management and is NET (National Eligibility Test) qualified. Her teaching experience spans 19 years. Her PhD focused on Human Resource Management and Organizational Behavior, with an emphasis on "Emotional Intelligence, Spiritual Intelligence, and Quality of Work Life of Management Teachers in Higher Education Institutions". She has published research articles in journals such as Asian Case Research Journal and International Journal of Emerging Technologies and Innovative Research. Research interests include Diversity and Inclusion, Neuro Linguistic Programming and Emotional Intelligence, Assurance of Learning under the AACSB accreditation, Cross-cultural study, Reverse Mentoring and Workplace Discrimination and Policy.

Balraj Verma is currently serving as an Associate Professor at the Doctoral Research Centre of Chitkara Business School, affiliated with Chitkara University, Rajpura, Punjab. He completed his PhD from Jaypee University of Information Technology (JUIT), Waknaghat, and holds a master's degree in Business Administration, bringing with him over 17 years of combined academic and corporate experience. His teaching portfolio includes courses such as Marketing Management, Strategic Management, Business Statistics, and Research Methodology. He has successfully supervised three scholars to PhD completion under his guidance, showcasing his proficiency in academic mentorship. His research contributions are substantial, with numerous publications in respected journals indexed in SCI, ABDC and Scopus. Additionally, he has authored and edited books and contributed chapters to leading international publishers. Dr. Balraj Verma is actively involved in organizing international conferences and serves as a resource person for Faculty Development Programs (FDPs), Management Development Programs (MDPs), and workshops focused on research methodologies. As a peer reviewer for esteemed journals including the Journal of Knowledge Economy (Springer), Economic Change and Restructuring (Springer), Electronic Commerce Research (Springer), International Journal of Information Management Data Insights (Elsevier), and S N Computer Science (Springer), he contributes significantly to maintaining the standards of academic scholarship in his field. His research interests span E-commerce, Retail Management, Technology Adoption, Aggregator Platforms Models, and Human-Computer Interaction etc.

Index

A

B

C

D

E

T

U

W

www.ingramcontent.com/pod-product-compliance
Lightning Source LLC
LaVergne TN
LVHW080608300926
849162LV00005B/1086
* 9 7 9 8 3 3 7 3 0 4 8 2 3 *